Praise for
Best of CALIFORNIA'S Missions, Mansions, and Museums

This guide is essential for anyone who wants to experience California's missions, mansions, and museums. It is full of little vignettes that inspire, educate, and enlighten the reader. Dahlynn and Ken McKowen have done a masterful job.

–Donald Murphy, former director, California State Parks

This comprehensive travel guide to California's rich diversity of historic and cultural treasures is a must for anyone interested in exploring the Golden State in-depth. It will prompt locals and tourists alike to not only read about these scenic and historic attractions, but to visit them as well.

–Christopher Craig, editor, Encyclopedia of San Francisco, *a project of the San Francisco Museum and Historical Society*

Wilderness Press's new publication, *Best of California's Missions, Mansions, and Museums,* is a wonderful addition to their list of well-known publications. This is the best guide I have seen on a behind-the-scenes look at the Golden State's historic and cultural treasures. This book will make you want to get off your butt, jump into your car, disregard gas prices, and take a long sabbatical to check out all the wonders that California has to offer. A wonderful addition to a traveler's collection.

–Jay Aldrich, Tourism & Public Relations, Autry National Center

Californians have always looked within themselves, beyond themselves, and to each other for inspiration. This book will help you find the true heart of California—yesterday, today, and tomorrow. Even California natives will find someplace new to discover and explore in this book. In its pages you come to realize that art, architecture, and inspiration are all around us.

–Joe D'Alessandro, president and CEO, San Francisco Convention & Visitors Bureau

NEW EXHIBIT
STEAMBOATS
OF THE
COLUMBIA RIVER
NEW EXHIBIT
COLUMBIA RIVER MARITIME MUSEUM

Best of OREGON and WASHINGTON'S Mansions Museums and More

Ken & Dahlynn McKowen

Best of Oregon and Washington's Mansions, Museums, and More:
A Behind-the-Scenes Guide to the Pacific Northwest's Historic and Cultural Treasures

1st EDITION 2009

Front cover photos copyright © 2009 by Ken and Dahlynn McKowen
Back cover photos copyright © 2009 by Ken and Dahlynn McKowen *(top and center)* and Shawn Shiflet *(bottom)*
Interior photos, except as noted on p. vii, by Ken and Dahlynn McKowen
Maps: Scott McGrew
Series design and book layout: Larry Van Dyke
Cover layout: Scott McGrew
Book editor: Laura Shauger

ISBN 978-0-89997-487-3

Manufactured in Canada

Published by: **Wilderness Press**
1345 8th Street
Berkeley, CA 94710
(800) 443-7227; FAX (510) 558-1696
info@wildernesspress.com
www.wildernesspress.com

Visit our website for a complete listing of our books and for ordering information.

Cover photos: *Front, clockwise from top:* Washington State capitol in Olympia, Science Fiction Museum and Hall of Fame in Seattle, Campbell Memorial Courtyard at the University of Oregon Jordan Schnitzer Art Museum in Eugene, and Shelton-McMurphey-Johnson House in Eugene
Back, top to bottom: Seattle Asian Art Museum, sculptures in the Chihuly Bridge at the Museum of Glass in Tacoma, and Shore Acres State Park

Frontispiece: *Top to bottom:* Keller House in Colville, Columbia River Maritime Museum in Astoria, and Sinnott Memorial Overlook in Crater Lake National Park

. . . I have wandered all my life, and I have travelled;
the difference between the two being this—
we wander for distraction, but we travel for fulfillment.
—Hilaire Belloc, "Places"

For my part, I travel not to go anywhere, but to go.
I travel for travel's sake.
—Robert Louis Stevenson, "Travels with a Donkey in the Cevennes"

Acknowledgments

We embarked on our journey knowing that it would require the assistance of many dozens of people to make *Best of Oregon and Washington's Mansions, Museums, and More* a reality. Beginning with managing editor Roslyn Bullas, our collaborators at Wilderness Press deserve a hearty thank you. They include our editor Laura Shauger whose attention to detail and her insistence that we include more first names, especially those of pioneer wives, added greatly to the book's readability. We thank Larry Van Dyke for his wonderful design work.

We traveled from our home in California to the Pacific Northwest several times over the course of more than a year, covering 10,000 miles, sometimes staying for a week, other times for a full month. We visited more than 200 museums, visitor centers, and historic homes. While we often stayed in hotels and campgrounds, we also enjoyed our visits with many of our friends who offered us a bed, a meal or two, a welcomed shower, and, most of all, ideas about what destinations we should include.

We would be remiss if we did not thank Joe and Annie Sullivan of Toutle, Washington. Besides offering us their guest bedroom, Annie steered us to the Veterans Memorial Museum in Chehalis. While we visited the Keller House in Colville, Washington, the Sullivan's daughter Addie and husband Eric Johanson, provided room and board. While we were in Washington's Kennewick area along the Columbia River, another lifelong friend Mike Brubaker and his family also provided a meal or two, a place to sleep, and a much-needed shower. Many other Pacific Northwest friends who offered their hospitality and enthusiastic support include Carol Gardner, Bryan and Shelly Anderson, Tom and Lynn Henze, Lenny and Harriet Garrett, and Terri Elders and her husband Ken Wilson. Dahlynn's mother, Scharre Johnson, became our clipping queen, sending us hundreds of travel articles from the *Oregonian* about Pacific Northwest travel destinations. Last but not least, our thanks to our neighbor Bill Falkenstein who takes care of our two dogs during our travels.

Needing to visit as many destinations as possible each day seldom allowed us to make concrete travel plans or appointments. Often we arrived unannounced, requesting access or tours to museums and historic homes. We were greeted by staff and volunteers who were always enthusiastic and helpful in accommodating our needs. More than one opened their doors to us after closing hours and even on days when they were not open to the public. We can never thank all of these people enough for their assistance.

As with our earlier book, *Best of California's Missions, Mansions, and Museums*, you, our readers, become our final collaborators. Our wish is that you enjoy and find useful our efforts to help your family and friends navigate the byroads of Oregon and Washington's fascinating history. Please let us know how we did.

PHOTO CREDITS

All interior photos were taken by Dahlynn and Ken McKowen, except for the following:

pages 13 and 55: Photos courtesy of Shawn Shiflet
page 49: Photo courtesy of Cindy Hanson, Oregon Coast Aquarium
page 185: Photo courtesy of John Larson
page 213: Photo courtesy of La Conner Quilt and Textile Museum
page 216: Photo courtesy of Snohomish County Airport, Paine Field
page 218: Photo courtesy of Microsoft Visitor Center

Oregon and Washington

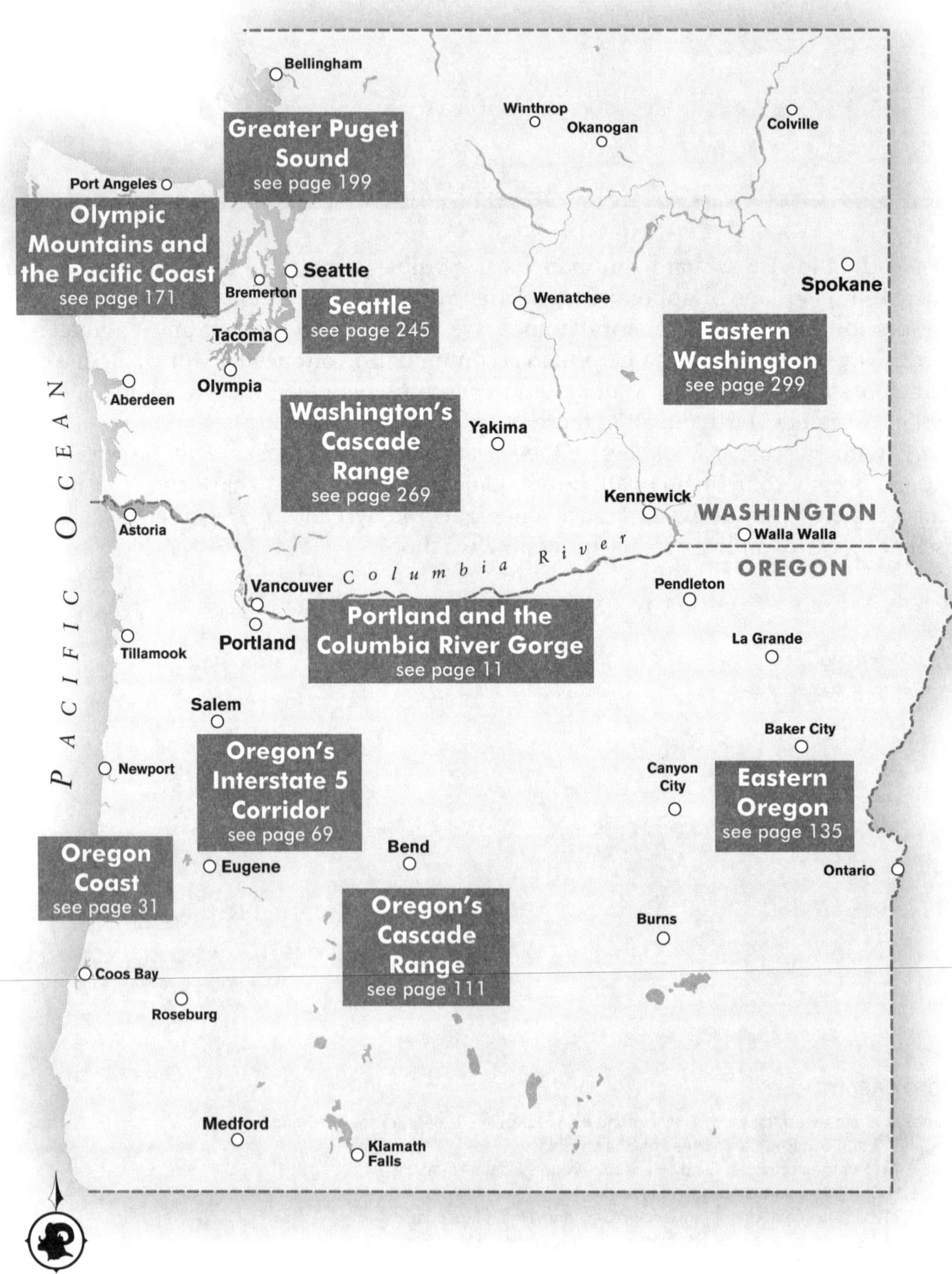

Bellingham
Winthrop
Okanogan
Colville
Greater Puget Sound
see page 199
Port Angeles
Olympic Mountains and the Pacific Coast
see page 171
Seattle
Bremerton
Seattle
see page 245
Wenatchee
Spokane
Tacoma
Eastern Washington
see page 299
Olympia
Aberdeen
Washington's Cascade Range
see page 269
Yakima
PACIFIC OCEAN
Kennewick
WASHINGTON
Astoria
Walla Walla
Columbia River
OREGON
Vancouver
Pendleton
Portland and the Columbia River Gorge
see page 11
Portland
Tillamook
La Grande
Salem
Baker City
Newport
Oregon's Interstate 5 Corridor
see page 69
Canyon City
Eastern Oregon
see page 135
Oregon Coast
see page 31
Bend
Eugene
Ontario
Oregon's Cascade Range
see page 111
Burns
Coos Bay
Roseburg
Medford
Klamath Falls

Contents

EASTERN WASHINGTON **299**

Destinations by Category

OREGON

Portland and the Columbia River Gorge

Mansions
Pittock Mansion

Museums
Oregon Museum of Science and Industry
Portland Art Museum
Hood River Museum
Columbia Gorge Discovery Center and Wasco County Historical Museum

More
Vista House at Crown Point
Bonneville Dam and Lock Interpretive Center

Oregon Coast

Mansions
Flavel House
Cape Blanco Lighthouse and the Hughes House

Museums
Columbia River Maritime Museum
Tillamook County Pioneer Museum
Tillamook Air Museum

Coos Historical and Maritime Museum
Bandon Historical Society Museum
Curry Historical Society
Chetco Valley Museum

More

Astoria Column
Fort Stevens State Park
Fort Clatsop National Memorial
Tillamook Cheese Factory and Visitor Center
Yaquina Head Lighthouse and Visitor Center
Oregon Coast Aquarium
Umpqua Discovery Center
Shore Acres State Park

Oregon's Interstate 5 Corridor

Mansions

Hoover-Minthorn House Museum
Stevens-Crawford Heritage House
Bush House Museum
Shelton-McMurphey-Johnson House
Beeman-Martin House

Museums

Museum of the Oregon Territory
Mission Mill Museum
Polk County Museum
Benton County Historical Museum
Lane County Historical Museum
University of Oregon Museum of Natural and Cultural History
University of Oregon Jordan Schnitzer Art Museum
Douglas County Museum
Jacksonville Museum and Children's Museum
ScienceWorks Hands-On Museum

More

End of the Oregon Trail Interpretive Center
Thompson's Mills State Heritage Site
Butte Creek Mill
Harry & David

Oregon's Cascade Range

Museums

Sherman County Historical Museum
The Museum at Warm Springs
A. R. Bowman Memorial Museum
Des Chutes Historical Museum
High Desert Museum
Favell Museum
Klamath County Museum

More

Newberry National Volcanic Monument Lava Lands Visitor Center
Crater Lake National Park Visitor Center

Eastern Oregon

Mansion

Adler House

Museums

Pendleton Round-Up and Happy Canyon Hall of Fame
Tamástslikt Cultural Institute
Eastern Oregon Fire Museum
Union County Museum
Eastern Oregon Museum
Baker Heritage Museum
Four Rivers Cultural Center and Museum
DeWitt Museum and Prairie City Depot
Kam Wah Chung State Heritage Site
Grant County Historical Museum
Harney County Historical Museum

More

National Historic Oregon Trail Interpretive Center

WASHINGTON

Olympic Mountains and the Pacific Coast

Mansions

Rothschild House
Polson Museum

Museums

Jefferson County Historical Museum
Makah Cultural and Research Center
Aberdeen Museum of History
World Kite Museum
Columbia Pacific Heritage Museum

More

Fort Worden State Park
Olympic National Park
Sol Duc Hot Springs
Fort Columbia State Park

Greater Puget Sound

Mansions

La Conner Quilt and Textile Museum
D. O. Pearson House
Kent History Museum and Bereiter House
Meeker Mansion
Bigelow House Museum

Museums

San Juan Historical Museum
The Whale Museum
Lynden Pioneer Museum
Whatcom Museum
American Museum of Radio and Electricity
White River Valley Museum
Naval Undersea Museum
Puget Sound Navy Museum
USS *Turner Joy* Naval Memorial Museum Ship
Tacoma Art Museum
Museum of Glass
Washington State History Museum

More

San Juan Island National Historic Park
Future of Flight Aviation Center and Boeing Tour
Microsoft Visitor Center
Washington State Capitol

Seattle

Museums

Burke Museum of Natural History and Culture
Museum of History and Industry
Seattle Asian Art Museum
Experience Music Project
Science Fiction Museum and Hall of Fame
Seattle Art Museum
The Wing Luke Asian Museum
The Museum of Flight

More

Pike Place Market
Seattle Aquarium

Washington's Cascade Range

Museums

Shafer Museum
Okanogan County Historical Museum
Leavenworth Nutcracker Museum
Cashmere Museum and Pioneer Village
Wenatchee Valley Museum and Cultural Center
Northwest Railway Museum
Veterans Memorial Museum
Pearson Air Museum

More

Mount Rainier National Park
Mount St. Helens National Volcanic Monument
Vancouver National Historic Reserve Visitor Center
Fort Vancouver National Historic Site

Eastern Washington

Mansions

Keller House
Campbell House
Presby Mansion
Kirkman House Museum

Museums

Stevens County Museum
Northwest Museum of Arts and Culture
Mobius Kids Museum
Yakima Electric Railway Museum
Yakima Valley Museum
Yakama Nation Museum and Cultural Heritage Center
American Hop Museum
Northern Pacific Railway Museum
Columbia River Exhibition of History, Science, and Technology
East Benton County Historical Society Museum
Fort Walla Walla Museum
Asotin County Historical Society Museum

More

Grand Coulee Dam and Visitor Center
Sacajawea State Park and Interpretive Center

1890 home of Ezra Meeker

Naval Undersea Museum, Bremerton

Garden pond at Shore Acres State Park

Introduction

Creating *Best of Oregon and Washington's Mansions, Museums, and More* was an easy decision to make following the publication of our national award-winning *Best of California's Missions, Mansions, and Museums*. During the past few decades, we have traveled extensively throughout both Oregon and Washington, and we have many friends who live here. So with the encouragement of our publisher—Wilderness Press—we enthusiastically began work on this new title for the Pacific Northwest. Since there are few missions in the Pacific Northwest, the "More" for this book allowed us to include destinations such as visitor centers, volcanoes, and other places we felt would appeal to our readers.

As with our California travel book, we were hoping to discover and share with our readers more about the history and cultures that make Oregon and Washington such special places to live and to visit. And we succeeded. We had never been to a glass museum, descended into the guts of a dam, or toured an aircraft manufacturing plant. While we had previously visited Seattle's Space Needle and Experience Music Project, and Portland's Oregon Museum of Science and Industry and Powell's Books, we discovered dozens of historic mansions and visited a long list of museums, many of which were previously unknown to us.

Oregon and Washington's history begins with the Native Americans who have lived in these forests and deserts for untold thousands of years. Salmon proved to be the glue that held so many of the early Native Americans together, spurring a large trading commerce that moved not only the dried salmon but also early European goods throughout the Pacific Northwest. As European explorers discovered and began to explore the western shores of the New World, word spread about the abundance of resources. President Thomas Jefferson, desiring to expand the borders of the U.S. to the Pacific Ocean and to find an inland water passage there, initiated the Lewis and Clark Expedition in 1803.

Spanish, Russians, French, British, and others through the 18th and early 19th centuries had attempted, in one way or another, to either settle the Pacific Coast or at least harvest its many economic benefits, from beaver and whales to timber and salmon. Ultimately, the British and the U.S. battled for control of the Pacific Northwest. In 1811, New York businessman John Jacob Astor funded the building of Fort Astoria for his Pacific Fur Company. The War of 1812 sent his fur company outposts into the hands of the British. Throughout the 1820s and 1830s the Hudson's Bay Company was the dominant force in the region, operating from its headquarters at what is today Washington's historic Fort Vancouver. Another treaty gave shared control of much of the Pacific Northwest to the U.S. and Great

Britain, which nearly sent them back to war, but the Oregon Treaty of 1846 resolved most of the issues. The only remaining problem was a dispute over the San Juan Islands that resulted in the Pig War, which wasn't really a war, but more of a peaceful military standoff.

During much of the 1840s, immigrants came mostly by wagon from the eastern U.S. to parts of California, Oregon, and Washington. The Oregon Trail, the best known of the trails, led thousands of new settlers here. California's Gold Rush spurred a more rapid settlement of the Oregon and Washington territories, but the government's offer of free farmland was a big enticement for more than a quarter million people between 1840 and 1860. The Native Americans certainly didn't enjoy the same benefits. They were moved to reservations, generally away from the more desirous fertile farmlands of eastern Oregon and Washington. The new population gains brought statehood to Oregon in 1859 and to Washington in 1889.

THE "BEST" SELECTIONS

Our intention with this book and with the geographic sections we have created is to provide a broad geographic and subject-matter selection of Oregon and Washington's mansions and museums. With such a large selection of mansions, museums, and more throughout the two states, we tasked ourselves with selecting the best, a personal process that is, by necessity subjective and limited by the available space.

Our decisions about which mansions and museums to visit was directed by our referencing maps, existing guidebooks, publications from state tourism organizations, lots of internet searches, suggestions from our many Oregon and Washington friends, and sometimes by seeing information signs along main highways and back roads. We were seldom disappointed in what we found, which is a bit of a two-edged sword. We visited many more places than we could write about—at least for this book.

We hit the road again, primarily during the summer of 2008, but we also made a final trip in February 2009, a couple of weeks before our manuscript was due. Altogether, in more than two months on the road, we traveled more than 10,000 miles; stayed in hotels, campgrounds, and with friends; and visited in excess of 200 parks, mansions, museums, visitor centers, and other places that caught our interest. During our adventures we discovered more than a few unexpected treasures, many of which were in out-of-the-way places.

The Best Mansions

Our definition of a mansion is likely more expansive and inclusive than most people's. During the mid-19th and earlier 20th centuries, leading citizens in many of the West's towns built what their neighbors thought of as mansions. Many were not as large and some not as fancy as many of today's larger, cookie-cutter tract homes. Essentially, for our book's purposes, we included historic homes—even smaller ones—that we found open to the public on a reasonably regular basis. There were always exceptions, and most of the exceptions we made were for historic homes located in small communities. Few if any tourists pass through these towns during winter and the locals are smart enough not to venture out any more than they must, so the homes remain closed. Some will arrange for a volunteer to open the homes and provide a personal tour, if you call in advance. If such accommodations are made, a donation greater than the minimal fees usually charged would be much appreciated. Most of these historic homes were generally built in the 19th and early 20th centuries and have survived the passing decades, being maintained by local historical societies, government entities, or under the umbrella of the National Trust for Historic Preservation. They operate with volunteers and little annual budget beyond the small admission fees and money raised through local fundraisers.

Most of the historic homes, especially those in smaller communities, serve dual purposes as local and regional museums. Such is a noble and often essential use because very few of these early homes, most owned over the decades by different families, still possess their original furnishings. Touring houses devoid of furnishings would be no fun. There are exceptions, as some families maintained their homes since their early days and have donated original furnishings along with the home to local preservation organizations, but those are rare.

With our final selections, we have attempted to provide a representative geographic and historic balance of the best mansions and historic homes across both Oregon and Washington.

The Best Museums

Selecting the best museums in Oregon and Washington was a challenge—there are so many from which to choose. After visiting 20, 40, 60, or more museums, it becomes evident that many possess essentially the same types of artifacts, although some of the collections represent more of a regional emphasis. It's mostly the eastern museums in Oregon and Washington that have the huge harvesters and other farming equipment that have been used in these farming communities for the past century or longer and won't be found in one of the big city museums. It seems most museums, especially the house museums, will have 19th-century tools, American Indian baskets, women's clothing, and various pieces of common home furnishings such as beds, quilts, and sofas. Yet many also have one or two artifacts found nowhere else, such as the skulls of the first two criminals hanged in a newly-formed county sitting in Oregon's Grant County Museum.

Yakama Nation Museum

We didn't allow size, budget, collection size, or a museum's ability to meet someone's standards to serve as our primary ranking criteria. In larger cities such as Seattle or Portland, dozens of museums exist, some large and some not. If we were to eliminate all or most of the natural history and cultural museums from our book that were smaller than the Burke Museum in Seattle, then we might not have included such gems as the Makah Cultural and Research Center in Neah Bay or the Favell Museum in Klamath Falls. Mostly, our choices were made based on the museums that we most enjoyed visiting. If we found two or more very similar museums in a reasonably small geographic region, then we generally selected only one, attempting to spread our selections throughout the two states. Then there are museums still on the drawing boards and not yet open, as well as those that were open but planned to close soon. One museum that needs to be mentioned is the Oregon Military Museum in Clackamas, which has a phenomenal collection of military equipment, including tanks, artillery, and especially historic firearms. They are in the process of moving into a larger facility, so they requested not to be listed.

The Best of More

The "More" category allowed us to include some of those special places that we discovered during our travels that didn't quite meet even our expanded definitions of mansions and museums. Without this bonus category we would have been hard-pressed to justify including such great monuments and vista points as the Astoria Column in northwestern Oregon or the Vista House at Crown Point perched high above the Columbia River. "More" allowed us to include the Boeing factory tour in Everett and Seattle's Pike Place Market, both fascinating places to visit.

View of Mt. St. Helens from the Johnson Ridge Observatory

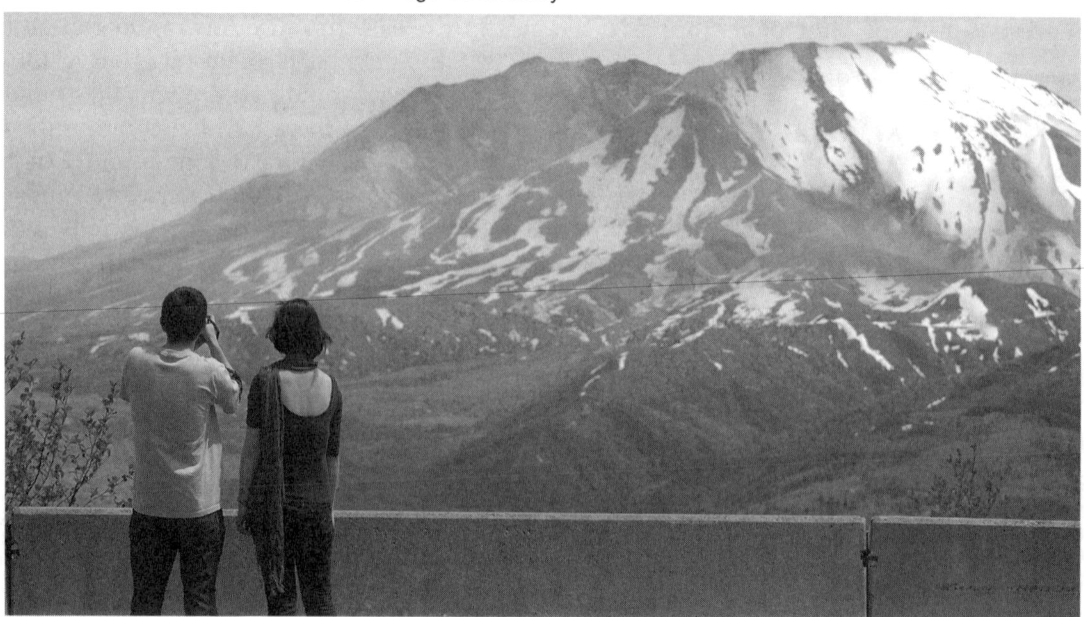

It became obvious during our travels that our "More" category could easily have become much larger than our mansions and museums categories. There really is so much more in the Pacific Northwest to experience. We could have easily included many more of the state and national parks that we visited or where we camped. Instead, we limited ourselves to a few state parks that included historic homes or military sites, and our national park and monument selections to the big ones: Crater Lake, Mount Rainier, and Mount St. Helens, all of which have great museums and visitor centers.

Many more of our "More" selections are included in the suggested area tours at the end of each chapter. They include the curious and fun such as the Astoria Column and the Harry & David factory and the historic such as lighthouses and visitor centers.

ABOUT THIS GUIDE

Oregon and Washington are often referred to simply as the Pacific Northwest, overlooking the fact that they are two states with similar, yet very diverse geographies. Both are bordered by the Pacific Ocean to the west and by desert to the east, and each state has distinct regions that are dominated by forests, agricultural lands, and deserts. For the purposes of this book, we took the liberty of consolidating some of each state's recognized geographic regions as we created our book, using names that best describe those chapters.

Portland and Columbia River Gorge begins in Portland and runs east following the Columbia River to The Dalles. The **Oregon Coast** includes the length of U.S. 101 as it meanders south from Astoria to Brookings. **Oregon's Interstate 5 Corridor** picks up just south of Portland and follows the freeway south to Ashland and includes numerous sites several miles east and west of this main north-south connector. **Oregon's Cascade Range** is less easily defined as the mountains meander southward from the Washington border. It covers the area east of the I-5 corridor to about Highway 97 that runs from Klamath Falls near the California border, through Bend, and with a little bump farther east to include Prineville. It ends west of The Dalles where the highway crosses the Columbia River into Washington. The book's **Eastern Oregon** section includes the remaining large and lightly populated area east of Highway 97 to the Idaho border.

Washington's **Olympic Mountains and the Pacific Coast** includes the Olympic Peninsula that is surrounded by the Pacific Ocean on the west, the Strait of Juan de Fuca to the north, and Puget Sound and the Hood Canal to the east. The section includes south along the Pacific Coast to the mouth of the Columbia River. **Greater Puget Sound** encompasses the San Juan Islands and the northern portions of the I-5 corridor from the Canadian border south to Olympia. The exception is **Seattle,** which has its own section as Washington's largest city. **Washington's Cascade Range** begins along the eastern side of the I-5 corridor, from the border with Canada south to the Columbia River, including Vancouver. **Eastern Washington** is by far the largest of the state's geographic regions, beginning in a ragged line north and south along the eastern side of the Cascades from near Yakima, then east to the Idaho border.

We have included maps, cross-references, and an index to help everyone find their favorite mansions, museums, and more. The tour suggestions for some chapters even include a few bonus destinations. We hope you enjoy them.

Special Features

Describing 137 mansions, museums, and more would be tedious writing and even more tedious reading if all we included were listings of collections and a few important dates. After all, numerous museums in Oregon and Washington possess many of the same kinds of artifacts, from natural history specimens and 19th- and early 20th-century technology to Victorian-era furniture and Native American artifacts.

In our description of each destination, we decided to focus not just on the collections, although we do cover the contents, collections, and furnishings of these mansions, museums, and more. Instead, we have devoted quite a few words to the history that surrounds these mansions and museums, as well as the visitor centers and other sites included in our "more" category. That way, in addition to learning about Oregon and Washington's histories by visiting some of the best cultural and historical sites, you'll learn quite a lot simply by reading the book. As you learn about the characters behind these places—folks like Ezra Meeker, D. O. Pearson, Alexander Pearson, Jr., D.C.H. Rothschild, Simon Shafer, Henry Pittock, and George Flavel—you'll begin to see a picture emerge of the people who created these two states and how their influence developed the Oregon and Washington we know today.

Nippon Kan Theatre screen, Wing Luke Asian Museum, Seattle

If you're up for the challenge, check out the trivia questions at the start of each chapter and see if you can come up with the correct answers about the mansions, museums, and more. If you get stuck, the answers are on page 339.

We also have included some special features throughout the book to help you choose the destinations that best suit your particular interests. If you're most interested in seeing a certain type of institution, simply turn to the section "Destinations by Category" (page xx), find the perfect mansion, museum, or more in the region you'd like to explore, and plan your trip.

If you have more time and would like to travel throughout Oregon and Washington to explore more of our listings, each chapter offers a selection of tours (daylong to weeklong) tailored to families, couples, and other individuals with specific interests, such as visiting historic homes or military museums. These tours include institutions covered in the book's listings, as well as other sites to visit and activities to do along the way. Each chapter ends with contact information for the regional travel bureaus where you can obtain additional information on accommodations and more.

A Final Word

Things change, and that certainly includes the institutions covered in this book. Even during the year we researched, visited, and wrote about these destinations, several changed their prices, one came up with new information that corrected some of their historical information, another was planning to move to a new building, and a couple closed temporarily because of budget problems.

Always check websites or call ahead to confirm the information we have included in this book. This is especially true regarding admission prices and hours of operation, as most organizations don't advertise price increases very loudly or broadly. During winter, you should also check in advance of your visit as many facilities, especially in the smaller rural communities of Oregon and Washington, close or significantly reduce their hours of operation.

The Pittock Mansion overlooks Portland.

OREGON

Lush rain forests, a long and ragged coastline, active volcanoes, and an expansive eastern desert plateau have attracted people to Oregon and Washington for eons. For thousands of years Native Americans have lived here, most along the edge of the Pacific Ocean or where rivers teeming with salmon offered bountiful food supplies. The imprint of the Pacific Northwest's Indian tribes remains today, most often apparent in the Native American names attached to towns, rivers, lakes, and roads.

Spanish, English, and Russian explorers and traders began arriving in larger numbers during the late 18th and early 19th centuries, although the Spanish may have passed near the coast as early as 1565, as they rode the Kuroshio Current around the Pacific Ocean from trading missions in the Philippines. In their attempts to spread their rule, Spain sent sea expeditions, including one led by Bruno de Heceta, who made landfall on the Olympic Peninsula in July 1775. The following month he sighted the mouth of the Columbia River, which separates Oregon and Washington. In 1776, English Captain James Cook sailed along the Pacific Coast, and during the winter of 1805–06, Meriwether Lewis and William Clark explored the mouth of the Columbia River. They were soon followed by trappers and traders working for companies such as Hudson's Bay Company.

During the mid-19th century, U.S. government offers of free land sent more than a quarter million emigrants across the Oregon Trail and into what was then called Oregon Territory. That great human migration permanently changed the face of Oregon as eastern Oregon agriculture, Pacific Coast fisheries, and the lumber industries emerged.

Portland and the Columbia River Gorge

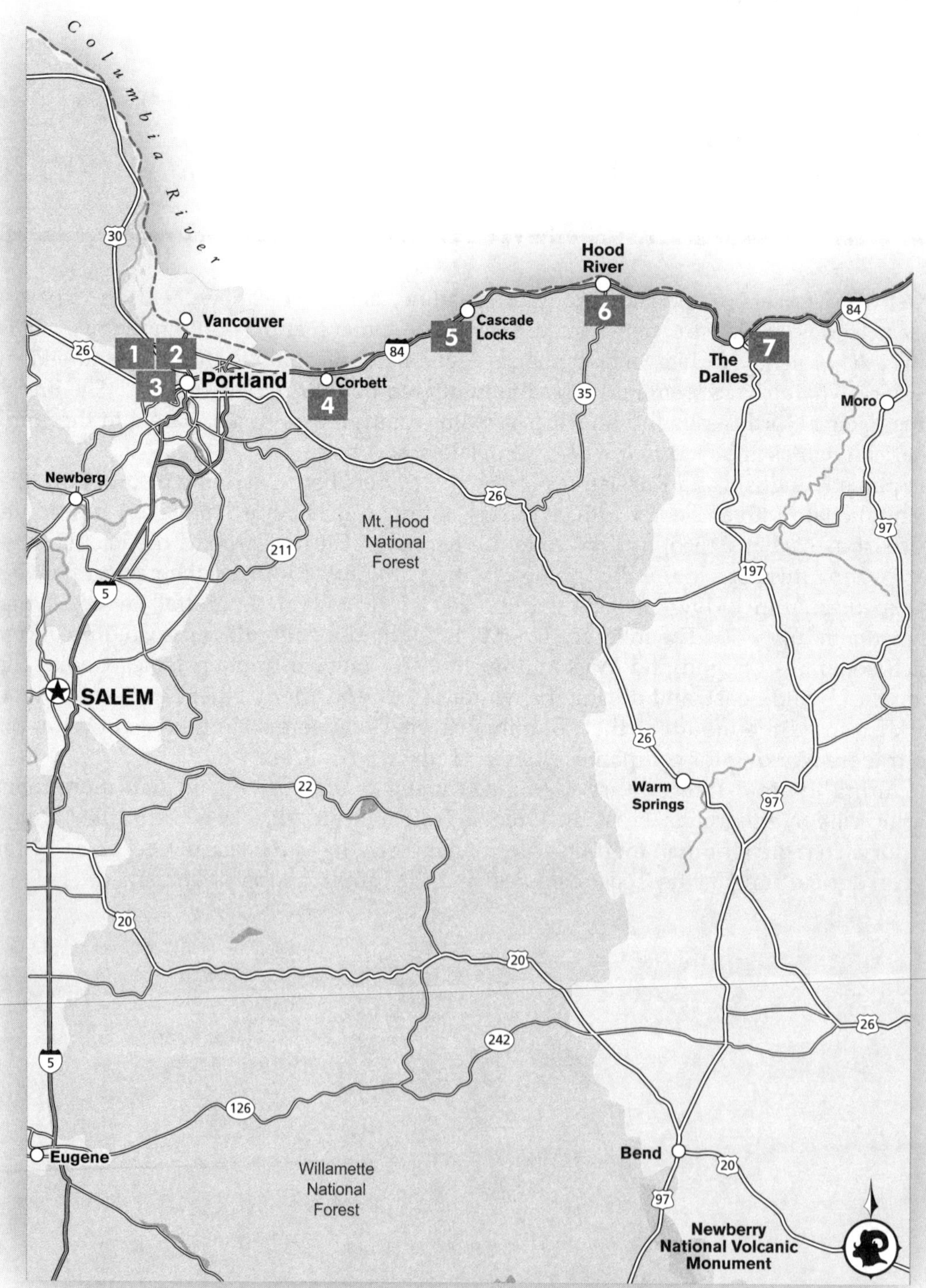

Portland and the Columbia River Gorge

The Columbia River runs southwest from Canada, through Washington, then heads west, serving as the natural border between much of Washington and Oregon. Near where the Deschutes River joins the Columbia, it begins its journey through a great gorge for the next 80 miles where the river canyon in places can be as much as 4,000 feet deep. Several dams have calmed the Columbia's once wild waters charging through the gorge as it heads toward Portland.

Columbia Gorge Discovery Center and Wasco County Historical Museum

The Columbia River is the only navigable river that passes through the Cascade Range from the Columbia Plateau to the Pacific Ocean. The vegetation changes dramatically, downriver along the Columbia Gorge, from the Celilo grasslands where annual rainfall is only 12 inches to coniferous forests near Portland that can receive 75 inches of rain annually.

Where the Gorge marks the boundary between Oregon and Washington, highways today parallel both sides of the Columbia River. The first highway construction began on the Oregon side in 1912, with the historic Columbia River Highway being completed from Portland to The Dalles in 1922. In the days when workers had only horses and primitive machinery to work with, the engineering and construction of a paved road that never exceeded a five-percent grade was nothing less than phenomenal. Today, most of the original road has been destroyed, much of it with the construction of Interstate 84. A few portions remain and some sections have been restored as the Historic Columbia River Highway State Trail. It's a very narrow and winding road, but you will gain an appreciation for the efforts that went into building it—and many of the views are spectacular.

Meriwether Lewis and William Clark traveled down the Columbia River Gorge in the early 19th century, having to battle rapids and waterfalls. Most of those have been either tamed or inundated by reservoirs created by dams, the first of which was Bonneville, which was begun in 1933. Today, locks along the river allow small ships and barges to make the long journey from the wheat fields of eastern Oregon and Washington to markets along the river and to the Port of Portland. Even though portions of the river's wild and scenic beauty have been impacted by dams, bridges, and other development, the Gorge continues to attract visitors. Places such as Multnomah Falls and the Vista House at Crown Point, and even the dams and their visitor centers, remain popular destinations. And the Columbia River and the Gorge are still quite impressive.

TRIVIA

1. **Which Portland museum is designed for kids?**
2. **Where can you learn about the first dam built across the Columbia River?**
3. **What mansion sits on a 1,000-foot-high bluff overlooking Portland?**
4. **Where can you see exhibits about the history of windsurfing that include the very first board built in 1964 by inventor Newman Darby?**
5. **Where can you get a glimpse back 15,000 years when a glacier dam broke, releasing the water from a 3,000-square-mile lake down the Columbia Gorge?**
6. **What historic national landmark, built as a rest stop in 1918, offers a spectacular view of the Columbia River?**
7. **Which museum has an underground tunnel connecting its two primary galleries?**

For trivia answers, see page 339.

1 Oregon Museum of Science and Industry

WHAT'S HERE: A treasure chest of science discoveries for kids and adults

DON'T MISS THIS: Any of the hands-on lab experiments

If you are anywhere near Portland, and especially if you are traveling with kids, then OMSI (pronounced OM-zee or OM-see) is a place you don't want to miss. The big museum sits beside the Willamette River below Interstate 5's Marquam Bridge. There are hundreds of things for kids to do here, although a few, such as the laser light show, the planetarium, and the submarine, require extra fees.

Just about everything here is hands-on. The main exhibit hall offers opportunities to launch water rockets that nearly hit the high ceilings. You control the amount of pressure and water loaded into your rocket and determine when to launch it. What makes the soda bottle rocket blast higher—more water and less air, or more air and less water? There's a Mercury space capsule that lets kids climb in and lie back, ready for launch. This one doesn't go anywhere like the soda bottle rockets do, but kids can get a sense of how an astronaut feels before blasting off.

Robots have come of age, at least in factories. You can sit at the controls of a giant robot arm and compete against a friend in a contest that measures your finesse in moving small objects. Tired of robots? Numerous stations allow visitors to do everything from design, build, and fly paper airplanes and helicopters to spend time in the inventor's ball room, which is filled with plastic balls that kids can shoot through various vacuum tubes and air guns.

In some of the labs, staff and volunteers assist kids—and adults—in learning about everything from static electricity in the physics lab with a real hair-raising experiment, to the power of vibration. With goggles on, youngsters have opportunities to try various experiments in the chemistry lab using real chemicals, while the laser and holography lab allows them to observe the refraction properties of water and learn how holograms are created.

When you tire all of the hands-on stuff, try a trip aboard the Motion Simulator that will surround you with sound and film projections as it takes you and about a dozen others on a trip down a volcano or on a high speed run around a racetrack. The OMNIMAX Dome Theater has a five-story screen with an IMAX projection system and a 15,000-watt surround-sound system. There are usually several different movies playing, which can make it difficult to choose.

Entrance to OMSI

If it happens to be a warm, sunny day, staff may even be outside playing with some of the more fascinating "toys" such as the model of an old castle-bashing catapult that shoots tennis balls great distances. They're likely to encourage you to help.

HOURS: September through mid-June: Tuesday through Sunday, 9:30 AM to 5:30 PM; mid-June through August, daily 9:30 AM to 7 PM. Closed Thanksgiving and Christmas.

COST: Adults, $11; seniors (63-plus) and ages 3–13, $9; OMNIMAX Dome Theater, adults, $8.50; seniors (63-plus) and ages 3–13, $6.50; parking, $2

LOCATION: 1945 SW Water Avenue, Portland

PHONE: 503-797-4000

WEBSITE: www.omsi.edu

2 Portland Art Museum

WHAT'S HERE: **Extensive collection of Asian, American, European, and contemporary art**

DON'T MISS THIS: **The special art shows when offered**

The Portland Art Museum uses 90 percent of its 112,000 square feet of galleries to exhibit a rotating selection of its 42,000-piece collection. And it's a collection that is representative of the world's history of art, including American, Native American, European, and Asian objects. Be sure to get a map of the museum because it's a very large place with numerous levels spread between two separate buildings connected by an underground link, itself a gallery of rotating art exhibits.

As with most large museums, the collection here far exceeds the gallery space that would be required to allow everything to be permanently exhibited for public viewing. Therefore periodically the staff selects a theme—be it a certain artist, a single medium, or a particular subject—and displays that part of the museum's collection in the galleries. It may be beaded bags from the Columbia River Plateau, or post–World War II European sculpture, or prints and drawings from such artists as Rembrandt, Matisse, or Picasso.

Asian art dominates the museum's main floor. From its earliest days, the museum and some of its founding trustees have had close connections with East Asian culture. This interchange has resulted in the donation of nearly 4,000 pieces, especially Chinese, Japanese, and Korean examples. While the Japanese print collection began with an initial donation of 800 pieces in 1932, it has grown to more than 1,800 today. The Japanese collection includes much more than prints, with numerous paintings and decorative arts from the Edo (1615–1868) and Meiji (1868–1912) periods. The Chinese collection has also expanded with ceramic pieces representing dancers, musicians, and court nobles, and the animals, including dogs, horses, and sometimes unidentifiable supernatural creatures, that are so prominent on many pieces. The collection also is rich in tomb objects from the dynasties of Han (206 BC–220 AD) and Tang (618–907).

If prints and drawings are of special interest, the museum's Vivian and Gordon Gilkey Center for the Graphic Arts houses more than 26,000 pieces of art. The center is open to the public for researching prints, drawings, and photographs that range from the 12th century to today's contemporary contributions. If you would like to view a specific piece for research or pleasure, an appointment is required. The expansive collection began slowly with its first 100 Giovanni Battista Piranesi prints donated in 1916. In 1932, another 800 Japanese prints were added along with smaller donations in subsequent years. Then in 1978, Vivian and Gordon Gilkey gifted 8,000 prints from their personal collection, plus another 6,000 in the years that followed.

The museum was founded in 1892 and has benefited from hundreds of donations, many of them made by Portland residents. The American art collection exhibited on the second level of the main building includes pieces from Gilbert Stuart, Erastus Salisbury Field, and the renowned 19th-century landscape painter George Inness. The works of Childe Hassam and J. Alden Weir in this collection include some that they painted in the early 20th century while visiting Portland.

The museum's largest galleries for contemporary and modern art are found in the Belluschi Building's Jubitz Center, which is connected to the main building by an underground passage. The passage isn't as ominous as it may sound. It, too, includes art exhibits that change regularly. The Jubitz Center has six floors of galleries, beginning in the underground link. Level one includes Impressionism and the School of Paris, along with the New York School. The galleries are relatively small as you ascend the stairway through successive floors. The art represents the changes that have occurred throughout Modernism's lifespan, which can be seen in different media, including paintings, sculpture, decorative arts, photography, and works on paper. Technology also surfaces in art with both video and sound works exhibited.

There is much more to see here, including Northwest art, Native American pieces, and a discovery center where kids can pursue some of their own artistic desires. The museum has an active acquisitions program, so there are always new objects to see.

Portland Art Museum

HOURS: Tuesday, Wednesday, and Saturday, 10 AM to 5 PM; Thursday and Friday, 10 AM to 8 PM; Sunday, noon to 5 PM. Closed most major holidays.

COST: Adults, $10; age 55-plus and students over age 18 (with ID), $9; ages 17 and under, free

LOCATION: 1219 SW Park Avenue, Portland

PHONE: 503-226-2811

WEBSITE: www.portlandartmuseum.org

3 Pittock Mansion

WHAT'S HERE: **Early 20th-century mansion constructed by one of Portland's most successful and influential businessmen**

DON'T MISS THIS: **The elaborate master bathroom shower**

The views of downtown Portland, its waterfront, and distant Mount Hood are quite spectacular from Henry Pittock's former front yard. His home is perched on Portland's West Hills, or Tualatin Mountains, 1,000 feet above the city. Henry Pittock had come to Oregon in 1853 when he was only 19 years old and in a financial state that he described as "barefoot and penniless." Seven years later he married a girl from Missouri, 15-year-old Georgiana Martin. Pittock worked as a typesetter, and within a few years he owned the newspaper, transforming it into *The Oregonian.* The daily newspaper, today the largest in the Pacific Northwest, became only a small part of his financial empire that included real estate, the manufacture of railroad equipment, banks, silver mines, sheep ranches, and the paper industry. He was 73 years old when he started planning his new home, completed his mansion in 1914, and lived it until his death in 1919. Members of the Pittock family continued living in the home until 1958.

The home's tours are self-guided so you can walk through the numerous rooms and spend as much time as you want reading the informational signage or enjoying the beautiful views. When you enter the home, one of the first architectural marvels you see is the grand staircase, its marble steps sweeping up

The Pittock Mansion's grand staircase

to the third floor. Most of the home's furnishings have been donated by various people, although there are a few pieces that belonged to the Pittock family.

The music room enjoys a truly inspirational 180-degree view of Portland, with five mountain peaks visible in the distance, including Mount Hood and Mount St. Helens. The room's walls have been returned to their original faux leather texture and the ceiling to its silver leaf, under a bronze glazing. The 1887 rosewood Steinway grand piano is one of the few original furnishings—Henry Pittock purchased it for his daughter Lucy. The carved walnut bench sitting beneath the window also belonged to the Pittocks. In the center of the room is a gilded harp that was made in Chicago in about 1890.

The Turkish smoking room features exquisite examples of plasterwork and parquetry. The room's walls are finished with a Tiffany glaze—carefully applied layers of silver, green, blue, and gold pigments. The oak floorboards were actually steamed and bent to match the room's round contour. In the nearby dining room, the drawers in the built-in sideboard were lined with velvet so the fine silverware would not be scratched. If you look in the sideboard's mirror, you'll be able to see Mount Hood in its reflection—at least on clear days. The Kerman carpet beneath the table belonged to the Pittocks.

The kitchen has been restored to reflect how it would have appeared when Henry and Georgiana first moved into their new home. Even the cookware and utensils are of the same time period. A photograph in the refrigerator room shows what the original cold food storage system looked like, an elaborate multilevel cooler that used a compressor located in the basement and ammonia as the refrigerant. The room's current Westinghouse refrigerator replaced the original in 1928. In the nearby central hallway, you, like the Pittocks' servants once could, can see the annunciator, a device similar to those found in most households where servants were employed. When someone in one of the home's numerous rooms required assistance, he or she simply pressed the servant's button in that room. The annunciator bell rang in the central hallway, tipping an arrow indicating where assistance was required.

The grand staircase leads up to several bedrooms and a sleeping porch. The south sleeping porch is furnished with a single bed that belonged to Henry Pittock. The rocker is one of Gustav Stickley's Arts & Crafts–style chairs, and the master designer even signed the chair. One of the bedrooms belonged to the Pittock's two nieces, who were orphans.

One of the more curious practices on display in the mansion, at least by today's standards, is the separate bedrooms for Mr. and Mrs. Pittock. The suite includes her sewing room and a shower that likely has few equals. To quote from the sign explaining the elaborate shower:

> The tile shower's horizontal pipes allow for a "Needle"-like spray from all sides. A "Shampoo" spray allows water to cascade from above while a "Bidet" fountain rises from the floor of the shower. Two mid-height shower heads, located on opposite sides, were operated by a handle labeled "Liver Spray." Finally, lower down the central pipe is a spout for gauging the temperature labeled "Test." It releases water on one's toe first before opening the master valve.

The master bath also includes a sitz bath for one's feet and a call button over the tub, should assistance be needed.

In the home's lowest floor (below the main entry-level floor), a small museum has been added. It includes photographs of the Pittock family and also of the home being constructed, including the quarrying of the 35-ton blocks of sandstone. This was also where the laundry facility and the servants' and tradesmen's entrance can be found.

HOURS: September through May, 12 PM to 4 PM; June through August, 11 AM to 4 PM. Closed Thanksgiving, Christmas, and the month of January.

COST: Adults, $8; age 65-plus, $7; ages 6–18, $5

LOCATION: 3229 NW Pittock Drive, Portland

PHONE: 503-823-6362

WEBSITE: www.pittockmansion.org

4 Vista House at Crown Point

WHAT'S HERE: **Historic highway rest stop and vista point, set high above the Columbia River**

DON'T MISS THIS: **Photos of Columbia Gorge travelers during the 1920s and '30s**

The view from Crown Point—the western gateway to the Columbia Gorge—is breathtaking and is situated far enough west where the great Columbia River has widened and its steep banks changed from desert browns to forest greens. The views are well worth the winding drive. The Vista House rests atop a point of basaltic rock sitting high above the river's churning waters.

This national landmark was constructed in 1918 as a rest stop and observatory for travelers on the old Columbia River Gorge Highway. Architect Edgar M. Lazarus designed Vista House as a German version of an Art Nouveau building, popular during the early 20th century. The Italian stone craftsmen, who at the time were building the walls and bridges along the Columbia River Highway, so closely cut and fit the monument foundation's stone that mortar and cement were not required. The two-story building is 55 feet high and 44 feet in diameter. The restored roof is covered with matte-glazed green tiles.

Vista House at Crown Point

Inside, the floors, the rotunda stairs, and the basement wainscoting are Alaskan Tokeen marble. The rare marble was quarried from Marble Island, located off the west coast of Prince of Wales Island near Ketchikan, and shipped to Vermont Marble Company in Tacoma for processing. Although the structure cost $100,000 to build, the final interior decorations, designed to complement the eight busts of four different Native Americans, were never completed.

Inside Vista House, a series of photo exhibits extol the beauty of the Columbia Gorge and provides a look at the early travelers who came here to admire nature's handiwork. Part of the exhibit is a series of postcards that some of those early travelers wrote to their friends and families. Friends of Vista House volunteers operate a gift shop and espresso cafe in the building's lower level from mid-March through October.

HOURS: Mid-March through October, daily, 9 AM until 6 PM; November through mid-March, weekends, 10 AM until 4 PM. Hours and days are subject to change.

COST: Free, but donations requested

LOCATION: 40700 E. Historic Columbia River Highway, Corbett. Take exit 22 from Interstate 84.

PHONE: 503-695-2230

WEBSITE: www.vistahouse.com

5 Bonneville Dam and Lock Interpretive Center

WHAT'S HERE: **Dam, power plant, fish ladder, fish hatchery, and visitor center**

DON'T MISS THIS: **The sturgeon at the fish hatchery**

Overlooking Bonneville Dam, the interpretive center provides films and exhibits about the construction and operation of the dam and its locks. Although the Bonneville locks were originally constructed in 1938, the U.S. Army Corps of Engineers built an even earlier lock in 1896. Before then, ships had to unload their cargo and portage it around the Columbia River's Cascade Rapids. That first lock and the rapids are now submerged beneath the waters behind the present-day Bonneville Dam.

The 1938 lock, also built by the U.S. Army Corps of Engineers, could hold two barges and a tugboat at one time. Over the years, new dams were built upstream with locks that could handle even larger vessels turning Bonneville's 1938 lock into a bottleneck. That changed in 1993 when Bonneville's 1938 lock was replaced with a much larger facility, allowing the 1938 facility to be closed. The new lock can hold five barge tows, the same capacity as the seven upstream locks, helping facilitate the flow of river traffic.

The locks are designed to raise or lower barges, ships, and even personal pleasure boats, approximately 60 feet at each of the dams, depending upon whether they are headed upstream or downriver. Those commercial vessels transport petroleum, wood products, and grain between Lewiston, Idaho, and the Pacific Ocean on the river highway known as the Columbia-Snake Inland Waterway.

The five-story visitor center and observation platform offers a great view of Bonneville Dam and of the navigational lock. Hang around long enough and you can watch the lock at work as it raises or lowers large barges and small boats the 60 feet in elevation difference between the dam and the river below. There are numerous exhibits in the visitor center that explain the history and the logistics of river transportation. You can discover how fast the big tugboats move when pushing five barges (3.5 miles per hour or 95 miles per day), how much fuel a tugboat uses each day when pushing those five barges (3,000 gallons per day), and that shipping by barge costs 2.5 times less than shipping by train and about 7.5 times less than shipping by truck.

After spending time at the visitor center, drive across the top of the dam to the Bradford Island Visitor Center. If you are here during summer, head over to the fish ladder facility where a window allows you to see the fish migrating upriver. At each of the fishways, a worker is always present counting the passing fish. Annually, between 700,000 and 1.5 million salmon and steelhead pass through the ladder. Some 24 million to 43 million fingerlings swim downstream each year.

One last stop you need to make before leaving is the Bonneville fish hatchery. The biggest attraction here is the sturgeon viewing center. The hatchery has been operating since 1909, making it one of the oldest in the state. There are several rearing ponds and creeks scattered around the hatchery. Stepping down into one of the small buildings allows for an underwater view of the sturgeon and salmon swimming in one of the ponds.

The visitor center offer various tours, including of the Bonneville dam hydroelectric power plant. Tour times change, so be sure to check the U.S. Army Corps of Engineer's website.

HOURS: Daily, 9 AM to 5 PM. Closed Thanksgiving, Christmas, and New Year's Day.
COST: Free
LOCATION: Cascade Locks
PHONE: 541-374-8820
WEBSITE: www.nwp.usace.army.mil

Bonneville Dam

6 Hood River Museum

WHAT'S HERE: History of the local Hood and Columbia rivers
DON'T MISS THIS: The original 1984 Darby plywood sailboard

The museum is located near the marina, emphasizing its relationship with the nearby Columbia and Hood rivers. It is easy to spot the museum's giant red paddle wheel. The diverse local history, the theme of the museum's collection, makes for a fun visit. There is a look at Celilo Falls—for thousands of years a primary fishing and trading center for many regional American Indian tribes—before The Dalles Dam (about 23 miles upriver) inundated the historic site. The Mount Hood Railroad exhibit includes part of a waiting room with a woman traveling with her daughter. A modern Mount Hood Railroad telephone booth proudly displays its hand-cranked telephone.

Women today can be thankful that modern clothing allows for wearing comfortable garments. Such was not the case in the late 19th century (and before), as the exhibit showcasing women's undergarments amply shows—comfort was not the most immediate concern. Other displays show the clothing worn by the different nationalities of women, including Hispanic and Japanese, who also settled here.

The museum shares the story of Shizue Iwatsuki, who at age 19, came to Hood River in 1916 for an arranged marriage to local farmer Kamegoro Iwatsuki. She became a local leader, organizing the Japanese Women's Society to help new arrivals from Japan adjust to life here. At the beginning of World War II, she and her husband were sent to Japanese internment camps. Following the war, they returned and continued farming. In 1950, Shizue took a correspondence course in Tanka, a more advanced form of haiku. In 1974 she returned to Japan for the first time in 58 years to be honored for an award-winning poem, which she read at the Imperial Palace in Tokyo.

The museum's exhibits continue, one telling the story of the area's apple-growing industry, another about music. If you look toward the ceiling in one of the galleries, you can see everything from oxen yokes to old hand augers. There are a couple of 19th-century Winchester rifles, and even a wooden military drill rifle that was used during the Spanish-American War. Moving into the 1930s brings a kitchen and everything you might find for meal preparation, and even some of the old wooden washing machines that were used by the Hood River Laundry Company. Part of the laundry exhibit features the company's horse-drawn sleigh delivery wagon. Thought to be a Studebaker, it actually had wheels

Hood River Museum entry gallery

attached for use during months when it didn't snow. It was pulled by a team of two white horses named Tom and Jerry.

Windsurfing on the nearby Columbia River has exploded in popularity since the late 1980s. Although others may disagree, the city lays claim to being the home of the sport that became known as windsurfing. In 1964, Newman Darby attached a sail to a rectangular piece of plywood that was beveled on its front and back leading edges, then used it for sailing on the Columbia River. He even had his sailboard design published in the August 1965 issue of *Popular Science.* Over the next few years, legal battles in England and the U.S. erupted among different parties about who owned the patent for the device. The museum features several board designs, including Darby's very first sailboard with a photograph of a woman riding it—a woman who later became his wife.

Other exhibits include children's toys, ranging from a Lincoln Log set and an Erector set to an old jack-in-the-box and an Atari 400 computer (with game cartridges). Scattered among the toys and Black Jack chewing gum are several dolls, including some from the early 20th century.

HOURS: March through April, daily, 1 PM to 5 PM; May through September, Monday through Saturday, 10 AM to 5 PM, Sunday, 1 PM to 5 PM

COST: Free, but donations accepted and used for public programs

LOCATION: 300 E. Port Marina Drive, Hood River

PHONE: 541-386-6772

WEBSITE: www.co.hood-river.or.us/museum

7 Columbia Gorge Discovery Center and Wasco County Historical Museum

WHAT'S HERE: **A look at the geologic and cultural history of the Columbia River Gorge**

DON'T MISS THIS: **The outside views of the Columbia River**

Two distinct, yet related, facilities are housed in this single building on a bluff overlooking the Columbia River. The Columbia Gorge Discovery Center is the official visitor center for the Columbia Gorge National Scenic Area. It takes visitors on a trip back to the time when volcanic eruptions and catastrophic floods created the gorge. Exhibits look at the great Columbia River and the habitat that exists along its winding course. Just across the facility's enclosed breezeway is the Wasco County Historical Museum, with more than

17,000 square feet of exhibits that tell the story of the people who live in one of the largest counties in the U.S.

Enter the Discovery Center galleries to see not only at the cultural changes but also the geologic changes that have occurred along the Columbia Gorge. Native Americans have occupied these lands for more than 4,000 years. During the late 18th century and early 19th century, an onslaught of explorers, trappers, and traders from Spain, Russia, France, England, and the U.S. entered the Pacific Northwest. Meriwether Lewis and William Clark passed through the area in 1806, trading with the Indian tribes for needed supplies and other items useful to their exploration. One transaction that Lewis included in his journal documented his trading a knife and 36 feet each of blue and white beads for a sea otter pelt that he wanted.

The story of the gorge's geology is fascinating—and violent. About 15,000 years ago, a glacier dammed a fork of the Columbia River creating an ancient 3,000-square-mile reservoir geologists call Lake Missoula. Perhaps 100 times over the next 2,000 years, an ice dam reformed and once again broke, allowing torrential floods to course down the Columbia. Geologists estimate that the largest of these floods was 1,000 feet deep and moved a volume of water ten times greater than the combined flows of all of the world's rivers at 60 miles per hour. The torrent moved huge boulders and scoured the bottom and side channels, creating what is here today.

Volcanic activity also played a key role in molding the Columbia Gorge. Millions of years ago, great flows of basalt oozed up from cracks in the earth's crust and flowed over much of eastern Oregon. Ultimately, the basalt covered 65,000 square miles and reached as far as the Pacific Ocean. Over millions of years, the Columbia River, aided by those catastrophic ice age floods, carved its way through the rock. During those same millions of years, more eruptions formed some of the Oregon's most famous volcanoes, including Mount Hood.

As you meander through the Discovery Center you will come face-to-face with a massive Columbian mammoth. These mammals could reach a height of 13 feet with curved tusks equally as long. To better illustrate how much larger mammals were several million years ago, an exhibit features the skulls of an ancient beaver and one of a modern beaver. It's like comparing a house cat with an African lion. There are also ancient bear skulls to show that the ancient beaver wasn't alone in its extraordinary size.

On the history side of the visitor center, exhibits explore the explorers, dissecting the planning that Lewis and Clark undertook for their journey of discovery. You can see receipts for $142.14 for 83 shirts and $246.63 for 16 coats. Some of the things they brought with them were of questionable need, such as satin pants, a crystal decanter, and musical instruments—at least until they ran

The facility houses the Discovery Center and the museum.

out of trade goods and still needed to trade for food or other supplies. For kids wanting to learn more about Lewis and Clark, there is a Kids' Explorer Room where young ones can literally dig into some of the explorers' history.

Exhibits look at one of the last battles between railroad tycoons who, in 1909, were competing to extend their lines up the Columbia Gorge to access commerce in central Oregon. James Hill's Great Northern Railway beat Edward Harriman's Deschutes Railroad by six weeks. Harriman at the time controlled Union Pacific and Southern Pacific. In the end, the two merged their lines.

The museum also looks back at the county's farming history and even early tourism with several recreated buildings. One is the Umatilla House, which could handle 300 guests in first-class comfort; the hotel owners kept up to 2,500 gallons of whiskey in the basement. Besides the Umatilla House, there is a newspaper office and a salmon processing plant. The Columbia River provided plenty of fish for nets and fishwheels, which were efficient, mechanical fish catchers that turned with the current and scooped up large quantities of migrating salmon. On a good day, a fishwheel could harvest 42,000 pounds of salmon—and there were dozens of them along the river.

The old sternwheelers that plied the Columbia were critical to moving agricultural products from central Oregon farms to coastal markets and shipping points. While the steam-powered ships of yesterday that the museum showcases are now history, modern barges move hundreds of millions of dollars in agricultural produce and other products down the Columbia River each year.

There is plenty more to see here, including a look at how the lives of the Native American tribes in this area, including the Wasco, Paiute, Teninos, and Warm Springs, were impacted by the changes that have occurred along the Columbia Gorge.

HOURS: Daily, 9 AM until 5 PM. Closed Thanksgiving, Christmas, and New Year's Day.
COST: Adults, $8; seniors, $7; ages 6–16, $4
LOCATION: 5000 Discovery Drive, The Dalles
PHONE: 541-296-8600
WEBSITE: www.gorgediscovery.org

Portland and the Columbia River Gorge Tours

Family/Kids' Day Tour

ESTIMATED DAYS: 1–2
ESTIMATED DRIVING MILES: 5

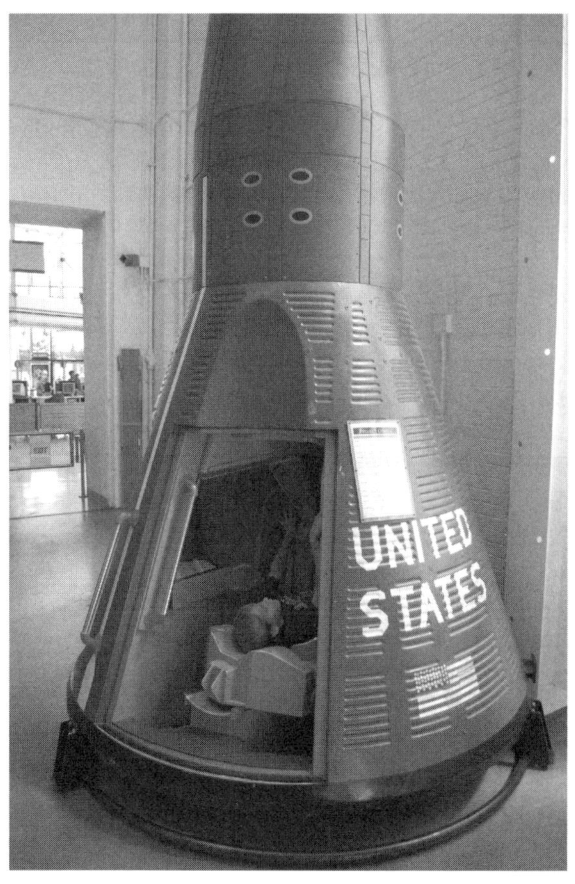

Blasting off at OMSI

Portland is a big city with a small city feel, and it's a playground for kids. A good start—or ending—is hands-on science fun at **OMSI,** the **Oregon Museum of Science and Industry** (page 13). Plan to spend a half day or longer here, especially if you attend one or more of the films at the museum's OMNIMAX Dome Theater. There are also the laser light shows, or you can visit the submarine (it's real!) or the planetarium. From here, it's about a 5-mile, 12-minute drive to the **Oregon Zoo** (www.oregonzoo.org) whose 64 acres will take you on a safari of sorts to such places as the Alaskan tundra; the jungles of Southeast Asia, Borneo, and Sumatra; and the plains of Africa. You will see animals ranging from orangutans and ocelots to crocodiles and leopards.

Romantic Tour

ESTIMATED DAYS: 2–3
ESTIMATED DRIVING MILES: 6

There is so much to see and do in Portland. The soaring vistas from many of the city's bridges are spectacular, but a better place for a gorgeous vista is from the cliff near the front of the **Pittock Mansion** (page 16). It's a bit of a twisting drive getting up here, but the mansion's beauty is magnified by the views of downtown Portland, the surrounding rivers, and snowcapped Mount Hood.

Although the mansion's grounds are quite attractive, it's time to head to the first of two great formal Portland gardens—the **Portland Japanese Garden** (www.japanesegarden.com). The garden is heavily influenced by Shinto, Buddhist, and Taoist philosophies with quiet pathways through forests of bamboo and gardens filled with pagodas, bridges, and water features. The **Portland Classical Chinese Garden** (www.portlandchinesegarden.org) offers much the same tranquility as you take relaxing strolls through gardens of jasmine, bamboo, and orchids.

From the gardens, drive to downtown and enjoy the treasures at the expansive **Portland Art Museum** (page 14). Not only is there an excellent and extensive collection of local and regional art, but hundreds of pieces from Asia, Europe, and other regions of the Americas. If you still have time, just a few blocks away is the largest independent used and new bookstore in the world—**Powell's Books** (www.powells.com). Located at 1005 W. Burnside, the store covers an entire city block. From the newest releases to a few million used books, chances are you can find a book on any subject imaginable. And be sure to stop by their coffee shop, which is a delight.

Pittock Mansion dining room

Columbia River Tour

ESTIMATED DAYS: 1–2
ESTIMATED DRIVING MILES: 85

It's a short drive east from downtown Portland along Interstate 84 to the beginning of the beautiful Columbia Gorge. Take exit 22 and follow the signs and the historic twisting, narrow road up the canyon wall to **Vista House at Crown Point** (page 18). The views both upriver and downriver are breathtaking, and inside Vista House you can gain a sense of the engineering that went into building the historic Columbia River Gorge Highway back in the early 20th century. Head back to Interstate 84 and continue east to the Bonneville Dam and the locks that raise and lower the thousands of boats and barges that travel the Columbia River each year. Along the way, don't miss a quick stop to see **Multnomah Falls** (www.multnomahfalls.org). At 620 feet, it's the second tallest year-round waterfall in the country.

The Columbia River Gorge is a favorite place for windsurfers and the **Hood River Museum** (page 21) highlights much of the early history of the area, including a look at where windsurfing was invented. For a more intimate and expansive look at the geology and history of the Gorge, continue east to the **Columbia Gorge Discovery Center** (page 22) located at The Dalles. This part of the Columbia River was one of several favorites of Native Americans who fished for salmon here for thousands of years before immigrants and dams changed everything.

View from the Vista House at Crown Point

Oregon Museum of Science and Industry's kid-friendly main gallery

Portland and the Columbia River Gorge Information Centers

Portland Oregon Visitors Association
www.travelportland.com
800-962-3700

The Dalles Area Chamber of Commerce
www.thedalleschamber.com
541-296-2231

Cashmere Chamber of Commerce
www.cashmerechamber.com
509-782-7404

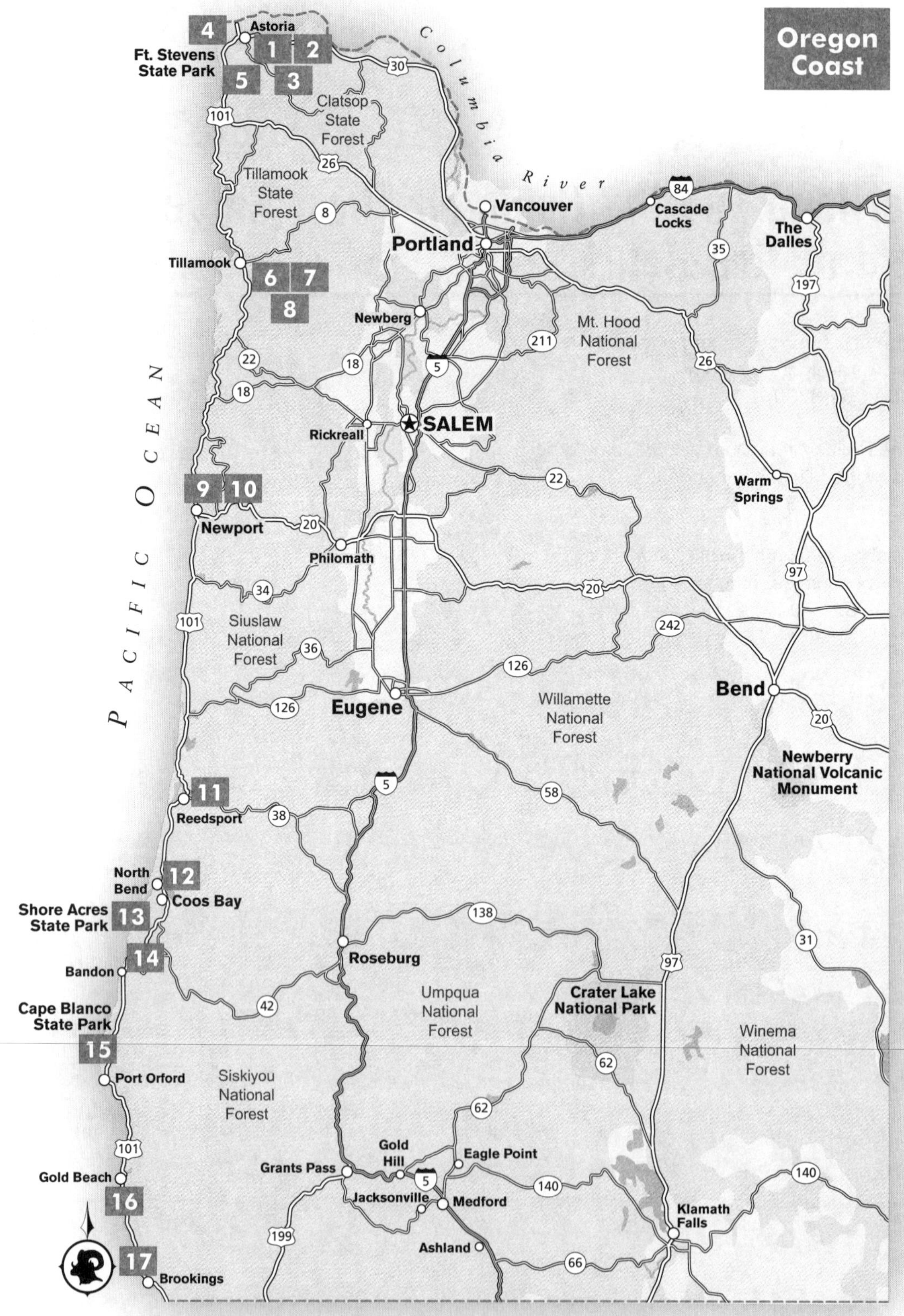

Oregon Coast
Astoria
Ft. Stevens State Park
Columbia River
Clatsop State Forest
Tillamook State Forest
Vancouver
Cascade Locks
The Dalles
Portland
Tillamook
Newberg
Mt. Hood National Forest
PACIFIC OCEAN
SALEM
Rickreall
Warm Springs
Newport
Philomath
Siuslaw National Forest
Eugene
Bend
Willamette National Forest
Newberry National Volcanic Monument
Reedsport
North Bend
Coos Bay
Shore Acres State Park
Roseburg
Bandon
Umpqua National Forest
Crater Lake National Park
Cape Blanco State Park
Winema National Forest
Port Orford
Siskiyou National Forest
Gold Hill
Eagle Point
Grants Pass
Gold Beach
Jacksonville
Medford
Klamath Falls
Ashland
Brookings

Oregon Coast

The mouth of the Columbia River marks Oregon's coastal boundary with Washington. In 1775, Bruno de Heceta was the first European to sight the river's mouth from the Pacific, but it wasn't until 1792 that the first ship successfully sailed across the treacherous bar and entered the Columbia River. American sea captain Robert Gray accomplished that feat, but only after nine days of trying. Since that first crossing, the treacherous Columbia bar has claimed more than 2,000 large ships.

Oregon's coast, trailing south from the Columbia River, is a jagged rift of rocky cliffs, with gaps that release numerous rivers to the Pacific. The Umpqua, Coos, Coquille, Rogue, Chetco, and smaller rivers flow down from the coastal mountains, some entering the ocean through narrow passages, others meandering into bays that serve as harbors for sport and commercial fishing. Coos Bay is the largest and deepest port between San Francisco and the Columbia River mouth.

View looking west from the Astoria Column

U.S. 101 traces much of Oregon's coast, rising well above sea level as it passes over some of the higher cliffs battered by the Pacific's unrelenting onslaught. The highway veers inland periodically through the green coastal forests of Douglas fir and Sitka spruce. Between the cities of Florence and North Bend, the land between U.S. 101 and the ocean turns into miles of shifting dunes, as the constant winds swirl sand into temporary mountains that attract thousands of recreational dune buggy enthusiasts each year.

Short drives west from U.S. 101 reveal numerous lighthouses that mark the Oregon Coast's most hazardous points, with names like Cape Mears, Yaquina Head, Haceta Head, and Cape Blanco. The coast, being mostly wild and unsettled, features numerous state parks, offering public access to some of the most beautiful meetings of land and sea to be found anywhere. A few early farmhouses that once graced the river valleys, such as the 19th-century Hughes House at Cape Blanco, still survive. Others, such as the Simpson mansion at Shore Acres State Park, remain now only as photographs, having lost their battles with nature, progress, or economic calamities.

TRIVIA

1 Where can you tour a historic lighthouse ship?

2 Where can you see a metal bathtub with an accompanying view of Astoria and the Columbia River?

3 What state park was once the only place on the U.S. mainland that a Japanese ship successfully attacked during World War II?

4 Where can you tour a hangar that once housed the largest aircraft in the world?

5 What is the oldest and highest lighthouse in Oregon?

6 What state park is the site of lumberman Louis Simpson's two mansions?

7 Where can you see one of the largest Monterey cypress trees in existence?

For trivia answers, see page 340.

1 Columbia River Maritime Museum

WHAT'S HERE: Maritime history focused on the mouth of the Columbia River

DON'T MISS THIS: The lighthouse ship *Columbia*

The city of Astoria sits at the mouth of the Columbia River, one of the most dangerous and deadly ocean gateways in the world. Since 1792, about 2,000 ships have sunk in and around the mouth with the loss of life in the thousands. Even modern-day navigational equipment has failed to stop the tragic loss of vessels and lives. Unlike most large rivers that empty into the oceans, the Columbia has no expansive delta to slow its flow into the Pacific. Instead, its channel dumps the massive river and all of the sediment it carries directly into the ocean, causing surges and waves that can easily reach a height of 40 feet. A slight shift in the winds can cause relatively smooth waters to transform into ship-battering waves in a matter of minutes, driving vessels onto the treacherous and changing sandbars.

The Columbia River Maritime Museum tells the story of this nationally important river with a special focus on the valiant efforts of the U.S. Coast Guard to save ships and rescue crews and passengers. A large relief map of the Columbia River mouth on the wall near the entrance shows where dozens of vessels have sunk over the years—making it obvious that there isn't a safe place anywhere around it.

And to further make its point about the life-ending dangers here, one of the first exhibits in the main gallery tells a harrowing story: A full-sized replica of Coast Guard motor lifeboat CG 36474 sits here at rest now. But on January 12, 1961, the original 36-foot wooden rescue craft was dispatched, along with three other Coast Guard vessels, to rescue the disabled and drifting fishing boat *Mermaid*. That night, even though they were battling 36-foot waves, all but two of the fishing boat's crew were successfully rescued, but at the cost of three Coast Guard men and three sunken Coast Guard rescue boats, including CG 36474.

The museum also looks at the history of the salmon fishing industry along the Columbia River. Initially, commercial salmon fishermen salted their catch and packed the fish in barrels for shipment to Hawaii and the East Coast, but too often the fish spoiled before reaching their destinations. The French came to the rescue in 1809, when their scientists, working to develop a way to preserve food for Napoleon's army, discovered food canning. The ability to can salmon allowed the fishing industry to thrive throughout the Pacific Northwest.

The lighthouse ship *Columbia* at anchor

OREGON COAST

The fishing industry wasn't limited to the fishermen and their boats. The museum looks at the different ethnic groups that came to this region to chase the American dream. Of the 7,000 residents of Clatsop County in 1880, more than 2,000 were Chinese immigrants, and they excelled as cannery workers. A good worker could cut the tail and head off a 40-pound salmon and gut it in 45 seconds. And he could do this to 1,700 fish during an 11-hour workday. By the 1930s, the salmon canning business was coming to a close. The museum tells about the overfishing, logging, mining, pollution, and dams on the upper Columbia that all contributed to the death of the commercial fishing industry and the end of Astoria's salmon canning operations. There still is commercial salmon fishing today, but it occurs offshore in the Pacific Ocean, not in the Columbia River.

The museum has one of the seven identical trollers built in 1945 at the George and Barker Cannery for the Columbia River Packers Association. It's a beautiful wooden boat that remains in excellent condition, even after 50 years of use. The museum also has the only remaining sailing gillnetter in existence. It was such a common-looking boat that most were allowed to rot away or they were converted to motor power over the years. Numerous exhibits describe how all the different fishing boats were used to catch fish and the tactics fishermen used to thwart their competitors. There were fishermen's drift rights (places in the river reserved for specific individuals) and corking—dropping their nets directly in front of another's set net in order to intercept all of the fish.

The museum includes exhibits on the river's history of boating, from towboats and tugboats, to getting through the locks. You can see the evolution of rain gear, from the early oilskins to rubber to today's polypropylene, PVC, and breathable, high-tech waterproof materials. Kids can take the helm of a towboat's wheelhouse, or go onboard the bridge of the destroyer USS *Knapp*. A large collection of naval ship weapons is also exhibited. There is a look at naval vessels named after local cities (USS *Astoria*) and their actions in World War II. The museum even has two Japanese surrender swords in its collection.

Part of the museum's entrance fee is a tour on the *Columbia,* the lighthouse ship that served as a floating lighthouse from 1950 to 1979, six miles off the entrance to the Columbia River. The *Columbia* is moored beside the museum and was the last active lightship on the West Coast. The interior of the ship looks much as it did while it was in service.

HOURS: Daily, 9:30 AM until 5 PM. Closed Thanksgiving and Christmas.
COST: Adults, $10; ages 65-plus, $8; ages 6–17, $5
LOCATION: 1729 Marine Drive, Astoria
PHONE: 503-325-2323
WEBSITE: www.crmm.org

2 Astoria Column

WHAT'S HERE: **A monument saluting the early pioneers who helped settle the West—and great views of Astoria and the Columbia River mouth**

DON'T MISS THIS: **The climb to the top of the tower**

Standing proudly on Astoria's highest point, the 125-foot-tall concrete tower provides unsurpassed views of the Columbia River and the surrounding forests—assuming you are willing to climb the 164 steps to its top. The Astoria Column was the last of 12 historical markers dedicated to the pioneers who came to the West. In 1925, Ralph Budd, president of the Great Northern Railway, began this project, placing the first marker in the series in St. Paul, Minnesota.

Fittingly, an immigrant Italian artist named Attilo Pusterla was commissioned to complete the 14 carvings on the Astoria Column that would represent significant historical events in the region. He worked with a bas-relief technique known as sgraffito, an Italian Renaissance process that combined paint and plaster carvings. The column was dedicated on July 22, 1926.

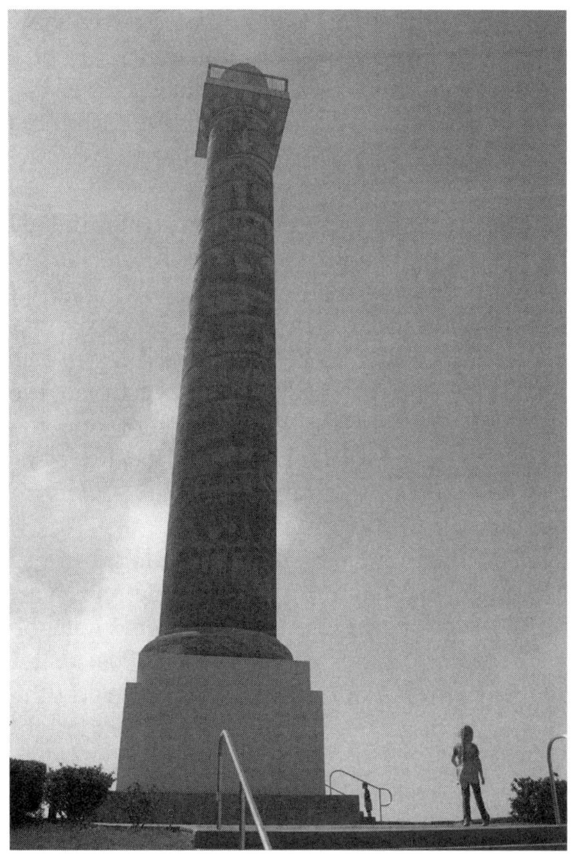

The Astoria Column stands 125 feet tall.

More than 400,000 people visit the column each year, and many make the climb to the top, trudging up all 164 steps. Coxcomb Hill, the site of the Astoria Column, reaches 600 feet above the city of Astoria, and the column another 125 feet. The artwork that wraps around the exterior of the column includes 12 panels and 200 different figures. If you could unwind it like a roll of paper, the piece would stretch out more than 500 feet. The text panels begin with "Before the White Man Came," and include Lieutenant William Broughton naming Mount Hood in 1792; Fort Clatsop being established by the Lewis and Clark Expedition; American Indians fishing and the boat building industry; the Overlanders crossing the Continental Divide led by Wilson Price Hunt; the coming of the pioneers in 1837–1848; the arrival of the railroad in 1893; and more.

HOURS: Daily, dawn to dusk
COST: $1 per car
LOCATION: 1 Coxcomb Drive, Astoria
PHONE: 503-325-2963
WEBSITE: www.astoriacolumn.org

3 Flavel House

WHAT'S HERE: **Restored and furnished 19th-century Queen Anne Victorian home**
DON'T MISS THIS: **The upstairs metal bathtub with a view**

When completed in 1885, this Queen Anne Victorian commanded an unobstructed view of the waterfront. Captain George Flavel was 62 years old when he, his wife Mary, and their two adult daughters Nellie and Katie, moved into their newly completed home. The captain had been a very prominent and successful river bar pilot on the nearby Columbia River and had invested wisely in real estate allowing him to afford many luxuries in life. His home proved to be the showcase.

Captain Flavel died in 1893, but the home remained in the Flavel family until 1934 when Patricia Jean Flavel, a great-granddaughter, gave it to the city of Astoria. It was to serve as a memorial to her pioneer family, but within two years the city was talking about razing the home because it could no longer afford to maintain it. Instead, the property was returned to Patricia who then donated it to Clatsop County to be maintained for public use. From 1937 through World War II, a series of different organizations occupied the house, including the local Welfare Commission, the Public Health Department, and the Red Cross. By 1951, there was again talk about tearing down the home, but local citizens organized and convinced the county to allow the Clatsop County Historical Society to manage the home; later the county transferred the title to the organization.

The home was built in the period when only a few homes had indoor toilets and gas lighting was being replaced by electric lights. The home's lighting was all originally gas. Although there was an electric company in Astoria offering electrical power when the home was constructed, power could still be lost several times a day in the 1890s. Water was a different story. Piped water was available, which made putting toilets inside the home—one upstairs and one downstairs—a reality, though few people at the time thought such a thing was appropriate.

The house was meant to inspire and impress those who visited. Its six fireplaces, each with its own custom mantel of various hardwoods, including walnut and cherry, plus tiles imported from around the world, were not the home's only heat source. The basement held a large furnace capable of burning four-foot-long logs, which provided a centralized heat source.

The home's first floor served as the primary entertainment area for guests. The formal parlor apparently was used when important guests visited the Flavels and for birthdays and other ceremonies. It's furnished with period pieces, including a lady's writing desk from about 1870. The music room was the largest in the 11,400-square-foot home. It contained the most furnishings and likely received the most use. This is where friends came to visit or have tea and where the Flavel daughters entertained guests with their piano recitals. The mahogany fireplace mantel cost $232 when the home was built. The other rooms on the first floor include the dining room, the library, the kitchen, and the butler's pantry.

Upstairs was the family's private area, with the exception of the guest bedroom. Each of the rooms has period-appropriate furnishings. The two daughters had their own bedrooms with a single "pass" bath with its ceramic basin. Apparently husband and wife had their separate sleeping chambers, with the captain's being the largest. The second-floor bathroom had hot and cold running water. There was originally a bathtub that likely only saw use from each of the family members once or twice a week.

The third floor is an attic that served as servants' quarters and is quite plain in its design. The attic also contains a stairway that leads to the cupola, which is likely where Captain Flavel was able to view traffic on the Columbia River with his telescope.

The outside grounds with their gardenlike setting cover most of a city block. The carriage house on the southwest corner of the property was built in 1887 and is where the family kept its carriages, sleigh, buggies, horses, and tack. It also became the residence of the family's hired caretaker. In later years it was the garage for their Studebaker. Today, the carriage house serves as a visitor center, gift shop, and place for visitors to purchase tour tickets.

HOURS: May through September, daily, 10 AM to 5 PM; October through April, daily, 11 AM to 4 PM

COST: Adults, $5; seniors and students, $4; ages 6–17, $2; family, $15

LOCATION: 441 8th Street (corner of 8th and Duane streets), Astoria

PHONE: 503-325-2203

WEBSITE: www.cumtux.org

The mansion's music room

4 Fort Stevens State Park

WHAT'S HERE: **Historic coastal defense fort from the Civil War through World War II**

DON'T MISS THIS: **West Battery Command Station**

Strategically situated near Oregon's most northwesterly tip, Fort Stevens was built to defend the Columbia River from attack during the Civil War. It was part of what would become a triad harbor defense system that included Fort Canby and Fort Columbia on the Washington side of the Columbia River. At the time, President Abraham Lincoln was concerned about both British and Confederate raiders sailing along the West Coast, so he ordered the construction of Fort Stevens, a nine-sided earthen fort surrounded by a moat. Fort Stevens was armed with 26 guns, including 17, 10-inch muzzle-loading Rodman cannons capable of firing a 128-pound cannonball more than a mile.

There was another flurry of construction near the turn of the century. Beginning in 1897, the military began an expansion and improvement program at the fort adding eight concrete gun batteries. Battery Freeman, named after Lt. Colonel Constant Freeman who served in the Revolutionary War and the War of 1812, was built inside the old earthworks. They added two 6-inch guns and one 3-inch gun. The historic earthen fort was leveled in 1940 and turned into a parade ground.

Battery Pratt was updated with two 6-inch rifles mounted on disappearing carriages in support of West Battery's six 10-inch rifles, which served as the fort's primary defenses. Battery Pratt was positioned to protect the adjacent Columbia River minefields during World War II. When a Japanese submarine surfaced in the Columbia River and fired on Fort Stevens on the night of June 21, 1942, it became the only attack against a U.S. mainland military target during World War II. While the shelling damaged some phone cables and a baseball field backstop, Fort Stevens' gunners were ordered not to return fire, fearful that the sub's crew could then better identify the different batteries' locations. The sub escaped unharmed.

The Fort Stevens Museum is located inside the War Games Building, which was constructed in 1911. It initially served as an enlisted men's dormitory, but following World War I, it was converted to a war games center that housed communications equipment and links to all of the bunkers. Today the building houses a number of exhibits, many of which are focused on uniforms and related military equipment dating from the Spanish-American War and World Wars I and II.

Photographs of the fort's big guns along with their gun crews provide an

Gun battery overlooking the Columbia River

idea of what was involved in firing them. A Swasey Depression Range and Position Finder is also exhibited. Each gun battery had two similar devices located nearby that would plot the location and distance of targets on the Columbia River. That data was transmitted to the plotting rooms where aiming and firing instructions could be provided for the guns.

Fort Stevens served as a military post until shortly after the end of World War II, when it was abandoned, later becoming a state historical site. The best thing to do while here is to pick up a trail guide to the fort's numerous gun batteries, bunkers, and post buildings. Exploring the old concrete fortifications and winding your way through the underground concrete bunkers, which are now mostly empty, is an adventure. There is, however, a remnant diesel-powered electric generator in the Steam Plant bunker. When built in about 1900, the steam plant produced the power to run West Battery. In 1920, the fort's central power plant took over, leaving this one to serve as a backup power supply.

It takes about two hours to walk all of the trails to each of the fort's different historical sites. Most are fairly level with one exception; behind West Battery a set of steps leads to the top of a high promontory with expansive views across the Columbia River.

Summer brings out historic encampments and battlefield reenactments. Check the park's website for updates and information.

HOURS: Museum: June through September, daily, 10 AM until 6 PM; October through May, daily, 10 AM until 4 PM. The park day-use area is open daily from 8 AM to 6 PM.

COST: $3 per vehicle

LOCATION: 100 Peter Iredale Road, Hammond

PHONE: 503-861-1671

WEBSITE: www.oregonstateparks.org

5 Fort Clatsop National Memorial

WHAT'S HERE: **Visitor center with numerous exhibits and a reconstruction of the Lewis and Clark Expedition's 1805 winter home**

DON'T MISS THIS: **The short walk to the reconstructed Fort Clatsop**

Through a series of exhibits and interpretive panels, the visitor center tells the story of the Lewis and Clark Expedition as it reached the West Coast. Leaving from near St. Louis on May 14, 1804, the Lewis and Clark Corps of Discovery finally arrived at the Pacific Ocean in December 1805 after covering more than 4,000 miles. They spent their last 600 miles on the Clearwater, Snake, and finally the Columbia River. Captain William Clark mistakenly thought they had reached the Pacific Ocean on November 7, but they were still in the Columbia River estuary.

They spent their initial 10 days here exploring the north side of the Columbia River, looking for a place to spend the winter. The party finally decided to cross the river because they had heard from local Clatsop Indians that there was better hunting over there. They found what they thought was "a most eligible site" and began construction of their small fort, which was about two miles from what is now the Lewis and Clark River. Their combination log fort and home served them through a very rainy winter, in which it didn't rain on only 12 days. Many of the rainy days found the members of the party remaining inside their shelters preparing clothing, food, and weapons for the long trip home.

Throughout the winter, they traded with the local Clatsop who Clark described in his journal entries as being quite shrewd bargainers. Food was never a problem here as it had been in the Bitterroot Mountains. They managed to kill more than 130 elk, 20 deer, and numerous smaller game, including waterfowl. Vegetables were rare. They traded with the Indians for wapato, a root that looks similar to a small potato.

They also had an opportunity to eat whale meat. Clatsop Indians described a "monstrous fish" that had washed up on the beach a few miles south (on today's Cannon Beach). By the time a party reached the beached whale, only bones remained—the local Indians had already removed the meat. Clark managed to trade for 300 pounds of whale meat and a few gallons of rendered oil. Lewis described the meat as: "not unlike the fat of Poark tho' the texture was more spongey and somewhat coarser. I had a part of it cooked and found it very pallitable and tender, it resembled the beaver or the dog in flavor." Obviously, members of the expedition were not choosey about food, especially when hungry.

Expedition member bunks at Fort Clatsop

As the expedition ran low on salt, a party was sent to the coast to boil seawater. A rotation of three men worked around the clock to keep five of the company's largest kettles boiling, producing about three quarts of salt each day. They made four bushels total, the equivalent of 32 gallons, most of which they put in casks for the trip home. That trip began on March 23, 1806.

The fort is a short walk from the visitor center. As you walk through the small fort, you'll see the cramped quarters, along with elk and beaver pelts like those that the party used to keep warm. The original reconstructed fort, built in 1955, burned to the ground in 2005. Another has since been reconstructed, based, like the first, on floor plan descriptions and dimensions that Clark drew on the elk skin cover of one of his journals.

Besides the short walk from the visitor center to Fort Clatsop, another trail leads down to the river's edge. Part of the trail is a boardwalk across a wetlands area. There is a dugout canoe and interpretive signs along the way—not to mention lots of wildflowers during summer.

HOURS: Mid-June to Labor Day, daily, 9 AM until 6 PM; after Labor Day until mid-June, daily, 9 AM until 5 PM. Closed Christmas Day.
COST: Age 16 and older, $3
LOCATION: 92343 Fort Clatsop Road, Astoria
PHONE: 503-861-2471
WEBSITE: www.nps.gov/lewi

6 Tillamook Cheese Factory and Visitor Center

WHAT'S HERE: **Cheese factory, restaurant, and gift shop**
DON'T MISS THIS: **The absolutely delicious ice cream**

This is a gastronomically-satisfying and educational stop, all in one. As early as 1855, Tillamook farmers had begun shipping their butter to Portland aboard the *Morning Star of Tillamook*, a schooner they had built. A replica of the ship sits outside the visitor center, and its image is still on the Tillamook product labels. Cheese production wasn't started until 1894. That year, T. S. Townsend established a commercial cheese plant in this small, coastal Oregon farming community. With orders in-hand from local farmers, Townsend headed to Portland where he purchased 30 cows and the required equipment for a cheese plant. He hired Canadian Peter McIntosh as his cheesemaker because McIntosh had experience with the cheddering process—and he had his own recipe.

Other local farmers joined in the cheesemaking process by creating numerous small plants around the county. In 1909, 10 of those independent cheesemakers banded together and formed a cooperative—the Tillamook County Creamery Association—that would control cheese quality, and just as important, market the cheese under a single brand. In the late 1940s, several large independent cheese producers joined the co-op and built a processing plant just outside of the town of Tillamook. That plant remains part of today's large-scale operations. In the 1950s, a small cheese shop was added to the factory to sell directly to the public. In 1979, the shop expanded to include the observation deck and a larger visitor center.

If you walk past the restaurant and gift shop toward the self-guided factory tour area, numerous photographs and graphics explain the area's history and the cheesemaking process. The observation deck allows for great views of the cheesemaking and packaging process. An introductory video explains some of the history behind this operation: It takes five quarts of whole milk to make one pound of cheese, and it takes ten quarts of milk to make a pound of butter. There are 198 dairy farms in Tillamook County, each averaging 82 acres and 100 milking cows, plus another 100 head of young stock and dry or pregnant cows on each farm. Farmers gross about $2,100 for each producing cow and pay out about $1,000 for feed, medical care, and other expenses. The average Holstein eats 90 pounds of forage and grain and drinks between 30 and 40 gallons of water daily. Another exhibit describes the different dairy cows, and there is a cow with the milking machine attached.

As you exit the exhibit area samples of the many cheeses are available; there is plenty available to purchase. One of the most popular products is Tillamook ice cream—and it's available in numerous flavors.

HOURS: Day following Labor Day through mid-June, daily, 8 AM to 6 PM; mid-June through Labor Day, 8 AM to 8 PM. Closed Thanksgiving and Christmas (tours are self-guided).

COST: Free

LOCATION: 4175 U.S. 101 North, Tillamook

PHONE: 503-815-1300

WEBSITE: www.tillamookcheese.com

Tillamook Cheese Factory

7 Tillamook County Pioneer Museum

WHAT'S HERE: **Wide range of artifacts reflecting regional history**

DON'T MISS THIS: **The extensive collection of wildlife specimens, from birds to bears**

Built in 1905, the Tillamook County courthouse served only three decades before being deemed too small, after which a new courthouse was constructed. That was the first step toward turning the old courthouse into a county museum that would house a collection of only 400 items. Today the museum possesses more than 35,000 artifacts and 10,000 photographs, many of which are exhibited throughout the courthouse's many rooms.

Several of Tillamook County's more prominent and important early families are represented in the museum's Pioneer Family Gallery. Photos of each member, along with short histories of their contributions, cover the walls. Joseph Champion was the first non-Indian settler in the county, arriving in 1851. He became the first schoolteacher of newly created Tillamook County, as well as the first county clerk and the first treasurer. Considering his many accomplishments, Champion was most noted for his "strong and legible handwriting." Warren Vaughn and Harriet Trask were the first couple to be married in the county in 1858. Harriet was almost 15 years old when Justice of the Peace Isaac Alderman conducted the civil ceremony. For anyone wanting more information about Tillamook's pioneer families, a series of storyboards in the gallery offers summaries of many family histories. This gallery also includes numerous personal items, such as the rolltop desk of Governor William Wallace Thayer, Oregon's sixth governor, who served from 1878 to 1882.

The old courthouse's large vault remains, but rather than being filled with money or valuable documents, it serves as a gallery for local Native American artifacts, from arrowheads and spear points to finely woven cedar bark baskets and whale bone war clubs. A story above the cases from a diary entry made by Warren Vaughn recounts a meeting with Tillamook Chief Kilchis, who is described as a "large, dark Indian with an imposing presence." Chief Kilchis is thought to have been part African and descended from a shipwreck survivor.

The military gallery features exhibits divided into the different war eras, including World War I and II, and the Korean and Vietnam conflicts. One of the most popular exhibits is the mannequin soldier holding a Thompson submachine gun. This gallery also displays a small portion of their gun collection. It includes a Peerless double-barrel shotgun from the first shipment of breech-loading shotguns that arrived in the county.

Typical 19th-century Oregon furniture

OREGON COAST

One of the more curious items in the museum is a log cabin, a large hollowed tree with a shake roof. It is a replica of the tree that Chief Kilchis offered as shelter to Joe Champion. The same area also features a blacksmith shop with its tools. An old buckboard seat is mounted on the floor in front of the display, which you can sit on; its spring suspension provides a sense of what a buckboard ride might have been like. Throughout the adjacent pioneer cabin's furnishings are numerous mountain lion skins; apparently, the cats were not tolerated in dairy country. In the same area, an exhibit case holds large pieces of beeswax, a major trade item even during the 16th and 17th centuries. The wax blocks stamped with numbers and designs in the exhibit have been scientifically dated to between 1500 and 1650 and are from Luzon Island in the Philippines. Tons of the wax has washed up on the shore from old shipwrecks.

The basement holds several vehicles, including a 1902 Holsman originally purchased for $1,100 and a 1909 Buick that cost $1,000. The stagecoach from the North Yamhill and Tillamook State Line is a design that is seldom seen. Unlike most stagecoaches with their covered passenger compartments, this one has no roof, which seems a very strange design considering rain is a common occurrence in coastal Oregon. The remainder of the basement includes saddles—this is still cow country—old washing machines, early radios, and various other farm-related items. There is even a "transportation basket." These casket-shaped woven baskets were used to transport bodies from the place of death to the mortuary, a kind of early body bag.

Walk the stairway to the second floor, passing a series of salmon and steelhead mounted to the wall, to reach a very large natural history museum with hundreds of animal specimens. The displays include numerous dioramas of different birds in their natural habitats—snowy owl in snow, waterbirds along a shoreline, marsh birds in a marsh. While there are weasels and beaver and seals, not all of the animals are native to the Pacific Northwest. There is also a polar bear, a grizzly bear, and a musk ox.

HOURS: Tuesday through Saturday, 10 AM to 4 PM
COST: Adults, $3; seniors, $2
LOCATION: 2106 2nd Street, Tillamook
PHONE: 503-842-4553
WEBSITE: www.tcpm.org

8 Tillamook Air Museum

WHAT'S HERE: Historic aircraft stored in a massive blimp hangar
DON'T MISS THIS: The Mini-Guppy

Driving on U.S. 101 south of Tillamook, the Air Museum is impossible to miss. Even from a distance, you instantly realize the building is big. The World War II–era wooden blimp hangar stands 192 feet high (over 15 stories) and is 1,072-feet long. Its doors are 120 feet high, which allowed the 8,252-feet-long K-class blimps that were originally assigned here to easily enter and exit. The U.S. Navy built 17 of these wooden behemoths along the coastal U.S. to house the blimps that patrolled the oceans and escorted convoys during World War II. The big blimps had a range of 2,000 miles and the ability to stay aloft for three days.

Outside the museum you will be greeted by the very peculiar-looking Boeing 377 Stratocruiser, better known as the Mini-Guppy. It looks like someone attached a little nose, wings, and a tail to a grain silo and called it an airplane. There were two other incantations of this aircraft known by equally fish-type names—the Super Guppy and the Pregnant Guppy. The Mini-Guppy had a 13-foot-wide cargo floor, and its inside diameter could handle Apollo mission rocket components, which it could fly from California to Florida in 18 hours, much faster than the three weeks it had originally taken by land.

Step inside the hangar and "amazing" is the only response. The wooden support framework that holds this structure together makes China's Bird's Nest Olympic Stadium look like a child's toy. This had to be an architect's nightmare and the construction crew's biggest puzzle ever. While many of the aircraft and other exhibits are in the wide open spaces of the hangar, many of the highly prized and meticulously restored aircraft are tucked under a set of suspended parachutes. Their main purpose may be keeping the birds roosting in the high support rafters above from bombing the aircraft.

The collection includes primarily World War II– and Cold War–era military aircraft. Among them are a Lockheed P2V-7 Neptune, a 400-mile-per-hour turbojet, antisubmarine patrol aircraft that had a range of 2,200 miles and carried six 0.50 caliber guns, torpedoes, mines, and depth charges. This aircraft began service in 1961 and did its job for 16 years patrolling over the Atlantic, Pacific, Arctic, and Mediterranean. An earlier P2V set a long-distance record in 1946, flying 11,235 miles from Australia to Ohio in a little more than 55 hours, without refueling.

Other aircraft include an A-7 Corsair, another Naval aircraft capable of carrying

One of 30-plus aircraft in the blimp hangar

a 10,000-pound payload. A-7s began their careers over Vietnam and ended them with the Iraq War. The museum holds the World War II version of the Corsair, the F4U-7 model with its unique "gull-shaped" wings and set-back cockpit that required a nontraditional approach to landing on aircraft carriers.

World War II caused some of the biggest-ever innovations in aircraft design in an ongoing attempt to create bigger, faster, and more capable aircraft. One of those designs was the P-38 Lightning. Known as the "forked-tail devil" to enemy pilots, the museum's P-38 is one of only a few that remain in flying condition. It has been named *Tangerine.* A pre–World War II aircraft in the museum is the Bellanca Aircruiser. Built in 1938, some consider it the most efficient single engine airplane ever built. It could hold 15 people, or with the seats removed, carry two tons of cargo. The Tillamook Air Museum has the last remaining Bellanca in existence.

A plane, often confused with the famous Japanese Zero, the Nakajima Ki-43 Hayabusa, named for the peregrine falcon but better known as the Oscar, was actually the Japanese military's most used single-engine fighter. In the latter part of World War II, it became outclassed by newer U.S. and Japanese fighters, and was used for kamikaze suicide flights. Also here is a Consolidated PBY-5A Catalina, one of the most famous seaplanes in the U.S. arsenal. The PBY first saw use in 1935. Slow by today's standards with a top speed of 179 knots, it carried five machine guns for defensive purposes. A Catalina was the first to sight the Japanese fleet heading toward Midway Island, providing the early warning that helped the U.S. victory that proved to be a turning point in the war.

There are many more aircraft, including a C-47 Skytrain, an F-14 Tomcat, a German BF-109 Messerschmitt, and even a MiG-17. As you wander through the big hangar, you will see numerous aircraft engines on display, military equipment, including a motorcycle, Jeep, spotlights, and even one of those big military olive drab canvas tents. Peek inside—if the jokester hasn't dismantled the exhibit you will see a GI sitting on a rather modern toilet.

There are many, many more aircraft here and additional exhibits (such as winter coats worn by pilots in the days when cockpits weren't heated) along with a gift shop and small cafe.

HOURS: Daily, 9 AM to 5 PM. Closed Thanksgiving and Christmas.
COST: Adults, $11.50; ages 65-plus, $10.50; ages 6–17, $7
LOCATION: 6030 Hangar Road, Tillamook
PHONE: 503-842-1130
WEBSITE: www.tillamookair.com

9 Yaquina Head Lighthouse and Visitor Center

WHAT'S HERE: Visitor center and museum, the historic lighthouse, and hiking trails

DON'T MISS THIS: The climb to the top of the lighthouse

Your first stop as you drive out to the Yaquina Head Lighthouse, if you don't count stops to admire the amazing views of the coast and ocean, is the visitor center. This isn't a small, pick-up-a-couple-of-brochures type of visitor center. It's a major interpretive center with wonderful exhibits that are both fun and very informative.

The exhibits follow the history of the area's development beginning with the building of the coast highway. While, today, Yaquina Head is protected as a natural area, between 1917 and 1983, its basalt (rock) proved to be an ideal, easily crushed material for road construction. Workers weren't gentle on the land. To get the basalt, they carved tunnels deep into the cliffs, packed them with explosives, and blew off large chunks of the cliffs, sometimes breaking nearby windows. You can still see drill holes in the cliffs above the visitor center.

Operated by the U.S. Bureau of Land Management, the visitor center identifies the changes that government has made to the headland and the way that people and their values have influenced those decisions. During the 19th century it appeared that government's job was to acquire new lands, then give away that land as enticement to bring settlers west. From the Midwest to the Pacific Northwest, land giveaways attracted thousands of people. As we moved into the 20th century, government leaders began to realize that some of these public lands should be saved for future generations to enjoy. Leaders looked for a balance between preserving resources and allowing some of those resources to be mined and harvested responsibly in order for the country to grow. One of the changes included the surveying and marking of U.S. Forest lands in an effort to reduce illegal or accidental harvesting of government-owned forests. The center includes a look at some of the forester's tools, including tree climbing gear and a branding ax that was used to smack a U.S. identity brand onto a tree's bare wood after part of its bark had been cut off with an ax.

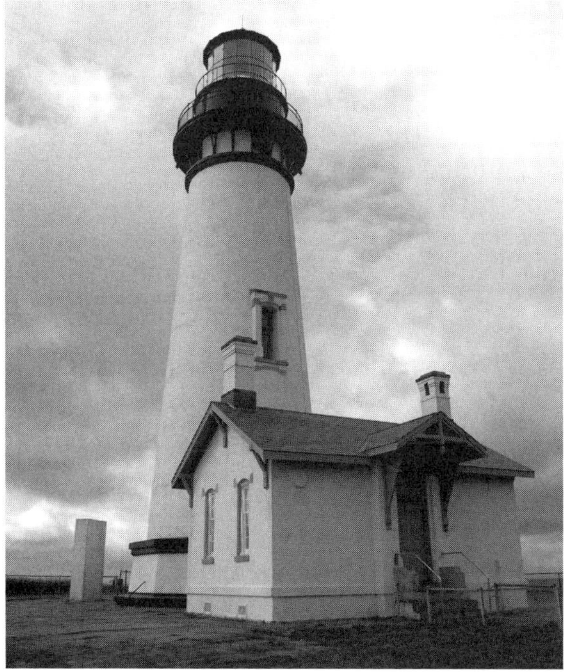

Yaquina Head Lighthouse

The visitor center's exhibits include a close look at the challenges that workers confronted during the construction of the lighthouse in the 1870s. Yaquina Head was isolated, so small boats brought in supplies and work crews. Weather was a major hindrance as high winds and high waves battered boats and crews, occasionally destroying the boats. Workers fought both wind and rain as they hand-dug down 11 feet for the tower's foundation. Pulleys were required to lift the heavy iron pieces to the top of the tower, and finally the French-made First Order Fresnel lens had to be carried by hand to the top and assembled. A model of the lighthouse offers a better perspective on its design and construction. Other exhibits include a look at how a Fresnel lens can greatly magnify the brightness of the lamp through its many prisms, and the very monotonous duties of the lighthouse keepers in making sure that their lifesaving beam of light was always shining bright.

The visitor center's exhibits on ocean wildlife are an excellent place to introduce kids—and adults—to the real treasures of the sea. Yaquina Head is a paradise for birds, those that inhabit the tidal zones and also the pelagic (open ocean) birds that come here in spring to feed and nest. There's a gray whale skull in the life-sized coastal cliff diorama that visitors can walk through; the life-sized wall mural of gray whales makes you feel almost as though you are underwater with these magnificent creatures. Back in the lobby area, puzzles and other hands-on activities are waiting for any kids who are interested.

The lighthouse is only a few minutes' drive from the visitor center. It's a short and level walk from the parking lot to the lighthouse. Inside are several interpretive panels, some of the old tools that were used here, and even a lighthouse keeper's writing desk. One of the exhibits answers the question about how high to build the lighthouse. The higher the light sits, the farther out to sea it can be seen—except when low fog settles in, then it becomes invisible. Designers made the decision that with Yaquina Head being 81 feet above the ocean, they needed to build the lighthouse about the same height, putting the light 162 feet above the ocean. At that height, the light can be seen from about 19 miles out to sea, not because the light doesn't shine any farther, but because beyond that distance the earth's curvature blocks the view. This is one of the few working lighthouses in which visitors can climb the spiral staircase to the top where the lens sits. The views of the coastline from the top are quite spectacular, so a little huffing and puffing is worth the effort.

Yaquina Head offers several miles of trails. If you'd like an even better view of the coast, hike to the top of Salal Hill, which sits on the inland side of the lighthouse. It generally doesn't takes more than 15 minutes to hike to the top, but the trail gets quite steep in places.

HOURS: Park open daily, dawn to dusk. Visitor center open daily: summer, 9 AM to 5 PM; fall, 10 AM to 5 PM; winter, 10 AM to 4:30 PM. Lighthouse open daily, summer, 9 AM to 4 PM; fall and winter, 10 AM to 4 PM.

COST: $7 per vehicle

LOCATION: Turnoff and entrance is on U.S. 101, 3 miles north of Newport

PHONE: 541-574-3100

WEBSITE: www.blm.gov/or/resources/recreation/yaquina/index.php

10 Oregon Coast Aquarium

WHAT'S HERE: **Fish, mammals, and birds of the Pacific**

DON'T MISS THIS: **An "underwater" tunnel adventure with sharks, rockfish, and bat rays**

Since the Pacific Ocean is Oregon's western border, it seems appropriate that the state have at least one excellent aquarium—and the aquarium at Newport certainly fits the bill. It's much more than a simple aquarium, because many of the exhibits are outside and offer close-up views of marine life, including sea lions, otters, and seabirds. You're going to want to spend a couple of hours or more here, especially if you have kids along.

The aquarium takes you through the various marine habitats with the Orford Reef and Halibut Flats. In one gallery kids and limber adults can crawl beneath one of the tanks and pop up inside a plastic bubble inside the tank for an entirely different perspective, surrounded by water and staring eye-to-eye with a giant crab. That is only a sampling of what lies ahead. Wander a little farther into the galleries to Passages of the Deep, a clear-acrylic tunnel that allows you to walk on the ocean floor as lots of sharks, bat rays, and dozens of species of rockfish swim all around you. It's quite exciting to see a large shark swim slowly over your head or look into the eyes of several of the aquarium's 500 different species while in *their* home. There's even the remnants of an old shipwreck on the sandy bottom.

The jellyfish exhibit is always popular. These squishy creatures spend most of their lives drifting with the ocean's currents. Since they are about 95 percent water and mostly transparent, they have few enemies in the ocean—there's not much worth eating and they are hard to see. Some jellies eat plankton and small fish, a few eat other jellies, and some hug the ocean bottom and eat algae. Some are harmless, while others have powerful stinging tentacles. The longest animal in the world is the lion's mane jelly, which has tentacles that have a powerful stinger and can reach 200 feet in length.

Passages of the Deep exhibit

Head outside to the various pools for more fun. At one time, sea otters were nearly extinct as their fur was a cherished commodity for 19th-century trappers and hunters. Why were they such a popular target of fur traders? A sea otter's pelt is extremely luxurious, averaging 1 million hairs per square inch. And these aren't tiny animals; adults can weigh up to 100 pounds, and they must eat the equivalent of 25 percent of their weight each day of crabs, clams, and shrimp to maintain those shapely bodies. They spend many hours each day grooming their fur coats. Scrupulously clean hairs and a thick coat prevent cold seawater from reaching their skin, ensuring they stay warm in the coldest water. The aquarium has two species, the northern and southern sea otter, swimming in one of its outside pools. The 12-foot-deep pool is surrounded by rocks and has several vantage points, including an underwater window.

Two of the most commonly seen marine mammals along the Oregon Coast are sea lions and harbor seals. Sea lions are heard before they are seen as they often bark nonstop as they lie out on rocks, docks, or anywhere else they find convenient. How do you tell them apart? Sea lions are usually more slender and darker in color. They also have prominent ear flaps and walk on their front flippers when onshore. Harbor seals have holes for their ears and push themselves along on their bellies. The 15-foot-deep pool includes haul-out rocks where the seals and sea lions can be seen from the underwater window and several above-water vantage points.

For bird lovers, the aviary offers a look at a few rare birds that only a few people ever see in the wild. This is one of the largest open aviaries you'll find anywhere. It includes a large pool—yes, these are seabirds—along with cliffs, shoreline rocks, and sand, making this a seabird paradise. The birds here include tufted puffins, common murres, black oystercatchers, rhinoceros auklets, and pigeon guillemots—not your common robins and blackbirds.

The aquarium offers numerous opportunities throughout the year to sleepover in the Passages of the Deep tunnel. You can fall asleep as sharks and bat rays swim just a few feet away. It's great fun for kids.

HOURS: Memorial Day weekend through Labor Day, daily, 9 AM to 6 PM; from Labor Day to Memorial Day weekend, daily, 10 AM to 5 PM. Closed Christmas Day.

COST: Ages 13–64, $14.25; ages 65-plus, $12.25; ages 3–12, $8.75

LOCATION: 2820 SE Ferry Slip Road, Newport

PHONE: 541-867-3474

WEBSITE: www.aquarium.org

11 Umpqua Discovery Center

WHAT'S HERE: Unique exhibits on the Umpqua River's natural and cultural history

DON'T MISS THIS: View of the Umpqua River from the boardwalk behind the museum

The Umpqua Discovery Center is a great kid's learning adventure—and not bad for adults, either. There are two distinct galleries, one on each side of the lobby. Enter the Tidewater and Time section to journey back through time when nearly 7,000 years ago the first Native Americans settled these rich tidelands along the Umpqua River. Their way of life was changed forever with the coming of European sailing ships, fur traders, and finally, settlers.

The most striking part of all the exhibits are the life-sized murals that seem to bring these times to life. The Confederated Tribes of the Coos Lower Umpqua and the Siuslaw Indians, descendants of these ancient people, have worked with archaeologists to recover and exhibit the artifacts found here. A carved harpoon head, a fishing net weight, pestles, and mortars seen here all played important parts in the lives of these ancient people. The mural shows one of them standing among the river rocks, spearing salmon, a mainstay of their diets. Other interpretive panels explain that the local Kuuich Indians trapped deer and elk in pits, while using their bows and arrows to hunt small game and birds, including ducks and geese.

There is a peek at the life of Jedediah Smith, the 28-year-old trapper and explorer who crossed the Mojave Desert into California in 1827. He continued his explorations along Oregon's south coast, encountering the Kuuich. In one pitched battle, 15 of Smith's party were killed, with only Smith and three others escaping to Fort Vancouver. Some Comanche killed Smith in 1831.

The settlers, men looking for free land to farm, brought quick and permanent changes. One of the museum's murals depicts a man behind his horse-drawn plow as his wife waves, holding her basket, likely filled with food for a hungry husband. While farming brought people, it was mines, lumber, and the shipping industry that ensured prosperity for the Oregon Coast. In a small room, you can hear firsthand what life was like during those earlier times from four elderly Oregonians whose photographs show who is giving the recorded talks.

The exhibits continue to the salmon industry, beginning back in the days when you could walk across the rivers on the backs of fish and never get your feet wet. Perhaps an exaggeration, but with millions of salmon seemingly there for the taking, the salmon canning industry

Totem pole outside the Umpqua Discovery Center

flourished. The murals depict the waterfront and sailing ships, as well as local businesses—a barbershop, milliner, and a general store. River steamboats added to the excitement as they moved goods and people back and forth between mining towns, lumber mills, and farms.

Exit the tidewater exhibit and enter a cave for a journey into the Pacific Northwest's natural history. One of the first things you'll encounter is a big bull elk, fortunately only the mural version. Now you're hiking along a forest trail to a switchback offering numerous encounters with nature. Inside the cave a black bear is hibernating, and you can hear the much-slowed heartbeat, down from its normal 70–90 beats per minute to as few as 8 beats each minute. You can also learn that black bears aren't always black and that a cub at birth weighs less than one pound, but as an adult, a male may weigh 350 pounds. There's also a look at bear scat to help discover what they have been eating.

Hike a little farther and you'll see more elk. A story tells how they lose their antlers each year—and how the raccoons gnaw on the discarded antlers for the minerals they contain. Kids can push buttons to hear the calls of birds such as quail, pileated woodpeckers, and an eagle, each very distinct. Look down at the trail where a small piece has been cut out and the underground world of salamanders and soil is revealed. A little farther along, you will encounter a cougar, sometimes called a mountain lion, Oregon's largest cat.

A few steps from the forest enter the science lab, which illustrates and explains the reasons for Oregon's rainy weather. The weather station helps you identify the many different types of clouds and looks at how the rains are monitored along with the changing river levels in order to predict flooding. Another exhibit explores coastal wind—one of the most powerful natural forces—and how it continually shapes the coastal strand with waves and wind-blown sand.

There's still more wildlife to experience, from deer and frogs to snakes and foxes. A beaver will greet you on your nature walk, as it sits quietly, perhaps contemplating the next tree branch it needs to chew through and add to its dam.

When you finally finish inside, head outside to the back of the museum where a boardwalk offers great views of the Umpqua River.

HOURS: Daily, October through May, 10 AM to 4 PM; June through September, 9 AM to 5 PM
COST: Adults, $8; ages 65-plus, $7; ages 6–15, $4
LOCATION: 409 Riverfront Way, Reedsport
PHONE: 541-271-4816
WEBSITE: www.umpquadiscoverycenter.com

12 Coos Historical and Maritime Museum

WHAT'S HERE: **History of Coos Bay, from the Native Americans to maritime explorers**

DON'T MISS THIS: **The 300-year-old Native American fish weir**

For centuries, ships of many nations had sailed along Oregon's coast and passed the extensive sandbar that screened from sight the body of water that would become known as Coos Bay. The first settlers here were only temporary, stranded for four months after their military supply ship *Captain Lincoln* wrecked on the North Spit in 1852. Following their rescue, word of the area's riches spread, bringing settlers who soon founded Marshfield, the first town on Coos Bay.

Even after the entrance to Coos Bay was discovered, getting into the bay by ship was not easy. A relatively shallow passage and shifting sands caused numerous shipwrecks. Since the *Captain Lincoln,* more than 160 vessels and 130 people have been lost on or near what's been referred to as the Coos Bay "wrecking bar." One of the more famous was the *New Carissa* that ran aground on the North Spit in 1999. Since it was leaking oil, the U.S. Navy attempted and failed to ignite the fuel onboard. The following day the Navy dropped napalm on the ship, but that simply broke it in half. Attempting to tow the ship's two parts out to sea so they could be sunk also failed. Finally with half of the ship now stuck on shore and the other half floating at sea, the Navy was able to sink the floating half with torpedoes. A salvage company didn't begin removing the remaining half from the beach until 2008.

As difficult as getting into Coos Bay by sea may have been, for many years that was the only way to get to there. Rugged mountains surround the bay, making it difficult to construct roads. It took travelers three days of stage rides, boat rides, and more stage rides in order to get from Coos Bay to Eugene, Oregon. By contrast, within 24 hours people could get to San Francisco with one boat ride, so that is where Coos Bay citizens often

Early dairy equipment

OREGON COAST

went for "culture," which included the San Francisco Opera. A small exhibit houses some of the early-day Coos Bay-to-San Francisco opera clothes and a pair of opera glasses.

In 1869 the U.S. government offered nearly 100,000 acres to the Coos Bay Wagon Road Company (a group of investors from Roseburg) to build a military wagon road from Roseburg to Coos Bay. The company was allowed to sell the land in 160-acre parcels at a maximum of $2.50 per acre to help pay for the construction of this first overland route between the two towns. Instead, the investors sold the land in several very large parcels at higher prices, sometimes even selling land they didn't own. The properties changed hands several times, and in the end, no one was sure who owned the road that was ultimately constructed. Finally, in 1915, a U.S. Supreme Court ruling allowed the government to pay the titleholders $2.50 per acre, so that it could become the official owner of its own road. The museum has numerous documents and photographs of the disputed mountain road.

While the museum has numerous shipwreck artifacts filling the exhibits, there is much more here to see and learn about life in the Pacific Northwest. One of those now-illegal Pacific Northwest practices was one of the ways they moved thousands of logs down small rivers toward the mills before the advent of logging trucks. "Splash dams" were built to raise the level of a stream and create a large pond or lake. Teams of oxen hauled thousands of logs from where loggers felled them to the pond where they were floated. When the reservoir filled with logs, the splash dams were simply blown up, allowing the torrent of water to carry the cascading raft of logs downriver toward the mill.

One of the older and quite rare artifacts found in the museum is part of a 300-year-old Native American weir uncovered in 1995 near Bandon. It is a section of lattice that was staked to the bottom of the river to restrict the movements of fish, allowing them to be trapped, netted, clubbed, or harpooned. It's a rare discovery, considering how quickly objects made from wood decay.

The museum includes many of the same artifacts found in other Pacific Northwest museums. You'll see logging tools, including pike poles, cant hooks, and axes. There is also old cranberry harvesting equipment, kitchen items from pioneer homes, early dairy-related tools and exhibits on gold mining, coal mining (this was a big coal mining area for many years), and even shipbuilding.

A new museum is scheduled for construction in 2010 on the waterfront south of the present museum.

HOURS: Tuesday through Saturday, 10 AM to 4 PM. Open Sundays from July 1 through Labor Day, 12 PM to 4 PM.

COST: Ages 13 and over, $4

LOCATION: 1220 Sherman Avenue, North Bend

PHONE: 541-756-6320

WEBSITE: www.cooshistory.org

13 Shore Acres State Park

WHAT'S HERE: **Ocean views and elegant gardens that were once part of a lumberman's mansion**

DON'T MISS THIS: **The largest Monterey pine in Oregon**

What is now Shore Acres State Park was once an estate that belonged to pioneer lumberman and shipbuilder Louis J. Simpson. It was actually Louis's father, Captain Asa Mead Simpson, who first came to California in 1849 looking for gold and finding it, but not in the gold fields. Instead, he found his wealth in the Stockton and Sacramento retail lumberyards that he opened in California. Looking for timber and sawmill sites, he opened a mill and shipyard—to build the ships to transport his lumber to distant markets—on Coos Bay. Eventually he had mills in several West Coast cities. In 1899, Asa's son Louis, arrived in Coos Bay to oversee his father's investments. Louis expanded his business interests to include a woolen mill and an ice plant, and he laid out the city of North Bend.

In 1905, Louis Simpson ventured out to the headland, where he crawled through the heavy undergrowth. Near the point he found the perfect place for his home. The land's owner, a "squawman" who lived alone in a small cabin, offered him the property for $4,000. Simpson quickly agreed and became the owner of 320 acres of coastal shoreline. He began building his summer home on the bluff, a three-story mansion with a heated indoor swimming pool. He also developed five acres of formal gardens that included a large pond.

In 1914, Simpson started building an addition that included a 75-foot-long Roman bath room with a large swimming pool that allowed guests to choose between hot or cold freshwater or seawater. Simpson initially furnished the home with Mission Style furniture, but when it became his year-round home, he replaced the original oak furniture with more formal furnishings, including Oriental carpets, sculptures, and paintings. Much of the new furniture came from his father's home in California following his father's death in 1915. On July 4, 1921, the home and all of its furnishings were destroyed in a spectacular fire. With little insurance to replace the contents, the Simpsons moved into the garden cottage, which remains today.

Shore Acres fountain and garden

Following the wreck of a schooner in 1923 that dumped its cargo of lumber on Simpson's shoreline, he decided to salvage the materials and build another home. The 224-foot-long house with its gymnasium and bedroom suites, each with a private bath, was never completed, even though Simpson, his wife Lela, and daughters, Geraldine and Barbara, lived in the home. Financial setbacks and the start of World War II forced Simpson to abandon the home and move to a small cottage on lower Coos Bay.

In 1942, Oregon State Parks purchased the property. The mansion had deteriorated to such an extent that it had to be razed. The gardens, however, were maintained and today feature year-round displays. From May through September, there are 5,000 flowering annuals and perennials. From August to mid-October, expect to see the park's 200 dahlias in bloom, and from April through mid-May, hundreds of rhododendrons and azaleas can be found in their colorful glory. The gardens also feature more than 600 rosebushes that bloom from June through September. Near the greenhouse is a giant Monterey pine, the largest of its species in Oregon.

On the bluff where Simpson's two mansions once sat, an enclosed observation building offers spectacular views of the rugged cliffs. It's a great place to see migrating whales from December through June.

HOURS: Park is open 8 AM to sunset.
COST: $3 per vehicle
LOCATION: Cape Arago Highway, 13 miles southwest of Coos Bay, Oregon
PHONE: 541-888-4902 or 541-888-2472
WEBSITE: www.oregonstateparks.org/park_97.php

14 Bandon Historical Society Museum

WHAT'S HERE: **Local history as seen through artifacts and a large photo collection**
DON'T MISS THIS: **The cranberry grader and separator**

Originally named Averill, this coastal town was renamed Bandon in 1889. In 1936, a catastrophic fire swept through the city destroying more than 20 buildings in the business district and killing at least nine people. When rebuilding began, the second building to be reconstructed was Bandon's City Hall, which today is the museum.

The museum focuses on the history of the Bandon area, from the people to the businesses that held the town together. Logging, fishing, and the cranberry industry thrived, and the museum focuses its attention on each of them. There are likely more period photographs in this museum than in any other museum this size. The photos, mostly of people, help add an extra dimension to the artifacts that fill the exhibit cases. For example, a small selection of the photos illustrate what the museum labels "Bandon's Other Business," illegal alcohol following the passage of the Eighteenth Amendment, better known as

Prohibition. Along with a number of old jugs and bottles, there are numerous photos of the local sheriff, collected evidence, and a number of producing stills.

Another series of photos takes visitors back to the very early 1900s as the automobile was making its entry into the lives of those living in Bandon. It was a time when asphalt was rare and dirt roads frequently turned to mud. There is a 1920 photo of William Prewett with his new car—stuck axle deep in a very large mud hole. Some of the other vehicles appear to be overloaded, while a line of four cars gets ready for the 1916 Fourth of July parade in downtown Bandon.

The museum's exhibits include some of the locals' hunting weapons and equipment, an 1894 National cash register, medical equipment, and a series of photos and newspapers reporting on the 1936 fire. You can see antique phonographs and a 1905 Princess music box. Old restaurant menus are always intriguing; you can read about what people ate and what they paid for their meals. An original menu board from the Bandon Wayside Motel offers a breakfast steak for 30 cents, a plain steak for 45 cents, bacon and an egg for 20 cents, and a hamburger for 20 cents.

Native Americans are not ignored as several exhibit cases include numerous baskets, arrowheads, and other items such as necklaces from the Coquelle and other tribes. Labels, photos, and maps show the conflict that existed between the local Indians and the settlers.

Surprising for some, mining was another of the industries that flourished here for many years. More surprising, coal was mined here, too. The Port of Bandon was once a major exporter of coal from the Lampa Creek, Riverton, and Beaver Hill mines. Gold also brought people here, and photos of old dredges show the types of equipment that was used.

Like some of those coastal communities farther north, the Bandon area was a dairy producer. The museum looks at dairy farming in the Coquille Valley. But cranberries also came into the agricultural realm of Bandon. A series of photos illustrating cranberry processing is accompanied by cranberry processing equipment, including a Baily's Cranberry Separator and Grader—along with a story about the 1926 cranberry crop that brought in $10,000.

There is a small display of women's fashion from the early 1900s and into the 1950s. One of the older items is a pair of lady's leather high-top shoes from about 1800. A small

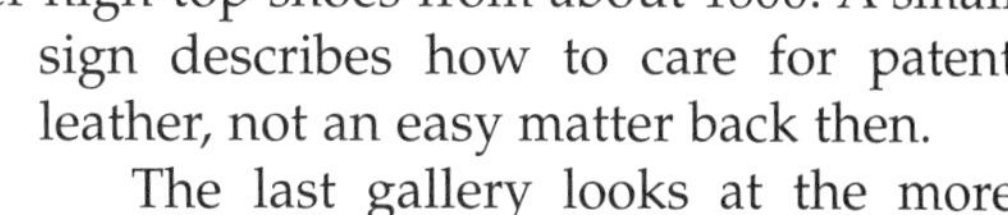

sign describes how to care for patent leather, not an easy matter back then.

The last gallery looks at the more recent history of Bandon with a couple of outboard boat motors, one from about 1916, and World War II military artifacts. Riverboats plied the larger local rivers, and a series of photos shows many of those old boats in action. There also is a small natural history area with various

Bandon's city hall is now the museum.

photographs of local birds and a skeleton of a gray grampus dolpin that was found at the mouth of the New River in 1990.

HOURS: Daily, 10 AM to 4 PM. Closed Sundays.
COST: Adults, $2
LOCATION: Corner of U.S. 101 and Filmore Avenue, Bandon
PHONE: 541-347-2164
WEBSITE: www.bandonhistoricalmuseum.org

15 Cape Blanco Lighthouse and the Hughes House

WHAT'S HERE: **Oregon's westernmost lighthouse and a historic ranch home**
DON'T MISS THIS: **The short climb into the lamp house**

As you head west toward Cape Blanco State Park, the historic Hughes House is the first structure you will encounter. It was constructed in 1898 and served as the home of Patrick and Jane Hughes and their family for 38 years. Cape Blanco was the site of several mini-gold rushes, as mining operations on the beach operated periodically from the mid-1800s to the 1940s. It was gold that caught Patrick Hughes's attention, but he wisely listened to his wife and instead decided on farming to support his family.

The Hughes home was no ordinary farmhouse, but a beautiful two-story, 11-room, 3,000-square-foot Victorian overlooking the Sixes River and their 2,000-acre farm. For carpenters and woodworkers who may be interested in early construction techniques, the house was framed with 2-inch by 8-inch Port Orford cedar, much heftier than today's 2-inch by 4-inch and 2-inch by 6-inch boards. At $3,800, it was not a cheap home for the time, but it was built to last.

The house was strategically located on a small terrace protected from some of the worst storms that came in from the southwest, although those blowing in from the northwest have a direct shot at the house. There is a large cast-iron cookstove in the kitchen. The second floor features a chapel with the original altar

The Hughes's family farmhouse

and a hand-painted ceiling. The home's heating was done with coal rather than cheaper firewood. First-floor rooms include the formal parlor, a room found in most Victorians. There is also a men's parlor, most likely where the men retired to smoke and take care of business.

There were seven children in the Hughes clan. One son, John, was a Roman Catholic priest whose parish was in Portland, yet he set up a chapel on the home's second floor. The altar is original, but the rug was likely taken from another room. The second oldest son, James, worked for 33 years as the lighthouse keeper at Cape Blanco Lighthouse. When another of the Hughes' sons, Francis, married Anna, she also moved into the home, and they used one of the rooms for their only child, Joseph.

The only person to have worked at the lighthouse longer than James Hughes is James Langlois, who served here for 42 years. The oldest standing lighthouse in Oregon claims other honors—it is the highest Oregon lighthouse, standing 245 feet above the Pacific. It is the most southern of Oregon's lighthouses, and was the first in the state fitted with a first-order Fresnel lens, although that was replaced with a smaller second-order lens in 1936. It also marks the westernmost point in Oregon. It is almost always windy and cold here, much different than back at the Hughes wind-sheltered home, so dress accordingly for the walk from the cliffside parking lot to the lighthouse.

HOURS: Cape Blanco State Park open daily. Gates to lighthouse open 10 AM to 3:30 PM. Tours April through October, Thursday through Monday, 10 AM to 3:30 PM. Hughes House closed Mondays, except for holidays.

COST: Lighthouse: Adults, $2; under age 12, $1; family, $5. Hughes House is free.

LOCATION: Approximately 4 miles north of Port Orford on U.S. 101, then 4.5 miles west on Cape Blanco Road

PHONE: 541-332-6774

WEBSITE: www.stateparks.com/cape_blanco.html

16 Curry Historical Society

WHAT'S HERE: **County history museum with many artifacts donated by local families**

DON'T MISS THIS: **Exhibit on the construction of the Rogue River Bridge**

This museum, located alongside U.S. 101, has captured the history of the small coastal communities of Curry County. This area has not always been the peaceful place it appears today, according to a story inside the museum. Beginning in about 1855, there had been ongoing tension and periodic hostilities between the American Indians and the immigrants who lived and traveled along the Rogue River. In 1856, on the north side of the Rogue River within a "gunshot" of the ocean is where the early settlers constructed what they called "Fort Miner." The fort was surrounded by a moat to further aid its defenses against local Indians. On February 22, 1856, as the townspeople celebrated George Washington's birthday, local constable Michael Riley headed upriver to serve a summons. On this day the tensions exploded. At the first gunshots, settlers retreated across the river to the safety of Fort Miner. The Indians burned 60 homes along the river, killed about 60 settlers and soldiers, and began what would be an unsuccessful siege of the fort that lasted 31 days.

Beyond stories of local history, the museum is filled with artifacts that helped the people of the area live better, more comfortable lives. One example is the WP Emerson piano that came around Cape Horn in the late 1880s, then traded hands and homes for a century before ending up in the museum. There is a short history of cast-iron stoves, the new cooking devices that became popular in the mid-1700s, especially after Benjamin Franklin improved the early designs with his "Pennsylvania Fireplace." One exhibit is filled with old logging equipment ranging from saws to brush hooks. There are also a number of photos of early logging operations. Native Americans have not been forgotten; besides the story about the Rogue River War, there is a nice collection of numerous types of Indian baskets.

Today, U.S. 101 crosses many magnificent bridges as it meanders along the Oregon Coast. During these early years, the only way to cross the Rogue River had been via toll ferries, which first began operating in 1857. With traffic becoming increasingly heavy, the county started a free ferry service in 1927. It wasn't until January 21, 1932, that the first bridge to cross the Rogue River opened, celebrated by a crowd of 5,000 people. That same

Safes and guns are included in the collection.

beautiful, seven-arch bridge remains the main U.S. 101 thoroughfare through Gold River. The exhibit includes photos of the bridge's construction.

The museum also includes a look back at how good fishing used to be with photos of anglers showing off their catches of very large salmon. There are also many more collections here, from medical equipment donated by local retired doctors to school desks to old safes. There's even an exhibit of those illegal stills that came into being during Prohibition.

HOURS: Tuesday through Saturday, 10 AM to 4 PM. Closed January.
COST: Donations requested: Ages 16 and over, $2; under age 16, $0.50
LOCATION: 29419 Ellensburg Avenue, Gold Beach
PHONE: 541-247-9396
WEBSITE: www.curryhistory.com

17 Chetco Valley Museum

WHAT'S HERE: **Historic farmhouse that is now a local museum**
DON'T MISS THIS: **The huge Oregon Heritage cypress tree in front of the museum**

Harrison G. Blake built his two-story home in about 1857. His wife Mary Giesel was one of only three in her family who survived an American Indian attack in 1856. In subsequent years, Blake used the home as a stagecoach way station and even as a trading center. Often the first few people to settle an area tend to become community leaders, and such was the case with Blake. He became Chetco's first postmaster, and he also served as the first member of Oregon's House of Representatives in 1874. Blake's home is the oldest standing building in the area and remains in very good condition, especially now, serving as the Chetco Valley Museum.

Chetco Valley Museum

Wandering through the two-story museum brings a few surprises. The museum holds numerous items donated by locals, with some related to early pioneer settlers. One of the more curious is a small trunk that came around Cape Horn in 1706. It has been speculated that Sir Francis Drake may have landed at various locations along California and Oregon, and the museum adds its own bit of intrigue with an iron mask of a lady, said to resemble Queen Elizabeth. Some think that perhaps it was a leftover from one of Drake's shore excursions.

There are many other things that you would expect to see in a small, local museum—old cameras, a cookstove, a Singer sewing machine made in 1887, numerous historic photos, patchwork quilts (some quite old), and more.

Down the hill a few dozen yards in front of the museum is a Monterey cypress tree that Harrison planted in 1857. Today the tree is designated as an Oregon Heritage Tree, and it is likely one of the largest in existence. It stands more than 130 feet tall with a trunk diameter of more than 18 feet. An early 1900s John Deere tractor beside the museum's parking lot looks as though it might still be capable of churning the soil with its steel-cleated rear wheels.

HOURS: Memorial Day through Labor Day only, Friday through Sunday, 1 PM to 5 PM

COST: Free, donations accepted

LOCATION: 15461 Museum Road, Brookings

PHONE: 541-269-2753

WEBSITE: www.curryhistory.com/currymuseums.html

Oregon Coast Tours

Mouth of the Columbia River History Tour

ESTIMATED DAYS: 1–2
ESTIMATED DRIVING MILES: 35

The mouth of the Columbia River is one of the most dangerous places in the world for boats and ships of all kinds. The **Columbia River Maritime Museum** (page 33) in Astoria highlights the history of this remarkable meeting of river and ocean. From the early European explorers who first entered the treacherous waters to the salmon fishermen who risked their lives here and the U.S. Coast Guard sailors and boats that made hundreds of daring rescue attempts, it's all captured here. Down the road a few blocks is the **Flavel House** (page 36), the Victorian home of one of Astoria's most successful 19th-century river bar pilots.

The Flavel House, Astoria

As dangerous a passage as the mouth of the Columbia may be, it was also a point that had to be protected during wartime to keep invading navies from entering the Columbia River and reaching Portland. Nearby **Fort Stevens** (page 38) is a concrete monument to the country's war efforts in protecting this vital waterway. Although the fort originally was built during the Civil War, the main portions that remain today are remnants of World War II. You are free to wander about and climb through the old gun emplacements and facilities—and tour the small museum.

Meriwether Lewis and William Clark's epic overland journey ended here near the mouth of the Columbia River in 1805. That winter their party spent their time in a small log "fort" they built south of Astoria along the shore of the Columbia River estuary. The original **Fort Clatsop** (page 40) is long gone, but the National Park Service has reconstructed and furnished the small fort (based on the expedition's notes and drawings) that served the exploration party during the winter of 1805–1806 as they prepared for their journey home.

Coastal History Tour

ESTIMATED DAYS: 1

ESTIMATED DRIVING MILES: 5

The Oregon Coast is as beautiful as any stretch of ocean shoreline in the world. While some early pioneers found that the coastal valleys provided a perfect place for raising crops and cattle, others needed the coastal lighthouses to help guide their ships along the treacherous headlands. One of the earliest and most successful dairy operations in this area is located in the tiny town of Tillamook—the **Tillamook Cheese Factory** (page 41). Take the short self-guided tour of the cheese factory, sample some cheese, and be sure to try their ice cream.

If you're flying high after all the great food at the cheese factory, head south a few miles on U.S. 101 and stop at the **Tillamook Air Museum** (page 45). Housed in a monstrous World War II–era blimp hangar, the building is impossible to miss. The 120-foot-tall hangar houses a great collection of World War II and Cold War military aircraft. And there's also the odd-shaped civilian Boeing 377, better known as the Mini-Guppy. It was used to ferry Apollo rocket components from California to the Florida launch site.

Drive back into town and stop by the **Tillamook County Pioneer Museum** (page 43) with its collection of artifacts that tells the region's story. Inside the historic courthouse museum, head upstairs if you're interested in wildlife. The museum houses one of the largest collections of animal specimens in Oregon.

Tillamook Cheese Factory visitor center

South Coastal Tour

ESTIMATED DAYS: 1
ESTIMATED DRIVING MILES: 60

Some of the best views of the rugged Oregon Coast can be seen at **Shore Acres State Park** (page 55) located about 13 miles south of Coos Bay. Besides the park's beautiful gardens, this is the site of one of the coast's earliest and grandest mansions. The mansion is gone, but the cliffs, crashing waves, and the barking sea lions remain. You can easily spend several hours wandering the park's trails, exploring colorful flower gardens, and relaxing on a comfortable bench next to the Asian-style koi pond.

Drive south for 53 miles and watch for the sign directing you to the **Cape Blanco Lighthouse** (page 58), the westernmost lighthouse in Oregon. The narrow road dead ends after about five miles at a small parking lot, a few hundred yards from the lighthouse. On the drive out to the lighthouse, stop by the historic **Hughes House** (page 58) for a quick tour of the late 19th-century farmhouse. It's tucked back against a hillside out of the prevailing wind and overlooks several hundred acres of farmland once owned by the Hughes family.

Shore Acres State Park

Family/Kids' Discovery Tour

ESTIMATED DAYS: 2
ESTIMATED DRIVING MILES: 78

About three miles north of the coastal town of Newport, take the turnoff to **Yaquina Head Lighthouse and Visitor Center** (page 47). The kids will love the adventure. The visitor center provides a good look at the coastal natural history, and there are plenty of places to hike. One of those hikes should be up the circular stairway to the top of the lighthouse. The views are hard to beat. And if that's not quite high enough, nearby Salal Hill offers an even more spectacular view of the coastline, both north and south—after the 15-minute hike to the top.

If you need a break from the hiking, take the short drive into Newport and drop into the **Oregon Coast Aquarium** (page 49). Here you can get really close to all the animals that live in the waters along the coast, from jellyfish to bat rays and sharks to sea otters. If you didn't see some of the more rare birds while out at Yaquina Head, you can see them here. The open aviary features tufted puffins, rhinoceros auklets, black oystercatchers, and pigeon guillemots. There's even an acrylic tube that allows you to walk "beneath" the ocean waters as sharks and other fish swim overhead.

The **Umpqua Discovery Center** (page 51) is a two-hour drive from Newport, along 70-plus miles of beautiful Oregon Coast. Located on the bank of the Umpqua River, the center is designed especially for kids, even the older ones. From Umpqua Indians, the first Native Americans here, to the early seafarers and pioneer settlers, half of the center offers a journey back through time with its innovative history walk exhibits. The other side of the center takes everyone on a short nature walk along a trail that features everything from black bears to snakes.

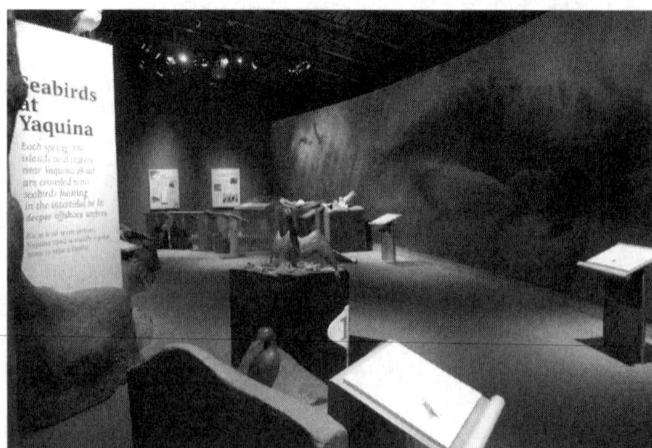

Yaquina Head Lighthouse Visitor Center

Oregon Coast Information Centers

Astoria and Warrenton Area Chamber of Commerce
www.oldoregon.com
800-875-6807

Lincoln City Visitor and Convention Bureau
www.oregoncoast.org
800-452-2151

Florence Area Chamber of Commerce
www.florencechamber.com
541-997-3128

Oregon Bay Area Chamber of Commerce
www.oregonsbayarea.org
541-266-0868

Brookings-Harbor Chamber of Commerce
www.brookingsor.com
800-535-9469

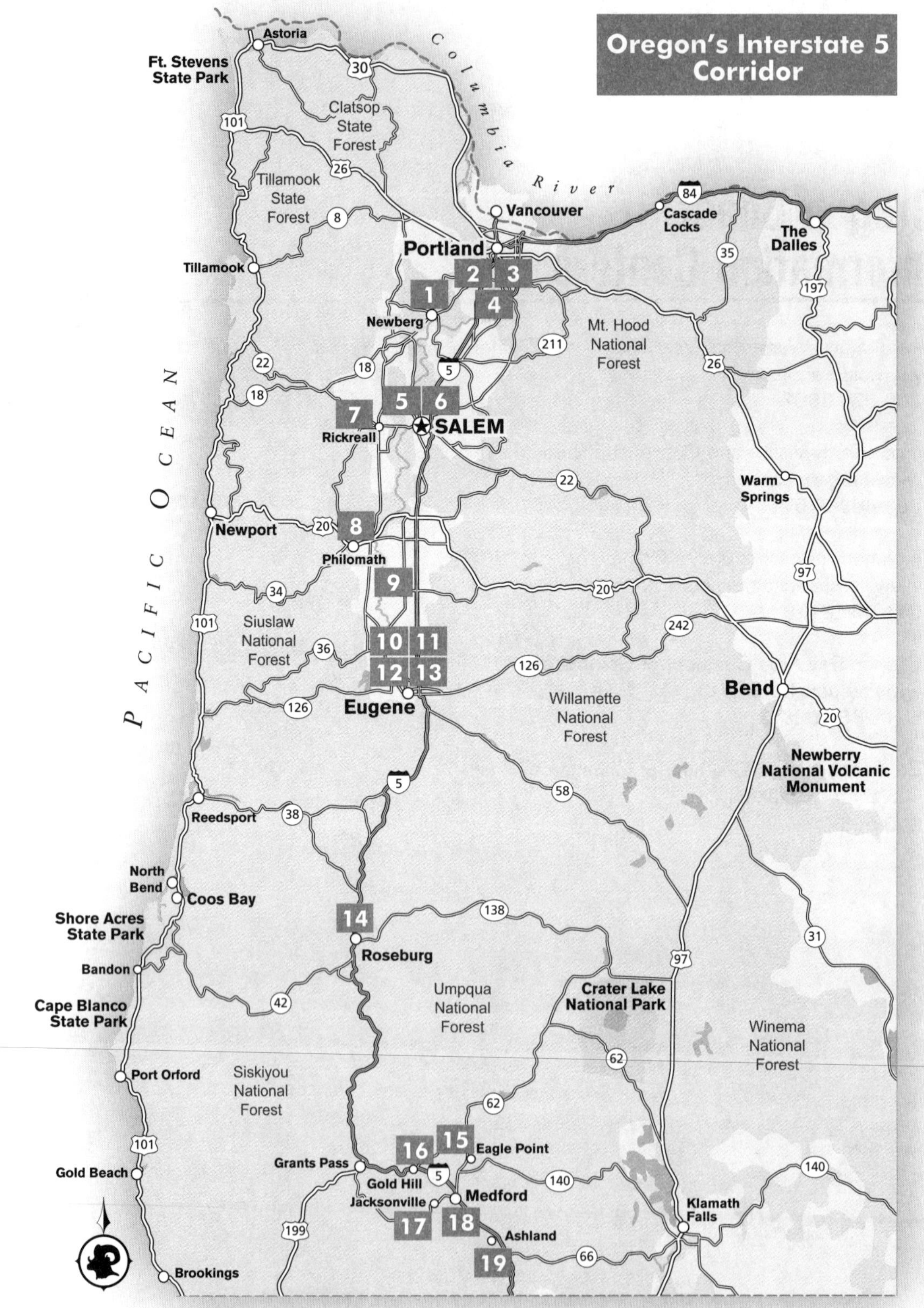
Oregon's Interstate 5 Corridor
Astoria
Ft. Stevens State Park
Columbia River
Clatsop State Forest
Tillamook State Forest
Tillamook
Vancouver
Portland
Cascade Locks
The Dalles
Newberg
Mt. Hood National Forest
Warm Springs
PACIFIC OCEAN
SALEM
Rickreall
Newport
Philomath
Siuslaw National Forest
Eugene
Willamette National Forest
Bend
Newberry National Volcanic Monument
Reedsport
North Bend
Coos Bay
Shore Acres State Park
Roseburg
Bandon
Cape Blanco State Park
Umpqua National Forest
Crater Lake National Park
Winema National Forest
Port Orford
Siskiyou National Forest
Eagle Point
Grants Pass
Gold Hill
Gold Beach
Jacksonville
Medford
Klamath Falls
Ashland
Brookings

Oregon's Interstate 5 Corridor

Oregon's Interstate 5 corridor includes lush forests, mountain passes, and miles of open valleys that have been transformed into thousands of acres of productive farm and dairy land. For this section, we begin our exploration along the I-5 corridor beginning near Newburg and Oregon City, both just south of the greater Portland metro area. Heading south, the interstate crosses numerous smaller streams and a couple of major rivers, including the Willamette and the Umpqua. It passes through most of Oregon's largest cities, including the state capital of Salem, as well as Eugene, Roseburg, and Medford.

University of Oregon's Jordan Schnitzer Art Museum, Campbell Memorial Courtyard

It also passes through the heart of the famous Willamette Valley, the destination for thousands of pioneers who came west over the Oregon Trail during the 1840s and 1850s. Free land was the attraction, and those early farmlands remain productive today. The Willamette Valley can receive up to 50 inches of rain annually, providing plenty of water for growing berries, grass seed, Christmas trees, and hops, which are used to make beer. More recently, the area has become one of Oregon's major wine-producing regions, producing many varietals, including Pinot Noir and Pinot Gris.

TRIVIA

1. Where can you visit a childhood home of President Herbert Hoover?
2. Where can you learn about the history of the Oregon Trail and also view Willamette Falls?
3. Where can you go on a tour and watch "America's Favorite Treats" being made?
4. What 19th-century Victorian Queen Anne Revival home did a 25-year-old architect design for a prominent physician?
5. Where can you see 10,000-year-old sandals made from sage bark?
6. Where can you purchase flour ground on a 130-year-old mill's still-operating, water-powered grinding wheels?
7. Which museum was once an 1880s Italianate-style courthouse built using 150,000 bricks?

For trivia answers, see page 341.

1 Hoover-Minthorn House Museum

WHAT'S HERE: Childhood home of U.S. President Herbert Hoover
DON'T MISS THIS: The fancier-than-normal woodstove

Bertie Hoover, as he was known to his friends, was destined to become the 31st president of the U.S. Herbert Hoover was born in 1874 in West Branch, Iowa, making him the first president to be born west of the Mississippi River. His father died in 1880 and his mother just four years later. At age nine, Hoover was an orphan, first living with his grandmother and then with an uncle. In 1885, at the request of another uncle, Hoover left Iowa to live with John Minthorn, a physician, and his wife Laura Ellen Minthorn in Oregon. The Minthorn's had recently lost their young son, and John's grief prompted him to ask his 11-year-old nephew to make the move.

The founder of the town of Newberg, Quaker Jesse Edwards, had built himself a new home in 1881, but sold it to John in 1885. The Minthorns moved in immediately before Hoover arrived. In his new home, Hoover registered for school at the Friends Pacific Academy where his classes included reading, arithmetic, geography, writing, spelling, and drawing. Like Hoover's parents, his new family raised him as a practicing Quaker. He helped with chores around the house, such as carrying in firewood and assisting with the horses.

In addition to being a doctor, John Minthorn had also served as the superintendent of the same school that young Hoover was attending. In 1889 the family, including Hoover, moved to Salem where Dr. Minthorn had taken a position as superintendent of the Chemawa Indian School, working for the Bureau of Indian Affairs. He continued his medical practice and also worked his way into real estate as president of the Oregon Land Company.

Hoover continued his education, but not in the usual manner. In Salem, while he took a job working in his uncle's real estate office, he did not continue his formal education by attending high school, but instead took night school classes. In 1891, Hoover started college at California's Stanford University, the first year the new school was open. He graduated four years later with a degree in geology. His succeeded in his desire to become a mining engineer, working in gold mines in Australia. He and Lou Henry married in 1899, and the young couple headed to China where Hoover, while working for a private company, became the country's leading engineer. He and his wife were caught in the Boxer Rebellion in 1890, but escaped unharmed.

President Herbert Hoover's childhood home

Hoover's growing reputation and experiences around the world helped lead President Woodrow Wilson to appoint him as head of the American Food Administration in 1917. With his influence continuing to grow, Hoover was a dark horse presidential candidate running in the California primaries. He lost that race, but by throwing his support to nominee Warren G. Harding, he secured himself a cabinet position as Secretary of Commerce in 1921. It wasn't long before Hoover was being referred to as the Secretary of Commerce and "Under-Secretary of Everything Else." In 1928 Hoover was elected president—the first person to go from a cabinet secretary position to the highest elected position in the country.

Hoover's boyhood home in Newberg was restored in the mid-1950s. On August 10, 1955, on the president's 81st birthday, he was in Newberg to help celebrate the opening of his old home as a public museum. Restoration of historic homes is generally guided by a combination of careful research and knowing the history of the era being researched. In this case Hoover's own memories helped to guide the home's restoration. The home's fancy woodstove (not including the gold-colored crown) was returned to the home during the restoration and is thought to be the original—at least Hoover recognized it when he returned for the home's dedication. Decades of layers of wallpaper and paint were removed in order to identify the original colors and patterns. Similar patterned replacements were used in the restoration. Hoover's original boyhood bedroom furniture set is back in his old bedroom. Much of the other interior furnishings were acquired from the region but are not original Minthorn or Hoover items.

The home is owned by the National Society of the Colonial Dames of America. The society's headquarters is in the Dumbarton House located in Washington, D.C.

HOURS: March through November, Wednesday through Sunday, 1 PM to 4 PM; December and February, Saturday and Sunday, 1 PM to 4 PM. Closed January.

COST: Adults, $3; seniors and students, $2; age 10 and under, $0.50

LOCATION: 115 S. River Street, Newberg

PHONE: 503-538-6629

WEBSITE: www.nscda.org/museums/oregon.htm#HOOVER

2 Museum of the Oregon Territory

WHAT'S HERE: **Museum explores the settlement and development of the Willamette Falls area**

DON'T MISS THIS: **The view of Willamette Falls from the museum's back windows**

The shore of the Willamette River in Oregon City marks the official end of the Oregon Trail. Many of those who came west, never ventured any farther, choosing instead to make this their home. The museum's exhibits showcase the people who stayed and the businesses they created. After you have walked past the window exhibits of early explorers, Native Americans, and more, you come to a sign for Kaegi's Pharmacy. The pharmacy has been recreated and includes a very large collection of 19th- and early 20th-century pharmaceuticals. Behind the counter and inside glass-fronted shelves, there are hundreds of early potions claiming to cure any ailment imaginable. One particular brand was made by S.B. Penich & Co. and named "Crude Drugs." They included such things as horehound, spearmint, chestnut leaves, and elecampane root. You can also find cystitis tablets, agrimonia, and alphozone tablets. If drugs couldn't fix you, then there was always the mid-1800s blood suction cup set that Dr. Andrew J. Clark used here in Oregon City.

The museum includes an early 20th-century office with typewriters and a duplicating machine. There is also a rather elaborate device called The Millionaire Calculating Machine. It was advertised for "working out the four simple rules," which appear to be addition, subtraction, multiplication, and division. While the basic instructions for solving the first three functions are each a paragraph in length, the division "rule" requires more than double the instructions of the other three combined.

At the window overlooking the Willamette River and Willamette Falls, a large photograph shows salmon fishermen in their small boats, likely a century or more ago. The area around the falls has changed significantly. Dams, locks, and industrial buildings including a power plant and a paper mill, now surround portions of the falls, although the view is still quite amazing. A map helps you locate present-day structures, including the fish ladder facility, the hydroelectric power plant, and even the site of the original power plant, dubbed Station A. It was from the generating facility here that electricity was first sent to Portland on June 3, 1889, the first-ever long-distance transmission of electricity. After your museum visit is completed, you can take the short walk down to the stone railing for an even closer view of the river and falls.

Willamette Falls was an impediment to river traffic, including the large rafts of

Museum of the Oregon Territory exhibit gallery

logs that moved along the river to mills. When the locks were finally completed, allowing boat and barge traffic to get past the falls, life was better for most. Unfortunately, the huge rafts of logs had to be unchained when they entered the locks and usually re-rafted when exiting in order to continue their journey.

With salmon and other fish so plentiful in Oregon's rivers, it wasn't long until sport fishing gained popularity. A small exhibit includes several fishing lures and flies, a rod, and a short newspaper story about British author Rudyard Kipling. Reportedly, the famous writer visited the Portland area in 1891 and declared: "I have lived! The American continent may now sink under the sea, for I have taken the best that it yields, and the best was neither dollars, love, nor real estate." The best, for Kipling, was fishing on the Clackamas River.

Additional exhibits reveal small pieces of the area's history, including the county courthouse, the arrival of Catholics, and a wagon with farm tools, including a corn planter, flail thresher, and hay fork. There is a look at Chief Lelooska, a name given to Don Smith when the Nez Pierce adopted him at age 12. Being of Cherokee descent, Lelooska studied Indian tribes throughout North America and carved the exhibit's totem pole in 1960. More Indian artifacts can be seen, including strings of beads and numerous fishing arrows.

HOURS: Tuesday through Saturday, 11 AM to 4 PM. Closed January.

COST: Oregon City Pass: Adults, $7; ages 6–17, $5. Also good at End of the Oregon Trail Interpretive Center (page 75) and at the Stevens-Crawford Heritage House (page 76).

LOCATION: 211 Tumwater Drive, Oregon City

PHONE: 503-960-0685

WEBSITE: www.historicoregoncity.org/HOC/

3 End of the Oregon Trail Interpretive Center

WHAT'S HERE: **A look at where the Oregon Trail ended**

DON'T MISS THIS: **The huge Oregon Trail map and the "Notice to Emigrants" on the walls outside the theater/supply store**

Resembling a giant wagon train, the interpretive center marks the end site of the Oregon Trail. Many immigrants never reached Oregon City, instead heading either north or south before arriving, but thousands more spent time here as they planned their next moves. Inside the visitor center, each section of the wagon train features a gallery, and there are actors in period costume who help tell the story of these early pioneers.

This site, which originally was called Green Point, was where Indians had gathered for thousands of years to fish at Willamette Falls. George Abernethy was the first emigrant to arrive here in 1840. He and his wife, Anne, claimed their 640 acres and built a cabin at nearby Abernethy Creek. Contrary to what one might believe, the first influx of emigrants began arriving here in 1843, not by "prairie schooner" as the wagons were often called, but by raft from Fort Vancouver. Soon, though, the pioneers were arriving by the hundreds in wagons. Those who pulled in as early winter approached often chose to remain until spring before moving on to their new homes. With food and other supplies guaranteed, they could take short trips to locate the land they wanted and then file their claims at Oregon City's Government Land Office. The big encampments that enriched George Abernethy came to an end in 1861 when floodwaters destroyed everything that he owned. Further, with a decade or more of improvements to the Oregon Trail cutting travel times in half, there was no need for the overwintering campground. Broke, George moved to Portland.

Take a walk along the front of the "wagon train" where a series of interpretive signs identify some of the more prominent early settlers here. Some of those included Abigail Scott Duniway, an early nationally known activist for women's rights who helped gain the right of women to vote only three years before her death. There is Lot Witcomb, the founder of nearby Milwaukie, Oregon, and the owner of a sawmill, gristmill, shipyard, and newspaper. And there is a short story about Dr. John McLoughlin, considered the father of Oregon, who ran the Hudson's Bay Company from Fort Vancouver from 1824 to 1845, helping many early emigrants.

Exhibit outside the interpretive center

Head inside the wagon train center and exhibits of interpretive signage and artifacts briefly discuss the reasons for the great migration west—free land! While Portland may be bigger and better known today, Oregon City has enjoyed many "firsts" during its lifetime. A small sign identifies some of those firsts: first sawmill, 1842; first pioneer lyceum and literary club, 1842; first town incorporated west of the Rockies, 1844; first capital of Oregon Country under Provisional Government, 1843; first Oregon paper mill, 1866; and first long-distance transmission of electricity, 13 miles from here to Portland, 1889.

As you wander through the "wagon train" you will see wagons, quilts, and more history. You can step outside through a side door to the Willamette Outpost, a general store. Inside, you can attempt to pack all the supplies you would need on your trip west into a wagon. It's not that easy.

The interpretive programs include both film- and actor-presented programs about *Going West*. The program is held in a theater that looks much more like a huge supply house filled with everything from sacks of flour to tools, iron pots, and ox harnesses—everything newly arrived pioneers could need.

The building across the patio-walkway from the "wagon train" also serves as a city and regional visitor information center, filled with brochures and other information.

HOURS: Tuesday through Saturday, 11 AM to 4 PM

COST: Oregon City Pass: Adults, $7; ages 6–17, $5. Also good at the Museum of the Oregon Territory (page 73) and at the Stevens-Crawford Heritage House (page 76).

LOCATION: 1726 Washington Street, Oregon City

PHONE: 503-960-0685

WEBSITE: www.historicoregoncity.org/HOC/

4 Stevens-Crawford Heritage House

WHAT'S HERE: **Home built in 1908 that today serves as a museum**

DON'T MISS THIS: **The family's original handwritten recipe cards**

Harley Stevens had this house built for his family in 1908; its "foursquare" or "classical box" architecture was popular in the early 20th century. Even though electricity had been generated locally since 1889, it must not have been dependable as the house boasted light fixtures for both gas and electricity. Stevens had come to Oregon at age 15, when he left New York and joined the Emigrant Escort Service in 1862. In 1871, he married Oregon City native Mary Elizabeth Crawford. They had only two children, Harley Jr. and Mertie.

After both of her parents' deaths, Mertie Stevens owned the house. Always thought to be small and sickly, she bequeathed the home to the Clackamas County Historical Society when she died in 1968 at the age of 96. Today, the house museum includes many of the items owned by both the Stevens and Crawford families.

In touring the home, it appears that many members of the family enjoyed collecting historic memorabilia. There is a little girl's rather large dollhouse that was thought to have been brought across the Oregon Trail. Normally, such large toys would never have been allowed, but this was a collapsible dollhouse, making it small enough to justify packing. Some of the many items you can see here include those early dress shirts with the separate starched collars and there is even a beaver fur hat. The beading set in the parlor was gifted to Mary Stevens (who was loved and respected by many) by the Chinese community. Traveling was part of her father Medorem Crawford's jobs, and his travel trunks have survived—not exactly portable luggage.

Since Mary used money she inherited from her father to pay for the house, she likely had a great deal of control over the home's design. Typically, houses of this era had small bedroom closets. Here, however, the closets are much larger. They have a passageway through them that allowed her the convenience of moving between bedrooms without having to walk into the hallway and expose herself in her bedclothes to guests. The piano in the downstairs parlor also belonged to Mary. Medorem purchased a piano for each of his daughters and had them shipped around Cape Horn. The one in this house still plays quite well.

Harley Stevens enjoyed collecting American Indian artifacts, among other pieces of history. The home has some of the Indian mortars and pestles that he acquired over the years, as well as a rare clay pot thrown by a slave before the Civil War. There are also more than 200 Victorian hats in the museum's collection that are rotated for viewing. This was an era when the automobile was becoming more and more popular, so Mary sported special driving clothes when out for drives in the country.

Mertie was a talented artist and several of her drawings remain in the home. Somewhere someone acquired what might be two odd flower vases, although nobody here seems to know for sure what they are. Some are convinced that they are spittoons for Victorian ladies.

The pocket doors in several of the rooms are made from old-growth Douglas fir, and they work exceptionally well. Walk through one such pair and make your way into the dining room. The table, chairs, sideboard, and other pieces were wedding gifts given to Harley and Mary. Harley was apparently a rather large, burly man, yet his teacup is quite dainty and feminine, at least by today's standards.

Step into what serves as the butler's pantry—although the family never had a butler—and take a look at the original family recipe cards. When we visited, a docent related a story about finally getting the courage to pick out one of the cards and read a recipe for Oxtail Soup. The first instruction was to get the ox. She put the card back.

Plumbing was an original part of the home, and this home had the first laundry room in Oregon City and indoor bathrooms as well. All the chamber pots you see in the home are simply part of the museum collection, not original to the house.

HOURS: Wednesday through Saturday, 12 PM to 4 PM. Closed mid-December through January.
COST: Oregon City Pass: Adults, $7; ages 6–17, $5. Also good at the End of the Oregon Trail Interpretive Center (page 75) and at the Museum of the Oregon Territory (page 73).
LOCATION: 603 6th Street, Oregon City
PHONE: 503-960-0685
WEBSITE: www.historicoregoncity.org/HOC/

5 Bush House Museum

WHAT'S HERE: **Italianate home built in 1878 by newspaper and business owner Asahel Bush II**
DON'T MISS THIS: **Japanese-influenced furnishings and motif**

Asahel Bush II was only 54 years old and a widower when his new home was completed in 1878. Although three of his children were adults, with two away at school when the house was finished, this newspaperman, banker, and businessman still had a 16-year-old daughter, Eugenia, living at home. Named after her mother, who died when Eugenia was only 18 months old, Eugenia lived with and cared for her father for the remainder of his life.

Growing up, Asahel, at age 17, become an apprentice printer in New York. In 1850, he passed the bar to become a lawyer, and quickly headed to Oregon via ship, by crossing the Isthmus of Panama. He settled in Oregon City and with his new printing press started the *Oregon Statesman* newspaper. When Salem was named the capital, he moved his newspaper operation there, starting what would become the Salem *Statesman Journal*. In 1859, Bush became Oregon's first official state printer. Four years later he sold his newspaper, and in 1867 he and partner William S. Ladd founded Salem's Ladd and Bush Bank. He later bought out Ladd, becoming sole owner. He was also active in politics, primarily in the Democratic Party. Bush married Eugenia Ziber, the daughter of one of his employees in 1854, and before she died at age 30, they had four children.

Besides daughter Estelle, who never lived in the house, and Eugenia who never left, Bush's two other children, Sally and A. N., returned to live in the home as adults after their father's death in 1913. Eugenia passed away here in 1932 at age 70. Sally lived here until her death in 1946, when she was 86 years old. Son A. N. moved back into the house when he was 90 years old, when his own house downtown was razed by the state in order to expand the Capitol Mall. A. N. Bush built the back porch and sunroom here to accommodate the elevator that he removed from his state-condemned home. He lived in his father's house until 1953, when he died at age 95.

Originally, Asahel Bush purchased 100 acres for his new home. The property, including a small house that the family occupied until their new home was completed, cost only $4,000. Victorian architecture was highly regarded during this time, and Bush thought the Italianate design, with its tall, narrow windows and hipped roof, suited his needs. During this same period in history, following the opening of Japan to international trade in 1868, Japanese style art and Asian designs found their way into homes throughout the U.S. and Europe. The home's rooms that visitors were most likely to see, especially if those visitors were business or community members rather than relatives and friends, included the parlor and the sitting room. Furnishings in those rooms most obviously illustrated the Japanese influence.

House tours take about 45 minutes. The ticket office is in the Bush Barn, operated by the Salem Art Association, located directly behind the Bush House. There is a small parking lot behind the home so you won't have to walk up the steep grassy slope from the parking lot on Mission Street.

HOURS: Tuesday through Sunday: March and April, 1 PM to 4 PM; May through September, 12 PM to 5 PM; October through December, 1 PM to 4 PM. January and February, please call for hours.

COST: Adults, $4; ages 55-plus and 13–21, $3; ages 6–12, $2

LOCATION: 600 Mission Street SE, Salem

PHONE: 503-363-4717

WEBSITE: http://salemart.org/index.php

Bush House Museum

6 Mission Mill Museum

WHAT'S HERE: Three pioneer houses and a 19th-century woolen mill

DON'T MISS THIS: Trying your hand at "carding" wool

This five-acre site is really two museums in one. The most obvious is the big red building complex that makes up the Thomas Kay Woolen Mill. The second includes several modest houses built by the Methodist missionaries, the founders of Salem. Over the years, these historic mission buildings have been moved to the mill site, providing a look at the simple living and work accommodations of the Methodist missionaries.

When you enter the large orientation center, you are met with several options. You can begin shopping immediately in the large gift shop, wander through the orientation center's historic interpretive exhibits and watch a film, join a guided tour, or choose to head out to the historic buildings on your own with an informational map in hand. If you are on your own, you will also be given a key that allows you to pass through the many buildings' locked doors, including those of the mill.

Your first stop should be the interpretive exhibits in the orientation center. They offer a glimpse into the history of the mill and the mission. Here you will discover that the industrialization and mechanization of the wool industry began in Salem in 1857, when the Willamette Woolen Manufacturing Company built its mill on Mill Creek. A ditch from the North Santiam River to Mill Creek ensured an ample water supply to run the mill, but apparently not fight the fire that destroyed the mill in 1876.

The building you are in was actually part of the Thomas Kay Woolen Mill, serving as Thomas Kay's wool warehouse. Kay, an English immigrant, founded the mill in 1889. The mill was running at full capacity by 1898, producing enough woolen cloth to supply clothing and blankets for 1,100 men heading north each week to the Klondike gold fields. The U.S. Army also relied on the mill for its heavy, olive drab-colored wool blankets and uniforms. Another popular product was the brightly colored Mackinaw fabric that many clothing producers used to make outdoor clothing favored by hunters, fishermen, and workers.

One of the first pioneers in the area was Jason Lee, arriving before the mills and establishing his Methodist mission on the banks of the Willamette River in 1834. He proved to be the driving force behind the pioneer settlement of Salem and the surrounding lands. A very elaborately designed musket is displayed that belonged to Josiah Parrish, a member of the Methodist mission and president of the Board of Trustees of Willamette University from 1869 to 1895.

The mill appears as if it is still active.

Head outside and begin your tour at the Methodist Parsonage. Built in 1841, it served as the home for missionaries who worked in the Indian Manual Training School. Its furnishings reflect the time when it housed the mission's minister and his family.

Moved from its original site in north Salem, the Jason Lee house is the oldest frame house still standing in the Pacific Northwest. Built in 1841, four families originally occupied the home. Jason Lee lived here with his second wife. Use your key to unlock the door and enter where you can see Lee's traveling desk, another resident family's bed, and the high chair that another occupant made for his son.

Next door is the John D. Boon House, Salem's oldest single-family frame house. The Boon family traveled over the Oregon Trail in 1845, and Boon was a cofounder of the Willamette Valley Woolen Manufacturing Company. This home also was moved to its present location.

The Pleasant Grove Presbyterian Church is often called the "Condit Church" after Reverend Phillip Condit, the founding minister who brought his family to Oregon in 1854. The community raised $1,378 and built the church in 1858. This simple church is the oldest surviving Presbyterian church in the Pacific Northwest.

Heading over to the mill, your first stop will be in the Mentzer machine shop. If you are on a self-guided tour, you will need your key to get into the machine shop, as well as into several more of the mill's exhibit rooms. The shop is named after millwright Wayne Mentzer who worked here from 1924 to 1984.

Your path takes you along the millrace to see the turbines and gears that transform the water's power into mechanical power that run the myriad machines inside the mill. Enter the "picker house" to see the most unglamorous job at the mill. Here, the raw wool came to be handpicked clean of burrs, bugs, and feces. In the dye house and scouring rooms, you will see the carbonizing bin, the scouring train, and one of the dryers. Carbonizing was a process that dipped the cleaned wool into steam-heated vats of sulfuric acid, a process that further weakened any remaining vegetable material such as burrs. Removed from the bath, heat was applied, which turned the unwanted contaminants to dust, leaving only pure wool.

As you wander through this huge mill, you will see everything it took to get that raw wool from the picker house to the final product—thousands of bolts of fine virgin wool cloth. Much of the mill looks as though the workers are merely out for a stroll. There are still large bags of wool and small pieces of wool scattered about the work areas. The water-powered machinery that did the carding, spinning, dressing, and weaving are still here and operational—and there are pieces of raw wool everywhere. The mill's different floors handled different parts of the process, including washing, drying, dying, weaving, burling, napping, shearing, mending, pressing, and the final inspection before it was shipped to markets across the country.

HOURS: Open for self-guided tours Monday through Saturday, 10 AM to 5 PM. House guided tours, 11 AM, 1 PM, and 3 PM. Closed Sundays and some holidays.

COST: Adults, $6; ages 55-plus, $5; students with ID, $4; ages 6–17, $3

LOCATION: 1313 Mill Street, Salem

PHONE: 503-585-7012

WEBSITE: www.missionmill.org

7 Polk County Museum

WHAT'S HERE: A collection from throughout the county, covering everything from farming to logging

DON'T MISS THIS: The 1912 Everitt touring car

The small size of this museum located at the edge of the Polk County Fairgrounds is deceiving from the outside. Polk County, Oregon, is named after James K. Polk who served as the 11th president of the U.S. from 1844 to 1849. It was President Polk who pushed a reluctant Congress to award territorial status to Oregon.

The museum's exhibits and collection appear to cover every aspect of Polk County. A covered wagon sits prominently inside the front entrance. Head to the left side of the museum where exhibits illustrate the early pioneer history of the area. There's George Gay, who arrived in Polk County by 1835. He came from Gloucestershire, England, going to sea at age 11, and arrived in Monterey, California, after serving nearly a dozen years at sea. He and a small party of men headed north to Oregon's Willamette Valley. They were attacked by Indians, and several of the party were killed; Gay was wounded but escaped. After traveling 500 miles in two months, Gay made it to what would become Polk County. He later built the first house of brick west of the Rocky Mountains—he molded and baked his bricks on-site.

This same part of the museum includes a look at the Old California Trail, which was also known as the Trappers Trail. It ran from Fort Vancouver, along the west side of the Willamette Valley, as it headed to California. It was actually an old American Indian trail, later used by the trappers and fur traders, and ultimately by some of Polk County's earliest pioneers.

Farming is the reason that settlers first came here, and the museum has its share of early farming tools, from scythes to brush hooks. There is a look at the hops industry, with photos and tools. Included are various beer bottles from the 1930s and '40s. Even tractors had designers, and the tractor seat exhibit shows off several seat designs, although all are still made of very uncomfortable steel.

The museum has a beautiful bright blue 1912 Everitt touring car that includes one of its advertisements: "Father, Mother, Son, or Daughter Can Drive THIS Car." A history shows that the vehicle was purchased in 1912 for $1,500 by Polk County residents Mr. and Mrs. John Ediger. Last used as a family car in 1925, it was converted to a pickup with a buzz saw attached. It sat unused from 1946 until

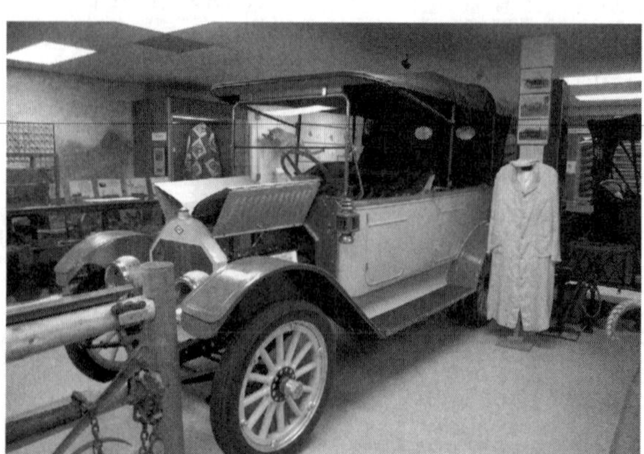

The museum's 1923 Everitt touring car

1959 when it was driven in a parade. Fortunately, the model on display has been restored to its original design. There is also a much more common 1919 Model T Ford.

The museum has a very extensive gun collection, much of it the gift of one man, Robert Tedd. Among the dozens of firearms, you will see a .69 caliber Harpers Ferry musket, an 1841 Eli Whitney Percussion rifle, and a .58 caliber Springfield. Many of the newer guns, such as the bolt-action Springfield 30-06 and the Remington rolling block .43 caliber rifle, include a sample of the round that each fires. Near the firearms display cases is a small gallery filled with skins and taxidermic wildlife, including a mountain lion and a black bear.

The museum's logging equipment exhibit is testament that timber is big business throughout much of the western half of Oregon. It includes everything from surveying equipment to those back-breaking whipsaws, from hard hats to old chain saws. You can see the difference between a bucking saw and a falling saw (before the invention of power chain saws), augers that were used to drill holes to place dynamite, and even a springboard. A springboard is a narrow board whose end loggers would stick into a cut made in the trunk of a huge old-growth tree. The logger stood on the extended part of the board so he could make his cuts above the unusable butt part of the tree.

The upstairs gallery includes representative "rooms" from past years. The drugstore features sample medicinals such as castor oil and a very old bottle of Campho-Phenique, along with a lot of chemicals and other "medicines" that have likely been banned by the Food and Drug Administration. There's a dentist's office, a beauty parlor, a schoolroom, and a dining room with red-and-white-checkered tablecloths. There is also a living room with a beautiful quilt draped over the couch, musical instruments, and a Victor High Wheel bicycle originally purchased for $125 in 1887.

HOURS: Monday, Thursday, Friday, and Saturday, 12:30 PM to 4:30 PM; Wednesday, 1 PM to 5 PM. Closed Tuesday and Sunday.

COST: Adults, $3; ages 62-plus, $2, ages 6–17, $1

LOCATION: 560 S. Pacific Highway (Polk County Fairgrounds), Rickreall

PHONE: 503-623-6251

WEBSITE: www.polkcountyhistoricalsociety.com

8 Benton County Historical Museum

WHAT'S HERE: **Historic building constructed in 1867 as Philomath College**
DON'T MISS THIS: **The second floor, which showcases changing art exhibits**

In 1865, successful negotiations with the Oregon Conference of the United Brethren and a community fundraising program resulted in eight acres being made available for a new school, which is where Philomath College would be built. Adjacent land parcels were sold to help pay the construction costs, although the deeds forbid grog shops, gambling establishments, saloons, and theaters from being built, all in an effort to safeguard the morals of local citizens and certainly the students. In 1867, with brick made on-site, the main portion of the new school was completed with its two-foot-thick walls. Soon after the turn-of-the-century, the building's two side wings were added.

The college served initially as an elementary and high school since there were no students ready for university-level studies. Once college courses were added, an emphasis was placed on the study of Greek, Latin, and the sciences. Low-paid teachers taught up to 10 courses daily, with student tuition ranging from $12 to $14 per term. Financial problems caused the college to close in 1929, but during the college's 62 years, 6,000 students enrolled and more than 1,200 became teachers. The building was used as a church until that closed in the 1960s. The historical society took over the building and started restoration efforts during the 1970s.

Today, with more than 100,000 objects in its collection, including 44,000 images, the museum periodically rotates many of its exhibits. The simple, tasteful exhibits include pistols, such as the H. Aston Co. single-shot percussion pistol. The Middleton, Connecticut, company's Model 1842, .54 caliber was issued by the U.S. Army during the Civil War and the Mexican-American War. Other Civil War memorabilia includes such things as an 1861 "forage hat" and a U.S. Naval sword. There are also more guns and swords from different eras, including a 1915 German bayonet, a 19th-century "pepperbox," and even a Belgium-made flintlock pistol.

The museum does not overlook the timber industry or the items that people used in everyday life over the past century and a half or so. You can see a sewing machine from the 1870s, a classic candlestick telephone from the early 1900s, and a 1940s-era FM radio.

A few of the museum's 100,000 artifacts

For the science buffs, the museum features a geology exhibit that focuses on "glowing rocks," those that exhibit fluorescence when exposed to ultraviolet light. In a dark room, samples of minerals, including fluoride, calcite, and apatite, are "illuminated" with ultraviolet light. At an atomic level, excited electrons release energy in the form of visible light in different colors, ranging from blue to purple to green to red. It's a fun exhibit.

HOURS: Tuesday through Saturday, 10 AM to 4:30 PM
COST: Free
LOCATION: 1101 Main Street, Philomath
PHONE: 541-929-6230
WEBSITE: www.bentoncountymuseum.org

9 Thompson's Mills State Heritage Site

WHAT'S HERE: **A restored and operating 19th-century gristmill**
DON'T MISS THIS: **The mill's basement "beaver holes"**

Flour mills created the economic lifeblood of 19th-century rural farms. Wagons would line up for miles as farmers hauled their summer grain harvests to the local mill to be ground into flour. Farmers for miles around the tiny Oregon town of Boston—its founders came from Boston, Massachusetts—welcomed Richard Finley's new mill that carried the town's name. The original mill burned to the ground in 1862, but the owners rebuilt a new mill that later became known as Thompson's Mills. Unfortunately, the town of Boston did not survive. In 1871, the Oregon and California Railroad laid its tracks about 1.5 miles away, and a train stop called Shedd's Station was established. Boston's businesses and its citizens abandoned their young town and moved closer to Shedd, many taking their buildings with them.

Thompson's Mills' silos next to the mill

The second mill survived and prospered as its owners expanded and improved their production capabilities. When the railroad arrived, allowing large shipments of grain to the Port of Portland, the mill's owner found himself selling flour to new markets as far away as China. All was going well until the 1940s when home-baked bread began going out of style, replaced by those packaged

OREGON'S I-5 CORRIDOR

loaves that were being mass-baked and sold in grocery stores. For this reason, local farmers began moving away from growing grain and instead started growing grass seed.

With local wheat supplies in too short of supply to keep the mill running full-time grinding flour, its owners switched to producing animal feed pellets. Still in operation in the 1980s, the mill added another product to its own lifeline—the water rights the mill owned, which provided the water to power its grinding wheels, were now used to also power electric generators. The generated electricity was added to the local utility's power grid, which provided extra income, but not enough. The mill finally closed in 2002, after 143 years of operation.

Today, the mill has been restored and is maintained as an Oregon State Heritage Site. And the fun part about visiting is that almost everything still works. The impoundment pond is kept full, providing the water that manages, with its 16 feet of head (drop), to provide enough power to turn the turbines that run all of the mill's machinery. Take one of the tours through the mill to see it in action. Peek through the basement trapdoor—don't forget to don your hard hat—for a much different view of the millrace, the turbines, and the guts and gears that transfer the water's force into a useable power that can run all of the upstairs machinery. Down here are the "beaver holes" that a couple of beavers gnawed through the wooden structure to escape after being trapped inside by one year's high water.

Back upstairs and outside are pieces of old machinery, including a turbine with adjustable blades and a set of grinding cylinders. They help illustrate how the two most important parts of the mill operated. Inside the main mill, the mortised timbers that make up the mill's support skeleton are all exposed for easy viewing. Staff have created a model that shows how the mortise, tenon, and pin structure is put together. The exhibits also show many of the early tools, some ingenious in their simplicity and efficiency, along with the processes required for a successful milling operation. There's a look at how grain is moved from one part of the mill to another with augers and chutes and small automated buckets as it is transferred from the outside silos to the mill and finally into the flour sacks. You can see the old canvas belts used to power the wheels and the millstones and cylinders that grind the different grains. The exhibits include a smaller working mill wheel that easily illustrates how grain is transformed from seed to flour.

On some of the spots where employees stood and worked for generations, you can see the layers of wood floor that have been worn through. One of the other fun things here is the old flour sacks. Each miller had its own designs with his own creative type and illustrations such as *Thompson's Best* and *Boston Roller Mills*. You can see some of the original flour sacks in the mill's tiny store.

HOURS: Park open daily. Mill tours offered throughout the day on weekends; weekday tours at 10:30 AM and 1:30 PM.

COST: Free

LOCATION: 32655 Boston Mill Drive, Shedd

PHONE: 541-491-3611

WEBSITE: www.oregonstateparks.org/park_256.php

10 Lane County Historical Museum

WHAT'S HERE: **Historic artifacts from throughout Lane County, from wagons to chain saws**

DON'T MISS THIS: **The hemlock tree discovered in 1960 with its carved 1867 inscription**

The museum's collection is quite diverse, and includes several historic wagons. Besides T. H. Williams's wholesale bakery wagon, which is painted black with yellow trim, you can't miss the big blue covered wagon that sits prominently in the center of the museum. It's one of the few original wagons to cross the Oregon Trail remaining—or at least the most important parts are original. The Conestoga wagon often seen in movies was bigger and used mostly during 1790 to 1820 when people were migrating west to Ohio, Indiana, Kentucky, and Tennessee. The covered wagon of Oregon Trail fame was smaller and simpler in design, more of a fancy farm wagon. This prairie schooner's undercarriage is the one that carried the Calvin Reed family to Oregon, with a stop along the way for baby Bianca to be born in 1850. They converted the prairie schooner to a farm wagon, then in the 1930s it was restored to its original state. Its red and blue pattern was common among prairie schooners. A bucket of tarry goop was hung from the rear axle and was used to periodically grease the axles and wheels. The wagon exhibit includes a very long list of supplies—about $600 worth—that the wagon would typically start with. Of the 2,000 pounds, more than half was food.

Other wagons are included in the collection. Stagecoaches were used nearly everywhere. There were two main styles—one was the larger Concord coach, and the other, which is in the museum, was the mud wagon. It was smaller and could carry 800 pounds of cargo on top. These coaches were built with leather suspensions designed to smooth the ride over the West's rutted, bumpy roads.

In 1960, a forester discovered a large hemlock with a long, partially healed-over scar on its side. Curious, he chopped away the newer growth, revealing a message that had been carved in the tree nearly 100 years earlier. It read:

JUNE 12 1867
SILAS R. CONDRA
BORN JULY 11, 1845
IN NOX CO. ILL.
CROSSED THE
PLAINS IN 1853

According to government documents, the Condra family registered as part of a wagon train in 1853. Eight-year-old Silas crossed the Great Plains with his parents, sister, and four brothers. They came from Knox County, Illinois, and staked a land claim near Halsey in Linn County. Silas apparently carved this message when he was 22 years old. The carved piece of the tree resides in the museum.

The lumber industry exhibits feature a look at the evolution of logging saws. Crosscut saws were used beginning in the early 1840s to cut already fallen trees into manageable lengths. By the 1880s loggers were using the saws, along with axes, to fell trees. They would drive wedges into the cut to keep the saw from binding to a halt. Next came the drag saw, also used to cut or "buck" already downed trees to length. A small gasoline engine powered the saw blade that was supported on a wooden frame. The heavy frames and saws were dragged to where the fallen trees lay. Finally, the predecessor to the modern chain saw came into action. The first were electric and were used as early as 1913, replacing drag saws. By the 1920s they began to take over tree felling duties. Many required two people to operate, and for some time they remained electric, plugged into generators that were moved from job site to job site by tractors.

Upstairs a series of exhibit cases holds additional parts of the museum's collection, including numerous children's shoes from the past century or earlier. There is a series of women's hats from past eras, including one described as a "wide, puffy hat of ivory straw, decorated with lace, black ribbon and feathers, c. 1910." A group of rocking chairs sits at one end of the upstairs walkway. They illustrate the many designs that the simple rocker has seen over the years. The oldest is from the mid-1800s.

HOURS: Tuesday through Saturday, 10 AM to 4 PM
COST: Adults, $3; seniors, $2; ages 15–17, $0.75
LOCATION: 740 West 13th Avenue, Eugene
PHONE: 541-682-4242
WEBSITE: www.lanecountyhistoricalsociety.org

The museum's 1850s prairie schooner

11 Shelton-McMurphey-Johnson House

WHAT'S HERE: **Prominent 19th-century Victorian home overlooking the city**
DON'T MISS THIS: **The attic retreat**

Eugene's most prominent architectural landmark is the Victorian Queen Anne Revival home that graces the side of Skinner Hill. Dr. Thomas W. Shelton purchased 320 acres from Eugene Skinner, half of his 640-acre land grant. The entrepreneurial doctor subdivided his property into parcels for residential and commercial development, retaining 4.5 acres on the side of Skinner Hill for his home. His other efforts included laying the city's first water mains along Willamette Street, which made sense since he was part owner of the city's water utility.

Dr. Shelton and his wife Adah had their house built in 1888. Architect W. D. Pugh, who graduated from college at age 17, was just 25 years old when Dr. Shelton hired him. Pugh sported a very prominent mustache in his attempt to appear older—thus more experienced—than he was. He also always wore a suit whenever in public—whether in his office or on a job site. The Shelton home was originally completed in 1887, but a disgruntled worker burned it to the ground before they moved in. It was rebuilt and the family moved into their new home in 1888.

Dr. Shelton and his wife had a daughter they named Alberta several years before the home was built. Alberta married Robert McMurphey in the home's parlor in 1893. Dr. Shelton had the unfortunate luck of contracting leukemia and dying that same year at the age of 49. Following the doctor's death, his widow moved to Portland, and Alberta and her husband moved into the Victorian. They had four daughters and two sons.

A couple of blocks away on Pearl Street, a young girl grew up admiring the Shelton's big green mansion. Eva Frazer received her undergraduate degree from the University of Oregon in 1912 and five years later graduated from Rush Medical School in Chicago. She married a newly graduated doctor, Dr. H. Curtis Johnson, she'd met while in school. He and Eva practiced medicine in Wisconsin for 25 years, then in 1950, they moved to Eugene, which proved to be perfect timing because the Shelton-McMurphey House was for sale. Eva paid $30,000 for the house, and wishing to continue her psychiatry practice, opened counseling offices in her new home. Her husband died in 1967, and she died here in 1986. She donated the home to Lane County for community use, and the City of Eugene is now the owner.

One of the more curious things about the house is its address—303 Willamette Street. Willamette Street never extended

The children's bedroom has been refurnished.

OREGON'S I-5 CORRIDOR

beyond its present-day dead end at the train depot a block or two down the hill from the home. Mrs. Shelton insisted on a Willamette Street address and apparently had the clout to get it. So you'll have to drive down a block from the depot to Pearl Street to get to the home—the road is behind the multistory retirement home at the corner of Pearl and 3rd streets.

After you enter the front door, the formal parlor is on the left. This is where members of the families that have lived here have been married—it is still available for weddings. The furnishings are not from the family, but have been donated by local families. The rest of the main floor's 2,000 square feet includes the sitting room, dining room, kitchen, and pantry. Adjacent to the bedrooms is a conservatory that was enlarged in 1919 so Robert McMurphey could use it for an office. The large cabinet in the dining room was used to exhibit the family's geology collection, among other things.

Walk up the stairs to the bedrooms. They've been furnished with pieces that reflect the time period. At one time the home was rearranged slightly to create a dorm of sorts for students attending the University of Oregon. The other bedrooms also have been furnished with period pieces that reflect how they could have appeared.

If you have an opportunity to get up to the third floor, which is the attic, do so. Although it may get moved, there is a very large model of the historic home stored in there. The attic also contains a small room that Dr. Curtis Johnson created for himself in the front turret. This is where he escaped to relax, play solitaire, and watch the city below through the room's small windows. It now holds a small display of his military memorabilia that he kept here. Johnson made the mistake of not putting a handle on the inside of his little retreat and one night he locked himself inside. He had to carve a hole with his pocket knife through the wall to escape.

HOURS: Tuesday through Friday, 10 AM to 1 PM; Saturday and Sunday, 1 PM to 4 PM

COST: Age 13 and older, $5; age 12 and under, $2

LOCATION: 303 Willamette Street, Eugene (Access is at the corner of Pearl and 3rd streets.)

PHONE: 541-484-0808

WEBSITE: www.smjhouse.org

12 University of Oregon Museum of Natural and Cultural History

WHAT'S HERE: **Significant collection of archaeological artifacts spanning 15,000 years**

DON'T MISS THIS: **The 10,000-year-old sagebrush bark sandals found in eastern Oregon**

Being associated with a major university offers certain advantages when it comes to acquiring artifacts, especially when they are archaeological and geological artifacts. It also allows exhibits to be changed periodically, offering new looks at different aspects of culture and history. With that as a backdrop, the museum's first exhibits look at the Native Americans and their relationships with the earth. Many of their villages were near the ocean's edge, a place where food was abundant. Inland, there were great fields of wild camas lilies and seed-bearing plants that Indians actively managed through burning to ensure these vital food sources for future generations. It was these same fertile valleys and fields that attracted pioneer farmers to much of Oregon. The museum maintains a close working relationship with the tribes in an ongoing effort to accurately tell the story of Oregon's first residents, including the Cayuse, Umatilla, Wasco, and Klamath from among the state's many tribes.

Exhibits look at the four regions of Oregon—the coast, the western valleys, the Great Basin, and the Columbia Plateau. The coast has changed over the past 10,000 years, as the Pacific Ocean has receded and risen moving its shoreline, eroding cliffs, and flooding low-lying areas. As the last ice age pushed its glaciers from higher mountains into the lower elevations, it carved great valleys and altered the courses of some rivers. Over millions of years, volcanoes flooded the Columbia Plateau with great fields of lava. Throughout that same geologic period, rivers carved their way through the great walls of rock, creating spectacular canyons and cliffs. Volcanoes also stamped their imprint on the Cascades, where continental plates collided. Half the state can experience rain every month of the year, while the other half is desertlike as the Cascades prevent the brunt of Pacific storms from moving farther inland.

One of the exhibits illustrates how the Indians modified not only their diets, but their movements, some migrating as each season's changes brought new opportunities for food. At times some of the most populated areas were places like Celilo Falls on the Columbia River when the salmon were swimming upriver to

Museum of Natural and Cultural History entrance

spawn. The museum shows how the Indians fished with traps, nets, and weirs (an enclosure), in addition to using spears.

The Native Americans who lived in these diverse climatic areas developed different cultures, from clothing and food sources to beliefs and ceremonies. The Klamath tell the story of the creation of Crater Lake. While terrorizing the people, Monadalkni, the Evil One, was confronted by Gmokemkts, the Creator. The two battled and eventually the Creator hit the Evil One so hard that he was pushed back into the earth and a mountain smashed in on top of him. The Creator then called for the rains that filled the great hole, creating Crater Lake. For the Klamath people, Crater Lake has always been a very powerful place.

Scientists believe that people have lived in the Great Basin for at least 15,000 years, their cultures changing little until the arrival of Europeans. One of the museum's most treasured artifacts comes from what has become known as Fort Rock Cave. A pair of 10,000-year-old sandals that were preserved under layers of volcanic ash from Mount Mazama (Crater Lake) were discovered here. The sandals fit neatly as one of the three distinct types of ancient sandals that have been found in Oregon. The two other types—multiple warp and spiral weft—are less than 9,000 years old.

The museum includes a science lab where visitors can see and touch animal bones, from skulls to femurs, along with sharks' teeth and more. The museum is constantly changing exhibits; you may enjoy a hands-on look at geology or perhaps learn about Polynesian tapa cloth, which was made from pounded bark and then woven into intricate geometric designs.

HOURS: Wednesday through Sunday, 11 AM to 5 PM
COST: Adults, $3; ages 63-plus and ages 3–18, $2; families (two adults, four children), $8
LOCATION: 1680 East 15th Avenue, Eugene
PHONE: 541-346-3024
WEBSITE: www.uoregon.edu/~mnh/

13 University of Oregon Jordan Schnitzer Art Museum

WHAT'S HERE: Extensive art collection with an Asian focus

DON'T MISS THIS: Second-floor balcony view of the Campbell Memorial Courtyard

The museum is named for Jordan Schnitzer, an alumnus and successful businessman. Built in 1932, the museum's exterior front wall features a very distinctive brick pattern. The museum underwent a major expansion that was completed in 2005, significantly increasing its exhibition space.

The museum's first major benefactor was Gertrude Bass Warner, who believed that greater cultural understanding among nations would be facilitated by the sharing of art treasures. She began collecting Asian art in 1904 on her first trip to Japan. Following her husband Murray Warner's death, Mrs. Warner donated her collection of art from Korea, Mongolia, Cambodia, and Russia to the museum. The largest part of her bequeathed gift came from China and Japan.

The museum's main floor is primarily administrative offices, a lecture hall, the museum gift shop, and a small cafe, while the exhibit galleries are upstairs. There are individual galleries focusing on Japanese, Chinese, and Korean art, with another gallery that combines American and regional art. No matter where you begin, there are many dozens of exquisite art pieces to enjoy. With the museum's extensive collection, it is expected that the pieces exhibited in the galleries will be rotated periodically.

The Japanese collection includes paintings, wood-block prints, Imari and Kutani ware ceramics, and lacquerware. You may see everyday items such as country textiles, including a fishmonger's jacket, or perhaps tea ceremony objects. Kimonos are well-known to be of Japanese origin, but in earlier times commoners were forbidden to wear silk garments. They used hemp and ramie until the introduction of cotton in the 18th century. Another of the restricted clothing items were those worn by the samurai or warrior who followed the Bushido code, the way of the warrior.

Folding panel screens are another of the art objects that originated in Asia. The museum's collection includes an exceptional 10-panel ink-on-silk panel screen from Korea's Joseon period that includes the 10 symbols of longevity. This particular art piece illustrates the mixing and exchange of art among different Asian cultures. Each of the symbols associated with longevity and immortality—deer, cranes, the sun, clouds, rocks, bamboo, pines, tortoises, fungi, and water—can be found in Chinese art. Only in Korea can all of

Front entrance to the Jordan Schnitzer Art Museum

the symbols be found on the same object, whether it be a large panel screen, ceramics, lacquerware, or furniture.

There is so much more here, from ceramics to wood-block prints to beautifully carved model pagodas. And as you move from the Asian galleries to the Jordan Schnitzer Gallery of American Art, you can view the largest public collection of Morris Graves's paintings. Graves was a self-taught American abstract painter and sculptor who died in 2001 at the age of 90. Moderism is well represented by artists, including C. S. Price, Mark Tobey, and Maude Kerns. You may also view a collection of paintings and drawings completed by artists from the 1930s working for the New Deal's Works Progress Administration.

Before you return to the main floor, take a short walk to the balcony that overlooks the Campbell Memorial Courtyard. The large garden pool below is a relaxing place to spend a few minutes reflecting on the art.

HOURS: Tuesday through Sunday, 11 AM to 5 PM; open Wednesdays until 8 PM
COST: Adults, $5; ages 62-plus, $3; ages 18 and under, free
LOCATION: 1430 Johnson Lane, Eugene
PHONE: 541-346-3027
WEBSITE: http://uoma.uoregon.edu

14 Douglas County Museum

WHAT'S HERE: **History of the Umpqua Valley and Oregon's largest natural history collection**

DON'T MISS THIS: **The logging exhibit that includes a 1951 Ford Short-logger**

The museum, which is a large, multidimensional structure, is difficult to miss, even from nearby Interstate 5. With many galleries to explore, one of the first exhibits explores 10,000 years of wine history, including a close look at how wine production has come to be such a big business in the Umpqua Valley. You start your trip back in history with the Egyptians who had to import most of their wine because their climate was not conducive to grape growing. The exhibit then covers the Greeks and Romans, who apparently enjoyed dining on lounge-type chairs and tossing bones, scraps, and other leftovers on the floor to be cleaned later. They also enjoyed great quantities of wine, with abundant toasts to Bacchus, the god of wine.

The museum also looks at modern grape growing and winemaking, including some of the specialized equipment such as destemmers for removing grapes from their stems. There is a wide variety of grapes grown in the region, including Cabernet Sauvignon,

Cabernet Franc, Malbec, Grenache, Viognier, Pinot Noir, Reisling, Syrah, and Pinot Gris, all of which can make excellent varietals.

Native Americans are an important part of the museum's exhibits, considering they were Oregon's first settlers. An excellent representative basket collection showcases the different basket styles and design patterns used by the Coos, Siletz, Klamath, and others. The interpretive panels tell tragic tales about the impact that the early trappers and settlers had on the local tribes. In 1836, the Hudson's Bay Company built Fort Umpqua on the Umpqua River as a trading post and as a storage facility for the furs. In those early days, the fort's traders could get $20,000 worth of furs from the Indians for as little as $2 worth of trinkets.

The museum takes a look at the early pioneers who came for more than the fur trade, an enterprise that died by the mid-1800s. For example, the Applegate family crossed the Oregon Trail in 1843. After losing two of their children while crossing the Columbia River, the Applegates and several others in their party blazed a new trail that soon carried their name, trying to avoid the hostile Cayuse Indians along the regular trail. They ended up in what would become Douglas County. The museum exhibits look at the increasing hostilities between the local Native Americans and the new arrivals, be they gold miners, farmers, or business owners, with numerous attacks by both sides and many deaths.

Going back many more years, tusks, jaws, and teeth from wooly mammoths are on display. For budding archaeologists, the museum has a rock structure with various artifacts and fossils buried in the sand pockets— kids can slowly brush away the sand and discover the ancient treasures. The exhibit discusses finding clues about the past through fossils.

The museum's natural history gallery is quite amazing. Just about any animal you can imagine that once lived in Oregon can be found here. While they may no longer be living creatures, the accompanying text provides much information about these animals and how and where they live. From otters to weasels, moles to frogs, bats to birds, they are all here. You can see animal skulls that illustrate the differences among herbivores, omnivores, and carnivores. Round one corner to be face-to-face with a very large elk.

Healthy forests are necessary for much of that wildlife and also for the timber industry to continue supplying building products for homes and businesses. Here is your chance to look at many of the different trees that grow so well in Oregon, from Douglas fir to Sitka spruce.

Move along through the galleries to a very comfortable looking living room. Let the kids take a seat in the overstuffed chairs and offer them a book from the bookshelf. When they open the books, they will be surprised with a hollow book filled with treasures such as a turritella shell. Hear an owl, but can't see it? Push one of the buttons on the panel to hear the sounds made by nine different

An early steam-powered tractor or steam donkey

owls, from a barn owl to a tiny burrowing owl. Those birds and more, such as an osprey with a fish in its talons and a turkey vulture, can be seen in the cases. There's also a gray whale skull, a harbor seal on a beach, and so much more.

Exploring David Douglas is an exhibit aimed at kids with hands-on learning activities based on cultural and natural history. Douglas was a Scottish botanist who came to the Pacific Northwest in 1824 searching for plant species unknown to Europe and Great Britain. The Douglas fir was named after him, although his rival Archibald Menzies was awarded the scientific name, *Pseudotsuga menziesii,* for the tree that Douglas introduced into cultivation. He also introduced numerous other species, including Sitka spruce, sugar pine, Monterey pine, and about 240 shrubs, herbs, and other trees. And while kids may not be out in the wilderness identifying newly discovered plants, they will be able to work with live animals, including turtles, frogs, and lizards, as well as fossils and pelts.

Trails and roads are explored along with the many different vehicles that traveled them, from horse-drawn wagons to a 1916 Dodge touring car. There are many more pieces of equipment outside, including an old John Deere tractor, a steam donkey, and other logging related equipment, from chain saws to logging trucks.

HOURS: Monday through Friday, 9 AM to 5 PM; Saturday, 10 AM to 5 PM; Sunday, 12 PM to 5 PM. Closed most major holidays.

COST: Adults, $4; ages 55-plus, $3; ages 4–17 and college students, $2

LOCATION: 123 Museum Drive, Roseburg

PHONE: 541-957-7007

WEBSITE: www.douglasmuseum.com

15 Butte Creek Mill

WHAT'S HERE: Historic gristmill that still operates and sells its stone-ground wheat

DON'T MISS THIS: Seeing the belts and pulleys in action as the miller grinds grain

It is rare for a business to remain in operation for more than 130 years in the same building, with essentially the same equipment and mode of power. A sailing ship brought the mill's most important piece of equipment from France to Crescent City, California. The special grinding stones were then carried by wagon over the mountains to the Butte Creek Mill, which began operation in 1872.

The mill was the center of local commerce. Farmers from miles around brought their grains here to be ground into flour so it could then be shipped to market. At harvest time, wagons loaded with grain would line up for miles awaiting the mill's services. The mill owner was usually paid by keeping every seventh bag of grain that was processed, flour that he sold here in his own store. Even the Klamath Indians traveled some 90 miles from Fort Klamath to trade for the ground flour.

Because this is still an operating mill, it is a fun place to visit. If you have an opportunity to take a tour, do so. You can go down to the guts of the operation where the penstock shoots water through a turbine that powers everything. When all the belts, wheels, and pulleys get moving, you will be amazed at the ingenuity and the simplicity of the entire operation. Some of the apparatus moves grain up and down the three floors of the mill, while another powers the original French buhr grinding stones.

Once the 1,400-pound grinding stones are set with the required "gap" to produce the correct grind, the grain is automatically poured from the hopper into the center of the stones. As the stones turn, the grain is ground and is slowly pushed outward where it is collected and bagged.

Beyond the grinding activity, take a look at the mill's construction. The big timber beams are mortised together, then pinned with hardwood pegs. Square nails hold the original whipsawed lumber walls to the frame. You can also see some of the old gears used to transfer water power from belt to machine. For the most part, the gear teeth are made of wood. The idea was that if a tooth broke, it could be quickly and easily replaced. If an iron tooth broke, the piece of machinery could be down for days waiting for parts and a welder.

Leave the grinding side of the mill and step into the store. It is filled with hundreds of items, most of them ground-something. You can get fresh spices and

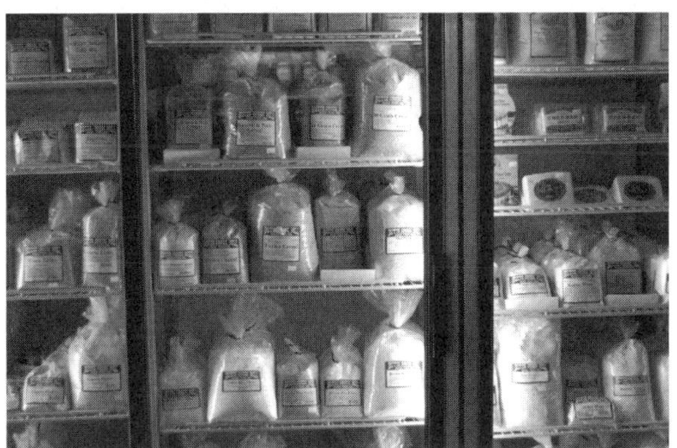

Freshly milled grains for sale

herbs such as coriander, cumin, mustard, and mace. And for fresh flour lovers, there is nearly anything you can imagine on the packed shelves and likely more than a few things you never knew existed. While there are many of the commonly found grains here such as oat bran, white rice flour, brown rice flour, potato flour, and barley flour, you can also find kamut flour, quinoa flour, and farina cereal. Most of the fancy ground grains are stored in a refrigerator to maintain freshness. If you can't make it into the mill's store, you can always order via telephone or online. Be aware, there often is only one person working in the store, handling both in-house customers and all of the telephone orders that come in. So be patient, whether you stop in or call in your order.

HOURS: Monday through Saturday, 9 AM to 5 PM; Sunday, 11 AM to 5 PM
COST: Free
LOCATION: 402 Royal Avenue N., Eagle Point
PHONE: 541-826-3531
WEBSITE: www.buttecreekmill.com

16 Beeman-Martin House

WHAT'S HERE: **Home built in 1901 by the owner of the Lucky Bart Mine**
DON'T MISS THIS: **Basement exhibits, including the barber's straight razor collection**

The small community of Gold Hill in southern Oregon was aptly named, considering millions of dollars in gold was taken from its surrounding hills. The history of Gold Hill began when, in 1857, Thomas Chavner purchased a land claim parcel in the area. One of his workers discovered a piece of gold-rich ore on this land, but Chavner and several partners didn't file a mining claim until 1860. The mine became known as "Gold Hill Lode" and produced more than $20 million (today's value). Chavner used some of his fortune to purchase 2,000 acres along the Rogue River, and he built a toll bridge across the river that the county finally purchased in 1888. A newer bridge replaced the original bridge in 1927, and it remains in use today.

Josiah and Hattie Beeman, owners of the Lucky Bart Mine in Gold Hill, built their home in 1901. Josiah actually leased the mine at first, purchasing it outright in 1897. So extravagant was the new home that it was the first in the city to have indoor plumbing. Very modest by today's standards, the home sits only a short distance from the Rogue River. Refurbished and opened as a museum in 1994, it houses an eclectic collection of Gold Hill history.

Before you go inside, walk around back. As a testament to the local history, a stamp mill has been moved to the property. The stamp mill was originally purchased in San Francisco in 1892 and shipped by rail to Gold Hill. Mules pulled the massive mill up Sardine Creek to the Lucky Bart Mine. The stamp mill actually operated, at least periodically, as ore became available from other mines, until 1975.

The house remained in the same family through three generations before coming to the local historical society and becoming a museum, although only a few of the artifacts inside are from the home. One piece is the hall coat tree and another is the woodstove in the kitchen. Although a more modern stove had been in the house, the old woodstove here now is the original.

Among the other things you can see is an antique piano, a 1949 Montgomery Ward television, and dishes from various past eras. Head downstairs into the basement for a treasure trove of tools, from axes and whipsaws to picks and wrenches, and a collection of electric line insulators, bottles, jugs, and more.

HOURS: Thursday through Saturday, 12 PM to 4 PM
COST: Free
LOCATION: 504 1st Avenue, Gold Hill
PHONE: 541-855-1182
WEBSITE: None

Stamp mill behind the Beeman-Martin House

17 Jacksonville Museum and Children's Museum

WHAT'S HERE: Local history museum in the original county courthouse
DON'T MISS THIS: The kids' museum next door

It's been tradition at the beginning of construction of many grand buildings to place a time capsule in the cornerstone. When construction of the Jackson County Italianate style courthouse began in the 1880s, several mementos were included in its cornerstone, including a set of false teeth, two quarts of whiskey, and a $20 Confederate bill. The whiskey is likely well-aged by now, considering that the courthouse was constructed in 1883.

Pioneer communities that had survived their infancy and appeared headed toward long-term prosperity built public buildings made of brick and stone, materials that symbolized their solid foundation and future longevity. Jackson County used 150,000 bricks to build its $32,000 courthouse, but unfortunately, county government and the court moved to Medford in about 1927. As such, the abandoned courthouse served as a community center until 1950 when the Jacksonville Museum opened.

While the museum exhibits cover numerous historical aspects of the area, several focus on Peter Britt. He accompanied his family and their friends from Switzerland when they emigrated to the U.S. in 1845. While living in Highland, Illinois, besides becoming a photographer, Peter Britt also became an U.S. citizen. Even as a citizen he never gave up reading and writing German, his native language. As thousands of others were attracted to the American West in the mid-19th century, so too was Peter. At the age of 33, he headed west on the Oregon Trail.

The discovery of gold was one of the things that in 1852 attracted Peter Britt to what would become Jacksonville. When financial success did not accompany either his mining or his mule packing enterprises, he returned to photography. In subsequent years, Britt became quite involved in meteorology and more importantly in agriculture. He had always been an avid gardener, and according to his family, an Italian from California sold him his first grape cuttings in 1854. Through the 1860s and into the 1870s, Britt planted extensive vineyards on his ever-increasing landholdings in the area. Experimenting with more than 200 different varieties, he sold Claret, Chardonnay, Muscatel, Zinfandel, and Port. He borrowed from California's wine making industry, purchasing fifteen 200-gallon storage casks along with a pair of 1,000-gallon redwood fermenting tanks. He sold his wine under his Valley View Vineyard label.

Britt's wine became very popular and was sold throughout the western states.

Some of Peter Britt's photo equipment

He used large wicker-covered (for cushioning) bottles to ship his wine. The bottles were called demijohns, and he would charge his customers an extra 75 cents per bottle if they chose to keep it or they could return the bottle and not be charged. While other winemakers ultimately exceeded Britt's production capacities by the end of the 19th century, he was still recognized as the father of the grape industry in the Rogue River Valley. The museum exhibits include several of his cameras and other items, including numerous photographs he took of the area.

The museum features much more, including a Native American gallery with baskets and other items from many different tribes, including those who lived along the Oregon Trail. Apparently, even with the limited space in their wagons for food and other supplies, some of the immigrants managed to find, trade, or purchase items from the Indians that captured their fancies as they headed west. Some of the local descendants of the early pioneers have donated baskets and other artifacts to the museum.

Head upstairs where many early local businesses are represented in mini-store fronts. Since gold brought many of the first pioneers to Jacksonville, there is a mining exhibit, including an assay office and an area where kids can pan for gold. Exhibits include a blacksmith shop, a laundry, a carpenter's shop that includes many hand tools, a hat store for the ladies, and the interiors of local homes. The Chinese exhibit includes numerous bowls, tea sets, and a couple of baskets.

Next door to the main courthouse museum is the jail. It's now a children's museum with numerous hands-on things to do. It's filled with lots of original and reproduction historic artifacts that the younger set can play with, including dress-up pioneer clothing. To give kids an idea of how hard a child's daily chores might have been in the 1800s, there are several buckets that would have been common back then in most homes. They were used to bring water into the houses, because most homes didn't have indoor plumbing. The buckets are filled with 15 pounds of a solid material, representing the weight of a bucket full of water that had to be carried from the outside well into the kitchens and bathtubs—at least when baths were taken. They can try their hands at lugging one or two of the full buckets around the museum.

There is also a giant Lincoln Log–type of set that has been turned into a log cabin. Upstairs a model train winds its way through a huge diorama that includes the nearby towns of Medford and Ashland. There's even a replica of Peter Britt's photography studio that includes a camera the kids can use to take their own pretend pictures, while you take photos of the kids in action.

HOURS: Wednesday through Sunday, 11 AM to 4 PM. Closed major holidays.
COST: Includes both museums: adults, $5; ages 65-plus and 3–12, $3
LOCATION: 206 N. Fifth Street, Jacksonville
PHONE: 541-773-6536
WEBSITE: www.sohs.org

18 Harry & David

WHAT'S HERE: The popular mail order gift food company's store and factory
DON'T MISS THIS: Take the factory tour

If you happen to be traveling along Interstate 5 in Oregon and see exit 27—take it. Within a few minutes, you are wandering through a cornucopia of delectable treats at the Harry & David Country Village (and factory). While there's nothing historic about the building, the company's story is one of early 20th-century entrepreneurial success.

In 1910 Samuel Rosenberg sold his luxury Seattle hotel and purchased 240 acres of pears in Oregon's Rogue River Valley. Following his death four years later, Harry and David, his two sons, took over the orchard business. They had studied agriculture at Cornell University and also knew something about marketing. They exported their extraordinarily delicious French Comice pears that they named "Royal Riviera" to the finer restaurants and hotels in Europe. Business boomed during the 1920s, until the stock market crashed and the Great Depression descended upon the country.

When their overseas markets collapsed, they changed tactics and went to San Francisco and New York City, seeking to establish new markets. Targeting big business owners, those who could still afford luxury, they pitched their pears as ideal business gifts, and soon orders once again came flooding in, marking their entry into the direct marketing business of fruit and food gift baskets. They followed with other marketing innovations, including their Fruit-of-the-Month Club, a sales practice now common for businesses selling everything from wine to books. Today Harry & David is one of the country's oldest and most successful catalog mail order companies—although today you can just as easily place your order online.

The factory tours are fun and take only about an hour. They can be popular, especially during holiday periods, so it's wise to make a reservation. You'll be boarding a small bus with a guide who will share the company's history as you take the short drive from the main store, past the corporate headquarter offices to the factory. Along the way, a video tells the story of how the company became, and how it continues to be, a success—quality products and unsurpassed customer service.

Although the tour route can be reversed, usually visitors next enter the bakery and candy factory. One of the first things you will see is the famous pear on the lobby floor—done in tile. For the most part you will be walking above the work areas, looking down on the machines and the people who make such

The Harry & David factory store in Medford

mouthwatering treats as their famous Moose Munch, a wickedly delicious combination of air-popped gourmet popcorn covered with buttery toffee and tossed with crisp nuts, some of which are covered in rich chocolate. These machines that can produce 200 pounds of the treat each hour.

Continuing with the tour you will see the bakery where everything from dessert bars to cookies are created. The ovens are from Sweden. Then there are the cooling areas and the blast freezer—most of the baked goods are shipped frozen. There is a machine that wraps hundreds of pieces of candy in foil each hour. Other machines pass candy along doing everything from picking up trays to automatically dipping and decorating chocolates. While automation is everywhere, there are still hundreds of workers busy filling, dumping, sorting, and monitoring everything going on. And they all appear to be enjoying their work. As you leave the bakery and candy factory, you will receive a small gift box of chocolate.

But the tour isn't over yet. Back onboard the bus, you will drive past some of the orchards on your way to the production facility where all the fruit, candy, and baked goods come together in those famous Harry & David gift baskets shipped all over the country. Off the bus once again and inside, you can see where the fancy bows are made—yes, most are still handmade—along with the dozens of workers responsible for putting everything together into baskets and boxes for shipping.

The bus takes you back to the Country Village where you can purchase additional gift baskets, try a few free samples, or enjoy browsing the store.

HOURS: Tours, Monday through Friday, 9:15 AM, 10:30 AM, 12:30 PM, and 1:45 PM
COST: $5 (redeemable as part of a minimum purchase at the store)
LOCATION: 1314 Center Drive, Medford
PHONE: 877-322-8000
WEBSITE: www.harryanddavid.com

19 ScienceWorks Hands-On Museum

WHAT'S HERE: Kids' hands-on science center

DON'T MISS THIS: The Black Bear Gardens in front of the museum

There are numerous kids' museums throughout the country, so what makes this one different? The founders of ScienceWorks visited more than 40 interactive children's museums and identified the best and most innovative exhibits, which they then recreated when they put the museum together in 2002—and it's definitely the kids who benefit, although parents also have a lot of fun.

Those interactive exhibits begin just steps past the entry desk. For example, the pulley chairs let one child sit in a chair while another child easily pulls them upward using a rope attached to a pulley system. Inside the Discovery Lab, there is ample time for experiments and an opportunity to work with critters such as snakes, lizards, and even the museum's bearded dragon, which is an Australian native. If luck holds, you can watch as the dragon stands on three legs, then raises one of its front legs and waves it in a slow circular motion. There's even a real beehive full of live honeybees. Fortunately, they are able to leave the hive through a tube to the outside of the building.

By riding the museum's special stationary bike, kids can see how much power, or at least how much pedal power, it takes to run an electric train and light a light. The sand pendulum lets you make fun designs in sand as a funnel swings in circles and ovals above a yellow board depositing dark sand as it moves. Another experiment has a sign that warns those with heart conditions to be careful; the glass ball is filled with streams of electrons trying to escape. Touch the glass ball and it glows as you create an easier path for the electrons to escape, causing lightning to move to your hand, through your body, and finally into the ground. Another experiment with electricity uses a small meter that allows kids to measure the amount of power that passes through their bodies as they place one hand on a copper plate and the other on an aluminum plate.

Magnetism is another phenomenon that allows for creative fun, and everyone can play with magnets and iron shavings to create hair and beards on painted faces. The giant bubble maker is always an attraction; kids can dip large wands into the huge trays of soapy water and make magnificent bubbles in different shapes. There is a climbing and play area for the smaller tykes, and kids of all ages can have fun floating foam balls on streams of air. And for those who can't get enough video-game practice, the flight simulator lets you attempt to fly and land a model air-

There is an endless array of kid-active attractions.

plane. For baseball players, there is a pitching cage with a radar gun that tells you how fast your fastballs really are. Randy Johnson has thrown a 102-mile-per-hour fastball. Think you can beat him?

There's enough going on here to keep a bunch of kids busy for several hours, and they'll be learning without even realizing it! Once back outside, take a few minutes to wander through the Black Bear Gardens across the plaza from the front entrance.

HOURS: Wednesday through Saturday, 10 AM to 4 PM; Sunday, noon to 4 PM
COST: Adults and teens, $7.50; ages 2–12, $5; ages 65-plus, $5
LOCATION: 1500 E. Main Street, Ashland
PHONE: 541-482-6767
WEBSITE: www.scienceworksmuseum.org

Oregon's Interstate 5 Corridor Tours

Oregon City History Tour

ESTIMATED DAYS: 1
ESTIMATED DRIVING MILES: 5

Oregon City marks the official ending point of the Oregon Trail. The **End of the Oregon Trail Interpretive Center** (page 75) offers live programs and demonstrations that focus on the early pioneers and their dangerous 19th-century journeys across the country. There is also a large visitor center with maps, brochures, and other travel-related information available here. Perhaps a ten-minute drive away is the **Museum of the Oregon Territory** (page 73) that offers a look at the region's history—and offers great views of adjacent Willamette Falls and the locks that allow small ships and barges to bypass the falls on their trips up and down the river.

Several historic homes are open to the public, including the **Stevens-Crawford Heritage House** (page 76) and the nearby **McLoughlin House** (www.mcloughlinhouse.org). Something not to miss is North America's only "elevator street"—**Oregon City Municipal Elevator,** www.orcity.org/publicworks/municipal-elevator. Aptly named Elevator Street, an elevator carries passengers up this "vertical street." The original elevator was constructed in 1915 and was designed to get pedestrians from the river-level part of the city to the bluff portion of the expanding town. That first elevator took up to five minutes to raise passengers the 89 feet to the top—and it had a trapdoor for escape should it fail, which it did routinely. The new elevator doesn't share those same design faults and can zip you up the cliff in less than 30 seconds. And it's still free.

The supply store serves as a theater.

The Mills Tour

ESTIMATED DAYS: 1 or 2
ESTIMATED DRIVING MILES: 40 or 240

Western Oregon has plenty of rivers that have provided the power to industrialize production of agricultural end-products. One of those products is wool, and the **Mission Mill Museum** (page 80) in Salem is the perfect place to see 19th-century technology in action. Several historic homes occupy part of the five-acre site, but the biggest attraction is the woolen mill. Walk over the millrace and see where water once passed to power the turbines, which turned the gears that operated all the machinery. Inside the mill, it appears that it has just shut down for the day and the workers have left. From bales of wool to finished bolts of fine woolen cloth and everything in between, the mill and its signage provide a close-up look at the entire manufacturing process.

For a different kind of mill, but one that still depends on water to turn its turbines and power the machinery, drive about 40 miles to the small community of Shedd. As pioneer farms expanded, a need for grist (flour) mills arose. **Thompson's Mills State Heritage Site** (page 85) is one of those 19th-century flour mills that local farmers came to depend on. The original mill burned in 1862, and the new replacement mill operated for 143 years before going out of business in 2002. Interpretive exhibits reveal the inner workings of the mill and demonstrations show what it was like to work here.

If you happen to be heading much farther down Interstate 5, about 200 miles farther south is the privately owned **Butte Creek Mill** (page 97). An operational gristmill that offers a large array of fresh stone-ground flours from wheat to barley, tours of the mill are offered and the "general store" is a delight to explore.

Power workings under Thompson's Mills

Family/Kids' Tour

ESTIMATED DAYS: 1
ESTIMATED DRIVING MILES: 18

While parents will likely enjoy the **Jacksonville Museum** (page 100) more than the kids, the youngsters will likely have a lot more fun next door at the Jacksonville **Children's Museum** (page 100). The county's historic jail now houses a museum designed especially for kids. Everything is hands-on, such as the filled "pioneer buckets" that weigh 15 pounds. Lifting and carrying the bucket offers a realistic look at pioneer life when children often had to tote many buckets of water each day from the well into the house. And yes, there is still a small jail cell here.

Drive to Ashland for more kid fun. The **ScienceWorks Hands-On Museum** (page 104) is true to its name. Here you will find everything from giant bubble makers and floating foam balls to a flight simulator and even a baseball pitching cage with radar to track the speed of your fastball. There are many dozens of other science-related activities, all of which will keep kids and parents busily entertained for most of the day.

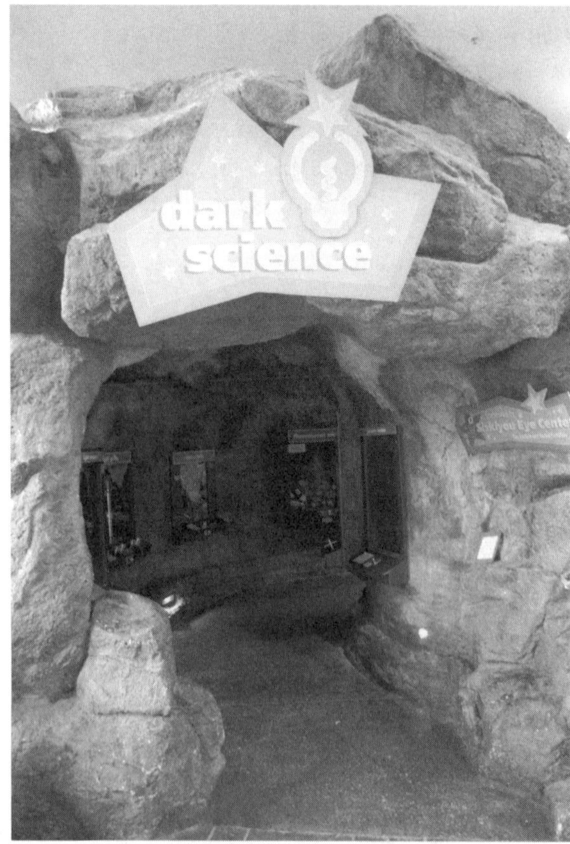

ScienceWorks Hands-On Museum

Oregon's Interstate 5 Corridor Information Centers

Salem Convention and Visitors Association
www.travelsalem.com
800-874-7012

Eugene, Lane County, and Oregon Visitor Information
www.travellanecounty.org
800-547-5445

City of Roseburg Visitors and Convention Bureau
www.visitroseburg.com
800-444-9584

Medford Visitors and Convention Center
www.visitmedford.org
800-469-6307

Ashland Chamber of Commerce
www.ashlandchamber.com
541-482-3486

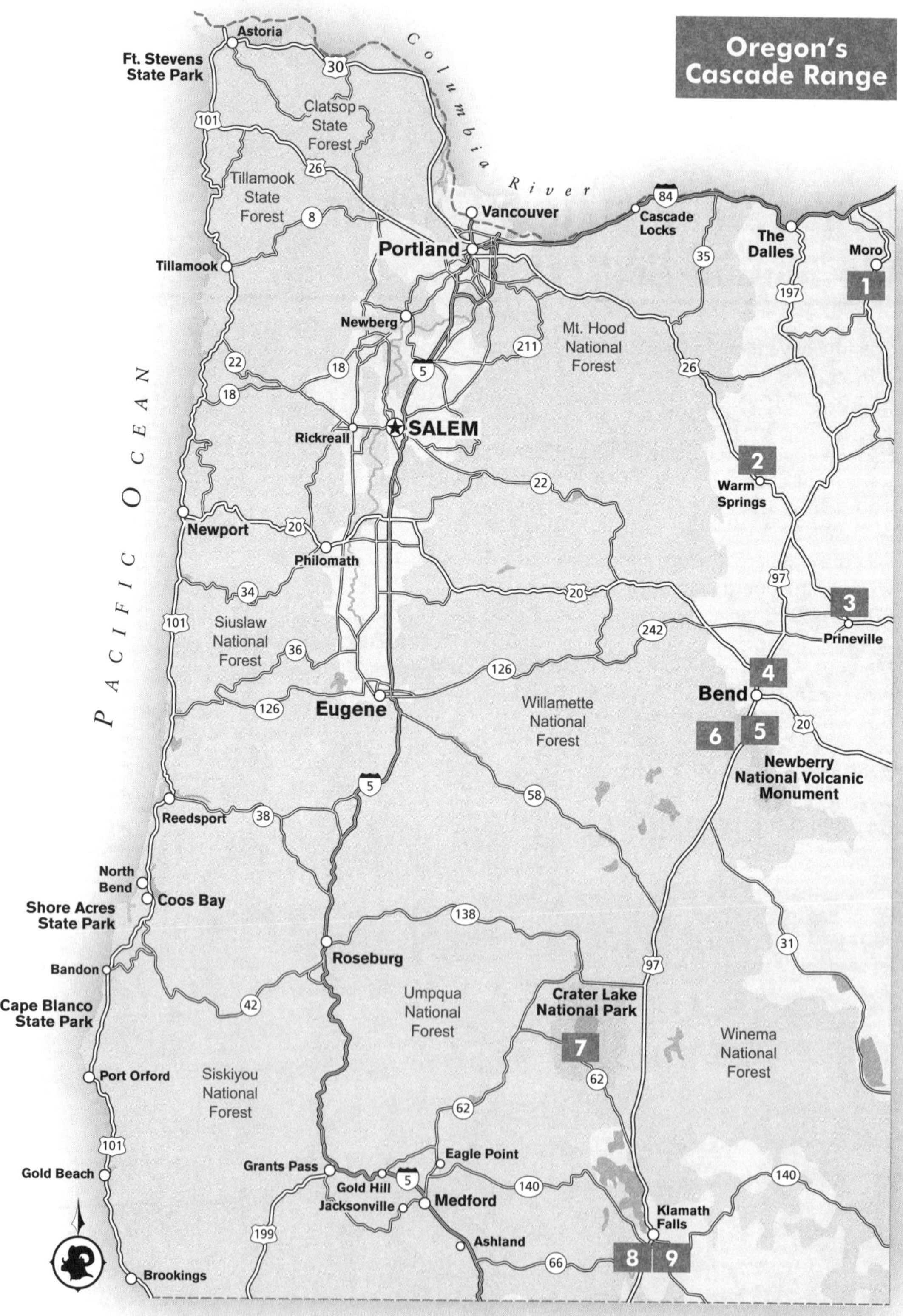

Oregon's Cascade Range
Astoria
Ft. Stevens State Park
Columbia River
Clatsop State Forest
Tillamook State Forest
Vancouver
Cascade Locks
The Dalles
Moro
Portland
Tillamook
Newberg
Mt. Hood National Forest
PACIFIC OCEAN
SALEM
Rickreall
Warm Springs
Newport
Philomath
Siuslaw National Forest
Prineville
Bend
Eugene
Willamette National Forest
Newberry National Volcanic Monument
Reedsport
North Bend
Coos Bay
Shore Acres State Park
Roseburg
Bandon
Crater Lake National Park
Umpqua National Forest
Cape Blanco State Park
Winema National Forest
Port Orford
Siskiyou National Forest
Eagle Point
Grants Pass
Gold Hill
Gold Beach
Jacksonville
Medford
Klamath Falls
Ashland
Brookings

Oregon's Cascade Range

Central Oregon claims a small portion of what geologists call the "Ring of Fire," the arc of volcanic mountains that essentially follows the edge of the Pacific Ocean's several tectonic plates. Those geologic plates have created the Cascade Range, a continuous stretch of mostly volcanic mountains that begin in Canada and stretch into Northern California. The only break in the mountain range is where the Columbia River passes through the Columbia Gorge.

The western side of the Cascade Range can receive more than 200 inches of snow in some years, while the eastern side may receive less than 12 inches of rain each year. Those conditions create marked differences in the types of vegetation found. On the west, Douglas

Ancient lava flows at Newberry National Volcanic Monument

fir, western hemlock, and red alder—all moisture-loving trees—grow prolifically. On the east, where the storms are blocked by the mountains, more drought-tolerant trees, such as Ponderosa pine and western larch are found.

Volcanoes are the landmarks most easily seen when traveling here. They are the tallest mountains and several, such as Mount Hood, Mount Jefferson, and the Three Sisters, can easily be seen from many miles away. Crater Lake is the most famous, a huge volcano whose violent explosion nearly 8,000 years ago spewed 150 times more ash into the atmosphere than Mount St. Helen's eruption in 1980. Evidence of thousands of years of eruptions is seen everywhere as volcanic lava flows cover vast areas of central Oregon.

TRIVIA

1. Where can you see a springtooth, a chisel plow, and a rodweeder?
2. Where can you learn what *yáamâ*, *i'ánk*, and *tuhudya* (from three Native American languages) mean in English?
3. What museum features a large volcanic rock with several initials and the year 1813 carved by members of the Pacific Fur Company?
4. Where can you see forest animals, a historic homestead ranch and sawmill, and Native American and early settler artifacts?
5. Where can you see spindle bombs, "squeeze-up," and pumice?
6. Where can you find the deepest lake in the U.S.?
7. Where can you see a "balloon bomb" that was once launched in aerial attacks by the Japanese against the U.S. during World War II?

For trivia answers, see page 341.

1 Sherman County Historical Museum

WHAT'S HERE: **Farming, from the people to the work, is the focus of the museum.**
DON'T MISS THIS: **The fancy farm worker chuck wagon**

Located in the small farming community of Moro, set amidst thousands of acres of wheat fields, the museum is a wonderful destination for learning about the agricultural history of the area, especially when it comes to grain farming. Sherman County averages only 11.5 inches of rain each year, yet it is the dryland cereal grain farming king. In mid-July and early August big combines harvest wheat fields that appear to go on forever.

The museum has numerous pieces of equipment that are used to farm dryland soils, each designed for uses that limit soil and moisture loss. The simple plow turns over soil, burying the residue from the previous year 10 to 12 inches deep. The springtooth smoothes the larger chunks of soil and pulls some of the weeds back to the surface to help control erosion. For very compacted soils, the chisel plow can cut through 10 inches of hard surface. When weeds begin to grow (before planting) robbing the soil of what little moisture it has, a rodweeder, invented in 1921 for dryland farming, can uproot weeds without going more than two to three inches deep. Disks are commonly seen working in spring, another way of reducing volunteer grasses. Often, though, farmers resort to using herbicides to eliminate weeds, thus delaying their initial tilling until soil conditions improve. Then there are harrows that further smooth the surface, fertilizer applicators, ground sprayers (or aerial sprayers), and drills—equipment that plants seeds in shallow, disked rows, usually seen working in early fall as planting gets underway each year.

The museum's focus may be farming, but its Native American and early explorer exhibit, Oregon Trails, Rails, and Roads provides an overview of the area's history. The exhibit includes maps of the early Indian trade trails. The four regional Tenino bands traveled and traded with each other and with other tribes, especially during the salmon runs that brought millions of the big fish up the Columbia River and its tributaries. Celilo Falls, now inundated by the water behind The Dalles Dam, was one of their traditional gathering areas. The treaty signed in 1855 caused the Tenino to be moved from their tribal lands to the Warm Springs Reservation, although they retained hunting and fishing rights on their ceded lands.

The museum's collection of Indian artifacts includes numerous historic photographs of villages and of fishing activities on the Columbia River and baskets from the nearby Klickitat. Best described as a food wheel, one of the graphics

Period kitchen exhibit

illustrates some of the different key foods that were available to the Tenino during each month of the year.

There is also a look at the early explorers, including John Frémont and Meriwether Lewis and William Clark, all before the Oregon Trail became the highway to a new life for thousands of immigrants. Some of the early dirt trails were transformed into trails of steel as railroads began to crisscross the state, connecting the agricultural regions in eastern Oregon and Washington with the markets and shipping companies in Seattle and Portland. As the 20th century unfolded, trails turned to roads as automobiles became common, along with the ferries needed to get them across rivers before many of today's bridges were built.

The museum's artifact collection grows as its time line travels through the 20th century. The emphasis is on farming, and wheat is the main crop. One exhibit illustrates with dozens of products the extent that wheat is consumed, from breakfast cereal and pancakes to pasta and beer. Artifact-rich exhibits show the lives of the settlers who have lived here for the past 150 years. Many pioneer descendants have donated clothes from earlier eras, including military uniforms. There are also numerous examples of the tools and equipment that have been used here, such as a very unusual, round, Lambert typewriter, part of an old farmhouse with its kitchen, and even a meat storage locker.

Growing, harvesting, and marketing wheat is the big story. Accompanied by plenty of photographs and artifacts—including combines and cookhouses from different eras—the story and the processes can easily be understood. A fanning mill that once belonged to immigrant Carsten von Borstel (1848–1936) is here. It was used to clean grain for seeding.

There is a look at the way the shipping of wheat has changed. Historically, threshed wheat was stored in burlap sacks. The sacks were stacked for storage or in horse-drawn wagons and later in trucks for shipping. All of that changed during the 1940s. Burlap was needed for the war effort, so farmers began storing and shipping grain in bulk, without the sacks. After the end of World War II, they decided that burlap sacks no longer made sense, so they continued shipping and storing in bulk—thus today's big silos, barges, and ships filled with loose grain.

Head to the outside shed on the side of the main museum to see a traveling cafeteria for farm workers and ranch hands. It's a wooden cabin set on an old wagon frame. Inside is the cook's stove and tools, along with table seating for a dozen workers. Old photographs show the fancy chuck wagon in action. A wash basin and bar of soap are set up outside for cleanup.

For those who know little about wheat farming, a display shows several of the different kinds of wheat grown in the area. There really is a difference, not only in how they look, but also in their yields per acre. The metal building outside the main museum and across the small footbridge provides a look at several generations of different pieces of harvesting equipment. Excellent written descriptions accompany most of the artifacts, explaining what they were and how they worked, including a look at the special equipment designs needed to work on the hilly farmland that is found here.

HOURS: May through October, daily, 10 AM to 5 PM
COST: Adults, $3; students, $1
LOCATION: 200 Dewey Street, Moro
PHONE: 541-565-3232
WEBSITE: www.shermanmuseum.org

2 The Museum at Warm Springs

WHAT'S HERE: **Culture, history, and traditions of the Confederated Tribes of Warm Springs**

DON'T MISS THIS: **The pictographs on the rocks near the exhibit's entrance**

The Warm Springs, Wasco, and Paiute tribes have joined together to create a tribal museum that showcases their traditions, culture, and sacred artifacts. You can sense that this is a special place when approaching the museum from the parking lot. Part of the building's form resembles a tepee and another portion looks like a longhouse, both traditional Indian shelters. The exterior's geometric brickwork is representative of a Klickitat basket design. Keeping with tradition, one part of the pattern is imperfect, with the symmetrical pattern purposely changed. Can you find it?

The sidewalk to the museum's entrance curves along a stream and into what is described as a circular stone drum. It then delivers you to very beautiful entry doors that blend with the walls, some of which are faced with volcanic rock from the reservation. The door handles resemble feathered bustles worn by male dancers. The stream continues inside, at least symbolically, in the form of the slate floor. Inside several treelike columns support the translucent roof.

Entry to the Museum at Warm Springs

An introductory video offers a brief overview of the tribes' histories. Tribal elders talk about the importance of language and traditions and how those have survived throughout extremely difficult times. The entry area into the main galleries is a cavelike room with pictographs and an exhibit that depicts the traditional uses of plants by the local Native

Americans. Once inside the main gallery, full-sized traditional dwellings have been constructed, including Warm Springs tribe tepees, a Paiute wickiup, and the wooden plankhouse favored by the Wasco. There is also a full-sized replica of a traditional wedding that includes the extraordinarily beautiful gifts associated with the ceremony.

An important part of the museum is the story of contact with Europeans, followed by the Americans. The story talks about the first horses that came from those brought to Mexico and Texas by the Spanish in the 1500s. The use of horses spread north and became an important part of the local Native American cultures. What followed, unfortunately, were the diseases introduced from Europe that decimated Native American tribal populations. The exhibit touches on contact with Meriwether Lewis and William Clark, the Treaty Council at The Dalles in 1855, the Indian Removal Act, and the U.S. recognizing Indian tribes as individual nations capable of making treaties—unfortunately most of those treaties did little to help the Indians. Schools were established that discouraged the young students, often forcibly, from practicing the dress and customs of their native cultures. Often, families secretly continued teaching those important cultural traditions in their homes.

The biggest and most tragic impact to Oregon's Native Americans came between 1840 and 1860 as more than 250,000 people crossed into Oregon via the Oregon Trail. All was not peaceful. From 1825 to about 1868, bands of Paiute raided pioneer settlements, taking horses and other things of value to their survival. General George Crook waged a war in 1866–68 that finally defeated the Paiute, who were later welcomed to the Warm Springs Reservation by the Warm Springs and Wasco. Congress passed the Dawes Act in 1887 designed to split the reservations into 160-acre parcels for the Indians, making those parcels available for sale after 25 years. Ultimately the Indians lost much of their land. The Indian Reorganization Act of 1934, sometimes referred to as the "Indian New Deal," righted some of the past wrongs, setting up funds to purchase lands for Indians, authorizing tribal organizations and incorporation, and expanding educational opportunities.

A part of the museum that both kids and adults find very intriguing is the language exhibit. It allows visitors to hear and learn words or phrases such as *deer* and *my mother* in three different Indian languages. For example, the English words for *deer* spoken in Shaptin (Warm Springs) is *yáamâ*; spoken in Wasco it's *i'ánk*; and in Paiute, *tuhudya*. Some of the museum's exhibits focus on the importance of family and the honored place that the elders share in the community. Part of this emphasis on family and their critical connection with nature is the celebration of each family member's "firsts," from the first kill of a deer (a boy's first hunt) to the first catch ceremony when the salmon return each year. You can make a similar connection with nature just outside the museum where cottonwoods shade Shitike Creek, which empties into the nearby Deschutes River.

HOURS: March through November, daily, 9 AM to 5 PM; December through February, closed Mondays and Tuesdays

COST: Adults, $7; ages 60-plus, $6; students, $4.50; ages 5–12, $3.50. Closed Thanksgiving, Christmas, and New Year's Day.

LOCATION: Warm Springs

PHONE: 541-553-3331

WEBSITE: www.museumatwarmsprings.org

3 A. R. Bowman Memorial Museum

WHAT'S HERE: **A nearly intact early 20th-century bank building, now a social history museum**

DON'T MISS THIS: **The old safe with its safe deposit boxes in place**

The corner of Third and Main streets has been a popular building site in the community of Prineville. In 1883, a single-story wooden building was erected here that did business as a drugstore. At the turn of the century, a larger two-story building known as Belknap Hall replaced it. Two years later that building was moved to West 2nd Street. The present building was constructed on the vacated corner lot in 1910. The new building served as the Crook County Bank for 22 years and also as two other short-lived banking companies. A. R. Bowman purchased the building in 1935 for his title and loan business, and 20 years later he used it for his insurance company.

Bowman became part of the local political scene and also was involved in much of the local development. He supported projects to improve irrigation and construct the Prineville Airport and U.S. Highway 26. The nearby dam on Crooked River that he backed was named after him—the A. R. Bowman Dam. He had graduated from the University of Washington in 1910 with a law degree, which allowed him to serve as the Crook County judge from 1936 to 1942. Following his death in 1970, his family donated the building to the county as long as they agreed to use it as a museum.

For history buffs, Bowman's purchase of the old bank building proved fortuitous because he never updated the building, making it the only commercial building in Crook County that has retained most of its original interior. Even though he didn't run a bank in his building, he allowed the bank's marble counters, the bronze teller cages, mahogany paneling, gilt and alabaster chandeliers, and etched art glass to remain unchanged. About the only difference today, besides all the historic artifacts and exhibit cases, is that the bank no longer holds large sums of money in its safe, so kids can wander inside and open the old safe deposit boxes.

The museum's exhibits include both the common items found in local and regional museums and more than a few surprises. The first surprise is the old Texaco gas pump sitting in the lobby with its label warning that its gasoline contains lead. In a nearby case, an exhibit features Tillman "Till" Glaze. He owned a livery stable and saloon in Prineville and was well known as a bandleader, composer, and violinist. His violin and its

The museum's military uniform exhibit

very intricately hand-tooled leather case were very important to him. Unfortunately, Glaze also was a gunfighter. He'd shot a couple of men in The Dallas, Oregon, but he was the one who got shot during a gunfight in Burns in 1894. His widow, Anne, gave his five-shot cap and ball revolver to a friend, and years later it found its way into the museum, along with his violin.

Curiosities not seen in most museums include the collection of mousetraps. Some are designed to catch several mice, others are similar to those used today, and a few have added benefits like being able to set them with your foot; some are even self-setting. There is also a collection of rifles, including a 45/70 Springfield Model 1884 and an 1873 Springfield Trapshoot shotgun, and a collection of barbed wire and branding irons.

The museum, which is named for A. R. Bowman, also possesses a few much older artifacts (other than Native American items) that reach back before the 19th century. The snuff box's information label says: "Snuff Box, belong to Grandmother Martha Gray about 1745." Nearby a button from a sleeve set is labeled as belonging to "Grandmother Mooney bro't from Ireland about 1745."

More contemporary items fill some of the exhibit cases such as the leather football shoulder pads from 1930, and a vehicle license plate that has no number, but is embossed with the words: THIS DRIVER IS REQUIRED TO DRIVE CAREFULLY. The official seal identifies it as from the U.S. Civilian Conservation Corps. The museum has even more things to see, including the hand-powered Engine No. 1 fire pump and past women's fashions and military uniforms.

HOURS: Memorial Day through Labor Day: Monday through Friday, 10 AM to 5 PM; Saturday and Sunday, 11 AM to 4 PM; remainder of the year: open Tuesday through Friday, 10 AM to 5 PM; Saturday, 11 AM to 4 PM

COST: Free, but donations accepted

LOCATION: 246 North Main Street (corner of Third and Main streets), Prineville

PHONE: 541-447-3715

WEBSITE: www.bowmanmuseum.org

4 Des Chutes Historical Museum

WHAT'S HERE: **Exhibits exploring the history of Bend and its surrounding region**

DON'T MISS THIS: **The volcanic rock with the year 1813 carved in its side**

Residing inside what was originally the Reid School, the Des Chutes Historical Museum easily fills the bottom two floors with its hundreds of artifacts. The three-story structure was built of local pink volcanic tuff. The stone is initially soft and easy to cut when first quarried, but hardens over time. Bend's new Reid School was completed in 1914 in time for school that year, about the same time that World War I was beginning in Europe. The school had 10 large classrooms and opened with 241 students.

The school was named after Ruth Reid, one of its first teachers. When she married, custom at the time dictated that she had to leave teaching, which she did. The school remained in use for 65 years, closing in 1979. The following year, the building reopened as a museum.

There is a little confusion over the year that trappers first came to this part of Oregon. Traditional thought is that the Hudson's Bay Company sent an expedition to the Deschutes River Basin in 1825. But members of John Jacob Astor's competing Pacific Fur Company established a fort near the mouth of the Columbia River (near what is now Astoria) in 1811. Two years later they were searching the upper Willamette tributaries for new trapping territory and may have dropped into the Deschutes River Basin. A large, soft volcanic rock with 1813 and several initials carved in it, now resides in the museum. It was found on the shore of the Deschutes River, about a mile south of Bend and may indicate when Astor's trappers were first here.

The museum's main hallway—remember this was a school—serves as an introduction to the area's history. You will see a full-length buffalo coat and a horse saddle that belonged to John Y. Todd, who in 1857 was the first man to bring cows east of the Cascades. The saddle may be the one that he rode when he and other ranchers ran 3,000 head of cattle to Cheyenne—a drive that cost so much that he had to sell his Farewell Bend Ranch. Bend's Old Mill District Shopping Center now occupies part of Todd's ranch property.

For anyone who has spent time in our national forests, Room #1 tells the story of the U.S. Forest Service. Congress authorized the creation of forest reserves in 1891, and by 1907 had renamed the reserves as national forests. From a uniformed employee standing behind a transit to the tools used by the organization's firefighters, there is much to see. Two key firefighter hand tools are part

Historic Reid School is now the museum.

of the exhibit—the Pulaski, a combination ax and heavy hoe or pick, and a McCleod, a combination rake and hoe. Communications gear fills another exhibit case. An operation of an early field telephone that could be attached to an existing overhead telephone line is explained. The operator dug a hole, filled it with water, and then stuck the radio's ground wire into it. The phone's "live" wire was then thrown over a telephone line connected to other phones down the line—all of the wires were uninsulated, so electrical contact was easy. To call someone, the operator simply cranked his phone the number of short and long rings that were assigned to that person's phone. The old schoolroom also has a number of other exhibits ranging from whipsaws and a chain saw to more early tools used by foresters and lumberjacks.

The museum's other rooms hold equally fascinating artifacts, especially those related to managing one's home from the late 19th to mid-20th centuries. A square piano that was built in 1865 in Albany, New York, and resided in the Stover household here in Bend provided music not just for the family but for the neighborhood. There is a wood cookstove with its cast-iron frying pans, and a special metal food storage safe designed to keep mice and other critters out of the food. Its black finish is described as being made to look like the "very popular Japanned tinware." There is the Sunshine double action—foot and hand—wooden washing machine and the ABC Electric Laundress, manufactured sometime after 1915 that had a wooden tumbler instead of an agitator and motorized top wringers.

Another classroom contains women's finery, from dresses to hats. There is a look at the men whose names have been attached to two nearby bridges. One bridge was named after Major General Alexander M. Patch, who trained combat engineers at Camp Abbot (Sunriver) in 1943, and later led the 7th Army in Europe during World War II. The second bridge is named for Technician Fifth Grade Robert D. Maxwell of Bend who received the Medal of Honor for giving his life to save his fellow soldiers in 1944.

Don't miss the telephone service-car. It's a 1907 Holsman Motorbuggy and served as the Pioneer Telephone Company's first company car. The open two-seater must not have been used much during winter. One of the exhibit cases holds a collection of dentist tools. Make note of the porcelain teeth and especially a tool called the Jaw Separator—it was to be used on "semiconscious" patients. For kids who have grown up with digital phones, the old PBX (private branch exchange) switchboard also includes a rotary dial phone—thus the phrase, "dial a phone number."

The museum also houses, appropriately, a schoolroom complete with desks, students, and a teacher. You can also find early business machines, cameras, and a collection of saddles. And don't forget to ask about the ghost of George Brosterhaus. One of the school's original building contractors, he fell from the roof and died on the stairway three floors down. Things around the museum sometimes get mysteriously moved—and George may be the culprit.

HOURS: Tuesday through Saturday, 10 AM to 4:30 PM
COST: Adults, $5; ages 12–17, $2
LOCATION: 129 NW Idaho Avenue, Bend
PHONE: 541-389-1813
WEBSITE: www.deschuteshistory.org

5 High Desert Museum

WHAT'S HERE: Extensive Indian exhibits, a pioneer town, wildlife, and kid programs

DON'T MISS THIS: Amphitheater nature programs and nature walks

Don't expect to get out of this museum quickly, especially if you have children with you. On the cusp of the high desert, one of the best museums in Oregon is actually located in a pine forest. The best place to begin? Check the museum's schedule for the daily special programs. There are live encounters with animals, from hawks and owls to a bobcat and porcupine. After that, perhaps head to the Hall of Plateau Indians, if the kids don't steer you to the wildlife or out the back door to the Homestead Ranch.

The Native American galleries are quite impressive. One of the first things you will likely see is the tule mat tepee, a structure used as a summer home for many of the Columbia River Plateau Indians. The museum's tepee was made by Yakama Indian James Selam and several family members. Continue to discover realistic full-sized dioramas. Near one are some of the ceremonial regalia used by members of the Plateau tribes that still practice the traditional Longhouse, Waashat, or Seven Drum religions. Believers are able to enhance their spiritual selves through vision quests, sweathouse purification, and various ceremonies, sometimes with the assistance of spiritual leaders.

For all of the Plateau Indians, either directly or indirectly, the migratory fish that crowded the region's great rivers were integral to life here. The museum offers a look at how salmon, sturgeon, and other fish affected the lives of the Indians. Fish that weren't immediately eaten were dried and saved for winter sustenance. It's all here, the baskets, the nets, the practices, and traditions associated with the annual fishing efforts. Other exhibits include an extensive collection of Native American clothing, a look at how they have maintained their cultural identity, and the service of Native Americans in wartime. Leave Native Americans and pass the Desertarium where the Gila monster enclosure allows visitors to see these very large lizards, which often tuck themselves under rocks. There are also other desert creatures, including snakes, spiders, and scorpions. Walking between the galleries offers an opportunity to see a couple of antique cars parked in the lobby areas, including a 1935 U.S. Forest Service fire truck.

A trappers' encampment

In the Hall of Exploration and Settlement you can experience the transformation of the high desert from Indian country to a traders' camp and fort, from a pioneer's wagon to a gold miner's sluice box on a creek, from a trapper's camp to a surveyor's camp, from a new settlement's mercantile to the buckaroo bunkhouse.

Head out the back of the museum to the High Desert Homestead Ranch, a look at what life was like in the 1880s. This replica ranch is similar to what many of these mini-communities looked like. Walk beyond the fence and if it's summer, there will likely be a garden growing. The log cabin looks quite comfortable, and hopefully the stove was able to keep everyone warm during cold winter nights. The barn sits next to the willow corral. These types of corrals were common because the building materials, willow and juniper, were plentiful along creeks. The branches were woven into the corral's walls and were strong enough to hold wild horses for training before they were transported to distant markets.

Just past the ranch is the Lazinka Sawmill—a real working mill that offers periodic demonstrations. On a slightly smaller scale, the nearby Changing Forest Exhibit features a full 1920s sawmill, including a boiler room needed to power everything. The Native American camp, where you can enter a tepee just like the ones the Plains Indians used, isn't far away. Walk a little farther back toward the main museum and stop by the otter exhibit to see the otter swimming in its private pool.

Nature trails and a wildlife observation area offer more things to do while visiting the museum. There is an outdoor amphitheater that features several programs each day, some that include the museum's wildlife. An indoor theater shows a 15-minute film exploring the pioneer's impact on the Native Americans. There are also changing exhibits throughout the year.

HOURS: Daily, 9 AM to 5 PM. Closed Thanksgiving, Christmas, and New Year's Day.
COST: Adults, $15; ages 65-plus, $12; ages 5–12, $9
LOCATION: 59800 South Highway 97, about 5 miles south of Bend
PHONE: 541-382-4754
WEBSITE: www.highdesertmuseum.org

6 Newberry National Volcanic Monument Lava Lands Visitor Center

WHAT'S HERE: Exhibits explaining the area's volcanic history

DON'T MISS THIS: A walk along the Trail of the Molten Land

The visitor center is hidden in a pine forest at the very edge of 50,000 acres of ancient lava flows. As you pull into the visitor center's large parking lot, the expanse of lava just beyond the visitor center isn't obvious. But imagine being inside a 17-square-mile caldera (volcano) that has spewed its contents from this 500-square-mile volcano, because that's where you are. Just to add to your queasiness, the volcano remains active today as its magma body lies a little more than a mile below the surface. And you're standing right in the middle of it.

The visitor center exhibits look at the history of firefighting efforts in this part of the Deschutes National Forest and offers lessons in vulcanology. An effective, albeit low-tech tool, the nearby Black Butte lookout tower served U.S. Forest Service fire observers for decades. The visitor center has a one-eighth scale model of the 83-foot tower that saw service from 1934 to 1990. It nearly reaches the visitor center's ceiling. This model was quite an improvement over the first three lookouts that were merely "crow's nest" platforms, and the fourth that wasn't much more. There are a few other U.S. Forest Service items in the display cases, but most of the exhibit area focuses on the geology of the area.

If you walk out behind the visitor center, Lava Butte, part of the Newberry volcano, juts up about 500 feet over the massive lava flows that surround it. The last time it erupted was 7,000 years ago, and the last time any portion of the Newberry volcano erupted was 1,300 years ago. According to geologists, that last eruption of Lava Butte was quite a show. It began with fire spewing skyward along the rift with small flows of lava coming from the fountains. Following a few days of preliminary fireworks, lava began to rise, forming Lava Butte and a cinder cone. The lava spewed out, first west then north, blocking portions of the Deschutes River and forcing it into new channels.

The reason geologists can speculate on what the last eruption was like is based in part on the types of lava that were spewed out. Each lava-type requires a different creation process. The exhibits include numerous examples. Pumice rock is a cellular glassy lava full of holes caused by the expanding volcanic gases. Spindle bombs are pyroclastic ejecta that consist of lava fragments that were liquid when ejected and formed into their football shapes as they cooled. Lava "squeeze-up" is viscous lava that pressure forces up through a

Lava Butte

fracture in the subsurface rock. There are also examples of lava drippings, lava bombs, and lava stalagmites.

Seeing lava samples in a display case is convenient, but if you head outside and hike one of the two trails behind the visitor center, you can see many lava forms in their natural states. Even now, centuries after the last eruption, only a few hardy plants are able to survive in this vast and rugged volcanic wasteland. When Lava Butte last erupted, the ground likely shook as the molten and glowing lava was being blown out of the central vent, adding layer upon layer, building the volcano higher with each pulse. Sulfur fumes and billowing clouds of smoke and ash would have engulfed the entire area.

The Trail of the Molten Land is paved. If you plan to walk off-trail very far, heavy hiking boots would be a giant plus since this is rugged terrain to traverse cross-country. In fact, these lands of lava were the training and testing grounds for the astronauts and their equipment in 1964 and 1966; everyone and everything was tested for the lunar explorers who were the first to walk on the moon. The lava field behind the visitor center covers 6,117 acres and consists of two types of basaltic lava. Since Hawaii has been a focus of vulcanologists (geologists who specialize in volcanoes, not Mr. Spock's genealogy) for decades, many of the terms for the types of lava come from Hawaii. One of the flows here, aa (ah-ah) has a very jagged surface. The other type is pahoehoe (PAH-hoy-hoy), a fluid type that cools with a smooth or rippled surface.

There is a road to the top of Lava Butte. From the summit you'll witness great views of Mt. Adams in Washington and Mt. Scott in Crater Lake National Park. Check at the visitor center for access. There is a timed reservation system for driving to the top on busy days, especially on summer weekends.

HOURS: Early May through mid-October, Wednesday through Sunday, 9 AM to 5 PM; from late June through mid-October, open daily, 9 AM to 5 PM

COST: $5 per vehicle

LOCATION: Highway 97 South, 11.2 miles south of Bend

PHONE: 541-593-2421

WEBSITE: www.fs.fed.us/r6/centraloregon/newberrynvm/index.shtml

7 Crater Lake National Park Visitor Center

WHAT'S HERE: Two visitor centers and a historic lodge overlooking Crater Lake

DON'T MISS THIS: Sinnott Memorial Overlook's exhibits and view

From nearly anywhere, it's a long drive to the high-mountain park, but the view from the rim of Crater Lake is something you will never forget. The water varies in color from the deepest blue to the brightest turquoise, with a few other shades thrown in for accent.

Crater Lake is the deepest lake in the U.S. From a geological point of view, the lake hasn't been here very long. It emerged perhaps a half million years ago when volcanic activity began creating Mount Mazama. Periodic eruptions pushed the mountain higher as lava, ash, and pumice built their way up to 12,000 feet. Other nearby mountains formed during that same time. Glaciers developed at different times, carving the U-shaped valleys nearby. It's likely that Native Americans witnessed the final series of violent eruptions 7,700 years ago as the volcano spewed out 150 times more ash than the 1980 eruption of Mount St. Helens produced. Mount Mazama's 12,000-foot peak was reduced by more than 3,000 feet as its ash covered eight of today's states and three Canadian provinces. If you drive out to the park's Pumice Desert, the expansive layer of ash you see is 50 feet deep.

After the caldera collapsed, a smaller volcano erupted inside forming what would become Wizard Island. It took a few thousand years for the bottom of the caldera to seal itself and cool enough so that it could hold water. For the next 5,000 years rain, melting snow, and runoff from springs filled the lake. Today, the lake elevation of 6,173 feet varies only about three feet each year. Since no streams flow either into or out of the lake, the closed system had no fish until humans introduced them. Today rainbow trout and kokanee salmon live in the 1,943-foot-deep lake.

Currently there are two visitor centers (a new one is being planned for one of the older existing buildings) and several other facilities that provide information about Crater Lake's natural and cultural history, but their exhibits are primarily interpretive panels and photographs. Throughout the day the Steel Visitor Center at the park headquarters shows an 18-minute film that provides an overview of the human history connected to the lake, from those Indians who could have witnessed the eruption to early settlers who during the 1850s promoted the lake as a natural treasure that needed to be protected.

One of the most popular stops is the Sinnott Memorial Overlook, which is cut into the cliff just behind the Rim Visitor Center. It's a short walk down a pathway to the overlook that offers not only spectacular views of the lake's pristine blue waters but also includes a number of

Crater Lake's Wizard Island

exhibits that tell about the more recent history of the lake, including the ongoing scientific research. For example, there is a look at the 1886 U.S. Geological Survey team that managed to launch their 26-foot boat *Cleetwood* onto the lake's waters. One of the things that the team did once on the lake was to drop a weighted wire over the side and determine that it was in fact 1,996 feet deep, a very accurate reading for having used such a primitive measuring device. One of the team members was William Steel, who later became the new park's founder and superintendent. They purposely sank their boat near Wizard Island when they completed their study. It was rediscovered in 1931.

Research has found that the lake's clear water supports a very active ecosystem. Because the lake is an isolated and unspoiled environment, it serves as a benchmark for monitoring outside changes such as global warming. Go 100 feet below the surface along the lake's shoreline, and a thick band of moss provides homes for many species of zooplankton. Hydrothermal activity on the lake bottom feeds communities of bacteria that in turn help support flatworms, nematodes, and earthworms. The bottom is also where some species of insect larvae develop until it's time for them to rise almost 2,000 feet to the surface where they shed their old bodies and become winged insects.

The park's lodge—a historic building itself—should not be missed, even if you aren't staying as a guest. After sipping a hot cup of coffee or cocoa on the porch overlooking the lake, wander back inside to the exhibits down the hallway. The lodge's construction story is told through a series of interpretive panels and photographs. Following two years of construction, that included the roof collapsing because of snow during the winter of 1914, Crater Lake Lodge opened on June 28, 1915. As the time line points out, there were many problems during the years that followed, but also many improvements. In 1917, the cesspool overflowed; 1922 brought workers to build the lodge annexes; the awning-covered lakeside porch was begun in 1928; and by the following year guests complained about there being too little furniture. In 1942 the lodge closed for World War II, and the following year an engineer reported that the lodge was "a fire trap of the worst sort." In later years the lodge's stone walls were found to be inadequately supported—some were simply hollow chambers filled with rubble. The National Park Service has since had a new foundation constructed, as well as adding support to the walls.

Access to Crater Lake is available all year, although the North Entrance Road and West Rim Drive close with the first snowfall. Other roads also close during winter, with some remaining closed until early July, depending upon snowfall. Highway 62 is open year-round.

HOURS: Park is open year-round. Steel Visitor Center, daily, 9 AM to 5 PM. Sinnott Memorial Overlook, late June through October (weather permitting), 9:30 AM to 5 PM. Crater Lake Lodge is open daily, 24 hours.

COST: Park admission, $10 per vehicle for a five-day pass; $5 for bicycles and motorcycles. Visitor centers are free.

LOCATION: Approximately 21 miles north from Klamath Falls, Oregon, on Highway 97, then west on State Route 62 for 29 miles

PHONE: 541-594-3100

WEBSITE: www.nps.gov.crla

8 Favell Museum

WHAT'S HERE: Extensive collection of Indian artifacts and western art

DON'T MISS THIS: The fire opal arrowhead

Located on the banks of the Link River, much of the museum's extensive collection of California, Pacific Northwest, and Alaskan Indian artifacts belonged to Gene and Winifred Favell. As you walk in, notice the stone wall—embedded among its many stones are numerous Native American mortars and pestles. The interior of the museum is in the shape of a wagon wheel, with the spaces between each of its spokes a separate gallery. The hub is a walk-in safe that houses some of the museum's most valuable artifacts.

Among the museum's thousands of artifacts are some that are lucky to have survived. One example is the trade item found by a 10-year-old boy in 1972 along the banks of the Rogue River. The buckskin shirt (or breastplate) has numerous metal phoenix buttons attached to it. The only set of phoenix buttons to ever be found along the Rogue River, they were used as Northwest Indian trade goods and had a value of one beaver skin each.

The bead collection is exceptional. Among the many exhibited items are stone beads and the more common glass beads used as part of regional trading. Dentalium shell necklaces that would have been owned by an Indian of wealth can be seen, as well as one dentalium necklace that had U.S. and English coins strung between the beads for an extra bit of fancifulness. The coins were minted prior to 1885.

The museum's artifact collection goes beyond just Oregon and Washington Indians. Alaska is represented with such items as a salmon killing club and an exquisite ivory scrimshaw cribbage board. There are tiny carved walrus heads and even a cross, likely indicating a connection to Christian missionaries. Effigies, such as birds, fish, and even humans, are represented here, and a feathered Spokane headdress sits among other elaborately decorated ceremonial items. There also is pottery and carved necklaces from the Southwest and feather baskets from California tribes.

The museum collection includes an atlatl, which is rare because they are made from wood. Before the development of bows that could extend a hunter's reach, Indians used the atlatl, a spear-throwing device that essentially extended the length of the thrower's arm, sending the weapon out at a greater speed and distance. Another exhibit includes what likely has been misnamed over the years as a "slave killer." Relatively rare, each of the stones is a similarly carved likeness of an unknown animal in profile, with a long, thick tail. Some people originally proclaimed these

Favell Museum entrance

to be clubs for killing slaves because some northern tribes had slaves and periodically sacrificed them at ceremonies. The stone devices are too delicate to have been used as a blunt-force bludgeon and more than likely could have served as some type of honor for one's skill, bravery, or accomplishments.

Wandering around the museum wagon wheel galleries reveals one surprise after another. In one, hundreds of arrowheads and spear points are shown. Included among them is a beautiful fire opal arrowhead. Another exhibit case contains a Sioux war shirt made before 1840 and still in exquisite condition. The dyed porcupine quill embroidery remains bright and colorful, even today. In later years, glass trade beads replaced the porcupine quills for the decorative embroidery, but usually with the same design motifs.

Art is found not only with the Indian baskets and pottery, but with the Western painters and sculptors. Here you can see the museum's own Charles M. Russell original oil painting, *The Scouts*. Russell painted it in 1891 for the owner of the ranch where he was working and was paid $10. The painting remained in the rancher's family until the 1970s, when the museum purchased it. Other artists' works are also exhibited, including an E. S. Paxon oil that was painted in 1899 entitled *Bound for Buffalo Country*. There are also wood carvings, bronze sculptures, and miniature dioramas.

HOURS: Monday through Saturday, 9:30 AM to 5:30 PM. Closed major holidays.
COST: Adults, $7; ages 6–16, $4
LOCATION: 125 West Main Street, Klamath Falls
PHONE: 541-882-9996
WEBSITE: www.favellmuseum.org

9 Klamath County Museum

WHAT'S HERE: County museum in a historic armory building

DON'T MISS THIS: Dozens of historic washing machines on the balcony

For decades, this building was used for everything from National Guard meetings to community dances, plays, and basketball games. The old armory building boasts a very efficient heating system. When the weather turns cold, a thermal well provides the heat source for the museum, as well as for most of the town's other government buildings. Just outside the museum's beautiful brick main entrance is the first piece of local history you will see—a very rustic log cabin. It originally was built on a ranch west of Tule Lake, California, about 32 miles from Klamath Falls, and about 13 miles from the Modoc Indian stronghold at Lava Beds. During the Modoc Indian War (1872–73) the cabin served as a fort, with rifle ports cut through the walls, although it was used primarily for storage. It was moved to the museum in 1974.

The interior of the museum is cavernous with a very high, arched ceiling. Several of the Native American exhibits showcase artifacts, documents, and the history of the aforementioned Modoc Indian War. One of the mortars used to lob explosive shells into Captain Jack's stronghold is here, along with Captain O. C. Applegate's campaign uniform jacket. There are photographs of the Indians involved, including the leader, Captain Jack; the U.S. Cavalry's Major General Edward Canby; and some of the people involved in the failed peace talks. In the end, the U.S. lost 83 men, including General Canby, and 46 were wounded. The Indians lost 13 in action and 4, including Captain Jack, hanged following their capture. The Indians never had more than 53 Modoc warriors, along with the women and children, while the U.S. military had more than 500 soldiers at the height of the conflict. The museum's collection includes numerous exhibit cases of Native American artifacts, from baskets to weapons.

In a different war, another rare artifact, and one little known to most people in the U.S., is a portion of a Japanese balloon bomb. During World War II, the Japanese military launched thousands of bomb-carrying, hydrogen-filled balloons from their country. The balloons were carried to the U.S. via the high-altitude jet stream that the Japanese had discovered. Several hundred made it to the mainland, but very few caused any damage, and only one proved fatal. One balloon landed in a tree near Klamath Falls and exploded when a young girl, with a group of other kids and adults on a picnic, pulled on the balloon, trying to

The cavernous Klamath County Museum

get it down. The six killed were the only casualties that the Japanese inflicted on the U.S. mainland during World War II.

There is much more to see here, including early medical equipment and false legs, a schoolroom display, antique stoves, and other 19th-century tools. Look up along the second-floor balcony for the large collection of washing machines—they aren't what your mother used unless she was washing clothes back in the late 19th and early 20th centuries. One of the oldest is an 1873 model Lovell's Family Washer. If you are curious about any of the others, the museum has catalog cards with descriptions of each.

HOURS: Tuesday through Saturday, 9 AM to 5 PM. Closed major holidays.
COST: Adults, $4; seniors and students, $3; ages 5–12, $2
LOCATION: 1451 Main Street, Klamath Falls
PHONE: 541-883-4208
WEBSITE: www.co.klamath.or.us/museum/index.htm

Oregon's Cascade Range Tours

Native American Tour

ESTIMATED DAYS: 2–3
ESTIMATED DRIVING MILES: 195

Native Americans were prominent throughout Oregon for thousands of years. Today numerous Indian reservation museums allow Native Americans to tell their own stories. The tour begins at one of those reservation museums, **The Museum at Warm Springs** (page 115). It showcases the history of the Wasco and Paiute tribes from their perspectives. Tribe members have reconstructed traditional dwellings, including tepees, a wickiup, and a wooden plankhouse. Exhibits explore the changes and relationships that occurred as pioneers began entering Oregon Territory in large numbers. Throughout the exhibits there are examples of the Indians' close relationship with nature.

Head south about 55 miles, and on the south side of Bend, the **High Desert Museum** (page 121) is tucked back into a stand of pines just off Highway 97. Although not operated by Native Americans, it has done a very good job of portraying the cultural lifestyles of Oregon's tribes. With full-sized dioramas and an extensive artifact collection, it does an excellent job of relating the changing world that Native Americans had to contend with beginning in the 18th and 19th centuries. And out back, the museum has recreated a sprawling pioneer village that includes a log cabin, operating sawmill, and a barn and corral.

If you're still heading south, drive another 140 miles to the very different **Favell Museum** (page 127) in Klamath Falls. It has a vast collection of Indian artifacts and western art, from paintings to sculptures.

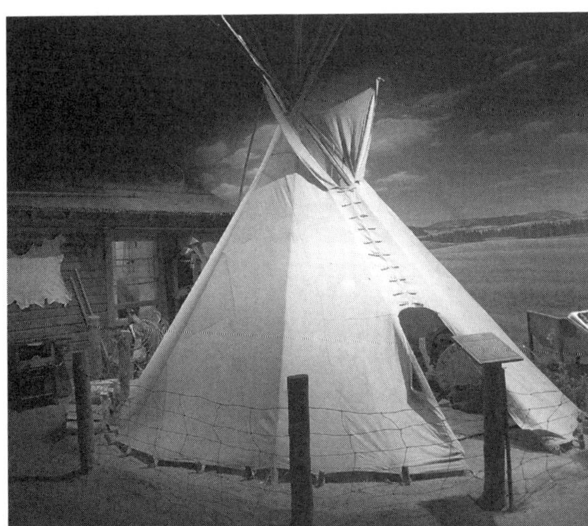

Indian encampment exhibit

Family/Kids' Volcano Tour

ESTIMATED DAYS: 2–3
ESTIMATED DRIVING MILES: 120

This is a great opportunity for kids to learn about volcanoes, because they will be in the middle of two very large ones. Driving along Highway 97 south of Bend, it's obvious that volcanoes have played a major role in forming the land. Stop at **Newberry National Volcanic Monument Lava Lands Visitor Center** (page 123), located about 12 miles south of Bend, for a close look at thousands of years of volcanic lava flows. The small visitor center offers examples of different types of lava and a little history, but the fun part is hiking the loop trails behind the visitor center. This is the same place where the Apollo astronauts practiced for traveling on the moon. There are nearby opportunities to explore volcanic caves if you'd like a little more adventure—check at the visitor center for more information.

Drive north about 120 miles and you'll find yourself at the edge of one of the most breathtaking views imaginable. At **Crater Lake National Park** (page 125) several visitor centers offer a look at one of the most beautiful volcanoes in the world, and the center of this volcano is home to the deepest lake in the U.S. There's even a boat tour available on the mostly inaccessible lake for a much closer look at Wizard Island, an ancient volcano within a volcano.

Lodge at Crater Lake National Park

Oregon's Cascade Range Information Centers

Visit Bend (Bend City Council)
www.visitbend.com
877-245-8484

Central Oregon Visitors Association
www.visitcentraloregon.com
800-800-8334

Discover Klamath Visitor and Convention Bureau
www.discoverklamath.com
800-445-6728

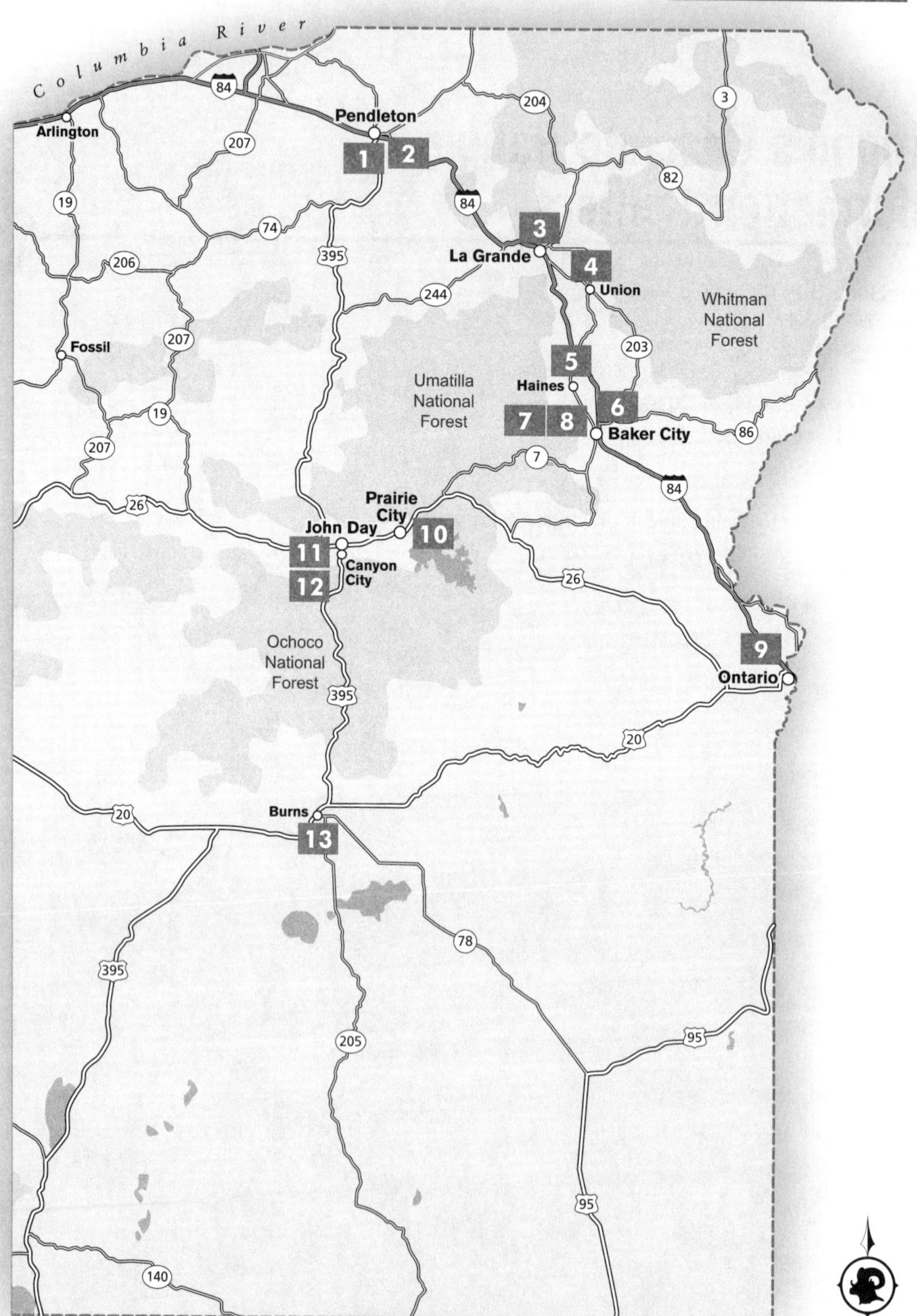
Columbia River
Arlington
Pendleton
La Grande
Union
Whitman National Forest
Umatilla National Forest
Haines
Baker City
Fossil
Prairie City
John Day
Canyon City
Ochoco National Forest
Ontario
Burns
1
2
3
4
5
6
7
8
9
10
11
12
13
84
207
204
3
82
19
74
395
206
244
203
86
7
26
20
78
205
95
140

Eastern Oregon

Visually, there are few similarities between eastern and western Oregon. Drive east from the Cascade Range and most of the great fir and hemlock forests for which Oregon is so well known vanish, replaced by much drier forests of pine and juniper. In far northeast Oregon, dry-farmed wheat fields begin to replace even those forests. In some areas of eastern Oregon rainfall is less than 10 inches annually, making much of this land a vast desert. Few crops can be grown here without irrigation, but there is water available in many areas of eastern Oregon. The Columbia River borders part of the state's northern border with Washington, and the Snake River separates much of northeastern Oregon from Idaho. It's colder here. Snow is much more likely to fall in eastern Oregon than along the Pacific Coast or in other places west of the Cascades, such as the Interstate 5 corridor's Willamette Valley.

Tamástslikt Cultural Institute

Oregon's northeastern border with Washington is part of the Columbia Plateau, one of the earth's largest areas ever flooded by volcanic basalt. For perhaps 15 million years, lava flowed from deep within the earth, filling the area nearly a mile deep with the outflows. The molten basalt gradually sank into the space vacated by the rising lava, creating the Columbia Plateau. Today as you drive through these wide open spaces, the volcanic activity is obvious. Places such as John Day Fossil Beds National Monument provide a look at fossils dating back as far as 54 million years ago. The lands around Baker City attracted miners looking to strike it rich, and many did. The city's downtown U.S. Bank proves that with its display of a five-pound gold nugget.

TRIVIA

1 Where can you see "War Paint," a famous bucking bronc now "preserved" for visitors' viewing pleasure?

2 What museum used to be a firehouse?

3 Where can you see some of the Oregon Trail's original wagon ruts, plus a life-sized diorama of a wagon train heading west?

4 Where can you see two criminals' skulls from a county's first hanging?

5 What historic Victorian home can you tour whose former owner left an endowment of $22 million to help pay the college expenses of the town's future high school graduates?

6 What Chinese doctor's office and general store was locked up and forgotten about for 20 years before its treasures were rediscovered in the 1970s?

7 Where can you see a quilt made in 1854 that future U.S. president Abraham Lincoln was said to have helped sew?

For trivia answers, see page 342.

1 Pendleton Round-Up and Happy Canyon Hall of Fame

WHAT'S HERE: **Cowboy rodeo history focused on the Pendleton Round-Up**

DON'T MISS THIS: **War Paint, the famous 1950s-era bucking horse**

This is cowboy country. For nearly 100 years, the famous Pendleton Round-Up has taken place here, and you can count on 60,000 or more visitors here each September for a week of cowboy everything. Count on several sanctioned Professional Rodeo Cowboy Association events happening each day, from bronc riding to calf roping, along with bull riders trying to stay on top of some of the world's meanest bulls. At night, the always popular Happy Canyon Indian Pageant takes place that features Native Americans representing life before, during, and after the influx of Euro-American immigrants. Plus, the annual Westward Ho! Parade goes through the town of Pendleton with its pack trains, stagecoaches, buggies, teams of oxen, covered wagons, and hundreds of Indians wearing full regalia.

Documenting a century's worth of Pendleton Round-Up and Happy Canyon events is what the Hall of Fame has done and continues to do. First thing inside the museum's door is the preserved bucking horse War Paint in his finest bucking pose. War Paint was one of the most famous bucking horses on the pro rodeo circuit during the 1950s and '60s. During his 20-year career as a bucking bronc, War Paint managed to rid himself of 90 percent of his riders before the buzzer.

When 60,000 people show up for a week of fun, it takes a load of volunteers to make everything happen. Since the first rodeo in 1910, it's been the efforts of community volunteers who have made the rodeo the success it is today. Each year about 20,000 hours of donated time are spent planning and putting on the rodeo. An exhibit recognizes the work of the volunteers, some of whom have done their jobs for the past 30 years, and a time line tracks the most significant events during each decade the rodeo has existed.

The exhibits also tell stories about rodeo life today. Some cowboys drive more than 100,000 mile each year participating in rodeos all over the country. During the 1920s, an escaped prisoner murdered the roundup president, while cowgirl Bonnie McCarroll suffered fatal injuries while riding a saddle bronc—after the accident, the roundup banned women from bucking events. The Great Depression slowed things a bit during the 1930s and in the 1940s the grandstand burned, while World War II caused the 1942 and '43 events to be cancelled. During the 1950s,

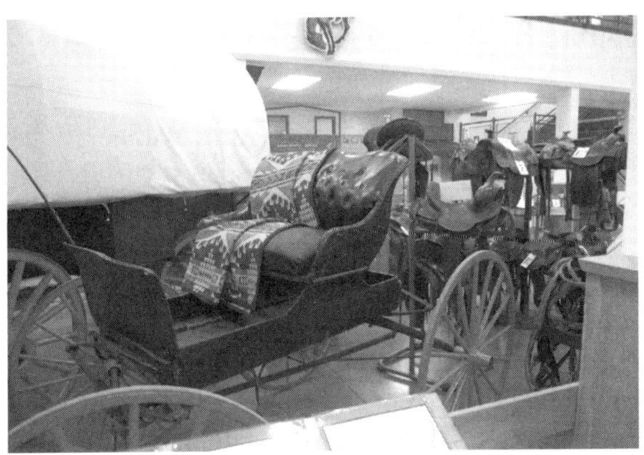

Hall of Fame's wagon exhibit

there were many improvements to the programs and to the facilities, and the 1960s saw the opening of the Hall of Fame with its first inductees.

In the center of the main gallery (there is a great view from the upstairs balcony), a full-sized tepee is set up, along with numerous saddles from some of the most famous saddle makers around. They include works from local masters Hamley & Company (more than a century old) and the Severe Brothers. The Smithsonian Institute has honored Duff Severe as a National Fellow "for changing saddle making from a craft to an art." One of the many saddles on display was won by Casey Tibbs in 1949 after being named that year's World's Champion Saddle Bronc Rider.

The museum well illustrates the participation of Native Americans in the roundup. Many who participate are from the Confederated Tribes of the Umatilla Indian Reservation. They host a tribal village where more than 200 tepees are set up as Indian rodeo enthusiasts and contestants gather to celebrate and compete.

There is more to see, including photographs of the rodeo champions, Native American costumes, the outfits worn by the Rodeo Queens over the years, and even a few firearms.

HOURS: Monday through Saturday, 10 AM until 4 PM

COST: Adults, $5; seniors (ages 60-plus), $4; students, $2

LOCATION: 1114 SW Court Avenue, Pendleton

PHONE: 541-278-0815 or 541-276-2553

WEBSITE: www.pendletonroundup.com (click "About" then "Hall of Fame" to reach the museum page)

2 Tamástslikt Cultural Institute

WHAT'S HERE: **The settlement of Eastern Oregon from the perspective of Native Americans**

DON'T MISS THIS: **The different native shelters behind the museum**

Representing the confederated tribes of the Cayuse, Umatilla, and Walla Walla, this is the only Indian-owned museum on the historic Oregon Trail. The museum provides a look at the early history of the Natitayt (the People) and the changes wrought by the coming of a quarter million immigrants looking to start new lives in Oregon Territory.

The interior of the museum is a series of galleries that circle the Coyote Theater, which is set in the center. One of the first things you will see is an Indian in full regalia sitting atop his horse, which is equally outfitted. The Indians who lived here were nomadic, moving from place to place as often as several times each year. Yet each subsequent year found them very near the same places they had been the previous year. Their movements were dictated by food availability. When the salmon were running, they would be near the Columbia and other rivers. Winter was the time when they moved little, remaining in protected valleys, gathering together for festivals, singing, dancing, and feasting.

The People passed on their beliefs, myths, and legends through oral teachings. They believed that all living beings were known through stories, and that storytelling was a way of teaching and learning.

Encounters with the immigrants wasn't as violent as Hollywood would have us believe. Most of the immigrants were farmers and lacked the skills to survive in the western wilderness. They often traded with the Native Americans; the Indians provided salmon, roots, and other food items, while the immigrants traded clothing, tools, and items the Indians could use. But there was periodic violence. As the number of immigrants increased, destroying grazing lands, fouling water holes, and killing too much wild game, the impacts sometimes became too much for the Indians to accept. A measles epidemic broke out in 1847, killing entire villages. A small band of Cayuse killed Protestant missionaries Marcus and Narcissa Whitman and 12 other people. A hastily formed militia attempted to capture the perpetrators, battling bands of Indians at several locations. The war ended in 1850 when the Nez Perce and Cayuse, who were not involved in the murders, captured the killers and turned them over to authorities, who promptly hanged the five Indians following a controversial trail.

Between 1778 and 1868, the U.S. government signed and ratified 367 treaties with various tribes. Those treaties recognized tribes as sovereign nations, but forced them to cede vast tracts of land while reserving their rights to fishing, hunting and gathering, grazing of stock, and self government. One of those treaty councils was held by Governor Isaac Stevens in 1855. At the meeting place, soldiers were met by 1,500 Nez Perce galloping at them in dramatic fashion, along with 400 Cayuse, Umatilla, and Walla Walla. More than 5,000 Indians attended the treaty meeting. While the governor initially insisted on only two reservation sites, the tribal leaders faced with threats of war and the taking of all their lands, were still able to negotiate a third reservation. In the end, the U.S. government ended up with 45,000 square miles of Native American lands.

Other wars followed as more settlers arrived, including the Nez Perce War in 1877 and the Bannock War in 1878. The Indians continued to lose. The General Allotment Act of 1887, essentially sold most of the Umatilla reservation lands to immigrants, reducing their original reservation from 510,000 acres to just 158,000 acres. By 1890, the Umatilla reservation, though much smaller, had become the largest livestock producing reservation in the U.S. Soon that changed as the reservation grazing lands were closed and the Indians were forced to give up their most precious resource—

Columbia River Plateau tule reed lodge

their horses. Most were sold, ultimately to slaughterhouses that turned a once proud heritage into dog food and fertilizer.

The reservations attempted to force tribal culture out of the Indians. Native children were required to attend reservation "Indian Training Schools," and they could not wear traditional dress, but instead had to wear military-style uniforms. They could not speak in their native languages nor engage in any culturally related activities or they would suffer severe punishment.

The museum's many collections help tell the story of the changes in Native American lives and cultures. They include Native American clothing, religious items from the early missionaries, as well as china, silverware, and other items from Fort Nez Perce and from some of the early pioneers. There are also early trade items ranging from beaver traps to glass beads. The last exhibit in the circle shows how Native Americans have adapted and blended both their ancient cultures and contemporary American lifestyles.

Step out behind the museum to a recreated village of traditional housing. It includes the familiar tepee, along with several other structures, such as a subterranean pit house that would have been used at least 2,500 years ago.

HOURS: April through October, daily, 9 AM to 5 PM, Saturdays, 2 PM until 5 PM; November through March, closed Sundays. Closed Thanksgiving, Christmas, and New Year's Day.

COST: Adults, $6; seniors (ages 55-plus) and students, $4

LOCATION: Umatilla Indian Reservation, 72789 Highway 331, Pendleton

PHONE: 541-966-9748

WEBSITE: www.tamastslikt.org

3 Eastern Oregon Fire Museum

WHAT'S HERE: **Original 1899 brick fire station that served the community for 100 years**

DON'T MISS THIS: **The 1925 Stutz fire engine, one of only nine ever built**

The museum is located in La Grande's original firehouse, which was built in 1899 at a cost of $2,700. It served the town's firefighting needs until 2002 when the active equipment was moved to a new location. The original Rescue Hose Company No. 1 was reinstated as a volunteer organization that today runs the museum.

As with most cities, especially in the West, La Grande's firefighting company began as a volunteer effort. By 1891, much of the city had burned at different times during the previous 17 years, some of it several times. An 1874 fire that started in the La Grande Brewery quickly spread, destroying 21 buildings, most of them businesses. The 1886 fire burned buildings on both sides of the street, including a hotel and railroad depot. The 1891 fire burned four blocks of businesses in less than an hour, including the hotel that had replaced the one destroyed in the 1886 fire. A second fire later in 1891 that destroyed six businesses appeared to be the final straw. The city spent $50,000 on a water supply system and started a volunteer fire department.

In 1887, Rescue Hose Company No. 1 was started with 47 personnel. It quickly secured 24 buckets and a small ladder, and the following year a hose cart was purchased. Money was always an issue when it came to buying equipment and paying salaries. Adequate funding became available in 1898, and the city accepted a bid to build its first fire station, which was completed in 1899. The second floor was added in 1913 and used to house the firefighters and the chief's office. Even in 1905, the fire department had only two fire carts, both pulled by hand, along with 1,000 feet of hose. Volunteers were paid $1 for each fire they fought.

By 1908, the town's 17 saloons often donated a keg of beer or more, along with cheese and crackers, to the firemen after each fire, depending upon its severity. Still, they had only hand-pulled hose carts, so in 1911, La Grande purchased its first motorized fire truck for $600. The American-LaFrance Chemical and Hose Wagon carried a 35-gallon tank that was filled with a combination of soda and water. At the fire, acid was dumped into the mixture and the resulting chemical reaction created the pressure needed to force the liquid from the tank, through a hose, and onto the fire. Since 35 gallons didn't go far when fighting a major fire, the truck's chemical tank was used as the first attack, followed with water as quickly as firemen could get hoses attached to the main water system hydrants.

Since the building has always served as the central fire station, most of its early alarm systems and other firefighting devices are here, along with many related items, including fire trucks that have been added to the museum's collections. Included with the "big" equipment is a hook and ladder cart that carried buckets suspended from hooks, lanterns, and a long extension ladder on top. There are also a couple of hand-pulled hose carts. A collection of nicely polished fire extinguishers lines one shelf, while nearby fire grenades mark a past effort at fighting fires. The grenades are softball-sized and shaped glass balls filled with a liquid chemical. They were designed to be thrown at the base of a fire, and when the thin glass shattered, it spewed out its contents, extinguishing the flames. Originally, they were filled with carbon tetrachloride, which was effective, but unfortunately the phosphene that was produced caused serious lung damage if it was breathed in. The grenades were common in homes, hotels, trains, factories, and schools before portable fire extinguishers became common.

1922 Model T Ford chemical truck

They were still being used into the 1960s, although they were filled with salt water or other less hazardous liquids.

Another interesting device displayed is a Lungmoter, essentially an oversized and fancy bicycle tire pump that was connected by a tube to a breathing mask and used to resuscitate nonbreathing victims. There was a regulator that controlled the amount of air pumped so that an infant's lungs wouldn't be exploded with too much pressure. The fire station's old alarm box system is still in place. It gave a general location as to where an alarm had been sounded.

Most of the fire engines in the bays have been well cared for over the years or they've been restored. The 1922 Model T Ford chemical truck was never a La Grande fire truck, but it now rests in the museum. It was powered by a 25-horsepower engine coupled to a two-speed transmission that allowed for a top speed of about 30 miles per hour. It was restored in 2002 and is used in parades. Other vehicles reside in the museum, including a 1948 Mack, a 1939 Seagrave, and a 1953 state police car.

The station's 1925 Stutz Model O fire engine has one of the best stories. It was purchased by La Grande in 1925 for $13,500, even though some fought the purchase because they thought the vehicle was unreliable. The city sold the fire engine in 1955 to an insurance company in Idaho, and it changed hands again in 1960, some say in a trade for a color television. La Grande's volunteer assistant fire chief Don Keeling located the engine in 1994 and arranged for it to be donated back to La Grande where it first served. Before returning home, it made a stop at the Nevada State Prison in 2000 where inmates completely restored it.

HOURS: Daily, 9 AM to 5 PM; Memorial Day through Labor Day, also open Saturdays, 9 AM to 3 PM. Closed Thanksgiving, Christmas, and New Year's Day.

COST: Free

LOCATION: 102 Elm Street, La Grande

PHONE: 541-963-8588 or 800-848-9969

WEBSITE: No website, but see www.visitlagrande.com/attractions.html#Morgan for area information

4 Union County Museum

WHAT'S HERE: **Large museum filled with eclectic collection of regional memorabilia**

DON'T MISS THIS: **Zack the cowboy talking about his long days working cattle**

The Union County Museum began in the First National Bank building, but has expanded into the two adjacent buildings in Union's historic downtown. The city brags that no one ever got away "scot-free" trying to rob a Union bank. In 1900 one group of men tried. They broke into the bank about 3 AM and dug through the brick surrounding the safe. Trying to pry open the safe that held $15,000 didn't work, so they attached three charges of nitroglycerin. When they set off the explosive, it destroyed most everything, but failed to open the safe. They disappeared into the night, having caused $2,000 in damage.

Wandering through the museum reveals numerous treasures. Among the musical instruments is a balalaika, a mandolin-type instrument with three strings and a three-sided triangular body. This particular instrument was made for the "Great Russian Orchestra" in about 1925. Another quite rare instrument is the Mandobass, an oversized mandolin that plays in a lower bass range than regular mandolins.

Mining has played a major role in the development of many towns in eastern Oregon, including Union City. One of the exhibits includes a large collection of minerals. Nearby, an old mine has been recreated in the museum that tells the story of gold's discovery. Inside are some of the tools used by miners, including a jug that likely held corn whiskey or some other equally potent liquid.

The museum features a large collection of late 19th- and early 20th-century women's clothing. One piece of interest, and not often seen elsewhere, is the "day-after dress," which were special dresses worn by new brides on the day following their weddings. This particular "day-after" dress belonged to Miskell Gale, and she wore it to the annual Silver Tea held in nearby North Powder each year. The dress had belonged to her mother. Miskell died in 2004 at the age of 105. Another of the museum's day-after dresses belonged to Clara Rudio who married Oregon's future governor Walter M. Pierce in 1887. Clara died just three years later giving birth to their first child. Walter, a Union County cattleman, served as Oregon's governor from 1923 to 1926, then served in the U.S. Congress from 1932 to 1942.

Some of the museum's galleries have been set up as period rooms, including a kitchen, a bedroom, and a bathroom. The kitchen includes a dining room table set with beautiful English china, and the bathroom has a tin bathtub.

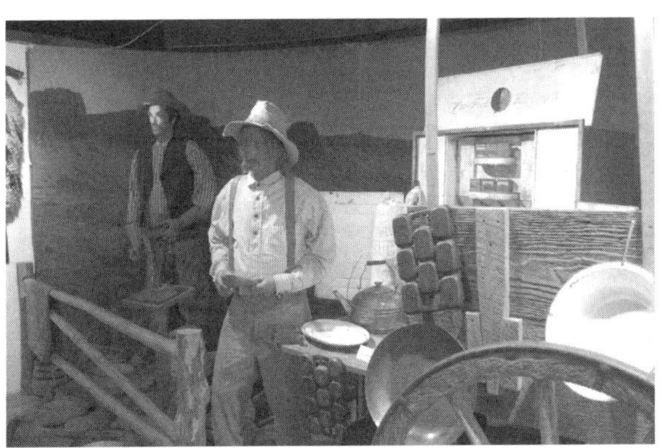

Cowboy Zack spins his tales.

The Chinese were prominent in the area. A green jacket belonging to Hop Lee, a Chinese man who lived and worked in the area, hangs in one of the cases. Nearby are letters written by some of the local Chinese. The letters are written in Chinese, but translations have been done. In one, Loung Lon tells a friend that he has been in Baker, Oregon, for a month and a half and has been sick. He collected money from friends so that he could buy "stuff" for New Year's. The letter was dated December 2 (no year).

As might be expected, a large portion of the museum is dedicated to cowboys and their lifestyle. One of the most famous rodeo cowboys to come out of Union was Ollie Osborn. Some of that fame came from the fact that Ollie was a woman. She was born in 1896 and by age 16, she was competing in local rodeos. She even performed at Madison Square Garden. Ultimately, her bronc riding landed her in the National Cowgirl Hall of Fame. She made other headlines also. During Prohibition, Ollie apparently produced moonshine, which she sold. In her 70s and 80s she loved entertaining young neighborhood girls with tales about her life. She died at age 92.

The museum has collected some of the local rodeo queen's robes and jackets, as well as bridles, lassos, and spurs. One bridle in the collection is hand-braided horsehair. Some of the horse's tail hair was dyed to form an intricate pattern. A more high-tech display shows a couple dozen Hollywood cowboys—and girls—from over the years, with buttons that can be pushed to identify the likes of John Wayne, Gene Autry, Roy Rogers, Clint Eastwood, and more. There are saddles and more cowboy paraphernalia among the exhibits.

Another exhibit identifies all of the "century farms" in the county. A century farm is one that has been owned and actively farmed by the same family for at least 100 years. Many family farmers lost their right to the title during the Great Depression when they were forced to lease their farms to others.

HOURS: Mother's Day through mid-October, Tuesday, Thursday, and Friday, 9 AM to 4 PM; Saturday, 2 PM to 5 PM

COST: Adults, $4; seniors (ages 60-plus), $3; students, $2

LOCATION: 333 South Main, Union

PHONE: 541-562-6003

WEBSITE: No website, but see www.visitlagrande.com for area information

5 Eastern Oregon Museum

WHAT'S HERE: **Extensive, eclectic collection of community ephemera**
DON'T MISS THIS: **The home-built snowblower behind the museum**

Haines is a very small community a few miles down the road from Baker City. In 1918, the Haines School was built, but without a gym for the students. Finally, in the midst of the Great Depression, the community decided it needed a gym. The school district combined its limited funding with the $2,100 available from the PTA, and construction was completed in 1932 for a total cost of $5,000. The gym was used for basketball games, dances, and community events for many years, until Haines students began attending high school in Baker City. In 1959 the building, no longer used by the school district, became the Eastern Oregon Museum, and since that time it has accumulated more than 10,000 artifacts.

Walking into the old gymnasium is like walking into the bay of a huge time machine that is divided into various themed sections. You are greeted by oxen yoke and Regulator clocks, old photos, and a quilt. Inside the cavernous building, the museum's logging and mining section includes gold rockers and gold pans, assaying equipment, and other hand tools used by miners. There are ore samples and assay equipment, as well as photographs and histories of the local mines. The beautiful Bourne Bar was taken intact from the gold mining ghost town of Bourne, Oregon, and moved here. Nearby is the full-color photograph (hand-painted) and advertisement for Madam Stella Darby, affiliated with the Cozy Room Bordello in Pendleton, Oregon. A story accompanies the bar: Just as in the movies, the bartender was constantly wiping the bar, but not to keep it clean. He was simply mopping up the gold dust that he "accidentally" dropped when weighing it for miners buying their whiskey. Likewise, bar girls sometimes put a streak of honey (the sticky kind) in their hair. When handling a customer's gold dust, they could run their hands into their hair, leaving behind some of the gold, which was washed out later. True? Who knows!

Cowboys certainly played a part of Haines's history—and still do. Branding irons, rifles, saddles, and more help tell the cowboys' stories. There's even a couple of cowboys playing poker. The museum's housewares and period clothing section has just about anything imaginable for a 19th- and early 20th-century housewife. From butter churns to coffee grinders, from beds to cookstoves, every home-care-related dream item can be found here.

The museum's wagon barn holds 19th-century vehicles from buckboards to horse-drawn sleighs. There is a blacksmith shop with its large bellows and dozens of tools and old horseshoes. Some

The eclectic collection includes butter churns.

of the items are more recent. The 1919 hay rake was pushed by a horse. The rake, once loaded, was lifted to get the teeth off the ground so the load could be transported to a place for stacking.

Ice was an important commodity for early communities. The North Powder Ice Plant operated from 1910 to 1937. The Pacific Fruit Express built an 18-acre pond and flooded it each year. In January, after the water was well frozen, horse-drawn ice plows harvested the ice—more than 30,000 tons each winter. The ice was cut into blocks approximately 22 by 22 by 18 inches. Some 12,000 tons were stored in a local ice warehouse. The rest was shipped by rail to other railroad ice houses in places like Laramie, Wyoming, and Wallula, Washington. During the summer of 1923, the North Powder Ice Plant iced 4,000 railcars of local produce for shipment. A lightning bolt struck the plant in 1937, burning it to the ground. It was never rebuilt because the ice was replaced by electric-powered refrigerator cars.

The Oregon Navigation & Railroad Company built the Haines Railroad Depot (now located next to the gym/museum) to provide a shipping point for the mining and timber industries needing to reach markets in Portland. After passenger service was discontinued in the early 1960s, the depot building was donated to the Eastern Oregon Museum. It was moved from its original site to the museum grounds soon afterward and has been restored. Inside are numerous items that would have been shipped via rail, including trunks and suitcases.

Outside, behind the main museum, is a home-built snowblower. It was built by local Champ Bond from various car and other parts and was used in the early 1960s to plow the Anthony Lake Highway. Although the black paint is peeling from the strange-looking vehicle's rounded plywood body, it's quite an ingenious contraption.

HOURS: Mid-May through mid-September, Monday through Sunday, 9:30 AM to 4:30 PM
COST: $2 per person; $5 per family
LOCATION: 610 Third Street, Haines
PHONE: 541-856-3233
WEBSITE: www.hainesoregon.com/eomuseum.html

6 National Historic Oregon Trail Interpretive Center

WHAT'S HERE: **A comprehensive look at the history of the Oregon Trail and the daily hardships the immigrants faced**

DON'T MISS THIS: **Viewing the actual Oregon Trail wagon wheel ruts that remain visible**

This is probably the closest you can come to experiencing what the early pioneers went through in order to cross the country by wagon into Oregon. The Oregon Trail began in Missouri and crossed the Rocky Mountains to Oregon's Willamette Valley. Much of the original trail was actually a series of winding trails that Indians had followed for thousands of years in their trading activities with different tribes. This was especially true for the annual treks down the Snake and Columbia rivers to the shallow rapids at Celilo Falls and The Dalles where they traded salmon, shell beads, and more.

The Oregon Trail was well-traveled long before the California Gold Rush. More than 11,000 emigrants had come west over the trail prior to 1849. Nine years earlier, Joel Walker was likely the first settler to have brought his family with him on the 2,000-mile trip. One estimate has 350,000 people making the trek between 1841 and 1866, with perhaps 10 percent dying along the way. Most died from disease, many from accidents, with perhaps only one percent at the hands of hostile Indians or criminals.

The drive from Interstate 84 up to the visitor center offers great views of the type of terrain that the wagons had to traverse. Pulled by oxen, which often became revered members of the family, the wagons could weigh up to 2,500 pounds. Most of the weight was food supplies that included flour, hard tack and crackers, bacon, sugar, coffee, tea, and saleratus (used as baking soda). Most of the wagons were only 4-feet wide, perhaps 11-feet long, with 2-foot-high sides. There wasn't much room left over for pots, pans, clothes, weapons, and tools for making repairs, let alone passengers.

The commanding views of the valley and Baker City below are worth the trip up here, but the visitor center's exhibits are excellent. One of the most dramatic is just inside the entrance where you are greeted by a full-sized wagon train that includes oxen, scouts, and even the pioneers walking beside the wagons as most did for 2,000 miles over five months. And many emigrants traveled much farther, beginning their journeys in Maine or New York rather than Missouri, the official starting point of the great trail west.

Life-sized wagon train diorama

The dioramas include a wagon that has broken down, as its owner attempts repairs, and another shows a mother grieving the death of her child at a trailside burial site. An interpretive sign tells of a child's day: "Get up at 4 a.m. Help fetch water, cook, clean up, and pack. Then walk for 10 to 20 miles, pick flowers, take a swim, and have a mock battle with buffalo chips. Schoolbooks and baths are rare. Go to sleep. Do it all over again 180 times."

Beyond the wagon train, the visitor center tells the entire story of this flood of immigants. It begins with the discovery of the Columbia River in 1792, then moves forward with the Lewis and Clark Expedition in 1803–1806, the trappers and fur traders with the Pacific Fur Company in 1811, missionaries such as the Whitmans who came in the 1830s, and finally those pioneer settlers who came first by the handful, then by the thousands each year beginning in the 1840s. All of these events and dozens more are chronicled in the visitor center's historical time line. The dates end with Ezra Meeker retracing his 1852 steps along the Oregon Trail and beginning his effort to save the historic trail in 1906, and finally the 1922 formation of the Old Oregon Trail Association.

Exhibits reveal those who tried to profit from the immigrants selling things that were "indispensible" for their long journeys, but proved worthless. The "Goodhugh's Airtight" was sold as a popular replacement cooking stove designed to save fuel and leave the heavy cast-iron stoves behind. The visitor center has one of these cooking jewels, which was nothing more than a smaller version of an iron stove. The trail became littered with Airtights.

The visitor center exhibits contain wonderful excerpts from many pioneer diaries. They deal with everything from why they left home seeking new lives to their daily encounters along the trail:

> As if we were all going to our grave . . . instead of starting on our trip of pleasure.
>
> —*Margaret Frink, 1850*

> We arrived at St. Joseph today. Was quite disappointed at the appearance of the place.
>
> —*Agnes Warner, 1853*

> It is death to every soul of you . . . to travel a distance so great as that through a trackless desert.
>
> —*William Sublett, 1842*

> A fine spree we had over the first fire we made of buffalo chips. The women did not like to touch it . . . for fear of getting their hands spoiled but this will wear off in a short time.
>
> —*John Newton Lewis, 1851*

> This route is the greatest one for wrangling discord and abuse of any other place in the world I am certain.
>
> —*Abigail Scott, 1852*

The exhibits track the changes of mind about the trip, from awe to boredom. And when boredom turned to murder, one panel explains emigrant justice. When a well-liked man named Donahue confessed to murdering Edward Wallace in 1852, his wagon train members voted, nearly unanimously, that he should be shot dead as punishment. Three of six handguns were loaded, the six weapons given to volunteers who were unaware which contained bullets. Upon a signal they fired at the blindfolded and kneeling man. Three bullets struck his body bringing death—and a quick burial next to his murder victim.

Native Americans along the trail often traded with the settlers. Another diorama depicts a trading event as the Indians offer salmon in exchange for an old shirt, beads, and a fishhook. The center's exhibits include a look at many of the trade items typical along the trail. But the forts along the way also provided opportunities for buying provisions, always at exorbitant prices.

There is much more here, including a 2-mile trail outside that winds down the hill to some of the old wagon ruts that still scar the hillsides more than 100 years after the passage of the last wagon.

HOURS: Daily, April through October, 9 AM to 6 PM; Daily, November through March; 9 AM to 4 PM. Closed Thanksgiving, Christmas, and New Year's Day.

COST: Ages 16–62, $5; ages 63-plus, $3.50 (some federal passes honored)

LOCATION: 22267 Oregon Highway 86, five miles east of Interstate 84, exit 302, Baker City

PHONE: 541-523-1843

WEBSITE: www.blm.gov/or/oregontrail/

7 Baker Heritage Museum

WHAT'S HERE: **Collections focused on the history of Baker, including its gold mining heyday**

DON'T MISS THIS: **One of the largest rock and gem collections in the western U.S.**

The museum occupies what was the Baker Municipal Natatorium, which was built in 1920. The natatorium, a building that houses a swimming pool, has been modified since becoming a museum. The pool that once covered most of the building's main floor is gone, and the replacement concrete floor is now exhibit space for the museum. A photograph on the wall inside the museum shows the old swimming pool in use, and a sign over the doorway into the main gallery says POOL ROOM.

When you walk into that main gallery, it's easy to scan the floor exhibits in order to get a sense of what is here: one of those old bicycles with the huge front wheels, some kind of warning tower with a light on top, various horse-drawn buggies, what looks like a 1920s-era car, and several exhibit cases. A closer look reveals much more.

One of the wagons, a buckboard-type vehicle with a roof and long seats in the back, was actually a horse-drawn school bus. The museum's stagecoach was drawn by a four-horse team and operated between the Cornucopia Mine and Baker in the 1880s and '90s carrying more supplies than passengers. The big bullwhip on the side of the stage is made of leather and is filled with fine lead shot to add weight and remain flexible so the leather popper at the business end could pop. There is also a chuck wagon, although with its bright green paint it doesn't appear to have spent too many days on the range.

The small, red handcart on display is left over from 1968 when Paramount was here filming *Paint Your Wagon*, starring John Wayne, Clint Eastwood, Lee Marvin, and many others. A magazine article in the exhibit was written by a local bow hunter and archery store owner about his role as an extra in the movie. In 1968, hippies found it useful to get jobs as extras in certain films, such as *Paint Your Wagon*. At that time, the towns around Baker hadn't yet experienced hippies and hippie living standards. The article's author writes about trying on costumes for the movie. He was quite surprised that the people in charge of costumes weren't the least bit surprised when the hippies dropped their pants to try on costumes and weren't wearing underwear. The wardrobe personnel had underwear on hand to give them since trying on film company costumes without underwear was not allowed.

Gold mining played an important role in Baker's early development. In 1897 there were 513 gold mines and claims in the Baker Gold District, with $3 million in gold having been taken out. That's about $100 million in today's world. Thus, the museum has many mining-related artifacts, some not often seen elsewhere. There are several round iron containers used to transport mercury, a very toxic mineral used to separate gold from other worthless materials. There's also a large copper and brass beakerlike container weighing 86 pounds that was used to transport nitroglycerin to the mines. The nitro was used to blast rock, but it was very volatile stuff, often exploding prematurely. It was ultimately replaced by dynamite, which is essentially sawdust soaked in nitroglycerin, a much more stable way to handle the highly explosive material. There are many more artifacts, from ore crushing stamp mills to maps and lists of the millions of dollars taken from the various Baker area gold mines.

The museum has one of the most extensive rock and mineral collections anywhere in the west. The collection was begun by two sisters, Mamie Cavin and Elizabeth Cavin-Warfel, about a half century ago. Many years ago, the Smithsonian offered $500,000 for the collection, which was turned down. There are actually two different collections, each donated by different families. The Cavin-Warfel collection (belonged to the

Baker Heritage Museum

two sisters) weighed in at 18 tons. The Wyatt Family collection consists of 2,000 agates, picture jasper, and cabochons. There is even a dark room that allows you to see the many minerals that glow beautifully in the dark when illuminated with a black light.

You will also find farm equipment, including the first wheat thresher to be brought into the valley. There is a gun exhibit upstairs, and also a look at different household furnishings that have been set up in room displays—a dining room, kitchen, bathroom, and more.

HOURS: Late March through October, daily, 9 AM to 5 PM
COST: Ages 16 and older, $5; ages 60-plus, $4.50
LOCATION: 2305 Main Street, Baker City
PHONE: 541-523-9308
WEBSITE: www.bakerheritagemuseum.com

8 Adler House

WHAT'S HERE: **Fully furnished home built in 1871**
DON'T MISS THIS: **The metal fireplace that looks just like marble**

Carl Adler left Germany in 1871 by sailing ship and ultimately landed in Astoria, Oregon, where he owned the Crystal Palace, a high-end gift shop. He met and married Laura Hirsch, also a German immigrant, but only after promising to close his business and move to Baker City so she could be near her sister. They moved here in 1888, where Adler once again opened a new Crystal Palace gift shop. Their three children were born here, with Leo being the youngest. In 1899, the family moved into their newly finished house, next door to Laura's sister. The Italianate home was to be Leo Adler's only home.

Ambitious and smart, young Leo began selling magazines on the streets of Baker when he was just nine years old. Over the years he expanded his enterprise, and by 1925 he had a magazine and newspaper distribution business that covered several states. He continued to expand until his sales territory covered seven states with 2,000 outlets, selling more than 3 million magazines each year. Leo was a multimillionaire. His father died in 1918 and his mother in 1933. Leo continued living in the family home, outliving his older sister and brother.

Leo didn't spend much of his money on himself. Instead, when not running his business, he was sitting on the boards of nonprofit organizations, including the Red Cross, Salvation Army, and Heart Association. He gave money to local organizations to do everything from building community baseball fields to buying fire trucks for the city fire department. When he died in 1993 at the age of 98, he left the city $22 million and instructed them to grant 60 percent of the interest earned from the endowment to graduating Baker High School students to help pay for college expenses. The remaining 40 percent of the interest was to be used for community projects. As for his house, he left it to the Baker County Museum Commission, likely expecting them to sell it. But they kept it as a historic home—and got a few surprises when they first entered it.

Leo had decided that after his parents' deaths he really didn't need such a large house with so many rooms and so much furniture. So he closed all of the rooms upstairs, rooms that had no electricity anyway, and used only the four back rooms on the main floor. All of the furniture in the closed rooms was left where it was. And he did little or no maintenance on the home during the next 60 years—cleaning wasn't Leo's strong point. The home used a coal-fired heating system that left many decades of black soot collecting on everything—drapes, walls, furniture, and carpets. Staff have cleaned the walls three times trying to rid it of the coal dust, but some still remains. The foundation needed repairs, the upstairs roof had been leaking, plaster was peeling away from the lathe, and the few times he went upstairs, it was only to store old mattresses and other junk that should have gone to the dump.

The good part of all of this is that the furnishings were found to be in excellent, almost new condition, once the coal soot was vacuumed from them. Leo used the dining room as his combination living room, dining room, and office. The den offered a little more privacy for his bedroom. He also used the kitchen and bathroom and the back door to come and go.

The home has a butler's pantry but never had a butler, and likely never had a maid, at least not a full-time live-in maid. If you look upward, the wallpaper on the ceiling in the pantry is original to the home, now well over a century old. The kitchen floor had two layers of linoleum, which was removed following Leo's death to reveal the tongue-and-groove redwood floor underneath. Leo's appliances were removed from the home because they were too new for the time period that the home is being maintained to reflect—about 1915. The icebox and stove were added, but almost everything else in the kitchen and pantry were as Leo had left them. Leo's back bathroom was likely a porch when the house was originally constructed, with the bathroom being added and the porch enclosed in later years.

Touring the remainder of the house reveals a few more of Leo's habits. He loved baseball, and over the years when the Yankees were nearly always winning pennants, he attended 20 consecutive World Series games in New York. In the family parlor, the fireplace that looks like marble is actually made of metal with a finish that can easily pass for stone. The Ludwig piano is thought to be one of the first 1,000 made.

Upstairs there is a World War I uniform that belonged to Stanford, Leo's older brother and a sergeant. The master

1871 Adler House

bedroom is furnished with the bed and dresser that were downstairs in what is now the office, which is where Leo slept. Here, there is an opera cape that looks like fur, but actually is made from feathers. Baker City did have an opera house. When you walk back downstairs, look at the red glass set above the front door. Gold is required to make ruby glass, a sign of wealth for some.

HOURS: May through September, Friday through Monday, 10 AM to 2 PM
COST: Ages 16 and older, $5
LOCATION: 2305 Main Street, Baker City
PHONE: 541-523-9308
WEBSITE: www.bakerheritagemuseum.com/adler_house.html

9 Four Rivers Cultural Center and Museum

WHAT'S HERE: **Museum exploring several different cultures in Oregon's Treasure Valley**
DON'T MISS THIS: **The very realistic sheepherder's camp diorama**

The museum takes its name from the four rivers that flow into western Treasure Valley—the Snake, Malheur, Payette, and Owyhee. Exhibits explore the five cultures that dominated the settlement of this part of eastern Oregon—Northern Paiute, Basques, Hispanics, Europeans, and Japanese-Americans. Each played an important role in creating all that exists here today.

The first of the five groups to settle here were the nomadic Northern Paiute who moved with the seasons following the changing natural food supplies. Those local to the Ontario region were known as the Agaiduka, or the Salmon Eaters. They spent the winter in the protected valleys near the rivers. Spring brought migratory waterfowl through the area as well as spring runs of fish up the rivers. In summer they moved to where new roots, berries, and other foods could be gathered and small game hunted. Fall brought hunts of antelope and rabbits, often by herding the animals into nets where they were killed with clubs. Fall runs of salmon provided plenty of additional food. Related exhibits include a life-sized diorama of a Northern Paiute camp with a woman and child making baskets, along with a prehistoric scraping tool, bone awl, and even the small remnant of a woven reed mat.

The museum's time line moves through the trappers who "trapped out" all the beaver by the 1860s. With the gold miners came the ranchers, developing the local cattle industry that sold its beef to the miners. Beginning with the 1862 Homestead Act, along with several more land-giveaway programs implemented in 1877, more than a million acres of what had originally been Northern Paiute lands, and even a previously established reservation, were made available to ranchers and settlers.

Transportation was key to the survival and prosperity of the newly arriving pioneers. They built roads and bridges, and where bridges weren't possible, enterprising individuals established ferries for crossing the rivers. With the connectors in place, stagecoach service became available, allowing passengers and mail to further connect the growing communities. There is a beautifully restored M.S.D. & D. stagecoach, loaded with trunks that showcase what was once a common mode of transportation.

But the railroad wasn't far behind. The Oregon Short Line steamed into operation on January 1, 1884, and began transporting livestock to markets in the Northwest's shipping centers. The railroad brought even more people and more of their possessions. In the early 1900s, it took horse-drawn freight wagons to get wheat, wool, and other products to the railheads for shipment to distant markets. One of those loaded freight wagons sits inside the museum.

With market transportation available, the Basque brought their sheep. The museum's sheep camp gives a good idea of what life was like out on the open grazing lands. The canvas tent holds a stove, pack saddle, and kitchen essentials, including cooking pots and food supplies such as flour, lard, and coffee. There is even a bottle of Kara syrup because pancakes were a common breakfast menu item. And more than a few sheep were appropriated for their fresh meat. The sheepherders generally worked alone, with a camp tender arriving every week or two to bring supplies.

Settlers began damming creeks and rivers in their efforts to provide irrigation for farming the dry, desert soil. Irrigation opened even more of the land to farming, especially after so many families arrived in response to the call of this "agricultural paradise" only to find 11 inches of rain annually to water the desert's sagebrush and bunchgrasses. They quickly discovered that with the native plants removed, soil turned to dust that blew everywhere. Unfortunately, unlike their Idaho neighbors, those on the Oregon side of the Snake River didn't have a dam that could be used to control irrigation waters.

The Owyhee Dam wasn't completed until 1932. With that came more farming and fruit orchards, followed quickly by the Great Depression. The migration that followed brought Mexican-American laborers seeking employment to settle among the Basques, Scots, and Japanese who had already settled throughout the area. With the outbreak of World War II, the Japanese, most of whom were U.S. citizens, were forced from their homes and moved to relocation camps. With the need for vast amounts of food to feed the troops, an experiment was approved that allowed 17 Japanese men to be released from the camp to work on farms in Malheur County. So successful was the program that by war's end, the expanded program had 5,000 Japanese

Basque sheepherder's camp

living around the Ontario area, the largest population of Japanese-Americans living free anywhere in the U.S. during that period. The museum displays many exceptionally powerful photographs of this era of the region's history.

The museum includes an exhibit that explores the reasons so many people left their ancestral homes and moved often thousands of miles to settle in a new and wild land. Many, such as the Basque, were looking to escape persecution; nearly all were looking for opportunities to make new and better lives for themselves and their families.

There is much more in this expansive museum from a look at cowboy poets and ethnic foods to traditional dances and clothing. The museum's diverse exhibits explore everything from hunting 12,000 years ago to the remnants of a mammoth tusk, tooth, and bone fragments found only a few miles away.

HOURS: Monday through Saturday, 10 AM to 5 PM
COST: Adults, $4; ages 6–14, 65 and over, and college students, $3
LOCATION: 676 SW 5th Avenue, Ontario
PHONE: 541-889-8191 or 888-211-1222
WEBSITE: www.4rcc.com

10 DeWitt Museum and Prairie City Depot

WHAT'S HERE: **Historic train depot that now serves as a local museum**
DON'T MISS THIS: **The railcar that was reputedly transformed from a cattle car to a rolling car of ill-repute**

Originally called Dixie and located about 2.5 miles above its present site on Dixie Creek, Prairie City was founded in 1862, the same year that the discovery of gold began drawing thousands of hopeful miners to the area. Unfortunately, the overzealous digging by miners apparently undercut many of the town's first buildings causing several to collapse. Although most likely weren't much more than shacks, the miners decided to move their shacks to the flat "prairie" downstream where they would be safe from the ever-expanding gold mining operations. By 1870 there were 110 buildings in Prairie City and 523 people; 304 were white and the remainder were Chinese.

By the late 1880s the area was in need of a railroad. The owner of the Oregon Lumber Company obtained a charter for a new railway that he named Sumpter Valley Railroad. It began operation in Baker, Oregon, in 1890, but it took 20 years before the line was completed and the Prairie City Depot built. Passenger service provided some income, but it was general freight and lumber that provided most of the railway's profit. Passenger service was suspended in 1933 as the Great Depression gripped the country. The lumber industry continued to support the line until 1947, when the last train rolled out of the Prairie City Depot.

Today, the restored depot is used partially to exhibit the historic ephemera that includes photos, collectibles, and mining artifacts from late 19th-century mining operations around Grant County. Many other items in the museum were donated by "Ma" Austin who lived in the town of Austin, about 18 miles northeast of Prairie City. The town was a favorite stop for the railroad folks because of the delicious meals that she cooked. One of Ma's tables on which she served her many guests between 1894 and 1935 resides in the museum, fully set and awaiting her food.

The main floor of the 60-foot-by-32-foot depot includes the depot's waiting room, the station agent's office, as well as the express office and the baggage and freight room. Upstairs originally was the station depot manager's home. It is now the local history museum.

Wander through the remainder of the museum to see everything from bedpans and frying pans to saddles and an old hand-cranked telephone. There is even the handwritten list of ring sequences needed to reach different people—two short rings to reach the DeWitts, one long and four short rings to get R. Johnson to answer his phone, and three short rings for the Blue Mtn. R. Station.

In front of the museum are several pieces of old gold mining equipment, including a monitor that once directed powerful streams of water against hillsides in order to wash out the gold. There is also a Sumpter Valley Railway car, SVR 2020, that looks like a cattle car. Rumor has it that before the demise of the railway in 1947, it had been converted into a rolling house of ill repute, used to provide weekend services to miners and loggers along the line.

HOURS: May 15 through October 15: Wednesday through Saturday, 10 AM to 5 PM
COST: Ages 10-plus, $3
LOCATION: Main and Bridge streets, Prairie City
PHONE: 541-820-3603
WEBSITE: www.prairiecityoregon.com/prairie-city-oregon-dewitt-museum.html

Did this car haul more than freight?

11 Kam Wah Chung State Heritage Site

WHAT'S HERE: **A fully furnished historic building that served as a combination Chinese home, store, and doctor's office**

DON'T MISS THIS: **The meat cleaver on the nightstand next to Doc Hay's bed**

Kam Wah Chung translates roughly as "Golden Flower of Prosperity." Locked and abandoned for 20 years or so following its owners' deaths, this treasure was nearly bulldozed in the 1970s to make way for a local city park. A city council member peeked inside the building shortly before it was to be razed and got the surprise of his life. It's as though the two Chinese owners had simply moved, leaving everything they owned in the building. Food, herbs, Chinese medicines, products imported from China, old catalogs, clothes, and record books—everything was just as it had been. His surprise led to the preservation of the building and its designation as one of Oregon's state heritage sites.

Gold was discovered in the area in 1862, and in addition to the thousands of Americans who were attracted by the possibility of easy riches, the Chinese also came in large numbers. When gold mining reached its peak in about 1880, more than 3,000 Chinese called the John Day area their home. Many Chinese lived in the Chinatown that developed around Kam Wah Chung & Co., including Lung On and Ing Hay, the latter known locally as Doc Hay. The two formed a partnership, and in 1888 purchased the lease for the only stone building in the area. Lung On, the businessman, and Doc Hay, the herbal doctor, maintained that partnership for 50 years.

The building was constructed in about 1870, the bottom floor made from local volcanic tuff and pine planking. It is not an impressive building by today's standards, but that was not the case in the late 19th century. As the only stone structure among dozens of wooden buildings, it became a community gathering site, a temporary refuge for new Chinese immigrants, a general store where imported Chinese goods could be purchased, and a place where the sick and injured could receive medical assistance. The building's upper level was added in the 1890s, but nothing more was done until the 1970s when it underwent a major rehabilitation as state property.

By 1920, the gold was gone and the population of John Day had been significantly reduced. About 35 Chinese were still living here, but with the exception Kam Wah Chung, few of the original Chinese buildings remained as dredging operations in the area required their removal. Even the Joss house was torn down and its shrine moved into Kam

Kam Wah Chung

Wah Chung.Today, the old dredger tailings have been leveled and turned into a small park that surrounds the historic site.

Lung On was the consummate entrepreneur, willing to try anything that could make money and quite successful. He sold supplies to the gold miners and Chinese-made and imported supplies to the local community. Lung On also built a gambling den; owned a horse racetrack; maintained a labor office and a contract office; invested in real estate, a mine, and the stock market; and opened the first car dealership in eastern Oregon. On top of all that, he had a catalog business that allowed his customers to order clothing from Chicago. Some of those catalog pages, such as the one advertising the snug fitting Jazz Model, are affixed to the walls. His entrepreneurial success allowed Lung On to maintain bank accounts in San Francisco, Portland, London, and New York. Leon, as he had become known locally, died in 1940.

Doc Hay, who died in 1952, depended on his skills as a "pulse doctor" to determine ailments and prescribe cures. By feeling a patient's pulse, the doctor could make a diagnosis and prescribe medicinal cures. He was always available, especially when a local "white" doctor wasn't, making him an important part of the community. His reputation became such that some people traveled great distances to be treated by the pulse doctor.

Walking through Doc Hay's home-based business reveals what life was like here a century ago. You can see food products recognizable today such as Wheaties and Skippy peanut butter, although with very different package designs. Then there are other products, from biscuit tins to pickle jars, that aren't likely to be seen ever again except in a museum. Tea and tobacco also appeared to be popular items for the general store. Doc Hay's apothecary contained more than 500 different herbs, along with animal parts such as bear claws that were important in Chinese medicine. Most of the herb boxes and bottles are labeled in Chinese, with red being the predominant color for labels.

Meat cleavers can be found in several places. Not only were they tools of the trade, but they served a useful self-defense purpose in times of need. Doc Hay kept one on the nightstand beside his bed, where it remains today.

The building also served as a temporary boarding house for Chinese travelers and newly arrived immigrants. The bunk area is still intact. Lung On often wrote letters home for those Chinese who weren't able to do so themselves, thus ensuring himself new and loyal customers.

Guided tours are the only way to enter the historic building. The visitor center, located about a half block away, has additional exhibits, including some that are temporary.

HOURS: May through October: Daily, 9 AM to 5 PM; last tour at 4 PM

COST: Free (tour tickets are required and available from the visitor center located about a half block away, just outside the park entry gate)

LOCATION: The end of Canton Street, John Day

PHONE: 541-575-2800

WEBSITE: www.oregonstateparks.org

12 Grant County Historical Museum

WHAT'S HERE: **Artifacts from local families collected over the years**

DON'T MISS THIS: **The skulls of the first two men hanged in the county**

The Grant County Historical Museum had a truly interesting beginning. Local service station owner Charles W. Brown simply wanted to help out a fellow local citizen who was down on his luck and needed money. Brown agreed to purchase his saddle, even though he wasn't in need of a saddle. A week later someone sold him an old Colt revolver. That was in 1925. Over the years others in the community, also needing extra money to help them through hard times, began showing up at Brown's business offering to sell him all sorts of old stuff. For many of them that "stuff" was junk and no longer needed; for Brown, his newly acquired "stuff" turned into a service station full of historic treasures. Those treasures ultimately became the Grant County Historical Museum in 1953, when Brown partnered with Herman Oliver and built the museum.

The museum is an eclectic collection of artifacts representing the county's history. Inside on one wall a sign proclaims Old Relics. Beneath the sign there are numerous exhibits that could be considered old relics, including geologic specimens and Regulator-style clocks hanging on the wall. Nearby, a piano with a *Grange Songster* music book awaits just the right player. If playing a musical instrument was not within the abilities of local music enthusiasts, perhaps the 1924 Atwater Kent Model 49 radio could substitute.

Portraits are a common item in most museums, especially smaller, regional museums that focus on local history. Two of the portraits in the Grant County museum create more questions than they answer. Joseph Caton Oliver was born in the Azores Islands on March 16, 1850, and came to the U.S. at age 16 as a stowaway on a sailing ship. How one could hide on such a small sailing vessel in 1866 during a long voyage halfway across the Pacific Ocean is itself a mystery. His future wife, Mary Elizabeth (Miller) Oliver, had a similar adventure, coming to the U.S. She was born in Germany in 1848 and orphaned at age 11. She sailed around Cape Horn two years later, landing in San Francisco.

A turn-of-the-century horseless carriage sits in the museum, last driven in a 1962 parade. The Orient Car was built by Waltham Manufacturing Company (not the Waltham Automobile Co.). The Orient Buckboard is not much more than a seat mounted on several boards riding on four wheels and powered by a small gasoline engine. Two people could ride in the vehicle as long as they didn't mind being quite cozy.

1906 Orient Car, Buckboard model

J. W. Snyder was the state agent with the job of eliminating moonshine from the county during Prohibition. He was apparently quite successful, arresting many of the same people several times. Some of the moonshine equipment that he confiscated over the years is here. Behind another counter is an extensive collection of rifles and shotguns, and there's even a "burp" gun. Actually, it's a Soviet machine gun developed during World War II that fired a 7.62-millimeter round from its 71-round magazine. It was captured in 1952 during the Korean War.

There are also typewriters and other office equipment. Unique is the buffalo coat that a Crow Indian made in Montana in 1873. It was owned by George Huntley of Prineville, Oregon. He donated the full-length coat in 1965—on his 90th birthday. A wooden high chair that has obviously seen much use now sits empty. Charles Osborn hand-carved the chair in 1895 while herding sheep. His 11 children sat in the chair, as well as 25 grandchildren and a number of great grandchildren.

For the more macabre-minded museum visitor, the Grant County Historical Museum fills the bill. The heads from several two-headed cows are mounted on the walls. Even more macabre are the museum's two human skulls. They belonged to two murderers, the first men hanged by the neck until dead in Grant County.

Outside the museum several historic buildings have been moved to the site. One is an old cabin where poet and writer Joaquin Miller lived for a while in 1865. Another building is the Greenhorn Jail that dates from 1910. Both structures are furnished, and the house appears much like a house in the latter 19th century might have looked. The jail houses a drunk passed out on the floor in one cell and a local prostitute standing next to a small table in the other cell.

HOURS: May through September: Monday through Saturday, 9 AM to 4:30 PM
COST: Adults, $4; seniors, $3.50; ages 7–18, $2
LOCATION: 101 South Canyon City Blvd., Canyon City
PHONE: 541-575-0362
WEBSITE: www.ortelco.net/~museum/

13 Harney County Historical Museum

WHAT'S HERE: **Collections of local history, including a quilt reportedly made by Abraham Lincoln**

DON'T MISS THIS: **The 10,000-year-old Indian sandals**

The town of Burns was named after Scottish poet Robert Burns, and it became the seat of government for Harney County in 1890. This area began as cattle country and remains so today, although logging also contributed to the town's growth. The site on which the museum is located has served many purposes and numerous owners over the years, but Brewery Hill seems to be a name that has stuck. After all, this was the site of a brewery in addition to a wrecking yard and a laundry. Like many county museums, the Harney County Historical Museum is a repository for the possessions of local families, many of whom have lived in the area for generations. Enter the museum and you can easily trace your way back over a century—and in some cases several thousand years.

Among the museum's pianos, family photographs, and clocks is a small exhibit of quilts. One of those quilts, a faded red, white, and somewhat ragged remnant of its original self, was reportedly sewn in part by Abraham Lincoln. A signed document states that the quilt was made in 1854 by Amanda Cowels. It further states that Abraham Lincoln stopped by the Cowelses' home for a visit, during which time he helped do some of the sewing. Furthermore, Jacob Cowels had raised the cotton that was used in the quilt's padding. The quilt and its story were passed down through several generations of the family until 1980 when one of the family members donated it to the museum.

Even the Internet has played a part in the museum's collections. A quilt purchased on eBay features pieces that originally came from the 1918 Harney County Annual Pioneer Reunion and the fourth annual Grant County Fair, along with a U.S. flag sporting 48 stars. The museum's collection includes several women's dresses, one of which is the white wedding dress worn by the city librarian Mrs. Jennie Dennison in the late 1890s. There are several other dresses and gowns from the late 19th and early 20th century.

The museum has its share of curious artifacts. One of more unusual is the ball of string that Mrs. Henry Steward started winding in 1947. By December 1964, it was 40 inches in diameter. The story that accompanies the ball of string explains that Mrs. Steward lost her son in World War II, so instead of knitting to maintain her sanity, she saved string and wound it into the 265-pound ball that the museum now displays on its main floor.

Mrs. Steward's 265-pound ball of string

Another item at the museum is a beautiful wood cabinet 1947–48 RCA Victor Model 8T530 television set with an advertisement that touts it as a "Powerful New De Luxe Table Television—Thrills, Fund, Gaiety . . . Presented at Their Best." It even promises a "Bright, Clear, Steady" picture and that its "Eye Witness Picture Synchronizer" will lock in a transmitting stations' signals. Its sound is described as the mellow tone of the "Golden Throat," using the largest speaker ever placed in an RCA Victor table model.

Edward Hines, the owner of the Edward Hines Lumber Company, donated much to the museum's collections, including items related to the logging and lumber industry. Nearby is an exhibit of very old fire extinguishers, something that the early towns never had enough of, considering that most usually burned at least in part during their early years—some more than once. Many of these early fire extinguishers used carbon tetrachloride as the firefighting chemical because it evaporated at room temperature. The same chemical was used by the medical profession as a painkiller and anesthetic during part of the 19th century until it was determined that more people were probably harmed or killed than were helped by the toxic chemical.

One case is filled with rifles, most made by Winchester, but a couple of Springfields and a Colt lightning magazine rifle are included. A story accompanying the case explains that one of the lever-action Winchesters belonged to a father and son who died fighting Indians. While one of the men was reloading the gun, it jammed—he bent the lever by pulling so hard on it. The Indians left the broken rifle behind in some bushes. A nephew discovered the weathered firearm in 1936.

Likely one of the rarest artifacts to be found in any museum can be seen here. A pair of ropelike sandals made from woven sagebrush bark was discovered in one of the locally well-known Catlow Caves. Someone has estimated that the sandals, along with several other artifacts found with them—bone beads, arrowheads, and baskets—may be up to 10,000 years old. The sandals were loaned to the museum by Sandy Morris, who along with two friends, discovered them and the other items.

The museum offers much more, from a birdlife diorama and a very large bird egg collection to a furnished kitchen and bedroom. In the back of the museum there is a door to the museum's wagon shed, but beware. There is a warning on the door about wasps in the room, which seems to be a seasonal issue. If you aren't allergic to or fearful of flying, stinging insects, the large shed has a nice collection of old wagons and commercial business signs that have been used around the county over the years.

HOURS: March through October, Monday through Saturday, 10 AM to 4 PM

COST: Adults, $4; couples, $5; family of four, $6; additional children, $0.50 each; children ages 13–16, $1; seniors (over 65), $3

LOCATION: 18 West D Street, Burns

PHONE: 541-573-5618 or 541-573-6239

WEBSITE: www.burnsmuseum.com

Eastern Oregon Tours

Historical Curiosities Tour

ESTIMATED DAYS: 2
ESTIMATED DRIVING MILES: 200

There is a lot of cowboy country in eastern Oregon, and one of the most famous of the region's cowboy towns is Pendleton. Sixty thousand people annually flock to the rodeo, the parade, and everything else associated with the Pendleton Round-Up, an event that has been going on for nearly 100 years. Stop by the **Pendleton Round-Up and Happy Canyon Hall of Fame** (page 137) for a look at the history of this famous cowboy gathering, including the stuffed body of War Paint, a famous 1950s bucking horse.

Then it's a 127-mile drive south along Highway 395 to the town of John Day where the **Kam Wah Chung State Heritage Site** (page 157) awaits. This is a time-capsule look at how two prominent Chinese, one a doctor, the other a merchant, successfully lived in a place and time of general discrimination against Asians. Doc Hay was one of the owners of this building that was locked-up and forgotten about for 20 years following Hay's death. It's full of Chinese herbs, merchandise, and more.

About a five-minute drive down the road is the **Grant County Historical Museum** (page 159). It has a small building that in 1865 was the residence of poet and writer Joaquin Miller. It also houses the skulls of the first two criminals hanged in the county.

Continue driving south on Highway 395 to the **Harney County Historical Museum** (page 161) where more curiosities await. The two-story museum holds a quilt that Abraham Lincoln helped sew, 10,000-year-old Native American sandals, and a 265-pound ball of string saved by a distraught mother whose son was killed in World War II.

The Kam Wah Chung kitchen

Immigrant and Indian Tour

ESTIMATED DAYS: 2
ESTIMATED DRIVING MILES: 170

Two cultures, the Native Americans and the overland immigrants, have predominantly inhabited Eastern Oregon. The **Four Rivers Cultural Center and Museum** (page 153) in Ontario provides a look at the Northern Paiute before and after the great American western migration along the Oregon Trail. Then head north on Interstate 84 to Baker City. On a bluff overlooking the valley, the **National Historic Oregon Trail Interpretive Center** (page 147) provides an in-depth look at the Oregon Trail and those who traveled it during the 1840s and 1850s. It also offers several miles of hiking trails that connect with parts of the original Oregon Trail.

Then it's another easy drive continuing north along Interstate 84 to the south side of Pendleton to the **Tamástslikt Cultural Institute** (page 138). The museum's galleries form a circle around the Coyote Theater and include a look at the history of the regional Native Americans, from their cultural practices to the wars and diseases that ultimately decimated the tribes.

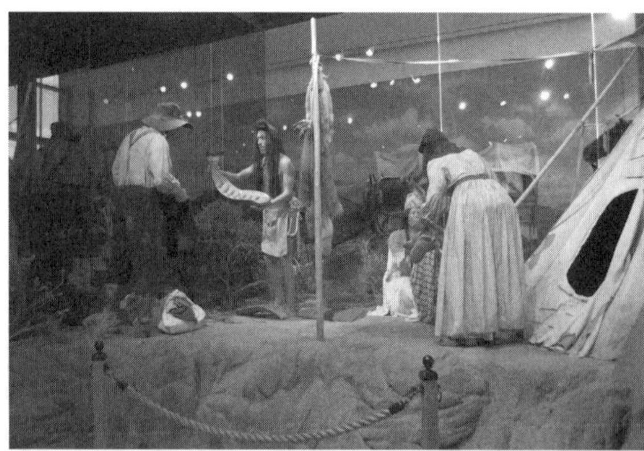

National Historic Oregon Trail Interpretive Center

Eastern Oregon Information Centers

Pendleton Chamber of Commerce
www.pendletonchamber.com
800-547-8911

Baker County Chamber of Commerce
www.visitbaker.com
800-523-1235

Grant County Chamber of Commerce
www.gcoregonlive.com
800-769-5664

Harney County Chamber of Commerce
http://harneycounty.com
541-573-2636

Fort Vancouver

WASHINGTON

Travel through Washington long and far enough and you can visit small towns and pulsating cities, high mountain glaciers, rocky deserts bisected by great rivers, forests as far as the eye can see, and a rugged coastline rivaling the most beautiful in the world. There is much more to Washington than its northern rain forests, Seattle's Space Needle, and Mount St. Helens.

The influence of Washington's original inhabitants is obvious nearly everywhere, from place names such as Seattle, Yakima, and Walla Walla to the state's 26 Indian reservations. Several of the Indian nations have created exceptional museums and visitor centers that rightly extol their cultures and histories, which are thousands of years old.

The timber industry remains important to Washington's economy. Drive through nearly any forested lands in the state and you will see that logging is still alive. Managed forests, many with signs indicating when they were last thinned or harvested, are common. Agriculture more than holds its own. Drive the open highways and back roads through much of the desertlike southeastern quarter of the state during July and August, and you will pass mile after mile of rolling hills covered in wheat. In these dry lands where irrigation is available, Washington's famous orchards cover thousands of acres. In other parts of the state, cherries, strawberries, blueberries, and the famed Walla Walla onions can be found in abundance. And in the last decade, Washington's vineyards have begun producing exceptionally fine wines.

Washington has always attracted the adventurers—the creative thinkers—willing to take chances. From the very first pioneers who traveled overland via the Oregon Trail or those who in more recent decades have landed at SeaTac Airport, entrepreneurialism and creativity have thrived here. Companies such as Microsoft, Boeing, Amazon, and of course, Starbucks, have gotten their start in the Evergreen State—and many more are certain to follow.

Today, hundreds of museums, stately mansions, log cabins, historic towns, and visitor centers help tell Washington's story of natural beauty and cultural diversity, of human perseverance and unrelenting creativity. Here, opportunities abound to learn, not only *about* the past, but *from* it as well.

Getting Around on Washington's Ferry System

The scenery around Washington's Olympic Peninsula and its inland waterways is truly spectacular as the blue-green waters of Puget Sound and the Strait of Juan de Fuca stand in contrast with its backdrop of the snowcapped Olympic Mountains. Driving the curving roads that wind around and over the waterways is something that few people do if there is a ferry that will get them to their destinations. Why drive between Bellingham or Seattle to places like Port Townsend, Bremerton, or Bainbridge Island when you can let the ferry do the work while eliminating several hours of driving from your journey? As a tourist you might enjoy the countryside, yet most visitors will sooner or later take advantage of the extensive and efficient ferry system.

It makes no difference if you are traveling in a passenger car, motorhome, kayak, or bicycle—the ferries can accommodate your travel needs. And if you're heading to the San Juan Islands or to Victoria, British Columbia, it's about the only way to get there. It's always wise to arrive at ferry terminals as least 30 minutes early, and during summer and peak commute times arriving an hour before the scheduled departure is not a bad idea. A few of the routes strongly suggest that you make reservations, so check the ferry website or call the information number. Reservations are especially important if you are taking one of the ferries to a Canadian port.

Heading to the San Juan Islands on a Washington State ferry

After you pay your fare at the kiosk for your vehicle and your passengers, simply drive forward where the vehicle lines are forming, stop, turn off your engine and wait. If you are walking or bicycling, pay inside the terminal and follow the folks walking to the loading waiting area. Bicyclists are usually allowed on and off before the motor vehicles. Some terminals have food service, but most don't. Fortunately, the ferries all have food available onboard.

When the ferry arrives, it will take a few minutes for the crew to unload all of the arriving vehicles before they begin loading for the return trip. The crew is very efficient and the process goes quickly. There will be plenty of people to direct you onto the ferry and tell you exactly where to go and where to stop and turn off your engine. Once parked onboard, you are free to head upstairs and grab any of the dozens of seats and enjoy the ferry ride to your destination—and even purchase a hot cup of clam chowder. Just before you arrive at your destination, head back to your vehicle and once the ferry is docked, a crew member will give the signal to start your car or grab your bicycle, and exit the ferry. Bikes go first. If you are in a car, just follow the line of cars in front of you. It's usually a pretty straight shot out of the terminal parking areas and onto a main street.

Ferry schedules vary significantly. Most terminals have ferries leaving at least every hour if not more often, but a few don't, especially on the San Juan Islands. Ferry schedules are available at the terminals, many businesses around the terminals, and also online. Be sure you fully understand the schedules and are aware of those peak travel times, because if you arrive too late, or don't have a reservation the few times you need one, you will have to wait for the next trip. Some of the areas with ferries include Seattle, Bainbridge Island, Bremerton, Edmonds, Kingston, the San Juan Islands, and Victoria, British Columbia. You can find out more about Washington's ferry system, by calling 888-808-7977 or visiting www.wsdot.wa.gov/ferries.

Olympic Mountains and the Pacific Coast

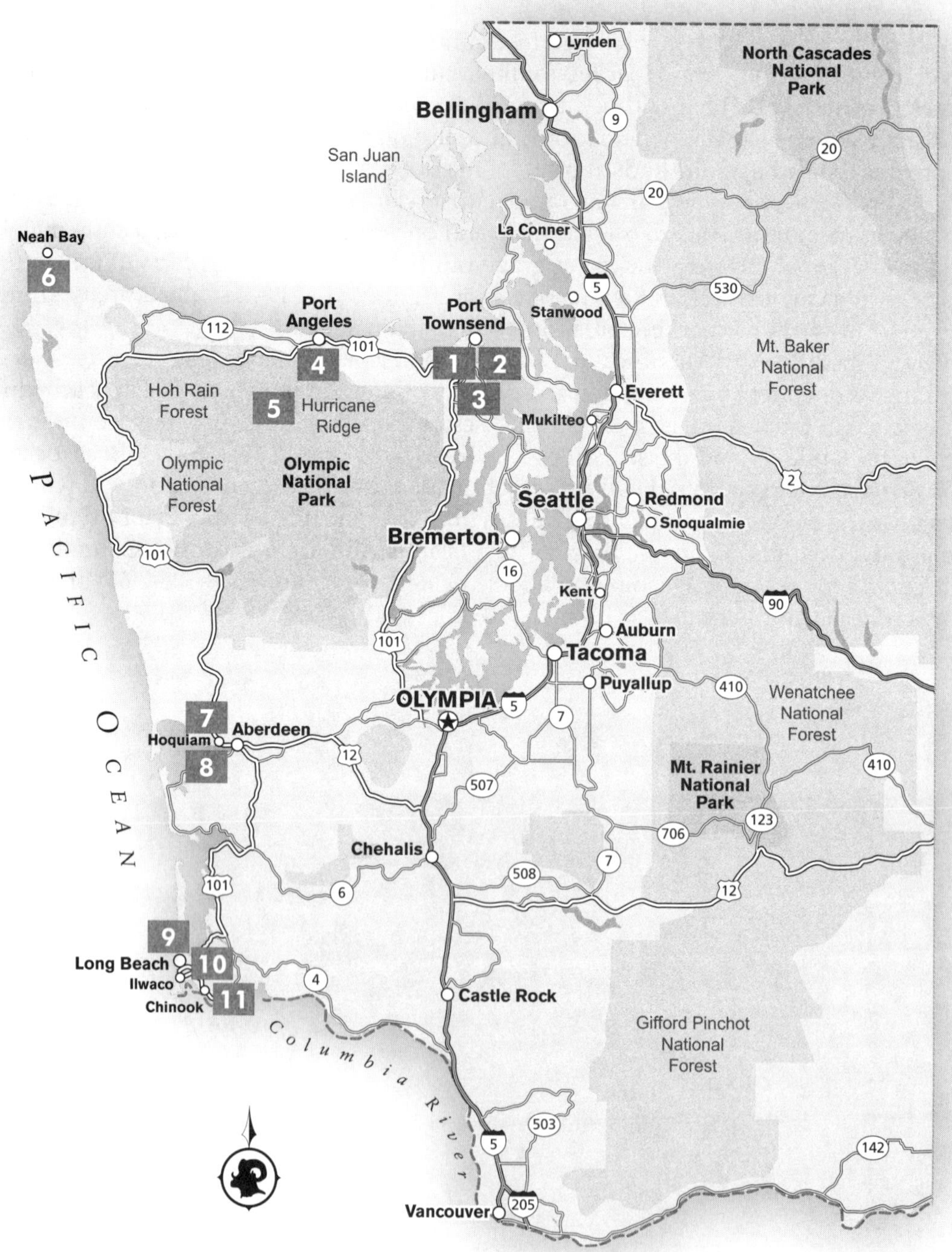

Lynden
North Cascades National Park
Bellingham
San Juan Island
La Conner
Neah Bay
6
Port Angeles
Port Townsend
Stanwood
1
2
4
3
Hoh Rain Forest
5
Hurricane Ridge
Everett
Mukilteo
Mt. Baker National Forest
Olympic National Forest
Olympic National Park
Seattle
Redmond
Snoqualmie
Bremerton
Kent
Auburn
Tacoma
Puyallup
OLYMPIA
Wenatchee National Forest
7
Aberdeen
Hoquiam
8
Mt. Rainier National Park
PACIFIC OCEAN
Chehalis
9
Long Beach
10
Ilwaco
Chinook
11
Castle Rock
Columbia River
Gifford Pinchot National Forest
Vancouver

Olympic Mountains and the Pacific Coast

It's no surprise that Washington's earliest settlements were sited along waterways that provided easy access to the Pacific Ocean. Washington's maritime history includes people such as the 16th-century mariner Juan de Fuca. He was the first to explore his namesake, the Strait of Juan de Fuca, the waterway that separates the U.S. from Canada and allows for ships to pass between Seattle and the Pacific Ocean. Others, including Lieutenant Peter Puget, who served under British Captain George Vancouver, would also

Totem poles at the center's entrance were made by Makah artist Frank Smith.

have their names attached to Washington's waterways and cities. Together they surveyed much of the Pacific Northwest's coast, with names like Puget Sound and the Hudson's Bay Company settlement of Fort Vancouver added to the world's maps.

The Olympic Mountains that cover the center of the peninsula are dominated by Mount Olympus, high enough at 7,962 feet to have its own glacier and to block much of the rain that pushes in from the Pacific Ocean. On the Pacific side of the mountains, the Hoh Rain Forest averages 142 inches of rain each year. On the northeastern side, towns such as Port Angeles and Sequim sit in a rain shadow and receive only 25 and 15 inches of precipitation, respectively, most as rain.

Beyond towns like Port Townsend and Hoodsport, there are many surprises. Drive west as far as you can along the Olympic Peninsula's State Route 112, which dead-ends in the small Indian community of Neah Bay. Take a short hike out to Cape Flattery and you will find yourself at the northwesternmost point of the continental U.S. Back in Neah Bay there is a excellent museum tucked into this remote Makah Indian Reservation fishing town that celebrates their history and culture. And the fishing here is excellent. Along Washington's Pacific Coast you can explore small towns like La Push and Westport, the sandy beach at Long Beach, or visit one of Washington's many lighthouses.

TRIVIA

1. What museum features a prominent exhibit of its town's historic red-light district?
2. Where can you see a shot-line gun used to aid passengers in escaping a stranded or sinking ship?
3. In what national park can you visit the Hoh Rain Forest, which averages 12 feet of rain each year?
4. Where can you see an item that has been used as a weapon of war for hundreds of years, a form of transportation, and as a child's toy?
5. Legend has it that the steaming tears from two dragons unable to win in battle created what special place?
6. Where can you see hundreds of objects discovered in an Indian village, which was buried by a landslide 500 years ago?
7. Which fort protected the Washington side of the mouth of the Columbia River during World War II?

For trivia answers, see page 343.

1 Jefferson County Historical Museum

WHAT'S HERE: History of Port Townsend and surrounding Jefferson County

DON'T MISS THIS: Exhibit on the town's red-light district

The restored 1892 Port Townsend City Hall building is home to the county's historical museum. It makes a great stage for showcasing the regional history—the local court remains as does the old jail in the basement, both of which are open to visitors. With more than 150 years of history, much of it tied to the town's wild waterfront and the nearby forests, there is plenty of material for the museum's numerous exhibits.

The Fire Hall Gallery offers a look at Port Townsend's maritime history. The wooden steering wheel from a very early Puget Sound ferry provides a centerpiece for the photographs and other artifacts, including the recovered remnants of long-ago sunken vessels. There is a wonderful and very long landscape photograph of the historic Port Townsend waterfront taken from the water and looking up the hill. Look carefully and you can identify some of the historic buildings that remain today. Since this was also the old Fire Hall, some of the city's early firefighting equipment is exhibited.

The Court Room Gallery features the area's history, from the Native Americans, early European explorers, Chinese settlers, and businesses, through the Victorian era. A small black, horse-drawn buggy is one of those exhibits that saw significant use; it served as a taxi able to carry four passengers in their own private compartment, while the driver directed his two horses through the town's streets from the outside seat. In 1890, for whatever reason, the taxi owner sold it to the City Transfer Company where the cute little buggy joined three others as part of the livery-transfer service. Ten years later the buggy was replaced by the automobile—a sign of the times.

Sin at Sea Level around the old city hall's basement jail cells includes an extensive exhibit on the area's early prostitutes and red-light districts. Names are named and photos displayed, along with the sad histories of some of the women who, for many personal reasons, chose this as a way of life. The women were referred to by many names besides their own—most not flattering. From the 1800s through the 1930s and beyond, the women earned low wages yet paid dearly satisfying the desires of sailors, loggers, soldiers, and businessmen. A few married, but the marriages were seldom happy or successful as the exhibit shows. The only people who prospered, at least financially, were the owners of the bordellos, saloons, dance halls, rooming houses, and theaters. They are the ones who could afford to build bigger businesses,

The wheel from an early Washington ferry

schools, churches and fancy Victorian homes, many of which still can be found today tucked along the city's hillsides. On a lighter note, the museum features a beautiful 1880s Steinway & Sons square rosewood piano.

When you are finished wandering the rooms of the museum, ask for a copy of Port Townsend's tour of historic homes and buildings. The small map features about 50 historic buildings, many within easy walking distance.

HOURS: Daily, 11 AM to 4 PM
COST: Adults, $4; ages 3–12, $1
LOCATION: 540 Water Street, Port Townsend
PHONE: 360-385-1003
WEBSITE: www.jchsmuseum.org

2 Fort Worden State Park

WHAT'S HERE: **Early 20th-century U.S. Army Coast Artillery Corps fort**
DON'T MISS THIS: **Touring the Commanding Officer's Quarters**

When the fort was commissioned in 1902, the troops were required to live in tents—not an ideal living arrangement during Pacific Northwest winters. Their mission was to guard the entrance to Puget Sound and the strategically vital Bremerton shipyard; to do this, the soldiers constructed 12 gun batteries near the beach. It wasn't until 1904 that the first barracks were built for the troops, with additional buildings added for administration, mess halls, a bakery, guardhouse, signal station, and the wharf that allowed supplies to be delivered.

Even today, the buildings that surround the large parade ground exemplify the simplistic organization and order the military demanded. The buildings, including the larger and more luxurious officers' quarters, have been restored and some are open to the public.

Each military post ensures that the facility's commanding officer lives in the biggest and fanciest house. The same was true here. Fort Worden's commanding officer's home is nearly 6,000 square feet, with a cross-gabled slate roof. It includes fireplaces in the parlor, dining room, and study, and the 10-foot-high rooms featured pressed tin ceilings, pocket doors, brass chandeliers, and Palladian-influenced windows. Inside, the elegance is even more obvious, especially when compared with the barracks that housed the enlisted soldiers.

The home's parlor served as a center for entertaining guests. Guests could relax on the Empire sofa while listening to music played either on the Beckwith organ or on the old phonograph sitting atop the corner table. The furnishings are highlighted by the Ispahan

Persian rug. The commanding officer's servants and a butler assisted in serving dinner in the dining room on Maddock English china and crystal glassware.

The other rooms include the butler's pantry, kitchen, upstairs bedrooms, and the sitting room for the lady of the house. The master bedroom features a carved black walnut bed and dresser. A sign of the times, the lady of the house's corset bag hangs on the bedpost. Some of her other garments that are exhibited—as though she has perhaps just left the room—include a velveteen hat with ostrich plumes and a silk and satin two-piece dress with luster beads that was handmade in 1898. The nearby guest room includes a "moss" rug weaved from scraps of wool and silk underwear. The home's bathrooms could not have been any more elegant with their Italian marble sinks; wood trimmed, gravity-fed toilets; and footed bathtubs. Look closely for the curling iron of the era (heated by open flame) and the shaving mug with its silver-handled shaving brush.

For those commanders with young children, the children's bedroom is markedly devoid of toys—play items were kept in the nursery for the kids. You can also see the sewing room, which originally was the servant's bedroom. It is much simpler in design and furnishings than the rooms of the commander's family living areas.

Just across the parade ground is another of the restored buildings, this one holding the Coast Artillery Museum. The museum houses a wonderful collection of military memorabilia ranging from different artillery rounds to uniforms. There is an interesting device called a shot-line gun. It's a miniature cannon mounted on a wooden cart that could be pulled to the beach by its crew of seven soldiers. After some setting up, a shot carrying a line was fired across a sinking and grounded ship. A heavier line was then attached to a block and tackle and secured between the beach and the ship so that sailors could be hauled safely to shore.

Many of the other exhibits show the changes that came to the military over the years the Army spent here at Fort Worden. With this still being an active post during the first part of the Cold War, there are military Geiger counters, manuals about fallout practice, and special canned Civil Defense food rations. There are also scale models of the coastal defense guns, a German machine gun from World War I, a Japanese machine gun from World War II, uniforms from different periods, and smaller weapons. Upstairs is a recreated barracks with its wall locker and single bunk that may bring back memories for military veterans.

When you finish visiting the Commander's Quarters and the museum, drive the short distance to the beach, passing through a small campground on the way. Along the beach some of the original gun emplacements (minus the guns) still exist and can be explored. There are also some great views of the Strait of Juan de Fuca and the entrance to Puget Sound.

Fort Worden's Commander's Quarters

HOURS: The park is open daily.
Coast Artillery Museum: daily, 11 AM to 4 PM, plus most holidays
Commanding Officer's Quarters: June through August, daily, 10 AM to 4 PM; March through May, September and October, weekends, 12 PM to 4 PM; and during some holidays

COST: **Museum:** Adults, $2; ages 6–12, $1; immediate family $5; active military, free
Commanding Officer's Quarters: Adults and teens, $2; ages 12 and under, free

LOCATION: 200 Battery Way, Fort Worden, Port Townsend

PHONE: 360-344-4452 or 360-385-0373

WEBSITE: www.parks.wa.gov/fortworden

3 Rothschild House

WHAT'S HERE: **One of Port Townsend's oldest homes open to the public**

DON'T MISS THIS: **The views of Port Townsend and the waterfront from the home**

One of Port Townsend's more successful merchants, D.C.H. Rothschild, had this home built in 1868, befitting his social standing as a community leader. His financial success came from his general mercantile stores that he started after emigrating from Germany. He was born in Bavaria in 1824 and upon arriving in the U.S. began several different successful businesses in California and Bellingham, Washington. Those businesses provided a solid basis for the two-story Kentucky Store he built on a pier that extended into Port Townsend Bay in 1858. Its location allowed trading ships to unload wares directly into his business, reducing shipping and handling costs for what he sold, which included everything from sewing supplies to boat parts. As time passed, he changed the name to Rothschild and Co. Mercantile.

A bachelor until age 39, Rothschild married 19-year-old Dorette Hartung in 1863. They lived on the top floor of his Kentucky Store for the first few years during which time their first three children were born. Seeking a more respectable and comfortable home for his family, yet one less flamboyant than the ones many of the other successful businessmen were having constructed, their five-bedroom home was completed in 1868. It's Port Townsend's second oldest home—and Washington's smallest state park.

It was a comfortable home with its back-to-back fireplaces in the dining room and parlor. Rothschild included a stone foundation basement where his Chinese cook hung curing meats from the wood beams and where he stored his crocks of sauerkraut and wine. The original bath was a tin tub with accompanying washstand. It was replaced by a more modern bathroom in later years. The building lot also held a stable, carriage house, a two-story washhouse, and servants' quarters.

Fortunately, little has changed either in the interior furnishings or the house itself, which is seldom the case for homes that are nearing a century-and-a-half of age. The economy, deaths, and family intentions have served to keep much of the home intact as an authentic 19th-century house museum. With his two sons as partners, Rothschild began moving away from general supplies and specialized in marine supplies, ultimately making a business decision to sell his mercantile in 1881 in order to focus on the marine shipping business. The timing proved less than ideal as competition was fierce and their business failed to prosper as his store had.

The elder Rothschild died in 1886, leaving everything to his family. The home remained virtually unchanged by the remaining family members as the adult children moved away to pursue their own lives. Mrs. Rothschild continued to live in the family home, caring for by her youngest daughter Emilie who never married. Following Mrs. Rothschild's death in 1918, Emilie remained in the house, keeping things as they had been. Following her death, the one remaining son, Eugene, chose to give the home and its contents to Washington State Parks.

The main floor is where the family lived and entertained its many guests. Apparently, Baron, as the senior Rothschild was known, enjoyed the company of many of the ships' captains who frequented his store, along with other leading citizens of Port Townsend. The front parlor overlooks the waterfront and bay down the hill, and the piano likely provided much entertainment over the years. There is also a single bedroom downstairs, along with the kitchen and dining room. Notice that there isn't a faucet over the kitchen sink. Instead, a small hand pump provided needed water from a spring that ran under the house.

Throughout the home, most of the furnishings and some of the wallpaper is original. There's even a wood tank toilet in the bathroom, a room that was originally only for bathing as an outhouse served the family needs until about 1914. One of the rarer items in the house is the Florence sewing machine. The sewing machine was operated by a foot treadle that transferred its power via leather belts to the working parts above. It seems likely that Baron Rothschild got a really good deal on the item because he was the exclusive territorial agent for sales of the Florence sewing machine, which he also sold in his mercantile. In the room that sometimes served as a master bedroom, but also as the youngest son Eugene's bedroom, the interesting floor covering is a woven grass mat that likely was purchased through local Chinese merchants or from a catalog. The four bedrooms upstairs have been furnished with additional items from the family illustrating what a local, well-to-do gentleman and his family would have used nearly every day.

The 1868 Rothschild House

HOURS: Daily, May through September, 11 AM to 4 PM
COST: Adults, $4; ages 3–12, $1
LOCATION: Corner of Taylor and Franklin streets, Port Townsend
PHONE: 360-385-1003
WEBSITE: www.jchsmuseum.org/Rothschild/house.html

4 Olympic National Park

WHAT'S HERE: **Wilderness beaches, active glaciers, lakes, rivers, and a rain forest**
DON'T MISS THIS: **The short hike along the nature trail at the Hoh Rain Forest Visitor Center**

Look at any map of Washington's Olympic Peninsula and what stands out is Olympic National Park. These rugged mountains drew several explorers and a few settlers, but very late when compared with other parts of the Pacific Northwest. A Greek navigator sailing under the Spanish flag first claimed and named the Strait of Juan de Fuca, a discovery that wasn't confirmed until 1787 when British Captain Charles Barkley rediscovered the passage. The first large and well-documented land exploration of the interior occurred in 1885, although a few other small parties had entered the rugged mountains earlier.

In 1938, President Franklin D. Roosevelt created Olympic National Park. Today, the park covers 1,400 square miles with 60 miles of Pacific Ocean frontage. About 95 percent of the park is designated as wilderness, which means the only way to see it is on foot. But there is much you can see and do via the few roads open to vehicular travel.

From Port Angeles near the park's northern boundary, Hurricane Ridge is one of the most popular destinations. Summer brings sometimes hundreds of carloads of eager explorers up the twisting 17-mile road from U.S. 101. A large visitor center serves not only as a place to learn about the park but also offers seasonal hikes and other interpretive programs. There are spectacular views from the visitor center of the surrounding mountains, and a couple of short hikes along the ridgelines offer even more spectacular vistas of the Strait of Juan de Fuca and Canada beyond. Hurricane Ridge is a popular winter destination for snowshoers and cross-country skiers, although be sure to call ahead about winter storm road closures.

While Hurricane Ridge offers access to beautiful alpine meadows and the treeless ridgelines, the visitor center at the Hoh Rain Forest is the access point to one of Washington's wettest places. The temperate rain forest here can receive up to 167 inches—14 feet—of rain each year. It's a one-hour drive from the nearest town of Forks to the Hoh Rain Forest

Visitor Center, but much of the 32 miles follows the meandering Hoh River with lots of places to stop for a little fishing or to take photographs. Come here prepared for rain every month of the year, especially if walking the visitor center's short loop nature trail is in your plans—and it should be! Sitka spruce and western hemlock are the dominant rain forest trees, and with all this rainfall some trees get really big, up to 300 feet tall and 23 feet in diameter.

There are three other information centers located around the sprawling national park, one in Port Angeles, another at Lake Quinault near the southwest corner of the park, and one more along U.S. 101 where the highway finally cuts back out to the Pacific Coast just south of Kalaloch. Each offers visitor information and wilderness permits if you are heading off on backpacking trips to visit one of the many glaciers found high up in the Olympic Mountains.

Less than half of the 60 miles of coastal national park lands are easily accessible by vehicle. From South Beach near the town of Queets, north to Ruby Beach, U.S. 101 allows easy access before it turns inland. For a more intimate look at this amazing meeting of land and sea, take the Highway 110 turnoff immediately north of Forks and head directly west toward the town of La Push. Just outside the tiny town are beaches within short hiking distances that few people visit. Just be certain to check tide tables if you decide to walk very far along the beaches that abut the steep cliffs or you could find yourself stranded for twelve hours or so until the tide goes out again. And be aware that unseen sleeper waves can suddenly crash high on the beach catching and pulling hikers into the cold waters. Waves can also move large logs, pushing them over onto unsuspecting log-hoppers, so watch the kids.

Another very popular summer destination in the park is Lake Crescent, which lies along U.S. 101 as the highway heads east toward Port Angeles. Fishing, swimming, boating, and hiking are the most popular activities. Anglers are often infatuated with the idea of catching one of the famed Beardslee trout. Generally, fishing licenses aren't required in the park, but always check the most current fishing regulations any time you plan to fish because there are numerous restrictions on hours, tackle, and closures.

The park is open during summer, but much of it, especially visitor facilities, is closed during winter. Always be prepared for inclement weather no matter the month or the weather forecast.

Pier at Lake Crescent Lodge

HOURS: Open daily during summer, with most visitor centers open from 10 AM to 5 PM, summer only

COST: Various fees for day-use, hiking, car camping, and backpacking (permit required for the latter)

LOCATION: 600 East Park Avenue, Port Angeles

PHONE: 360-565-3130 or for recorded road and weather conditions 360-565-3131

WEBSITE: www.nps.gov/olym

5 Sol Duc Hot Springs

WHAT'S HERE: **Natural hot springs in a swimming pool setting**

DON'T MISS THIS: **The pull-out picnic areas along the Sol Duc River**

The local Quileute Indians likely used these naturally occurring mountain hot springs for thousands of years. They called the steaming springs *si'bi'* or "stinky place." Another story has the Indians calling this place "Sol Duc," which meant "sparkling water." Whichever version is true, they also believed that two dragonlike creatures fought over the land, and if you look around today, perhaps some of the legend is true! After all, that green lichen hanging from the surrounding trees does look like dragon skin lost in the heat of battle. Alas, after battling each other to a draw, with neither dragon able to claim victory, they crawled back into their respective caves and cried. It's those hot tears that fill the Sol Duc Hot Springs.

In the 1880s, long after the dragon war, things began to change. Theodor Moritz apparently nursed a local Indian back to health, and in return, the Indian introduced him to what was referred to as the "firechuck," or magic waters. Moritz quickly staked a claim to the land and built what served as hot tubs, which began attracting visitors looking for cures for whatever ailed them. One major endorsement came from Michael Earles who owned Puget Sound Mills and Timber Company. He claimed the sparkling mineral waters cured him of what was supposedly a fatal disease.

Perhaps the claim was self-serving because following Moritz's death in 1909, Earles purchased the hot springs and surrounding land. He then built a road to the springs from Lake Crescent and spent several years, along with a part of his personal fortune, building the most elegant resort he could. It included a hotel, landscaped grounds, golf course, tennis courts, croquet courses, theater, bowling alley, and card rooms. For those desiring more than a few days soaking in the healthful mineral waters, Earles constructed a three-story sanitarium with beds and medical support facilities for 100 people.

In 1916, Earles's dream went up in smoke when sparks from a defective flue ignited the hotel's wood-shingled roof. Apparently, it was too early in the season for the water to be turned on without pipes likely freezing, and so the resort had no ability to fight it. As the fire raged on, electrical wires shorted causing the electric organ to begin playing Beethoven's *Funeral March*. Whether that last part is true or not, the hotel was reduced to ashes in three hours.

The resort was rebuilt four years later, although not on the same grand scale. In the 1980s it was rebuilt once more and continues in operation today as part of Olympic National Park. It has a few modern conveniences, including cabins, a restaurant, a paved road from Lake Crescent, as well as the hot springs and pools.

The bubbling mineral waters have been tamed and channeled into three different large circular pools, which draw many people here each year. Here's where you have to make a decision about how much heat you can stand. One is kept at 99°F, another at 101, and the third at about 104. Each of the pools has steps for easy entry (the deepest is three feet), and the largest pool also has a ramp for wheelchair access. There is a freshwater pool that can vary between 50 and 85°F.

So if you don't believe the dragon story, where does all the hot water really come from? Underground water, along with additional infiltrating surface rain and melting snow, seeps deep into the underlying sedimentary rocks. There it mixes with the hot gases and rocks, ultimately being forced back to the surface through larger cracks and fissures. There is more than enough mineral water available to refill each of the pools after they are drained nightly. The pools also are closed twice each day to allow for a "resting" period during which time they are tested for cleanliness.

Whether you visit the hot springs for the day or come for a longer stay in one of the cabins or nearby campgrounds, there is plenty to do besides soaking in the hot pools. The national park features several picnic areas along the road into the resort, where depending on the time of year, you can sit and watch salmon fighting their way through the Sol Duc River's rapids and waterfalls heading upriver to spawn. There are hiking trails everywhere leading higher into the Olympic Mountains or back toward Lake Crescent. The resort also has an RV campground, a small restaurant, and a gift shop.

Sol Duc Hot Springs restaurant and gift shop

HOURS: Pool hours vary so call ahead: approximately, from the end of March to first of May, 9 AM to 8 PM; May through most of September, 9 AM to 9 PM; end of September to end of October, 9 AM to 8 PM.

COST: There is a vehicle fee (good for seven days) to enter Olympic National Park in addition to the following pool fees: ages 13–61, $11; 62 and older, $8; 4–12 years, $8; under age 4, free.

LOCATION: 12076 Sol Duc Hot Springs Road, 30 miles southwest of Port Angeles off U.S. 101, in Olympic National Park

PHONE: 866-476-5382

WEBSITE: www.visitsolduc.com

6 Makah Cultural and Research Center

WHAT'S HERE: **Makah Indian Nation museum with extensive exhibits and artifact collection**

DON'T MISS THIS: **The "soft" Indian artifacts recovered from a village buried 500 years ago**

As you near the end of Washington's Highway 112 as it enters Neah Bay and the Makah Reservation, one of the first buildings you will see is the Makah Cultural and Research Center and its Museum of the Makah Indian Nation. The museum is a showcase for an extensive collection of "soft" goods recovered from an Indian village that lay buried for 500 years. Scientists speculate that in the 15th century, an earthquake triggered the massive mudslide that suddenly buried parts of a village near Lake Ozette, leaving its houses and their contents intact and protected for centuries. The site was originally identified in 1947, and in 1966–67, the Makah tribal government gave permission for Washington State University archaeologists to excavate a part of the Ozette site. In 1970, severe weather-caused erosion revealed more artifacts, requiring that archaeologists be called in to recover and preserve these important vestiges of Makah life that existed before the arrival of any European influence.

For 11 years a variety of scientific disciplines carefully collected and documented thousands of artifacts. Rather than the traditional shovels and trowels, they used streams of water to remove the clay deposits. For the first time large numbers of well-preserved organic materials had been recovered, some well-worn with use, others in various stages of development. The Ozette houses were uncovered, and archaeologists were able to dig deeper, into late prehistoric, early historic, and pre-contact periods, creating a stratigraphic representation of Makah history. The digging recovered 55,000 artifacts, and the museum's numerous exhibits reveal many of the most important items.

Entering the museum's galleries is like taking several steps back in time. A whale skeleton is suspended above the eight-man wooden dugout canoes, the kind traditionally used to hunt whales and seals in a time-honored and traditional manner. And as Makah life necessarily focused on the seasons, so do the museum exhibits. They begin with spring when hunting whales and seals dominated much of the tribe's activities. Sea lions, so prevalent today along the rocky coast, were not a primary target of Makah hunters, though a sea lion's gut was useful for bow strings and its stomach could be used as a container. Much preferred were the fur seals whose meat was also more edible and whose skins were warmer.

The ocean and rivers provided much of the Makah diet. Salmon, sea bass, snapper, rock cod, lingcod, and halibut were all caught. Some were taken by spear, and others were caught with hooks made from bone and other natural materials. Sea otters, likely more plentiful 500 years ago, were hunted not for food but instead for their warm hides and for their teeth, which were used as decorative art inlays.

Whale hunting represented the ultimate challenge, both physically and spiritually, for the Makah. Canoes would carefully approach a whale and thrust a long harpoon into it. Bladders were attached that would serve to help keep the animal afloat while hindering the wounded whale's movements, tiring the big mammal as it attempted to dive and escape. Once the whale was killed with a special harpoon, one of the Makah crew would dive into the frigid water and attach a rope to the animal so the crew could tow it to shore and share its meat with the village.

The museum's replica longhouse provides a look at how the Makah's four-season design adapted to the local weather patterns. Present-day Makahs built the house using only materials and tools that would have been available to them 500 years ago. Whale bones and rocks would have served as water drains around the outsides of the house, while the roof and wall planks could be removed during warm summer days and replaced during winter to maintain warmth.

Exhibits include hundreds of artifacts from the 11 years of archaeological recovery efforts that took place beginning in 1970. Blade fragments, harpoons, a sea mammal hunting bag, and more are here. One of the most intriguing artifacts is the 500-year-old blanket. It was made from dog hair, cattail fluff, and woodpecker feathers woven together with cedar bark. Strips of cedar were cut from live trees and then pounded to a soft, flexible texture that allowed it to be woven like cloth. The blanket's delicate plaid design pattern is one reminiscent of Scottish Highlander and the Gaelic cultures. There are also cedar bark sleeping mats and cradles, and carved wooden boxes.

A whale swims above dugout canoes.

One exhibit shows the steps required to construct one of the small cedar storage boxes, from carving the wooden sides to putting in the pins that hold it all together. Dog hair was another specialty item; the Makah raised dogs specifically for their hair that was woven into cloth. In later years they changed to using sheep's wool.

The Makah Cultural and Research Center has some of the best examples of pre-European Native American cultural artifacts made from organic materials, which seldom lasted beyond a few years. From wooden harpoons and bows to the day-to-day tools that women used to store and prepare foods, the museum is a true cultural treasure.

HOURS: Daily, 10 AM to 5 PM
COST: Adults, $5; students and elders, $4
LOCATION: Makah Indian Reservation, Neah Bay
PHONE: 360-645-2711
WEBSITE: www.makah.com

7 Polson Museum

WHAT'S HERE: **Historic home owned by the heir to the Polson Logging Company**
DON'T MISS THIS: **The HO-gauge model railroad display of the Polsons' logging empire**

Nova Scotia–born Alexander Polson headed west in 1876, learning the lumber trade along the way. Six years later he landed in Hoquiam, and in 1886 he and his brother Robert founded Polson Brothers Logging Company. It became the largest lumber producer in the Pacific Northwest with hundreds of employees, 12 logging camps, and even their own 100-mile-long railroad.

Owning a successful lumber company brought certain advantages for Alexander and Robert Polson, besides the obvious wealth. When Alexander's son Arnold married, Uncle Robert gave the newlyweds a new home directly across the street from their lumber business headquarters—and not just a small bungalow, but a 6,500-square-foot, 26-room colonial revival mansion. Robert even closed the mill for a day to regular work in order to set up for a special mill run for the home. Polson wanted the floorboards in each room to stretch the full width of the rooms, so he had his workers cut clear, kiln-dried hemlock lumber into tongue-and-groove flooring planks that were up to 40 feet long. As you tour the home, look at the floors; there are no end-butted floorboards in any of the large rooms.

Arnold Polson, Alexander's son, became heir to the Polson Lumber Company and continued living in his wedding present home until 1965, when he finally left the area.

The home stood vacant until 1975 when the family donated it to the local community to be used as a museum. Unfortunately, since the Polsons took their furnishings with them, little of their family furniture or personal items remain in the home. Yet, the family had a series of photos taken in 1942, documenting how each of the rooms appeared, and those photos, with the exception of the kitchen, are posted in each of the rooms. The upstairs master bedroom has been refurnished, but with locally donated pieces.

One notable exception to there being no Polson furnishings in the home, is the 1930s-era dollhouse that Ben Brunstad—the master builder of Arnold Polson's home—made for the family's two daughters, Jacqueline and Shirley. While it is more of a cabinet with five, glass-fronted doors, inside each of the cubbyhole rooms are miniature furnishings that Mrs. Polson collected from around the world. And there's even a flashlight on the house that you can use to better see what's inside.

For kids of all ages, a large HO-gauge model railroad has been designed and constructed to resemble the expansive Polson logging operations from 1915 to 1925. The upstairs setup includes timber falling and skyline operations on a mountainside, the railroad with trestles, the log transport system via steam locomotive and a river to the mill, the mill town, and finally the loading dock where the finished lumber was prepared for train and ship transport.

Many of the remaining artifacts in the museum are from families who have lived in Grays Harbor County, some for many generations. There is a nice collection of Native American baskets, spear points, and more. One curious item is the large red, neon "405" sign hanging in one of the rooms. The room focuses on the most popular forms of recreation during the town's logging and lumbering heydays—bars and houses of prostitution. The sign is from one of the last remaining brothels that operated locally until the mid-1950s.

The old elevator that sits in the hallway was operational in the house up to the 1940s, but the family had it taken out sometime before they moved away. And there are lots of old photographs throughout that show what life has been like in Grays Harbor County for the last 100-plus years.

The outside museum grounds offer opportunities to learn more about the local history. A blacksmith shop features occasional demonstrations, and when the roses are in bloom, it's a very pleasant place to spend some time. The site of the rose garden was once where the elder Polson's home was located—not far from their son's wedding present home. There is also a short trail, perhaps a quarter mile total, that meanders to the top of the hill near the home, which offers viewpoints of the local area. About halfway down the trail, local Eagle Scouts have built a deck around a very special tree. The 6.5-foot diameter fir is the last remaining old-growth tree to be found anywhere near town. The only reason the Polsons never logged the tree and

Mr. and Mrs. Arnold Polson's wedding present

turned it into lumber was that its top was blown out by a lightning strike, making the tree essentially worthless to them. There is also a nearby walking trail loop around Hoquiam's waterfront. It has 12 interpretive signs that explain the area's history.

There are plans to construct additional buildings on the expansive grounds in the very near future that will house some of the larger pieces of logging equipment the museum owns.

HOURS: April 1 through December 31, Wednesday through Saturday, 11 AM to 4 PM, Sunday, 12 PM to 4 PM; December 26 through March 31, Saturday, 11 AM to 4 PM, Sunday, 12 PM to 4 PM; Wednesday through Friday by appointment

COST: Adults, $4; students, $2; under age 12, $1; families, $10

LOCATION: 1611 Riverside Avenue, Hoquiam

PHONE: 360-533-5862

WEBSITE: www.polsonmuseum.org

8 Aberdeen Museum of History

WHAT'S HERE: **Exhibits ranging from logging to restored fire engines in a 1922 military armory building**

DON'T MISS THIS: **A mounted 127-pound king salmon**

The Spanish Colonial Revival architecture of this historic building creates an imposing site in Aberdeen's downtown. From 1922 until 1978, twelve different National Guard companies occupied the Armory, the purpose of its original construction. Its first occupant, following the building's dedication on July 4, 1922, was the 489th Company Coast Artillery Corps. Even during its use as an armory, the building's expansive interior design allowed the community to use it for local events.

Two years prior to the last National Guard unit leaving the Armory, Carl and Charles Swanson purchased the building from the State of Washington. The building saw little use for several years. Then in 1981, the Swanson brothers donated the old Armory to the City of Aberdeen to be used for public purposes. Today's museum shares the building with several other organizations, including the Grays Harbor Genealogical Society, although the museum's exhibits use the largest portion.

The exhibits offer a look back at the area's history, some quirky—at least by today's standards—but all interesting. The Red Hat Society ladies would be delighted to see the women's hat exhibit, along with an old Montgomery Ward & Co. catalog—it's filled with red hats.

The beautifully restored 1926 Ahrens-Fox fire truck served the city of Aberdeen from 1927 until 1969. For its time—at least back in the 1920s—it was a powerful firefighting machine, able to pump out 1,000 gallons of water per minute with its 130-horsepower engine. Its versatility contrasts sharply with "Old Tiger," a hand pumper that was manufactured in Boston in 1855 and shipped around Cape Horn to San Francisco where it was used before being purchased by the City of Salem then by the City of Astoria. In 1888, Aberdeen's treasurer arranged for the purchase of Old Tiger, along with 400 feet of hose. Since the old, brittle hose immediately broke into four-foot sections when it was unrolled for the first time, locals assumed the treasurer knew very little about fire equipment. It fought its last blaze in 1906, apparently with little success, because the Shannon rooming house the firemen were attempting to save burned to the ground.

Across the main gallery, the museum puts the spotlight on the role of churches in the town's early history, with a pulpit and several stained-glass windows from some of Aberdeen's early churches. Nearby is a large exhibit area dedicated to the local logging industry with dioramas of logging operations and the equipment used by loggers over the years. The exhibits include numerous explanations about how such things as a high lead cable system is used to move entire logs safely down mountainsides to waiting transports. There's a pair of logger's pants from 1914 and plenty of photos of old-growth logs being transported—one huge log at a time—on logging trucks.

There is much more here to see, including a barbershop, an auto repair garage, a 19th-century kitchen, a hand-cranked wooden-tub washing machine, and old business office and printing equipment. The museum has the Whiteside Funeral Chapel's (established 1880) elegant, horse-drawn hearse. For those who died, either in logging accidents—a frequent occurrence during the early years—or from old age, and could afford fancy transport to their final resting places, the hearse was the way to go out in style.

HOURS: November 1 through February 28, Tuesday through Saturday, 10 AM to 5 PM; March 1 through October 31, Tuesday through Saturday, 10 AM to 5 PM, Sunday, 12 PM to 4 PM

COST: Free but suggested donations: families, $2; individuals, $2; seniors, $1

LOCATION: 111 East Third Street, Aberdeen

PHONE: 360-533-1976

WEBSITE: www.aberdeen-museum.org

Aberdeen's 1926 Ahrens-Fox fire truck

9 World Kite Museum

WHAT'S HERE: **The history and accompanying collection of kites from around the world**

DON'T MISS THIS: **The World War II barrage kite**

Throughout its long history, the kite has served in wars, commerce, religion, celebration—and in making millions of people smile. Stroll through the World Kite Museum, located in kite-crazy Long Beach and you can't help but smile.

While today's kites are mostly playthings flown on breezy days at parks and beaches, the history of kites goes back a couple thousand years through many cultures and countries. While the inventor of the kite is unknown, kites were popular as long as 2,800 years ago in China where silk for both the cloth covering and the string was available. Bamboo, whose strength, combined with its light weight and flexibility, allowed for the construction of these wonderful flying devices. As with anything useful, whether for pleasure, business, or warfare, kite technology spread from Japan, Thailand, and Korea to India, North Africa, and even to Easter Island. Kites came to Europe a little later, but the first drawings of kites were printed in England and the Netherlands in the 17th century. Even America's Benjamin Franklin got into the kite act in 1750, proposing that a kite flown during a thunderstorm could extract electricity from the air. His theory was correct, and fortunately for him, he never attempted to prove his theory, at least not in the manner often depicted, or he likely would have received the last deadly shock of his life.

In 1826, Englishman George Pocock patented a kite-powered buggy, that unfortunately exists today only in drawings. The lightweight buggy was towed by a kite, although the driver had to remain alert for overhead trees and church steeples. Never destined to become a commercial success, Pocock did drive one of his Charvolants for 100 miles across the English countryside. Using two large kites, it was capable of reaching 20 miles per hour in his horseless carriage, allowing him to pass the mail coach, that era's fastest passenger conveyance. He passed the Duke of Gloucesters's royal coach, a breach of royal etiquette. What stopped him temporarily was the toll keeper who could not figure out what fee to charge his strange device, because tolls were based on the number of horses passing.

The museum is filled with amazing exhibits of kites from around the world. There are the World War II target kites that today are rare collector items. The museum features videos about the use of kites in World War II. The U.S. government commissioned Paul Garber to find

One of the museum's many fanciful kites

a way to teach Navy gunners to identify and shoot down enemy aircraft; he discovered that by using two strings he could control a kite, causing it to dive and dip just like real fighters. He painted pictures of Japanese aircraft on his kites and flew them for the gunners, training that proved much more practical than having sailors shoot at passing clouds. The museum also has a very large barrage kite that was flown over U.S. and British ship convoys, essentially setting up a flying minefield to defend against attacking enemy aircraft. The 2,000-foot-long piano wire that held the kites to the ships was strong enough to destroy a plane's wings.

The museum takes you through the rapidly changing design of newer kite shapes and the use of exotic materials that allows for highly maneuverable kites. There are photographs of large oceangoing freighters using huge kites to help pull them along, saving expensive fuel. And then there's Alexander Graham Bell's tetrahedral kite, which he developed for a kite contest at the 1904 Louisiana Purchase World's Fair in St. Louis, Missouri.

Walk over to the exhibits of Japanese, Chinese, and Korean kites and it is more like you have entered an Asian art museum. Their early kites were brightly painted with designs meant to frighten away evil spirits often for various religious purposes. In China, on a son's seventh birthday, his father made a special kite of woven straw. With as much string as he could find, the father flew the kite as high as possible, sending away any bad luck the boy might have. And in Asia they weren't shy about using kites to gain advantages during warfare. In the 1590s, Korean Admiral Yi Sun-sin flew kites that gave orders and other instructions to his armies in his seven-year war against Japan.

With many dozens of kites suspended on walls and overhead, it's almost dizzying walking through the museum. There are fuzzy hawk kites, frogs, hummingbirds, bugs, and bees, along with flying pigs and fish. There are even kites used for fishing.

The museum has stations for kids to make their own small kites, and since the museum is only a few blocks from the beach, there is almost always a breeze blowing, beckoning kite flyers.

The museum also has periodic kite design and building classes. Each year, the third full week of August is the International Kite Festival—a perfect time to visit Long Beach and the World Kite Museum.

HOURS: May through September, daily, 11 AM to 5 PM; October through April, Friday through Monday, 11 AM to 5 PM

COST: Adults, $5; seniors, $4; children, $3

LOCATION: 303 Syd Snyder Drive, Long Beach

PHONE: 360-642-4020

WEBSITE: www.worldkitemuseum.com

10 Columbia Pacific Heritage Museum

WHAT'S HERE: History of the Pacific Northwest

DON'T MISS THIS: The room-sized model of the Columbia River estuary

Nearly two centuries before there was a museum here, the Lewis and Clark Expedition camped on this site. Today, the museum highlights not only that expedition but the people who lived here before the first Americans passed through, as well as the many who followed.

Before the trappers and Lewis and Clark arrived, the Chinook Indians lived here, their rich culture easily sustained by ample food supplies and moderate albeit often rainy weather. Diseases that accompanied Euro-American explorers and trappers decimated the Chinook people, just as they had all Native American tribes. Because the Chinook and most tribes in the Pacific Northwest had well-established and regularly used trading routes, the deadly diseases were likely spread more quickly.

The museum's Exploration Gallery begins with the maritime explorers who came here in the late 18th century. It also looks at the 18 days that Lewis and Clark's Corps of Discovery spent in the area, including November 18 and 19, 1805, when Clark walked where the museum now sits. Near Ilwaco, one of the expedition members killed a California condor that was feeding on a beached whale. Other exhibits reveal the more recent history of Oregon's coastal communities. The 26-foot *Monomoy* surfboat built of oak and cedar was used as a training boat and served early rescue personnel along Ilwaco Beach (later named Klipsan Beach). There are lots of photographs of the boat in action through the decades. Inside the boat are the oars and life jackets from the 1940s, much different from today's bright orange vests. There is even an earlier cork life vest (circa 1904) displayed that once saved the life of local fisherman Clyde Woodham. Nearby is another rowing vessel, a 5.5-foot model of the *Sector*, the boat that Gérard d'Aboville rowed across the Pacific Ocean in 1991, starting in Japan and landing here in Ilwaco. The museum also has a video of his adventure that visitors can watch.

A narrow gauge railroad operated on the Long Beach Peninsula from 1889 to 1930. The museum's courtyard includes a rare clearlight passenger coach from the Ilwaco Railway & Navigation Company and the old Ilwaco freight depot. Walk inside the depot and you will be greeted by a 50-foot-long diorama of the peninsula as it appeared in 1925. And for model railroad buffs, the diorama includes a working N-scale model railroad. Being

Columbia Pacific Heritage Museum

located on the peninsula, the IR&N never connected directly with another rail line, so passengers and freight transferred to ferries to make further connections. Unfortunately, the two bays that surround the peninsula—Baker and Shoalwater—were so shallow that they could only be accessed at high tide. The changing tides therefore dictated the ferry and thus the railroad's schedule. IR&N gained nicknames such as the Clamshell Railroad and the Railroad that Ran by the Tide.

Since this is a coastal community, exhibits explore the whaling industry. There are also looms, period clothing, cranberry harvesting equipment, and a look at some of the local businesses such as the barbershop, tobacco shop, newspaper, and more.

HOURS: Tuesday through Saturday, 10 AM to 4 PM; Sunday, 12 PM to 4 PM. Closed Mondays from Labor Day until Memorial Day.

COST: Ages 18–54, $5; ages 55-plus, $4; ages 12–17, $2.50

LOCATION: 115 SE Lake Street, Ilwaco

PHONE: 360-642-3446

WEBSITE: www.columbiapacificheritagemuseum.org

11 Fort Columbia State Park

WHAT'S HERE: **Nearly intact historic coastal defense fort near the mouth of the Columbia River**

DON'T MISS THIS: **Views of the Columbia River**

The Columbia River proved to be a boon to Washington and Oregon commerce, but a headache for national defense purposes during the 19th and 20th centuries. Fort Columbia was the military's answer to defending the mouth of the great river from enemy ships that might choose to attack the U.S. In 1896, the new fort at Chinook Point became one of several coastal defense sites that were constructed. It added its coastal defense guns to those of nearby Fort Canby (now Cape Disappointment State Park), which was constructed originally during the Civil War in 1862, and of Fort Stevens on the Oregon side of the Columbia River. Today, little of Fort Canby remains, unlike Fort Columbia, much of which remains intact.

At the beginning of the 20th century, Fort Columbia became very active, mostly with soldiers training on their coastal defense guns. Since there was never any kind of enemy attack, either during World War I or World War II, the fort proved to be a relatively peaceful assignment for the soldiers here. There was one scare though. On June 21, 1942, a small Japanese submarine shelled the harbor defenses. With such incentive, and after being up all night, the following day the men of Battery C shot the highest scoring seacoast artillery practice round in the U.S.

Given the remoteness of the fort, living conditions were not too bad, even for the enlisted men. Food, including local fresh farm products, was trucked in, and during their off-duty time some soldiers played on the fort's baseball team, traveling to other military outposts and nearby towns for games. Musical entertainment was brought in, and on special occasions, girls from nearby towns were also brought on post for dances.

Twelve original buildings still stand and many have been restored, including the commanding officer's home. What you see in the home today is similar to what would have been here during the early 1900s, much of it donated by locals, others who actually lived in the home, and the military. The post's officers and their wives were not without luxuries. On exhibit is a set of gold-trimmed white Haviland china manufactured in Limoges, France. It had been presented to the wife of Captain F. W. Phisterer, the commanding officer of the 63rd Artillery, Coastal Artillery Corps from 1906 to 1909. Throughout the home you will see similar fine furnishings. In the master bedroom, Captain Phisterer's dress uniform is on display.

Since this was the commanding officer's home, he not only had to have accommodations for in-laws who might come to visit but also for visiting dignitaries, who often were officers coming here on inspection tours. The home's guest bedroom hosted such soldiers, including generals Dwight D. Eisenhower, Douglas MacArthur, and George C. Marshall, all early in their careers.

Wander through some of the other buildings for a look at how the enlisted soldiers lived here—as compared with commanding officer. There are numerous exhibits, including the enlisted men's bunk area (with beds made up military style), the barbershop, and the mess hall. During the early years, the three meals served here each day were family-style with the food placed on the table and everyone helping themselves. In later years the more modern serving line approach was adopted.

Throughout its relatively short history, the fort was constantly undergoing change. With the advent of World War II, some of the original buildings were moved, new structures constructed; the ordinance warehouse was converted to a theater, and the concrete gun emplacements made more sound. A couple of historic photos show one of the new gun sites after a gun carriage fell on it, severely damaging much of its intended support structure. The old concrete gun emplacements remain.

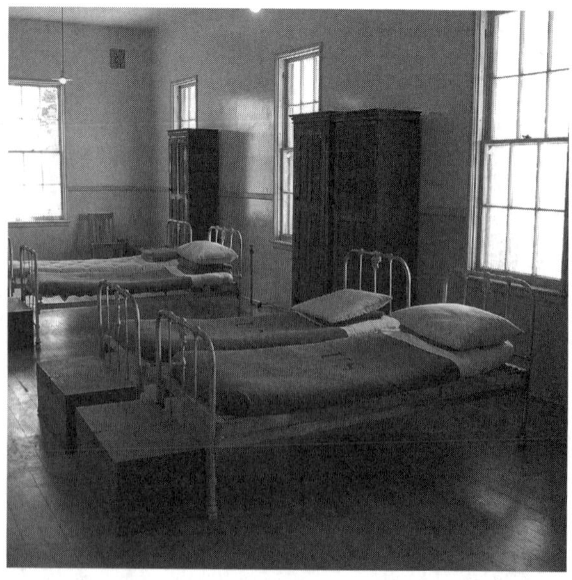

Fort Columbia's enlisted soldiers' barracks

The outside grounds, with the stark white buildings, appear much as they would have during the fort's operational years, without the soldiers, of course. Trails wind to the lower batteries below the main parking lot and down to the shore of the Columbia River. This is a day-use park with no camping facilities. Several of the restored military housing units are available for rent. Reservations can be made up to nine months in advance by calling 360-226-7688.

HOURS: Park: summer, daily, 6:30 AM to 9:30 PM; winter, 8 AM to 5 PM
Interpretive Center: July, 11 AM to 4 PM; August, 11 AM to 5 PM; September, 11 AM to 4 PM
Commanding Officer's House: August through Labor Day, Friday through Monday, 11 AM to 3 PM

COST: Free day-use

LOCATION: 2 miles west of the Astoria Bridge on U.S. 101, Chinook

PHONE: 360-642-3662 or 360-902-8844

WEBSITE: www.parks.wa.gov

Olympic Mountains and the Pacific Coast Tours

Maritime History Tour

ESTIMATED DAYS: 1–2
ESTIMATED DRIVING MILES: 2

Port Townsend is one of those charming little coastal towns that has something for everyone. There are plenty of antique shops, used bookstores, and quaint places for eating and drinking—and great views of Puget Sound and the ferry terminal. Its **Jefferson County Historical Museum** (page 173) is located in the historic City Hall building that was constructed in 1892. The museum looks at not only the local history ranging from undertakers to the red-light district but also the town's rich maritime history.

Uphill a few blocks away, the **Rothschild House** (page 176) provided its owner a panoramic view of the waterfront—and his maritime shipping and mercantile businesses. The home stayed in the family following their father's death in 1918, and it passed to Washington State Parks as a house museum following his daughter's death. The home and its furnishings are virtually unchanged from the time Emilie Rothschild died.

Another few blocks away, **Fort Worden State Park** (page 174) has retained much of the historic fort that was commissioned here in 1902. The fort's many historic buildings serve numerous purposes today. Some are open as vacation rentals, some are used for various meetings and conventions, and still others serve as museums and house museums. The Commander's Home is one of those that is a house museum, and just across the large parade grounds, another of the buildings serves as the Coast Artillery Museum filled with the fort's history.

Carriage at Jefferson County Historical Museum

Family/Kids' Fun Tour

ESTIMATED DAYS: 2–4
ESTIMATED DRIVING MILES: From 25 to about 130

Port Angeles is the Olympic Peninsula's largest city. From here you can see across the Strait of Juan de Fuca to Canada's picturesque city of Victoria, British Columbia, on the southeastern tip of Vancouver Island. It's also a place to catch a ferry over to Victoria—always a fun trip for adults and especially kids who can wander about the ferry, grab something good to eat, or play video games (but be sure you take valid passports with you). Head more than a few miles either south or west from Port Angeles and you will quickly find yourself in **Olympic National Park** (page 178). If you'd like even more spectacular views of British Columbia and the Olympic Mountains, drive up to the park's Hurricane Ridge. It's a mostly twisting road that seems to climb forever (about 25 miles) to the visitor center. Let the kids burn some energy by taking a short hike out along one of the ridges and you won't be disappointed with the views, the summer wildflowers, and the deer that often browse in the meadows.

If you drive west along U.S. 101 (yes, it does run east and west up here), about 30 miles away you will come to **Sol Duc Hot Springs** (page 180), also part of Olympic National Park. Stop at some of the pullouts along the road into the park to watch steelhead swimming upstream in the Sol Duc River. The historic site offers several hot mineral pools to soak tired, sore bodies and a cold pool for kids to use if the hot pools get to be too much. There are cabins and camping so you can stay longer than a day, but be sure to make reservations well in advance.

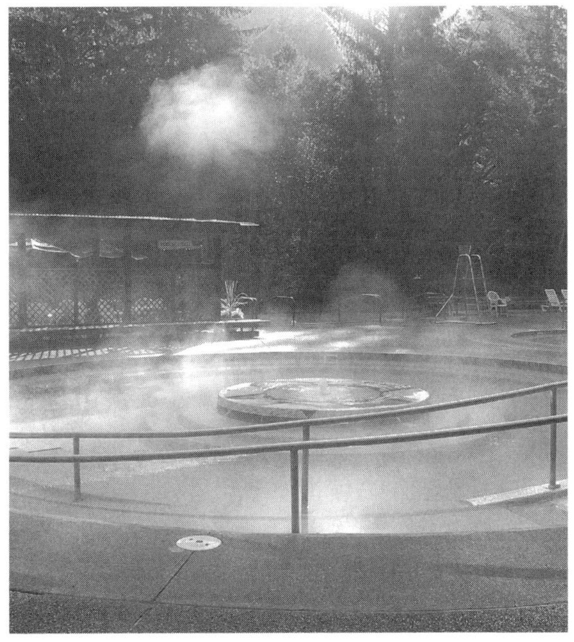

Hot mineral pool at Sol Duc Hot Springs

Head back to U.S. 101 and go west again. After about 15 miles, turn north onto Highway 113. Ten miles later head west again, but on Highway 112 toward Neah Bay, the westernmost point of land in the continental U.S. As you enter the small town, which is part of the Makah Indian Reservation, the **Makah Cultural and Research Center** (page 182) is on the left. It is well worth the time to visit. The museum houses Makah artifacts that are hundreds of years old—not just the stone points found everywhere but "soft" goods that were recovered from an Indian village buried in a massive slide in the 15th century. The museum does an excellent job of displaying and interpreting hundreds of artifacts from its even larger collection.

Afterward, continue driving into town. Whether you have your own boat or rent one at the docks, this is a great fishing spot, and kids are almost always guaranteed to catch fish. If you'd rather hike, continue on the main road and stop at the parking lot and then take the short hike out to that westernmost point of land. *Be careful not to leave anything of value visible in your car!*

Olympic Mountains and the Pacific Coast Information Centers

City of Port Townsend
www.enjoypt.com
360-385-2722

Olympic Peninsula Visitor Information
www.olympicpeninsula.org
800-942-4042

Long Beach Peninsula Visitors Bureau
www.funbeach.com
800-451-2542

Greater Puget Sound

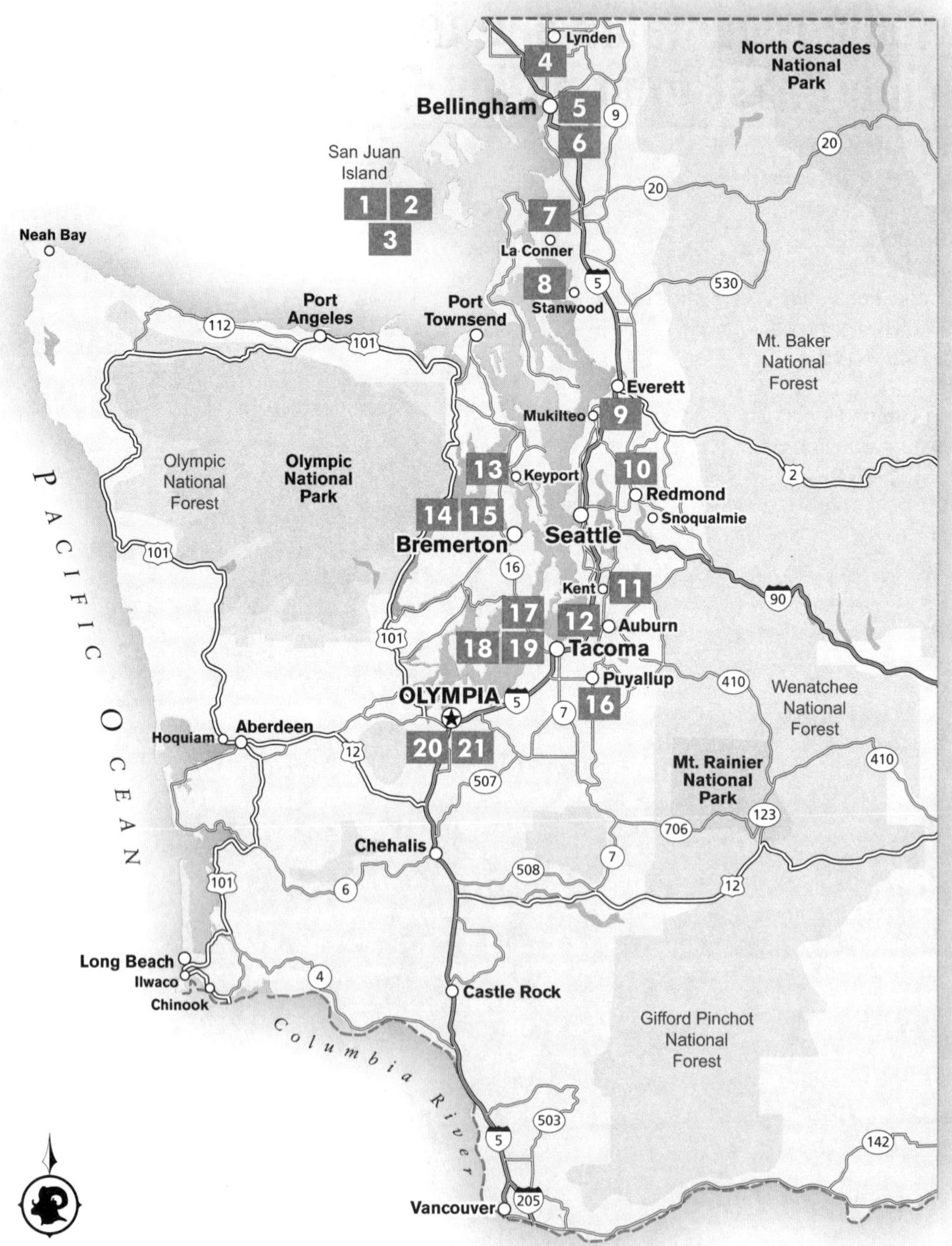

Lynden
North Cascades National Park
4
Bellingham
5
6
9
San Juan Island
1
2
3
20
7
Neah Bay
La Conner
5
530
8
Stanwood
Port Angeles
Port Townsend
112
101
Mt. Baker National Forest
Everett
Mukilteo
9
Olympic National Forest
Olympic National Park
13
Keyport
10
Redmond
2
14
15
Seattle
Snoqualmie
Bremerton
PACIFIC OCEAN
101
16
Kent
11
90
17
12
Auburn
101
18
19
Tacoma
Puyallup
410
Wenatchee National Forest
OLYMPIA
5
7
16
Hoquiam
Aberdeen
12
20
21
Mt. Rainier National Park
410
507
123
706
Chehalis
7
508
101
6
12
Long Beach
Ilwaco
Chinook
4
Castle Rock
Gifford Pinchot National Forest
Columbia River
503
5
142
205
Vancouver

Greater Puget Sound

Water is what the Puget Sound region is all about. From Native American dugout canoes to today's extensive ferry system, nuclear submarines, and weekend sailboats, water transportation has existed here for thousands of years. In 1792, George Vancouver named Puget Sound after one of his lieutenants, Peter Puget. Originally controlled by Great Britain through the Hudson's Bay Company, it became the property of the U.S. with the signing of the 1846 Oregon Treaty.

Puget Sound is a veritable maze of waterways and islands. Hood Canal, Whidbey Island, Tacoma Narrows, Admiralty Inlet, Kitsap Peninsula, Deception Pass, and more were scraped, carved, and molded by three different ice ages. The oldest glacier, during what is referred to as the Wisconsin Glacial Episode, formed 70,000 years ago, and the last ice age ended 10,000 years ago.

Washington State Capitol in Olympia

The area surrounding the Seattle metropolitan area is where the largest concentrations of Washington's population live. Many thousands of people live and work on the 15 prominent islands, from McNeil Island, where most residents are incarcerated in the state corrections center, to Bainbridge Island with its very busy ferry terminal. The U.S. Navy is also a prominent player with its naval shipyard at Bremerton.

Although far northern mainland towns such as Bellingham, along with the San Juan Islands, generally are not considered part of the greater Puget Sound, we have included them here for convenience. With Interstate 5 as the connector, it's a relatively short drive between Seattle, Bellingham, and the Canadian border. The island of Anacortes, the main ferry port to the San Juan Islands, is connected by bridge to the mainland.

Geology, geography, and politics created the San Juan Islands. The 450 islands in the San Juan Archipelago were formed by glaciers, but when the U.S. and Great Britain settled on a boundary in 1846, they forgot to specifically address the San Juan Islands. Confusion, mistrust, a murdered pig, and the resulting bloodless (except for the pig) Pig War, finally resulted in agreement on where the border should be—12 years later!

Today, of the 15 islands that have ferry service, nine are part of the Canadian Gulf Islands and six are part of the Washington State's San Juan Islands. San Juan Island is one of the most popular tourist destinations. Portions of the British and American forts that "battled" over the pig are here as part of San Juan Island National Historic Park. The island's Friday Harbor is a quiet town with lots of history, numerous restaurants, and many small shops.

Country roads are lightly traveled, though hilly, making for pleasurable bicycle riding. And there is always a chance to catch glimpses of the orcas, or "killer whales" as they are often called, plying the open waters or within easy sight of shoreline viewing points.

TRIVIA

1 Where can you learn more about a 1913, seven-horsepower Indian motorcycle that only cost $250 new?

2 Where can you see RCA's first AC-powered radio, built in 1926?

3 What museum and accompanying tour takes visitors through the world's largest building?

4 Where can you see an SRC, an ROV, and DSRV?

5 What is the name of the destroyer that came under attack in the Gulf of Tonkin, marking the official U.S. entry in the war against North Vietnam?

6 Where can you see a giant puppy named Leroy?

7 A large Tiffany chandelier is located inside the fourth-tallest masonry dome in the world, which is part of what historic building?

For trivia answers, see page 344.

1 San Juan Island National Historic Park

WHAT'S HERE: **The 19th-century camps built by the British and English as a result of the Pig War**

DON'T MISS THIS: **The 330-year-old bigleaf maple at English Camp**

What today is called the "Pig War" wasn't really a war between the U.S. and Great Britain, but it could have easily become one—and it all started over a pig. On June 15, 1859, Lyman Cutlar shot a pig that belonged to the Hudson's Bay Company. The pig had been rooting its way through his San Juan Island garden, and that didn't sit well with Cutlar. Unfortunately, that single act was the straw that nearly broke the camel's back as the U.S. and Great Britain had been bickering for 20 years about the boundary between Canada and the U.S. And even though the two countries had finally decided on the 49th parallel, they were still arguing over the San Juan Islands because the islands had not been specifically addressed in the treaty.

When British authorities threatened to arrest Cutlar, the U.S. Army, reacting to protect a U.S. citizen, sent troops under the command of Captain George Pickett to the island. Britain responded in-kind, sending three war ships to the island. The face-off took place on the Cattle Point peninsula and continued for three months. The confrontation eased with the arrival of U.S. Army Lieutenant General Winfield Scott. He helped negotiate a truce that essentially split the island with the Americans remaining at Cattle Point and the Brits establishing their camp on Garrison Bay, about 13 miles to the north. The resulting occupation lasted 12 years, ending only when Germany's Kaiser Wilhelm I was brought in as arbitrator and awarded the San Juan Islands to the U.S. In the end, the pig was the Pig War's only fatality.

Today, San Juan, Orcas, Shaw, and Lopez islands are the largest and the most heavily populated. Traveling to the islands on the ferry with a passenger vehicle costs about $40, in addition to $11 per passenger for the round-trip. If you decide to take bicycles, then it's $2 per bike plus about $11 per adult. If you're planning to bring your car, ferry reservations are highly recommended (www.wsdot.wa.gov/ferries).

Once on San Juan Island, getting to American Camp and English Camp, both part of San Juan Island National Historic Park, can be a challenge if you didn't bring your car or a bicycle. If you are on a bicycle, be aware that the ride from Friday Harbor to American Camp is six miles and from Friday Harbor to English Camp about nine miles—in opposite directions. And the island has a lot of

American Camp visitor center

hills, but if you aren't in a hurry and don't have young children riders, the bike ride is a lot of fun. Bikes can be rented at Friday Harbor (www.islandbicycles.com) as can mopeds, with taxis and shuttles also available. For more information on transportation contact the San Juan Island Chamber of Commerce (www.sanjuanisland.org).

A number of historic buildings remain at both sites. It's best to stop by each of the camps' visitor centers for maps, directions, and a list of activities and programs for the day. The visitor centers are only open during summer. English Camp features many more historic buildings that have survived the past century, including the original enlisted men's barracks, which is now the park's visitor contact station. English Camp is also adjacent to the shoreline where the British were able to easily supply their soldiers.

By the time Captain William Addis Delacombe arrived at English Camp with his wife in 1867, the camp was well established and reasonably comfortable. Not far from the shoreline, the captain decided to create a formal "Gardenesque-style" English garden that would help remind his wife of home. It also served a dual purpose of warning the enlisted men that they were trespassing on officer territory. The original garden has long since disappeared, but in 1972 it was recreated from historic photos and remains today. For panoramic views of the island and Vancouver Island, hike the 1.25 miles to the top of Young Hill; the short trail has an elevation gain of 650 feet, most during the last half mile, so take your time.

American Camp has several buildings, including the officers' quarters near the main parade ground. A self-guided walk from the visitor center leads to the remnant redoubt (earthen fortification) on a hillside overlooking the Strait of Juan de Fuca. The redoubt, requiring significant hand labor, was built under the direction of Lieutenant Henry M. Robert. The defensive positions were never completed and when finally abandoned, the soldiers nicknamed the site "Robert's Gopher Hole." Lieutenant Robert later gained fame when he created *Robert's Rules of Order*, an introduction to parliamentary law.

HOURS: American Camp Visitor Center is open year-round (call or check website to confirm times because there are seasonal changes). American Camp is generally open daily, year-round, from 8:30 AM to 4:30 PM. Closed on Christmas, New Year's Day, Memorial Day, and Thanksgiving.
English Camp is open from late May to early September only, 9 AM to 5 PM

COST: Free

LOCATION: American Camp: 6 miles southeast of Friday Harbor on Cattle Point Road
English Camp: 9 miles northwest of Friday Harbor on West Valley Road

PHONE: 360-378-2902 or 360-378-2240

WEBSITE: www.nps.gov/sajh

2 San Juan Historical Museum

WHAT'S HERE: **Century-old farmhouse, now San Juan Island's history museum**

DON'T MISS THIS: **The 1894 San Juan jail, condemned as Washington's worst jail in 1971**

The house that serves as the San Juan Historical Museum was built in 1894, and served as the James F. King home for more than 30 years. The King family farmed the 445 acres surrounding the home where they raised cattle and sheep and maintained orchards. During the 1930s the house changed hands and the new owners used it as a boardinghouse for young schoolteachers, as well as living here while they continued farming and dairy operations. In 1966, George Peacock, a retired Detroit teacher, purchased the home and donated it to the San Juan Historical Society.

The museum is filled with treasures collected mostly from families who have lived on San Juan Island for several generations. There are a couple of exhibits featuring a local gentleman named Jim Crook. He lived at the far end of the island and was likely one of the most self-sufficient farmers around. He came to the island in 1873 with his parents, traveling over the Oregon Trail. Crook remained here for his entire life, making do with whatever he could, growing his own food and making his own clothes from the wool of his sheep. Crook wanted an automatic carding machine used to process raw wool but couldn't afford the $20,000-plus catalog price tag, so he used the catalog's pictures as a guide and built his own from scrap metal and wood. The museum has one of his homemade suits, which looks more like it was made from a burlap sack.

There are numerous pieces of furniture in the museum, as well as several musical instruments. One is an 1895 Miller organ that was used in the island's Valley Church, and there is a circa 1880 Edisonphone that played cylindrical records—and several of the records accompanying the machine still have their original boxes with Thomas A. Edison's name and photograph prominently displayed.

The Kings constructed three structures in addition to their house—the carriage house, root cellar, and the milk house, where the dairy's milk processing took place. It holds a few artifacts, including a cream separator and old milk cans. Outside the stone root cellar is a large piece of rudder from the China clipper ship *America* that was built in 1874. By 1914 she had long been retired to barge duty when she ran aground, suspected of smuggling coal out to a German cruiser in the strait. Inside the root cellar are medical devices and various historical scenes of the island.

1894 James F. King home

The first San Juan County jail was built in 1894 for the grand total of $234.50. The diminutive jail was likely quite adequate for the time as there were few people living on the island at the end of the 19th century. It had served so well that it was still being used in 1971, when it was finally condemned, the inspecting authorities citing it as likely the worst jail in all of Washington State. It was moved to the museum grounds in 1981 and now has a few exhibits about some of the local lawmen, murderers, and their victims.

Another of the non-King era buildings is the large barn at the back of the property. The original barn burned to the ground in 1936 in what was described as an amazing nighttime event as flames filled the sky. Today's replacement barn is a storage facility for numerous pieces of equipment from a grain harvester to Jim Crook's wool picker, which processed the fibers in preparation for carding—a machine that Crook also made himself.

One final building not to miss is the log cabin, which was also moved to the museum site. It was originally built in the 1880s on a nearby homestead. Edward Scribner raised his family—all nine children—in this tiny home.

HOURS: Mid-April through October: Wednesday through Saturday, 10 AM to 4 PM, Sunday, 1 PM to 4 PM; November through early April: Open by appointment

COST: Adults, $5; seniors, $4; age 17 and younger, $3; families, $10

LOCATION: 405 Price Street, Friday Harbor

PHONE: 360-378-3949

WEBSITE: www.sjmuseum.org

3 The Whale Museum

WHAT'S HERE: **An in-depth look at the natural history of whales**

DON'T MISS THIS: **Full-sized whale models and skeletons suspended overhead**

Three pods of orcas live around Washington's San Juan Islands, and Friday Harbor's Whale Museum does a great job telling their story—along with the more complex story about the many species of whales found throughout the world. The museum's main floor is mostly a gallery and gift shop with some great educational materials and whale watching tools. Upstairs is where the main exhibit hall is located, with a theater that shows films about current whale-related research.

Walk upstairs and you enter a different world. With the blue-and-turquoise painting scheme covering the walls, ceiling, and stairs, you could easily imagine that you are entering the whales' domain. At the top of the stairs, Native American art and imagery cover the walls. In the main gallery, whale and dolphin skeletons are suspended from the ceiling in a room filled with dozens of exhibits. One exhibit explains the origin and geography of the Salish Sea, a name not found on most maps. It refers to the inland waterways that make up this northwest corner of North America, including the Strait of Juan de Fuca, Strait of Georgia, and Puget Sound. It was named after the first inhabitants of these lands.

More exhibits tell the story of the evolution of cetaceans (whales, dolphins, and porpoises), the only marine mammals that are fully aquatic and unable to live on land like seals and other similar sea mammals. The largest cetacean is the blue whale, which can reach 110 feet in length and weigh 200 tons. The smallest is the very rare vaquita porpoise that lives in the Sea of Cortez. It might reach 5 feet in length and weigh 110 pounds. Many whales travel thousands of miles during annual migrations between feeding areas and their birthing waters. They've evolved into sleek, albeit extremely large missiles for many, that allow for minimal amounts of energy to propel them forward. Cetaceans are the only fishlike creatures that have flukes—tails that are moved up and down instead of sideways.

There are two kinds of whales: those with teeth that eat small fish and squid and those without teeth. Instead, they have baleen, which are hundreds of long, narrow plates attached to their upper jaws that allow them to pass large quantities of sea water through their mouths and filter-feed mostly on krill and small crustaceans. The largest—the blue whale—is a baleen whale that can eat up to 40 million krill per day or about 8,000 pounds of the tiny animals. The biggest toothed whale is the sperm whale. The museum has a collection of sperm whale teeth, which generally grow only in the whale's lower jaw. Sperm whales can dive for more than two hours and as deep as one mile, and with up to 26 pairs of teeth they can easily catch large squid, although they'll settle for fish, octopus, or other such aquatic life.

Those with weak stomachs may want to bypass the brain exhibit that shows the various size relationships of whale, dolphin, and human brains. There's also a comparison of human, dolphin, and river otter skeletons. You can see the different species of lice and barnacles that attach themselves to whales, or listen to the amazing communication noises that whales make.

Since the waters surrounding the San Juan Islands are best known for the three pods of Orca, or "killer whales" as they are commonly called, there is a large amount of information here about their tracked histories. Included are identifying photos of the numerous members of the J, K, and L pods as they are known within the scientific community that tracks them. The museum is a great place to find the best Orca-watching places around the islands, one of which is at Lime Kiln Point State Park on the western side of San Juan Island. Whales sometimes come within a few dozen yards of the shore, and even when farther offshore, it is a thrill to see a six-foot-tall

Whale skeletons in the main gallery

dorsal fin breaking through the water's surface, or even better several members of a pod breaching or spy-hopping.

The museum exhibits also touch on seal hunting, both the commercial and often controversial seal-taking that has been allowed in Canada and the history of Native American hunting. The exhibits include seal skin clothing used by northern Indians and a look at the products that come from seals.

HOURS: July and August, daily, 9 AM to 6 PM; March through June and September through October, daily, 10 AM to 5 PM. Call ahead for winter hours.
COST: Adults, $5; students and seniors, $1; families, $5
LOCATION: 62 First Street, Friday Harbor
PHONE: 360-378-4710 or 800-946-7227
WEBSITE: www.whalemuseum.org

4 Lynden Pioneer Museum

WHAT'S HERE: **An expansive collection of Lynden's history**
DON'T MISS THIS: **The horse-drawn wagon collection**

The museum's street-front brick facade, although attractive and interesting, does not adequately ready visitors for what is inside. This is one of the largest and best county museums you will find in Washington. One of the first things you will see is a life-sized farmstead with its barn and portions of the farmhouse, including the necessary outhouse. The barn's doors are open and the flood of old farm equipment and tools—from plows to pitchforks—is spread out for easy viewing. Interpretive panels accompany this and the other exhibits, in this case explaining the process of growing crops, from plowing to harvesting.

The farmhouse kitchen includes the wood-burning stove, icebox, a set table, as well as many of the 19th and early 20th-century kitchen gadgets used to create meals meant for hard-working farmers. The Victorian parlor is accompanied by an explanation about its use—a meeting place for neighbors and friends—and also about how a proper Victorian woman should act:

> While walking down the street, her feet should be moderately turned out; steps should be equal, firm, and light. Proper young ladies do not wear cosmetics. Unmarried women under the age of thirty must be accompanied by a chaperone—a married woman—whenever in public. Ladies should never speak loudly or laugh

boisterously. Ladies should go quietly along, seeing and hearing nothing that they should not.

Contrasting with the Victorian home is the log cabin, its walls covered with newspapers, its tiny bed draped with an old quilt, and simple children's toys.

Wander deeper into the museum and you will see the Fred K. Polinder wagon collection. Polinder arrived in the area in 1901 at the age of 12. Witnessing the advent of steam-powered farm equipment, airplanes, and automobiles, he missed the old horse-drawn wagons so much that he began collecting them. Most of his extensive collection was either destroyed or damaged in a fire, but over several years he meticulously restored each of his prized wagons. In 1975, he donated his extensive collection to the city of Lynden for safe keeping.

Most of the horseless carriages in Polinder's collection look as though they just came off a showroom floor. And accompanying most are signs explaining what they are, who they belonged to—and, for some, what kind of automobile ultimately replaced them. The Black Coach was a very elegant coach with deluxe additions such as mud flaps and even rubber tires. It served the well-to-do merchants and others who could afford such luxury. One of the more curious is the English hunting cart that originally was owned by Elbridge Amos Stuart, founder of the Carnation Evaporated Milk Company located in Carnation, Washington. It has different hubs with offset spokes, and there is a back door under the seat for hunting dogs. The 1880 red carriage (Red Rover) was a passenger carriage designed for those with money. It featured a special fold-down step, a glass-enclosed cabin for passengers, the finest springs possible, and even a light for night driving. There are other work wagons, including a heavy dray, a gasoline delivery wagon, and a milk wagon.

The museum's collection moves forward with automobiles from the 1920s and '30s. Lynden's first fire truck is here, a 1929 Reo, and there is a 1926 Studebaker club coupe, along with a 1913, seven-horsepower Indian motorcycle that sold originally for $250. Gas-powered vehicles required repair shops—and the museum has an auto repair shop complete with all the wall advertisements, tools, products, a cash register, and even a gas pump needed to get the car and motorcycle here back in top running condition.

Since this was a farming community, there is plenty of farm equipment, from tractors and a real threshing machine, to a steam tractor, one of the earliest powered vehicles used on farms. These smoke-spewing beasts so frightened horses that they were often required by local laws to have a team of horses pulling them on public roads to reassure oncoming horses that all was okay, even though their top speed was perhaps three miles per hour.

Step deeper into this expansive museum and you will encounter a military area with old uniforms and a World War II military Indian motorcycle that was used

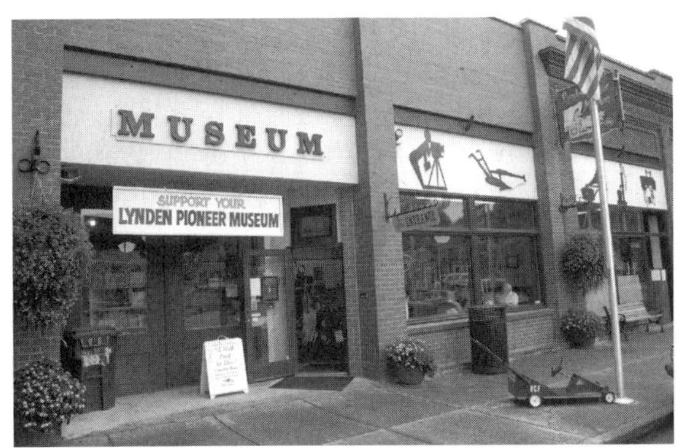

Lynden Pioneer Museum

in Holland during the French Liberation. There is a chicken egg incubator, egg sorter, and even a 1950s-era soda fountain.

Then when you think you're about finished, there's Lynden's historic business district from around 1900, which includes 26 different stores, shops, and service providers. Walk down the street past the drugstore, millenary shop, department store, and more. They are filled with merchandise that they would've had for sale back in the early 1900s. And there's even an upstairs to the town, along with part of a church with the stained glass from a local church, and a funeral home with a coffin. There's a barbershop (although the sign says closed) and the dentist's office of Ralphy H. Huey.

Plan to spend a couple of hours here, especially if you can get one of the "old-timers" who work here as docents to give a personal tour. Their personal stories about the old days of Lynden are priceless.

HOURS: Monday through Saturday, 10 AM to 4 PM; Sunday, 1 PM to 4 PM
COST: Adults, $7; students and seniors, $4
LOCATION: 217 Front Street, Lynden
PHONE: 360-354-3675
WEBSITE: www.lyndenpioneermuseum.com

5 Whatcom Museum

WHAT'S HERE: **Four different museums clustered in the city's museum complex**
DON'T MISS THIS: **Touring the Whatcom Museum's Old City Hall Building**

The largest and most impressive of the city's four-museum complex is certainly the Old City Hall Building. As the town's original city hall, it was born from controversy and funding shortages, and in 1962 it was partially destroyed by fire. Constructed in 1892, this city hall looks nothing like most city halls. The large Victorian building, with its central clock and bell tower and the four corner cupolas, each four stories tall, is highlighted by the gray Chuckanut sandstone trim that contrasts so nicely with the red brick walls. Its duties as city hall ended in 1939, and after escaping the wrecking ball, it became an official city-funded museum.

The restoration and the interior remodeling following the fire turned many of the original city hall offices into the larger open galleries of today's museum of art and cultural treasures. Some of the more elaborate original features remain, including the rich maple-paneled hallway on the first floor, the cedar doors, the oak and mahogany balustrade, and the iron columns in the second floor's main gallery.

The museum is a wonderful collection of everything from woodworking tools to fine art, all expertly displayed. For woodworking buffs, while many museums exhibit dozens of old hand tools, here the tools are accompanied by partially completed pieces that demonstrate how the tools were used and what they contributed to the construction of fine furniture. From beading planes to backsaws, there's plenty to see. And even if you aren't a woodworker, you can't help but be impressed by the wood-paneled walls and staircases found throughout the museum.

The fine art galleries feature important works by Northwest artists, including paintings by 19th- and 20th-century artists such as Sidney Laurence, James Everett Stuart, Mark Tobey, Philip McCracken, Helmi Juvenon, and Wesley Wehr. Many pieces are periodically rotated and new temporary art exhibits are featured during the year.

Since this is a Victorian building, it is only right that there be examples of Victorian home furnishings from the 19th century. A fully-furnished parlor and bedroom are presented, and their luxury contrasts sharply with the old homestead cabin exhibit showing bare-minimum living standards that were likely more common, especially in areas outside the main cities. Not to be excluded, there are several exhibits showing the traditional ways of the Native Americans of the region, groups that spoke some 40 different languages. Baskets, boats, and more illustrate the rich cultures that flourished in these lands for thousands of years.

For more than a century the logging industry has been the primary mover and shaker of industry in the Pacific Northwest, so it's only right that they be included in the museum's exhibits—and they are. As many as six different mills dotted Bellingham Bay in 1925. That rich history is included in part with dioramas that represent different periods of logging, from those mid-19th-century days of broad-bit axes and mules dragging logs from the woods to the more recent transporting of logs via trains, trucks, and balloons. The exhibits also include numerous historic photos depicting life in the lumber camps.

The Whatcom Museum Campus includes three additional museums within a block of the city hall museum. One block east, the newest addition includes a spacious art museum and a children's museum with its family interactive gallery. The ARCO Exhibits Building is just across the street from the city hall museum. Its 3,000-square-foot gallery is used to showcase the works of contemporary artists of local and national prominence.

1892 city hall, now a museum

Next door, the Syre Education Center has both classroom space and permanent exhibits focused on the Northwest. The Children's Hour exhibit features 19th- and early 20th-century children's toys from dolls to trains. Another exhibit features the birds of Washington. With such diversity of climate and landscape, from rain-swept ocean beaches to snow-covered volcanoes, there is great diversity among the bird species—and you can see many of them here. From peregrine falcons, bald eagles, and barn owls to pheasants, avocets, and sandpipers, there are dozens of examples to help you better identify birds in the wild.

HOURS: Tuesday through Sunday, 12 PM to 4 PM
COST: Free
LOCATION: 121 Prospect Street, Bellingham
PHONE: 360-778-8930
WEBSITE: www.whatcommuseum.org

6 American Museum of Radio and Electricity

WHAT'S HERE: **More than 2,000 artifacts related to the history of radio and electricity**
DON'T MISS THIS: **Archie Frederick Collins's wireless telephone from 1909**

The museum is filled with technology that is fun, even for nontechie types because so much of what's here, in one form or another, has always been part of our lives. The museum begins with exhibits about 17th- and 18th-century experiments with electricity. Although not often exhibited, the museum has a first edition of William Gilbert's (1544–1603) *De Magnete*, published in 1600. The book was the first to explore electricity using scientific methods. The book coined the word *electrica* for the attraction created when amber or other substances were rubbed, creating what we know today to be static electricity. Gilbert also created the very first electrical measuring device he called the Versorium. His day job was serving as Queen Elizabeth I's personal physician. Other exhibits include a look at the Leyden jar, discovered in 1745, that allowed static electricity to be stored for research purposes, as well as Benjamin Franklin's experiments proving that lightning was indeed electricity.

The exhibits move on to the wireless age of radio, circa 1818 to 1920. There is a small device identical to the one used by Heinrich Hertz when he became the first to send and receive radio waves, proving their existence in 1864. Hertz's name is forever attached to the measurement of radio and audio frequencies. Fans of old ocean liners will be interested in the recreated *Titanic's* wireless room; it is as close to how the original appeared, though the original has been at the bottom of the Atlantic Ocean since 1912.

Many early radios—not much more than cylinders wrapped with copper wire—demonstrate the advancement of radio technology leading up to World War I. Although still very primitive, being nothing more than on/off Morse code devices, the military's dabbling in radios began the road to replacing carrier pigeons, smoke signals, and human runners in future wars.

Another of the museum's curiosities—and the only one known to exist in the world—is a Collins wireless phone from 1909. Archie Frederick Collins invented what was supposed to be a long-distance wireless telephone, a primitive predecessor to today's cell phones. Even though he won awards for his invention and it worked over short distances, Collins ended up in prison. His business partners (possibly with his knowledge, but no one is certain) significantly exaggerated the phone's long-distance capability in an attempt to increase the company's stock value.

During the 19th century, people everywhere wanted music in their homes. If they lacked a piano or other such instrument, the next best thing often was the era's version of a music box, one that allowed the playing of different melodies. The museum has many working examples. One is the Criterion music box, manufactured between 1890 and the 1920s, with an advertisement claiming that it furnished the "Sweetest Music Ever Heard." The museum also has an amazing collection of other music-making machines, including early Edison phonographs. The old recorded cylinders may reproduce and play scratchy, low fidelity music, but that they even still work at all is amazing.

One of the special time radio receivers that told its recipient the correct Paris time is displayed in the museum. When the Eiffel Tower in Paris was completed in 1889 for the World's Fair, it was decided that the tower would not be dismantled afterward, but that it would be required to serve some beneficial purpose. A radio transmitter was placed on top that broadcasted time signals, essentially the very first community timekeeping device in the world.

A curious and fun sound transmitting machine in the museum is the Victor Theramin. It's one of 500 made in 1929. Wave the handheld wand in different configurations and speeds, and you can create varying sounds of weird electronic music. Another of the more curious devices is what amounts to the first self-contained home movie player. A concealed projector projects a silent film onto a pop-up white screen, all of which is contained inside a single cabinet. The film provided a cue at its beginning, warning the viewer to turn on the phonograph recording that then roughly synched sound with the movie. Within a short time someone figured out how to attach a sound track directly to a strip of movie film, ending this projector's useful life.

A small sampling of the radio collection

During the first years of broadcast, radios in the U.S. were powered by DC current, essentially batteries. With the advent of AC electricity being made available on a wider scope, RCA manufactured the first AC-powered radio in 1926—and, of course, that very first radio is in the museum's collection. From that point, everyone had to have a radio. Along the museum's wall there are dozens of antique radios, the kinds that Americans used to listen to music, plays, and President Franklin D. Roosevelt's famous fireside chats in the 1930s and 1940s.

These old radios used lots of vacuum tubes. The museum's collection includes 30,000 tubes, along with a few of the old tube testers. Some of the oldest and most curious are on display. The museum staff occasionally does repairs on tube radios for the public. And with all this radio technology at hand, the museum operates its own low-power community radio station in Bellingham, KMRE 102.3 FM.

HOURS: Wednesday through Saturday, 11 AM to 4 PM
COST: Adults, $5; under age 12, $2
LOCATION: 1312 Bay Street, Bellingham
PHONE: 360-738-3886
WEBSITE: www.amre.us

7 La Conner Quilt and Textile Museum

WHAT'S HERE: **Extensive collection of quilts exhibited in a 19th-century Victorian home**
DON'T MISS THIS: **The mural painted in the home's cupola**

This Victorian mansion has its own patchwork history. It began when George and Louisa Gaches built this three-story Victorian home in 1891. George and his brother James operated a local mercantile and shipped hay and grain from the nearby Swinomish flats. Deciding to move to Seattle, the Gaches sold their home sometime around 1900 to Dr. G. E. Howe who turned it into a small hospital. It changed hands again in 1909, becoming the home of L. W. and Julia Vaughn.

In 1940, Louise Bettner acquired the home in a sheriff's sale and once again the Victorian changed uses, becoming the Castle Apartments. It changed owners at least one more time before a fire destroyed much of the third floor in 1973. The following year the newly formed La Conner Landmarks, a nonprofit group, borrowed money and purchased the fire-gutted mansion. After its restoration, it initially housed the Valley Museum of the

Northwest. In 1997, the La Conner Quilt and Textile Museum rented the Victorian mansion; they purchased the grand building in 2005 for their permanent home and museum.

The La Conner Quilt and Textile Museum is one of only a handful of museums in the U.S. dedicated to the art and craft of quilt making. What makes the museum fun, even for those who aren't that enthusiastic about quilts, is the ever-changing exhibits. About every eight weeks new quilts, from the museum's permanent collection and from local, national, and international quilt and textile artists, are hung throughout the museum's three floors. Most of the quilts shown are from contemporary quilters, but others are much older examples of the craft.

There remains a sense of the home's history as you wander around looking at the numerous quilts. Part of that is helped by the photos of the Gaches family, several more of the home during various times in its history, and a spectacular image of the mansion while it burned in 1973. Though not having anything to do with history or the Victorian's roots, the interior of the cupola was painted in 1978 by then 22-year-old-student Craig Bartlett. He had just returned to college in Washington State after a one-year study visit to Sienna, Italy. The white clouds on the blue-sky background are reminiscent of Italy. Craig eventually moved to Los Angeles where he works as a writer, director, and producer of animation for television and film.

The second and third floors are used for additional gallery space for the dozens of quilts that are exhibited here at any one time. The stairs are a little narrow and steep—a throwback to their late 19th-century design—but well worth negotiating to the upper levels.

The museum presents several programs and special events each year. The three-day quilt festival in September is the biggest event of the year—and also their biggest fundraiser. There is also the Textile Enrichment Series, an educational program designed for all ages. It includes a series of workshops and other presentations by exhibiting artists and world-renowned quilt and textile instructors.

The 1891 Gaches Mansion

HOURS: Wednesday through Sunday, 11 PM to 5 PM. Closed January 1–16 and major holidays.
COST: Adults, $5; under age 12, free when accompanied by an adult
LOCATION: 703 S. 2nd Street, La Conner
PHONE: 360-466-4288
WEBSITE: www.laconnerquilts.com

8 D. O. Pearson House

WHAT'S HERE: **Historic Victorian home built by the town's first mayor**
DON'T MISS THIS: **The Floyd Norgaard Cultural Center next door**

D. O. Pearson built his Victorian home with its mansard roof in about 1890—historical records are a little vague on the exact date. He arrived in the area in 1866 with his mother and sister where they met his father and two older sisters who had preceded them from their home in Massachusetts. Two years later, 19-year-old Clara Stanwood traveled from her home in Lowell, Massachusetts, and soon after her arrival here, she and Pearson married.

Pearson initially farmed land on Whidbey Island, Washington, but in 1877, he leased land in nearby Centerville at the mouth of the Stillaguamish River. He constructed a wharf, warehouse, and store, even though Centerville hadn't yet become a regular steamboat stop. Pearson also took over the job of postmaster—actually he was the seventh postmaster in seven years—and when his superiors requested that he change the name of Centerville to something less common, he named his town Stanwood, after his wife.

His business ventures proved successful as his store and warehouse met the growing needs of the nearby logging camps, shingle mills, and farmers who could use his wharf to ship wood products, oats, and hay to outside markets. Pearson was successful enough financially and known well enough locally that he became involved in politics, running in the 1890 election for state representative. He lost, although he was elected mayor in 1903 when the town was incorporated.

But changes were coming to Stanwood. The following year the Seattle & Montana Railway (later named the Great Northern Railroad) laid tracks within a mile of Stanwood as it headed north from Seattle. With a partner, Pearson attempted to take advantage of the new railroad by selling nearby land parcels, but the Panic of 1893—caused in part by railroad overbuilding and shaky financing schemes—caused his efforts to fail. In 1898, the Klondike gold strikes attracted many of Stanwood's men north. Some of those who managed to strike it rich returned to their small Washington hometown where they purchased land and built new businesses.

By 1906, Pearson had built his third store, moving it away from his riverfront property because the area had become industrialized with too much noise, smoke, and pollution for his liking. In 1910, Pearson's wife Clara died; Fred Pearson, the couple's third son, joined his father as a business partner. When fire destroyed Fred's home in 1920, he and his family moved into the Pearson mansion. D. O. Pearson died in 1929, and Fred continued to manage the store until his own death in 1954.

The 1890 home is well furnished; however, most of the furnishings come from other pioneer families. There are a few exceptions such as the floral-print rocker that D. O. Pearson used and the Civil War–era drum that also belonged to him. The kitchen was one of the home's rooms that was redone over the years, so the wood-burning stove that currently occupies space there is not original. Yet the Pearsons may well have used a stove very similar to this in the years following the home's completion.

As you tour the upstairs bedrooms, you will see kids' toys, baby cribs, musical instruments, and many more historic items that families, whose local roots go back several generations, have donated. One of the most useful items is the white porcelain hot water bottle found on one of the beds that surely warmed feet during cold winter nights.

The Floyd Norgaard Cultural Center is located behind the main home and is used for special temporary exhibits, many tied to the history of Stanwood. It also has an area where a 19th-century kitchen has been reconstructed and filled with kitchen tools from that era. Since all of the things here are not part of the museum's historic artifacts, kids (and adults) are encouraged to try their hands using some of those early kitchen gadgets, including hand-powered mixers and apple peelers and slicers.

HOURS: Sunday, Wednesday, and Friday, 1 PM to 4 PM
COST: Free, but donations accepted
LOCATION: 27108 102nd Avenue NW, Stanwood
PHONE: 360-629-6110
WEBSITE: www.sahs-fncc.org/sahsplaces.html

Interior of the D. O. Pearson mansion

9 Future of Flight Aviation Center and Boeing Tour

WHAT'S HERE: **A museum of Boeing aircraft technology and history, plus the option of touring the production facility**

DON'T MISS THIS: **The tour through the Boeing aircraft production facility, the largest building in the world**

This is actually two separate facilities. The first is a museum that features primarily a history of Boeing and a look at some of the aircraft engine innovations the company has developed over the years. The second and more fascinating part is a tour through the actual Boeing aircraft production and assembly facility. At 472 million cubic feet, it is the largest building in the world. If you decide to take the Boeing tour (an additional fee), you will be assigned a tour time. Since the theater (the first stop) can accommodate 240 people, the wait usually isn't long enough to spend much time in the Future of Flight Aviation Center. The tour requires about one-third mile of walking, including a couple of stairways, and an elevator ride. You can return following the factory tour.

Your first stop will be the theater for an introductory film about Boeing. The company is now beginning work on its newest airplane, the Boeing 777 Dreamliner. The film shows a time-lapse assembly of a complete 777, a fascinating process that includes subcontracted work to companies with manufacturing facilities in several different countries. The "parts"—tail assemblies, cockpits, fuselages, wings, etc.—are flown in from wherever in the world they are built, and essentially bolted together at the Boeing plant. It's a bit more complicated than that, especially the final assembly, but Boeing has significantly and successfully redesigned Henry Ford's original assembly line production process for something a lot bigger than a Model T Ford.

Following the film you will board a bus for a short drive across Washington's only privately owned freeway overcrossing to the assembly plant. Off the bus and down a short stairway, you enter the bowels of the facility, the belowground half-mile-long service access hallways that allow for maintenance of water, fuel, power, and other required resources without interrupting the production process above. Board an elevator and head up to the overhead walkways for a bird's-eye view of the entire production facility. The guides will explain everything as you go, including how Boeing's modified assembly line process is put to work here. Below you will see a series of Boeing 777s or 737s in various stages of dress as wings, engines, fuselages, wiring, seats, and the remainder of the 3 million required rivets and fasteners are

The Boeing aircraft production facility

applied. The planes are marked as to which airline is purchasing what jet so that any of the dozens of required options that can be ordered are assured of making it into the right aircraft.

For the Boeing 777, about every three days a new plane rolls out of the assembly plant and onto the tarmac outside. Each new aircraft is towed across that same freeway overcrossing that your tour bus came over and into the paint shop in order to receive its official colors and logos before test flights are begun and the new owners take possession. The freeway crossing is scheduled for nonpeak traffic hours so as not to disrupt commuter traffic flows by gawkers confused at seeing a big jet driving on the road a few feet above their heads.

The Boeing factory tour requires that you leave backpacks, purses, cell phones, cameras, and food behind. While you can leave such items locked in your car, there is a computerized locker system that allows you to lock your valuables in the lobby. It costs $1 and assigns you a locker, but it can take several minutes to get one if the plant is busy. Kids, at least four feet tall, are allowed on the tour. Restrooms are not available on the one-hour tour.

The bus will return you to the Future of Flight Aviation Center where you can spend more time perusing the exhibits, including jet engines and, for the daydreaming kid in all of us, a cockpit that you can sit in. Meant mostly for kids, there is a computer terminal where you can design your aircraft. Nearby is the two-passenger XJ5 flight simulator, although an extra fee is charged for this. And don't miss taking either the stairs or the elevator upstairs to the observation deck for great views of the Paine Field runway and the Cascade Range in the distance.

HOURS: Daily, 8:30 AM to 5:30 PM. Boeing tours begin at 9 AM with the last tour at 3 PM. Closed Thanksgiving, Christmas, and New Year's Day. Closes early on Christmas Eve and New Year's Eve.

COST: Adults, $15; ages 65-plus and active military, $14; ages 15 and under, $8. Must be at least four feet tall for the factory tour.
Gallery only (no Boeing factory tour): Adults, $9; ages 6–15, $4; under age 6, free

LOCATION: 8415 Paine Field Blvd., Mukilteo, approximately 30 miles north of Seattle

PHONE: 888-467-4777 or 800-464-1476 for Boeing tour information and reservations

WEBSITE: www.futureofflight.org

10 Microsoft Visitor Center

WHAT'S HERE: **History of personal computing, focused on Microsoft**

DON'T MISS THIS: **The newest software products, including games, are available to try out**

Microsoft has traveled a long and very successful road since its founding in 1975. To document and share that road, the company that boasts subsidiary offices in more than 100 countries and regions from Algeria to Zimbabwe has a facility open to the public that is part visitor center, part software promotion, and part museum. And while much of the center is a high-tech delight, many of the exhibits aren't much different from any other museum.

For those who can remember the 1970s, the first of the time line exhibits will bring back pleasant memories—or maybe a hearty "thank you" that we no longer have to rely on that decade's technology. Analog was the name of the game, and the exhibits include examples of that old technology, from a reel-to-reel tape recorder and movie projector to the eight-track tape, an LP by Bonnie Rait, and reggae artist Jimmy Cliff's psychedelic album cover, *The Harder They Come*. If you could flip through the pages of the museum's copy of *Life* magazine's *The 70s* issue, it would reveal a lot more about life in the 1970s.

Obviously computers are the focus of much of the exhibits. An Altair 8800 computer holds a key position in the exhibit—and it even includes the programmer's instruction manual. To refresh old memories, in 1975, the Altair 8800 was advertised in magazines such as *Popular Electronics* as a kit computer for hobbyists. The designers expected to sell hundreds but instead sold thousands. Coincidently, it was based on the Intel 8080 CPU, and the 8800's first programming language was Altair BASIC, Microsoft's founding product.

As the story goes, when Microsoft cofounders Bill Gates and Paul Allen saw the advertisement in *Popular Electronics*, they contacted the Altair 8800's company founder Ed Roberts and asked if he would be interested in an "interpreter" they were developing. Not having actually developed an interpreter, Gates and Allen quickly modified an earlier programming effort and surreptitiously tested their new product on Harvard's PDP-10 computer. They never had an opportunity to test their punched-tape program on an Altair computer. As the plane landed in Albuquerque for their demonstration appointment, Allen was still writing program code. It wasn't until the actual demonstration when they discovered that their little 4K program worked on the Altair 8800. And as they say, "The rest is history." Today we com-

Inside the Microsoft Visitor Center

plain about support after purchasing a product; that first programmer's manual included a note that stated if you had any questions you could call the program's creators (Gates and Allen)—and it provided their phone numbers.

Technology took off after people realized the potential market for personal computers. Radio Shack was an early leader with its TRS 80 Micro Computer System. The early models looked like nothing more than a keyboard plugged into a small television set. For the Apple followers there is also a Macintosh in the time line. Introduced in 1984, it was the first personal computer to use a mouse and a graphic interface rather than the IBM PC's command line interface—making it much more user friendly. The introduction of Microsoft Windows in late 1985 competed directly with and dominated the Mac operating system. To this day, people argue about which one is better.

Microsoft quickly enhanced their Windows operating system with the introduction of business software, beginning with Word and Excel. The exhibits include packaging for many of its subsequently released software packages such as Windows 95 and photos of Bill Gates throughout the years of Microsoft's development and growth. And Microsoft's entertainment software is not ignored. From X-BOX to Movie Maker, there is something for everyone—and you can even try them in one of the several stations available for visitors.

HOURS: Monday through Friday, 9 AM to 7 PM

COST: Free

LOCATION: 15010 NE 36th Street, Microsoft Campus, Building 92, Redmond
Check website directions. The campus building numbering system can be confusing for first-time visitors.

PHONE: 425-703-6214

WEBSITE: www.microsoft.com/visitorcenter

11 Kent History Museum and Bereiter House

WHAT'S HERE: Historic early 20th-century home and museum

DON'T MISS THIS: Copy of the 13th Census of the U.S. (1910) that identifies all who lived in the home, including servants

The Kent Historical Society has established its headquarters in this 3,500-square-foot home that Emil Bereiter built in 1908. Bereiter was part owner of the Covington Lumber Company, and the home he built reflected his wealth at the time. As Kent's mayor in 1912, Bereiter lived here only a short time. Someone working for his lumber company stole a large amount of money and headed south. Bereiter, intent on retrieving what was rightfully his, pursued the thief, but lost him somewhere in California. While there, Bereiter became ill and returned home, but he never recovered, dying in 1914.

In later years, Kent's once grandest home passed to the ownership of Japanese-American Ernest K. Saito. The Saito family owned the White River Packing Company where locally grown lettuce was packed and shipped. The day following the bombing of Pearl Harbor, the F.B.I. interrogated Mr. Saito about his loyalty. Ultimately, he was cleared of any treasonous activities but was still sent to one of several Japanese internment camps after President Franklin D. Roosevelt issued his *Executive Order 9066* in February 1942. The order, among other things, prohibited West Coast Japanese and Japanese-Americans from owning property. Saito transferred title of his home to his stepdaughter Thelma, the daughter of his Caucasian wife. The museum has on display copies of the declassified 1942 F.B.I. notes and orders regarding the detention of Mr. Saito. A photograph shows Thelma Saito, in a better time, with her attendants after having been crowned Miss Lettuce Queen during the 1935 Annual Lettuce Festival.

The City of Kent purchased the home in 1996 and began restoration and renovations, readying it to serve the public as a museum. During that same time, Stuart Nakamura began work on a public art piece entitled *Another Place, Another Time*. It is located on the outside lawn, just to the side of the main home. It honors the local history of the Japanese-Americans, recognizing the national tragedy of *Executive Order 9066* that sent 110,000 Japanese Nationals and Japanese-Americans who lived in California, Oregon, and Washington to war relocation camps. Several of the exhibits in the house show the impact of that order on the local Japanese-Americans and on the remaining non-Japanese-Americans, many of whom were friends and had worked together for years. One of the letters from an interned local man described

1908 Bereiter House

the hardships he faced in the camp and how much he missed his home. Others who were imprisoned asked for assistance in trying to locate their cars that were left behind or to find money they were owed for work completed before they were forced to move to the camps with only a suitcase or two.

Local Kent residents have donated the furnishings inside the home's many rooms. The wood-paneled study served as Emil Bereiter's office when he worked at home, and while the wooden desk, filing cabinet, and typewriter did not belong to him, they are very similar to the kinds of furnishings he might have used. One thing that remains original and intact is the extensive tile work in the bathrooms. Considering its age, the tile remains in remarkably good condition. One of the bathrooms even has some early 20th-century self-grooming accoutrements, including men's razors, an electric hair drier, and a curling iron.

HOURS: Wednesday through Saturday, 12 PM to 4 PM. Closed holidays.
COST: Free
LOCATION: 855 E. Smith Street, Kent (Parking is available behind the house via East Temperance Street.)
PHONE: 253-854-4330
WEBSITE: www.kenthistoricalmuseum.org

12 White River Valley Museum

WHAT'S HERE: **History of the White River Valley, from Native Americans to farming**
DON'T MISS THIS: **The fully restored caboose near the back of the museum**

The first settlers in Washington's White River Valley found black bear, deer, elk, and huge flocks of ducks and geese everywhere. During spring, summer, and fall migrating coho, Chinook, and sockeye salmon filled the meandering White River. The river flooded its temporary banks almost yearly, often changing course, and leaving behind rich soil to be farmed. With the U.S. government encouraging people to settle the West, a dozen or so families claiming their 160 or more acres, laid claim to most of the White River Valley by 1855. The government ignored the local Native Americans who had lived on this land for thousands of years.

While some of the pioneer families prospered, life was not without its difficulties. Inside the museum is a small, 11- by 14-foot furnished log cabin that was home for one of those early farmers. The cabin itself has seen a long, meandering journey. First serving as a farmer's family home in 1890s, it became a Finnish sauna at a logging camp in 1912, and later was moved to another location for use as a residence. The last owner moved it to his property in 1955, before finally donating it to the museum. Interpretive signs on the cabin quote from some of the early farmers about life out here:

> We have got three hundred and twenty acres of good land and a small frame upon it, but we have no furniture except what we make ourselves, but it is as good as our neighbors have and we know it is our own.
>
> —*Eliza Jane Jones,*
> *letter home, November 12, 1854*

The museum includes a gallery of local Native American artifacts. Numerous photographs from the very early 19th century show what life was like for the Muckleshoot Indians. They still fished for salmon on the nearby White and Green rivers, often from dugout canoes such as the one in the exhibit. Traditional dress, such as the skirt and cape shown in one of the photographs, was still a part of Indian life. The skirt and cape were made from the inner bark of Western red cedar trees, pounded flat and woven together. They were designed to shed the rain, a constant companion here.

Hop farming became a big industry in the White River Valley after the first plants were brought here in the mid-1860s. Whether good or bad, it also afforded jobs for many of the local Indians who planted, tended, and harvested the hops. It also proved to be a profitable enterprise for local farmers. While Great Britain grew more hops, the crop had become so prohibitively expensive there that it could be grown in Washington instead and shipped to England—at a profit.

The museum includes exhibits on the issei, the Japanese immigrants who moved here. Many arrived soon after 1900, coming to farm and raise their families. A Japanese family's farmhouse has been reconstructed inside the museum. The 1920 census showed that the area had 590 residents of European heritage and 332 of Japanese ancestry. Euro-Americans owned 50 of the 56 farms they operated. Japanese operated 52 farms, but owned none because they were prohibited by law from owning their own land at the time. There were 25 European immigrant farmers, 22 of whom had become naturalized U.S. citizens; none of the Japanese had become citizens because that, too, was prohibited by existing law. In 1942, 300 Japanese families, some of whom were first arrested and questioned about their loyalty, were moved to relocation camps following President Franklin D. Roosevelt's order at the outbreak of World War II. They were scattered into camps throughout the West. After the war, only about 25 of those families returned to the White River Valley.

Wander farther into the museum to see a one-room schoolhouse and a reconstructed facade of the Tourist Hotel built

Wagon loaded with strawberries for market

in 1905 for train travelers. It boasted 24 rooms, a stylish saloon, four shops, and plenty of the best liquor and cigars. One exhibit focuses on the local bad guy. In 1902, Harry Tracy escaped from Oregon Penitentiary, killing three guards and another inmate, then traveled through this area, holding a local family hostage for awhile until the father was able to provide him a Colt .45 revolver. Not long afterward, Tracy was wounded by deputies, but killed himself with the revolver in order to avoid capture. The exhibit includes several guns used in the White River Valley—including the one used by Tracy.

The Northern Pacific caboose shows what life was like for the conductor and others who lived and worked aboard the train. A sign advises that, because the caboose toilet emptied directly onto the tracks below, it was seldom used because of the lack of water needed to keep it clean. One wonders about the alternative on a fast-moving train.

Near the caboose is an exhibit of terra cotta from the Green River Valley. Nearby Auburn in the early 20th century was an important clay-producing area, for making pots and garden sculptures. There is also a general store, drugstore, and a look at the old Auburn train depot.

HOURS: Wednesday through Sunday, 12 PM to 4 PM
COST: Adults, $2; children and seniors, $1; free on Wednesdays
LOCATION: 918 H Street SE, Auburn
PHONE: 253-288-7433
WEBSITE: www.wrvmuseum.org

13 Naval Undersea Museum

WHAT'S HERE: **The history of U.S. Naval submarine warfare and underwater research efforts**

DON'T MISS THIS: **World War II Japanese Kaiten, a manned "suicide" torpedo**

Across Puget Sound from Seattle, Bainbridge Island and the nearby huge Bremerton Naval facility are familiar to many people. From the base, nuclear submarines occasionally cruise through the nearby waterways heading toward the Pacific Ocean. Therefore, it seems appropriate for a museum that focuses on the history of submarine technology to be nearby. Pulling into the parking lot at the Naval Undersea Museum in Keyport —an official U.S. Navy museum—you will be greeted by the sail from a retired nuclear submarine and by the *Trieste II*, one of the U.S. Navy's famed deep-diving subs.

Inside this huge museum, four primary exhibit areas demonstrate different aspects of undersea technology and the ocean environment. An introduction leads through the lives of the Trident Family, telling the stories of sailors who patrol in their Ohio-class submarines, sometimes called *Trident* subs because they carry Trident nuclear missiles. There are also stories about how their respective families deal with the long absences that seldom include any kind of contact between themselves and the sailors.

The ocean environment section offers hands-on experience with everything from the sounds of the sea to an experiment that demonstrates the positive, negative, and neutral state of buoyancy—the basis of how a submarine works. And if you don't think it's noisy under the ocean, the Sounds of the Sea exhibit will prove you wrong with its recordings of the sounds of whales, snapping shrimp, and even underwater earthquakes.

Much of the museum focuses on what the Navy does best—designing and building submarines and torpedoes. The exhibits have some of the earliest torpedoes and mines used in U.S. warfare. It includes a Civil War–era spar torpedo, a small explosive canister that was attached to the end of a long pole mounted on the bow of a small boat. The idea was to ram the pole and its explosive end into an enemy ship without being seen or blown up by your own device. It became obsolete in 1866 with the invention of the self-propelled torpedo. The museum's collection of torpedoes include the Mark 18, the U.S.'s first electric torpedo developed in World War II, and the Mark 48, the Navy's current standard torpedo carried by today's nuclear-powered submarines.

Wander to another part of the museum and submarine technology is in the spotlight. The exhibit includes rescue chambers and control rooms, including the fast attack USS *Greenling's* (SSN 614) periscope that looks outside over the parking lot. The assortment of dials and controls include a look at its ballast control panel and the fire control panel. The SRC, or Submarine Rescue Chamber, can take its two operators and more than a half dozen sailors down to 850 feet below sea level in an effort to rescue anyone who might still be alive in a sunken submarine.

The Diving Technology exhibit area is a wonderful collection of smaller underwater rescue and work vehicles. The CURV III is a Navy ROV (remotely operated vehicle) that can descend with its lights and cameras to locate and retrieve errant torpedoes and most anything else from the ocean bottom. Navy Seals use SDVs like the museum's Swimmer Delivery Vehicle Mark 7 to drop its teams where they are needed. And for movie buffs, the DSRV (Deep Submergence Rescue Vessel) was designed to be transported by air, surface, or underwater vessel to rescue sites. The one here is a half-scale model that was used in the 1990 movie *The Hunt for Red October*. Its real counterpart is actually 49 feet long, carries 24 men per trip, and can operate at depths of 5,000 feet.

Several examples of diving suits can be seen in the diving technology area. There are several displays focused on the Navy's women divers and the early discrimination women encountered when trying to become members of the elite

A decommissioned nuke sub's sail

diving corps. Since the 1970s, when they were finally allowed to work as divers, fifteen women have been elected into the Women Divers Hall of Fame.

Highlighting the dangers involved in the undersea service is a panel that lists more than 400 U.S. subs built during World War II. Fifty-two of their names and hull numbers are printed in red indicating those that never returned from their last patrols.

HOURS: June through September, daily, 10 AM to 4 PM. Closed Tuesdays October through May.
COST: Free
LOCATION: 610 Dowell Street, Keyport
PHONE: 360-396-4148
WEBSITE: www.history.navy.mil/museums/keyport/index1.htm

14 Puget Sound Navy Museum

WHAT'S HERE: **Exhibits focus on the rich naval heritage of the Pacific Northwest and adjacent Puget Sound Naval Shipyard**

DON'T MISS THIS: **The outside fountains that appear like submarines surfacing—or volcanoes erupting**

The museum is difficult to miss as you drive toward the ferry terminal in Bremerton; it looks like a miniature White House with the black sail of a nuclear submarine rising from the blue and white tile "ocean" in front. That sub is what remains of the USS *Parche* (SSN 0683), the most decorated warship in the history of the U.S. Navy. The building that houses the museum was one of the first structures at the Puget Sound Naval Shipyard. Built in 1896, it served as the commander's quarters and as an administrative headquarters. Since the commander's home was a center for entertaining VIPs and dignitaries, both foreign and national, the home saw its share of elegant parties.

Unfortunately, because of shipyard expansion in 1910, the home that had served at least eight shipyard commanders, was relocated to what is today Dry Dock 5. In the mid-1930s the house was moved to Farragut Avenue and used mostly for administrative purposes. Building 50, as it was officially known, was moved one last time to its present location in 2006, and given to the City of Bremerton for use as a cultural heritage museum. In spite of its mobile life, the old home has retained most of its historical integrity. Photos in the museum show the original location of Building 50 overlooking the dry dock.

The museum highlights the historical importance of Bremerton's Puget Sound Naval Shipyard. In 1888, President Grover Cleveland appointed a commission to locate a site for a Navy yard and dry dock. The Bremerton site was approved by Congress in 1891, and the site's original promoter, Navy Lieutenant Ambrose Wyckoff, was given command of the new facility's construction. When the first dry dock was completed in 1896, it was the largest in the country at the time. Its first customer was the USS *Monterey*. During that first year of operation, 22 ships were worked on at the dry dock, including the battleships *Oregon*, *Wisconsin*, and *Iowa*. By 1913 a second and larger dry dock was constructed to meet the growing demand.

World War I brought tremendous growth to the shipyard as it became a maintenance and construction facility for new war ships. Its number of workers grew from 1,500 in 1916 to 6,500 by 1918. As would happen in World War II, with men being drafted and enlisting in the military, women took over their jobs. Only six women worked here in 1914. By 1917, that number was up to several hundred as submarines, sub chasers, minesweepers, and hundreds of other, mostly smaller boats were built here. The museum has dozens of great period photographs and numerous artifacts that help tell this story.

The end of World War I brought even more work to the shipyard as the Navy decided to increase the size of the nation's Pacific fleet. Not only did the shipyard begin building light cruisers, but it also started repairing and converting aircraft carriers. One of the tools built here in 1933 was the huge hammerhead crane—the iconic symbol of today's Puget Sound Naval Shipyard. Today the shipyard appears as busy as ever with aircraft carriers and nuclear submarines, including ballistic missile subs, lined up awaiting conversion, repair, or dismantling. This process includes the deactivation of nuclear reactors as old ships are scrapped.

There are many interesting historical items in the museum. One is a small piece of shrapnel that was found on the USS *Tennessee*, left over from the December 7, 1941, attack on Pearl Harbor. If it had slammed into a ship's bulkhead anywhere near you, you likely would not have thought that it was so small.

And for anyone who has ever seen a movie about aircraft carrier flight operations and wondered what all those sailors working on deck were doing, there is an exhibit that shows the different colored jerseys they wear and the jobs associated with each. One curious machine the museum has looks very much like a typewriter, but it's called a "graphotype" and was patented in the 1930s. Typing on the keys created stamped metal identification tags that were used to label the hundreds of miles of pipes and cables that ran through a ship. They were also called dog tag machines.

Puget Sound Navy Museum

HOURS: Monday through Saturday, 10 AM to 4 PM; Sunday, 1 PM to 4 PM. Closed Tuesdays from October through May. Closed Easter, Thanksgiving, Christmas, and New Year's Day.

COST: Free

LOCATION: 251 1st Street, Bremerton

PHONE: 360-479-7447

WEBSITE: www.history.navy.mil/museums/psnm/psnm.htm

15 USS *Turner Joy* Naval Memorial Museum Ship

WHAT'S HERE: **The U.S. Navy destroyer that came under attack in the Gulf of Tonkin, thus officially marking the beginning of the war against North Vietnam**

DON'T MISS THIS: **The boat tour available from the destroyer dock to see the nearby Bremerton Naval Shipyard**

Built in Seattle and commissioned in 1959, the USS *Turner Joy* is tied forever to the Vietnam War. It's appropriate that the last of the Forrest Sherman class destroyers now sits at peace near its birthplace. She began service in 1960 as the flagship of an antisubmarine destroyer group attached to the aircraft carrier USS *Hornet*.

Nearly four years and several deployments later, USS *Turner Joy* was in Southeast Asian waters and came to the rescue of the USS *Maddox* that was attacked by several North Vietnam high-speed surface vessels. Two nights later it was purported, but never confirmed, that *Turner Joy* came under attack and retaliated, firing its guns at ghostly radar images throughout much of the night. True or not, based on the incident the U.S. Congress passed the Gulf of Tonkin Resolution, which allowed President Lyndon B. Johnson to legally and officially begin the U.S. war against North Vietnam.

USS *Turner Joy* made several additional forays into the Vietnam conflict, first in support of U.S. and South Vietnamese troops with its 5-inch guns, but later along the coast of North Vietnam during operation Sea Dragon, attacking primarily surface supply vessels. During one battle the destroyer took a direct hit from a North Vietnamese shore battery damaging the fantail, and a follow-up airburst took out the ship's air search radar. After repairs and other deployments, she later returned to Vietnam, firing some of the last hostile U.S. rounds at the North Vietnamese between December 1972 and January 28, 1973, when a negotiated ceasefire was signed ending U.S. participation in the conflict.

The majority of the restored USS *Turner Joy* is open for tours, from the boiler room to the bridge. You can wander through the ship's corridors where its crew of 275 sailors and 17 officers worked, ate, and slept. Yellow signs throughout the ship offer information about the different compartments and the ship's operations. One describes the difference between miles per hour and knots when describing the ship's maximum speed of more than 32 knots (about 37 miles per hour). Another describes the commanding officer's stateroom where his dress uniform hangs, which the captain used when in port, while using his sea cabin near the bridge while at sea. Another sign describes the ship's "escape trunk," a simple shaft with a ladder that dropped three decks from the topside deck to the lower levels. It allowed sailors in the bottom decks to escape when battle damage required a quicker escape than was possible through the ship's many sealed hatches. You can also walk past the sick bay, the engineering room, and the ship's store where sailors could purchase personal items from Almond Joy candy bars to postcards.

Be sure to wear comfortable shoes and clothes that will allow you to easily climb ladders and climb through narrow hatches. And watch your head—bulkheads don't give much when hit by bare heads.

If you would like to see and experience more Navy history, a one-hour tour boat ride leaves from the USS *Turner Joy*'s dock. It skirts the tall hull of the *Turner Joy* before heading down to the nearby Navy shipyard where numerous war ships are anchored, some mothballed, others awaiting refitting and repairs. The tour boat captain offers insightful banter about the history of the shipyard and shipbuilding in the Bremerton area. You can make reservations at the USS *Turner Joy* office.

HOURS: May through September, daily, 10 AM to 5 PM; October through April, Saturday and Sunday, 1 PM to 4 PM. Closed New Year's Day, Thanksgiving, and Christmas Day.

COST: Adults, $8; ages 62-plus, $7; ages 5–12, $6; military in uniform, free

LOCATION: 300 Washington Beach Avenue, Bremerton

PHONE: 360-792-2457

WEBSITE: www.ussturnerjoy.org

USS *Turner Joy*

16 Meeker Mansion

WHAT'S HERE: **Elegant and fully furnished Victorian mansion**
DON'T MISS THIS: **The stencil-painted ceilings**

Ezra Meeker had lived many of his 60 years in a log cabin, and that seemed to fit him just fine. That all changed when Ezra took his wife Eliza Jane with him on a trip to London where he was seeking additional markets for his hops crop, a business that had made him wealthy. On this particular trip, his wife had the opportunity to be presented to Queen Victoria and became quite fond of the finery that the queen possessed. Back home in Puyallup, she informed her husband that they needed to live in something fancier than a log cabin—something that better fit their status in the community. Ezra agreed, but he insisted that if Eliza wanted it, then she would have to pay for the home herself. She did, and three years later, in 1890, they moved into their new 17-room Italianate Victorian home—and the home's legal title remained in her name.

Ezra Meeker, who also was the town's first mayor, fell in love with the historic Oregon Trail. When he took up his crusade to save and mark the trail in 1906, much of it was already gone, covered by time and new development. Meeker was 76 years old when he first traveled the remnants of the Oregon Trail with a dog, a driver, and two oxen pulling a wagon. He started his journey from his front yard (a small Oregon Trail monument marks the site today), and traveled to Washington, D.C., via New York City. Meeker mistakenly assumed this would be his first and last trip in his effort to gain official national recognition for the trail and begin efforts to preserve this national treasure. Meeker lived to age 98, but before he died, he traveled the trail twice more, once by automobile in 1915, and in 1924 he traced its meandering path by airplane.

When Eliza Jane died in 1909, Ezra soon moved. He sold the home to the Ladies of the Grand Army of the Republic, and it became a retirement home operated by this Civil War widows' organization. In 1970, the home was donated to the Meeker Historical Society.

Upon entering the front door, one of the most striking aspects of this home is the extensive use of fine wood paneling and trim. The craftsmanship is clearly evident in many of the walls, windows, the wainscoting, and especially in the grand staircase, which is made of beautiful contrasting cherry and ash and leads to the second floor. The original staircase was built without the use of nails, depending only on the fine joinery to keep everything together. The entry hallway ceiling is one of those historical treasures that careful restoration work can reveal. The original stencil

Meeker Mansion

painting was unknown to anyone because over the decades it had been covered by numerous layers of paint. Most of the rooms have been painted in their original colors—again by laboriously scraping away numerous coats of paint to discover their first coat.

The many rooms in the mansion have been furnished with period furniture. The only pieces that originally belonged to the Meekers are the dining room table, a piano in the drawing room, and the oak bed and dresser in the master bedroom. The upstairs master bedroom is octagonal in shape, with cherry wood used throughout. The upstairs bath is across the hall—it was the first home in town to have an upstairs bathroom. The billiard room is accented with bird's-eye or curly maple, and while the billiard table did not belong to the Meekers, it dates back to that time period. The room features photos of two of Ezra's cross-country adventures to mark the Oregon Trail.

As with nearly all homes of this type and age, the areas frequented by the hired help did not receive such exquisite finish detailing. The back hallway used by the servants has cedar and fir, rather than cherry and oak. The kitchen and butler's pantry lack the fancy wood-paneled walls and stenciled ceilings. They were utilitarian food preparation and storage areas, from the built-in flour sifter to the vented food storage cabinets.

Outside on the grounds, the original parcel's three acres has been reduced in size. Gone are the stable and the heated conservatory. Only a few of the original trees remain—the ginkgo, Empress of China, and the holly grove. The home's exterior light tan and brown paint is the same as its original colors. Modern painters have had trouble repainting over some of the still remaining original paint. It was a mixture of three tons of white sand and three coats of pure linseed oil.

HOURS: Wednesday through Sunday, 10 AM to 4 PM. Closed mid-December to March 1 (open by appointment).

COST: Adults, $4; seniors and students, $3; children, $2; half price on Thursdays

LOCATION: 312 Spring Street, Puyallup

PHONE: 253-848-1770

WEBSITE: www.meekermansion.org

17 Tacoma Art Museum

WHAT'S HERE: **Extensive collection of Northwest art**

DON'T MISS THIS: **The big pup named Leroy**

The Tacoma Art Museum has only been collecting art since 1963, making it a relative newcomer. Yet in that short time it has become a leading exhibitor of Northwest artists and has managed to put together an excellent collection of Japanese wood-block prints. The museum also has the largest collection of glass art by Tacoma native Dale Chihuly, including about 40 pieces that he donated in honor of his parents and brother and another 39 pieces from the *Niijima Floats* series.

The museum's permanent collection of "works on paper" includes 1,900 prints. The collection features works by national and internationally acclaimed artists, including Allan D'Arcangelo, Vito Aconci, Barbara Kruger, and Ed Ruscha. But the most important part of the collection is the more than 300 Japanese wood-block prints, with the gems of the museum's collection being its 266 *ukiyo-e* prints. Most of the collection was donated by a single person who was aided in her selections by one of the world's foremost experts on *ukiyo-e,* a Japanese word meaning "pictures of the floating world." They were produced between the 17th and 20th centuries and feature images of landscapes, the theater, and city life. Another part of the collection came from a donation made by Al Buck, a descendant of Alfred E. Buck, who was the U.S. ambassador to Japan from 1898 to 1902. These late 18th- through early 20th-century prints are in excellent condition because the family stored them carefully.

European paintings are found in nearly every important art museum, and the Tacoma Art Museum is no different. French and German pieces from artists like Eugene Louis Boudin, Edgar Hilaire Degas, Camille Pissarro, and Pierre-Auguste Renoir can be found here. Renoir's oil painting *Heads of Two Young Girls,* also known as *The Two Sisters,* is one of two favorites of visitors. The other is *Dancers,* a fan-shaped painting on silk done by Degas. In 1995, two Degas bronze sculptures were added to the museum's growing collection.

Leroy the Big Pup is one piece of the museum's collection that is impossible to miss. The huge puppy, made from archival cardboard, glue, and wood screws, is generally found in the front lobby, but occasionally it wanders to other parts of the museum—with the help of museum staff.

The museum sponsors up to 15 exhibitions annually that feature Northwest artists. There are also traveling exhibits and loans of national and international art.

Tacoma Art Museum

HOURS: Tuesday through Saturday, 10 AM to 5 PM; Thursday, 10 AM to 8 PM; Sunday, 12 PM to 5 PM. Open Mondays, June through August, 10 AM to 5 PM. Closed Thanksgiving, Christmas, New Year's Day, and Martin Luther King Jr. Day.

COST: Adults, $7.50; ages 65-plus, students, military, $6.50; under age 5, free; family (two adults and up to four children under 18), $25

LOCATION: 1701 Pacific Avenue, Tacoma

PHONE: 253-272-4258

WEBSITE: www.tacomaartmuseum.org

18 Museum of Glass

WHAT'S HERE: **Collections and special exhibitions of creative art glass**

DON'T MISS THIS: **The Chihuly Bridge of Glass**

Even the building that houses the Museum of Glass is eye-catching. The front of the museum faces the Tacoma waterfront, and the iconic 90-foot-tall cone that sits tilted above the main building is part of the museum's overall design. While the cone appears to be made of glass, its stainless steel form is reminiscent of the sawdust-burning stacks that once spewed smoke skyward at every lumber mill throughout the Pacific Northwest. And once inside the museum you will discover that the cone serves a purpose specific to the creation of blown glass.

Three exhibit halls and a 130-seat theater with short films, ranging from an animated history of glass to specific glass artists and their work, help fill this 75,000-square-foot building. One of the main attractions is the Hot Shop Amphitheater that can be found in the bottom of that cone visible outside. Here, some of the best of the Pacific Northwest's glassblowers are hard at work showcasing this fascinating art. It's an ongoing show that may include a dozen people working individually and often as teams creating wonderful glass shapes, from art pieces to scientific flasks and twisty tubes. With its several ovens heating glass red-hot so the glassblowers

The museum's dome and glass towers

can perform their magic, it gets warm in here, so it's best to dress in layers, allowing you to shed pieces as needed.

The exhibits are the other attraction. The good thing for visitors is that these are constantly changing exhibitions of contemporary and historic glass art. Return in a month or six months and you are likely to see new pieces displayed, such as the *Lino Taglianpietra in Retrospect: A Modern Renaissance in Italian Glass*. But rest assured, unless you are a follower of glass art, whatever the exhibit, the pieces featured are like nothing you've ever experienced. These aren't the relatively simple works of weekend glassblowers featured at most community events; the pieces here can range from exquisite and detailed tiny thimble-sized creations to complex monster pieces that can easily overwhelm the largest dining room table. The best glass artists in the world combine form, color, and texture to best take advantage of bending, reflecting, refracting, transmitting, and enhancing light. And the Museum of Glass brings the best to its exhibit space.

There is one restriction: While you are allowed to photograph the glassblowers at work in the Hot Shop, you can't photograph any of the exhibit pieces. But there is an alternative if sharing the beauty of this glass art with friends and family is important. Outside the museum, walk up the ramp or stairs to the top of the main building. Along the Chihuly Bridge that crosses above the freeway to the Washington State History Museum are dozens of colorful examples of glass art, including two tall blue crystal columns that spiral skyward. The bridge is named for Dale Chihuly, a renowned Washington-based glass artist. Since injuries have limited his glass-blowing abilities, he has excelled at putting together teams of artists to create exceptionally beautiful and complex glass sculptures. The roof of the covered pedestrian bridge is a collage of multicolored glass shapes, while the wall is full of large cubbyholes, each featuring its own glass artwork. Here you have an opportunity to take all the spectacular photos you wish.

There is a hands-on gallery in the museum, designed primarily for the younger crowd. A large room filled with art projects is open for kids to design (on paper) their own glass pieces, among other art programs. Periodically, the museum's glassblowers will create glass reproductions of the best of the kids' often whimsical and colorful art drawings, be they dogs or cats, trees, people, or anything else that emerges from the minds of children. There is someone on hand to provide assistance as needed to help bring out everyone's best creative side. Adults can even create their own art, if they feel so inclined.

HOURS: Memorial Day through Labor Day: Monday through Saturday, 10 AM to 5 PM; Sunday, 12 PM to 5 PM; between Labor Day and Memorial Day: Wednesday through Saturday, 10 AM to 5 PM; Sunday, noon to 5 PM

COST: Adults, $10; ages 13–17, military with ID and ages 62-plus, $8; children ages 6–12, $4; families (two adults and up to four children under age 17), $30; third Thursday each month 5 PM to 8 PM, free. Closed Thanksgiving, Christmas Day, and New Year's Day.

LOCATION: 1801 Dock Street, Tacoma

PHONE: 253-284-4750

WEBSITE: www.museumofglass.org

19 Washington State History Museum

WHAT'S HERE: **Exhibits with thousands of well-organized and -presented artifacts from Washington's past**

DON'T MISS THIS: **The model railroad**

Plan to spend some time here because there is that much to see and experience. The Great Hall of Washington History is the first gallery you encounter with its dioramas depicting the Native Americans and early explorers who passed through the area. The British had already penetrated the Northwest into Canada, establishing trade agreements with the Indians. Such efforts to establish permanent settlements, in what President Thomas Jefferson clearly expected to be part of the emerging U.S., pushed him to begin sending U.S. settlers into these wild lands. The Lewis and Clark Expedition in 1804–1806 was the first attempt by the U.S. to reach the Pacific Ocean overland; the great, undiscovered inland waterway they were hoping for didn't exist.

As you read some of the exhibit labels in this part of the museum, the politics that guided the Lewis and Clark Expedition begin to emerge. The U.S. wanted to establish trade relationships with the Pacific Northwest Indians and keep the British from expanding their influence. The two Nez Perce chiefs who accompanied the expedition as interpreters—in addition to Sacajawea—hoped that by helping the U.S. government, they would gain an ally against their Blackfeet enemies to whom their British trading partners had been supplying weapons.

The exhibits continue describing the transformation of what were originally Native American lands into the Oregon Territory and then to Washington Territory under U.S. control. With these geographic reorganizations came a growing influx of pioneer farmers and businesses. A covered wagon with all of the cargo that a family might bring on their 2,000-mile trip across the Great Plains and the Rocky Mountains to Oregon can be seen. The wagons were often so overfilled with clothes, furniture, spare parts, and the suggested 200 pounds of flour and 75 pounds of bacon for each person, that most family members walked the entire distance. Contrary to many myths, of the 53,000 people who traversed the Oregon Trail, only three percent perished along the way, a mortality rate that was the same as if they had stayed home. And 90 percent of those who died did so from disease, primarily cholera. Very few encountered hostile American Indians along the way.

The museum features life-sized dioramas.

These thousands of pioneers helped to create new frontier towns, which greet you as you continue through the museum's main galleries. What followed was the building of the great Transcontinental Railroad, which only served to increase the number of newcomers. As the Northern Pacific Railway grew, it expanded its promotional efforts to England, Scotland, and Europe, encouraging more people to take advantage of opportunities for riches in this new land. The museum has a full-sized train car with passengers for a look back at what life was like.

The museum shows how industry has transformed Washington over the past century. It begins with shingle mills and the lumber industry and continues through today to include aircraft manufacturing and nuclear development. There's a look at the economic booms and busts, including how during the Great Depression, Seattle's radicals formed the nation's first Unemployed Citizens Leagues (UCL). The UCL created co-ops and bartering systems to aid the destitute. Employed members volunteered two days of their services each week to those in need, everything from shoe repairs to auto repairs. They also collected and distributed tons of fish, potatoes, and fruit, along with thousands of cords of firewood to those in need.

The Great Depression ended with the beginning of World War II; Washington State's part in the war is addressed, from Japanese internment camps to the making of plutonium at Hanford for the atom bombs dropped on Nagasaki and Hiroshima. Despite the hardships many people faced during World War II, for some people it presented many opportunities; Patricia Koehler was 18 years old when she was hired to work in the Kaiser shipyards. Within a year, through hard work and night courses, she became a journeyman electrician, and in a single week made $80, her biggest paycheck ever. The museum shares her story and many others.

Agriculture is the key to much of Washington's riches today. The museum takes you through the Yakima Valley apple orchards and into the packing plants, then out across the great wheat farms to the east. And, of course, the fishing industry is not overlooked. There is even a mechanical fish-cleaning machine designed to eliminate the need to hire Chinese workers. Discrimination became rampant for a time, as anti-Chinese sentiment turned to creating legislation in 1853 that denied Chinese men the right to vote.

Timber has always been an economic mainstay in Washington. It was also of strategic importance during World War I as the Allies needed aircraft to break the great battlefield stalemates. Aircraft then were built ideally of Sitka spruce, and the Pacific Northwest had ample supplies. More exhibits introduce you to the early nightlife in Seattle, into Roslyn Mine #3 where coal was mined, and to the loggers who cut giant Douglas fir trees using nothing more than hand tools and muscle.

There are lots of hands-on exhibits for kids (and adults) in the history lab, including an opportunity to travel through time and connect the past with the present. Kids and adults can solve "History Mysteries," using historical evidence. The Puget Sound Model Railroad Engineers Club has created an 1,800-square-foot permanent layout of HO model trains that depict north Tacoma in the 1950s. And there's even more!

HOURS: Wednesday through Friday, 10 AM to 4 PM, with extended hours and free admission Thursday from 2 PM until 8 PM.

COST: Adults, $8; seniors, $7; military and ages 6–18, $6

LOCATION: 1911 Pacific Avenue, Tacoma

PHONE: 1-888-BE THERE (1-888-238-4373)

WEBSITE: www.washingtonhistory.org

20 Washington State Capitol

WHAT'S HERE: **Working place for state legislators and the governor**

DON'T MISS THIS: **The Tiffany chandelier suspended below the dome**

Washington's state capitol sits near the center of a large campus of other government buildings on a hilltop overlooking Budd Inlet's West Bay. It took six years and more than $7 million to complete the legislative center in 1928. At 287 feet, it is the fourth-tallest masonry dome in the world, surpassed only by three cathedrals in Europe. While the exterior of the capitol is constructed of Washington-quarried sandstone, what is most striking is the extensive use of marble throughout the interior of the public areas of the building. The main corridors are gray marble from Alaska, while the House, Senate, and State Reception Room are clad in different marbles from Italy, Germany, and France. It is estimated that to duplicate this building today, the cost would exceed $1 billion.

The marble is a perfect backdrop for the capitol's extensive lighting, including the largest chandelier ever made by Tiffany Lighting Company. Stand in the center rotunda and look up. The 10,000-pound chandelier is suspended from a 110-foot chain above the bronze replica of the state seal set in the floor beneath the interior dome. Replica Roman firepots rest on pedestals around the rotunda gallery. The ancient Romans lit their firepots burning moss or oil to notify the Senate when it was time to convene. That part of legislative tradition has been left to the Romans. For a better view of the chandelier and its Greco-Roman style figures, head to the fourth-floor balconies.

Inside the capitol's rotunda

If the legislature isn't in session, you can peek inside the Senate and House chambers. If they are in session, the fourth-floor galleries are open to the public year-round. Although you can't get to it, the capitol's cupola had its original lantern restored in 2004 after 30 years in storage. It once again burns brightly at night. Although it's not visible from the ground, the fifth-floor roof has solar panels that produce enough electricity to power the exterior lights even on cloudy days.

Touring the capitol is easy. You can go on your own, but taking one of the guided tours will provide much more information about the building's history. Meet the tour guide at the foot of the rotunda steps on the north side of the building, immediately inside the main entrance. A good place to start any visit to the capitol campus is the visitor information center located at 14th and Capitol Way (360-586-3460). They can guide you to the best places to park.

HOURS: Daily guided tours on the hour, 10 AM to 3 PM. The capitol is closed Thanksgiving, Christmas, and New Year's Day.

COST: Free

LOCATION: 416 Syd Snyder Avenue SW, Olympia

PHONE: 360-902-8880

WEBSITE: www.ga.wa.gov/Visitor/index.html

21 Bigelow House Museum

WHAT'S HERE: One of the Pacific Northwest's oldest surviving homes

DON'T MISS THIS: Land documents signed by four U.S. presidents

While not fancy by today's standards, when it was built in about 1860, the Bigelow House was perhaps the finest home in Olympia. The architecture is described as Carpenter Gothic, a style that was popular during the mid-19th century. Over the home's first 140 years, many changes were made by various Bigelow family owners. Since the home has come to be owned by the nonprofit Bigelow House Preservation Association, a few of those changes have been reversed, including raising ceilings back to their original 10-foot heights and changing wall colors to their 19th-century beginnings.

Daniel Richardson Bigelow left his New York home in 1850 with his Harvard degree in-hand. After his new law practice had failed to flourish as quickly as he thought it should in both Indiana and Wisconsin, he headed to the new Oregon Territory. He arrived in the tiny frontier town of Olympia in late 1851 and immediately went to work. Not only did he pursue his law practice, but he also got himself heavily involved in the budding town's politics.

Ann Elizabeth White had come to the Oregon Territory with her mother and four siblings in 1851 (her father was already here) when she was only 15 years old. By age 17, she was teaching school and two years later she and Daniel Bigelow married. The Bigelows apparently moved to their land claim on the eastern shore of Budd Inlet sometime before 1860, living in a log cabin (that is still on the grounds) while their new home was being built. They reared their eight children in their home overlooking Budd Inlet and the growing city of Olympia.

Although it's difficult to imagine today considering that this suburban neighborhood has hundreds of homes, when it was built, the Bigelows' home was one of the few in the area. In fact, Daniel Bigelow would often walk down the open hillside to his canoe on Budd Inlet and paddle around the spit to his law office. Perhaps all that exercise is why he lived until age 81 in 1905. His wife Ann Elizabeth lived until age 90, passing away in 1926.

One of the benefits of having had the Bigelow family reside in the home through four generations is that many of the original furnishings still remain. In fact, by today's standards the family might be considered pack rats because they saved almost everything, even items brought to the Oregon Territory in the 1850s and much of everything acquired over the next century or more. Examples include the parlor's pine parlor desk with its burl veneer, which they got about the time they moved into their new home; the upholstered platform rocker, also in the parlor, that according to the family history was used by suffragist Susan B. Anthony when she visited in 1871; and Daniel Bigelow's Steinway square grand piano purchased for $800 in 1870.

What was originally the dining room, but later became the Bigelow library, houses the owner's large law desk, which rests on a pedestal of drawers. Daniel brought the desk with him when he first traveled to Oregon Territory in 1851. He is thought to have brought the shotgun hanging on the wall on his journey as well. Look closely at the framed documents hanging on the library walls. They are the official General Land Office documents granting several properties to Daniel Bigelow, as well as to some of his other family members. They have been signed by Abraham Lincoln, Andrew Johnson, Benjamin Harrison, and Ulysses S. Grant—quite a collection of U.S. presidential autographs.

The kitchen was remodeled a number of times, but some of the earlier belongings are displayed. Look for the strange contraption that appears to be a cross between a hand-cranked meat grinder

Bigelow House Museum

and a music box's insides. It's actually an automatic knitting machine designed to easily make socks and other useful items. An 1871 advertisement, found in the house along with the mechanical device, reveals that it sold for $25 and was available via mail order from Boston and St. Louis.

HOURS: Weekends, Memorial Day through Labor Day, 12 PM to 4 PM
COST: Ages 13 and older, $3; ages 12 and under, $1
LOCATION: 918 Glass Avenue NE, Olympia
PHONE: 360-753-1215
WEBSITE: www.bigelowhouse.org

Greater Puget Sound Tours

Technology Tour

ESTIMATED DAYS: 2–4
ESTIMATED DRIVING MILES: 185

If you are interested in technology, then there is plenty to explore in the Puget Sound area, beginning with the **American Museum of Radio and Electricity** (page 210) in Bellingham. The museum holds some of the earliest attempts at experimenting with electricity and broadcast radios. Examples include a first edition *De Magnete*, published in 1600, and the only Collins 1909 wireless telephone known to exist. And for radio vacuum tube aficionados, the museum's collection includes 30,000 of the glass curiosities.

More advanced technology can be explored at Boeing's **Future of Flight Aviation Center** (page 216) in the town of Mukilteo. The museum lets you explore jet engines, cockpits, and more. But take the Boeing factory tour for a look at how Henry Ford's assembly line has been significantly modernized for the manufacture of Boeing 737s and their newest 777 Dreamliner. The 90-minute factory tour begins with a movie and continues with a bus ride to the factory. Considering Boeing's factory is the world's largest building by volume, wear comfortable shoes as there is a lot of walking (disabled access available with advanced notice). Also be advised they have many restrictions, including a height requirement for children, so be sure to check their website first.

Nearby Redmond is home to one of the most successful technology companies in history. The **Microsoft Visitor Center** (page 218) is relatively small considering the giant size of its namesake. It includes a look at "old" technology, from eight-track tapes to the Altair 8800 computer that started Bill Gates and partner Paul Allen on their way to fame, fortune, and the world's largest computer software empire.

Naval Undersea Museum's deep divers

In 1964, a U.S. destroyer came under attack and returned fire at ghostly radar images in the Gulf of Tonkin following an earlier attack on another U.S. vessel. The event marked the official beginning of the U.S. war against North Vietnam. That destroyer, the **USS *Turner Joy*** (page 227), is now a museum and memorial and is open for tours in its Bremerton home port.

Another aspect of naval technology, undersea rather than on the surface, can be found in Keyport's **Naval Undersea Museum** (page 223) just across Puget Sound from Seattle. The focus here is on both undersea exploration and the Navy's use of underwater technology over the past century. The earliest weapon is a Civil War–era spar torpedo, an explosive attached to the end of a long pole, which was mounted to the bow of a small watercraft and shoved into the side of an enemy ship where it exploded. It became obsolete soon after its invention, for obvious reasons. Here you can see subs, including the deep-diving *Trieste II*.

Southern Peninsula History Tour

ESTIMATED DAYS: 1–2
ESTIMATED DRIVING MILES: 42

Washington's state capitol

Victorian mansions can be seen throughout the Pacific Northwest as many of the early pioneers who were successful in business were building their new homes when such architecture was popular. One of the best examples is the **Meeker Mansion** (page 229) in Puyallup. Built in 1890 by Ezra Meeker's wife Eliza Jane because he refused to pay for it, the home has been well maintained and is fully furnished, although only a few of the pieces belonged to the Meekers.

About 10 miles away, the **Washington State History Museum** (page 234) tells one of the most complete stories about the forty-second state in the Union. From Native Americans, the British trappers, and the Lewis and Clark Expedition to the Oregon Trail, the development of agriculture, and the fishing industry, the museum has exhibits representing almost every aspect of Washington's history.

When you've finished with history, walk across the nearby pedestrian bridge that crosses the highway below and enter the world of art glass. The exhibits begin on the bridge and conclude inside the **Museum of Glass** (page 232). Not only are there plenty of exhibits of both old and new glass, but you can also watch demonstrations of glassblowers working their magic with the molten substance.

A final stop should be the **Washington State Capitol** (page 236) in Olympia. The building's dome, at 287 feet, is the fourth-tallest masonry dome in the world. You can marvel at the huge Tiffany chandelier suspended below the dome—or better yet, take one of the guided tours.

Greater Puget Sound Information Centers

Bellingham Whatcom County Convention and Visitors Bureau
www.bellingham.org
800-487-2032

Tacoma Regional Convention and Visitor Bureau
www.traveltacoma.com
800-272-2662

Olympia-Lacey-Tumwater Visitor and Convention Bureau
www.visitolympia.com
877-704-7500

San Juan Islands Visitor Bureau
www.visitsanjuans.com
888-468-3701

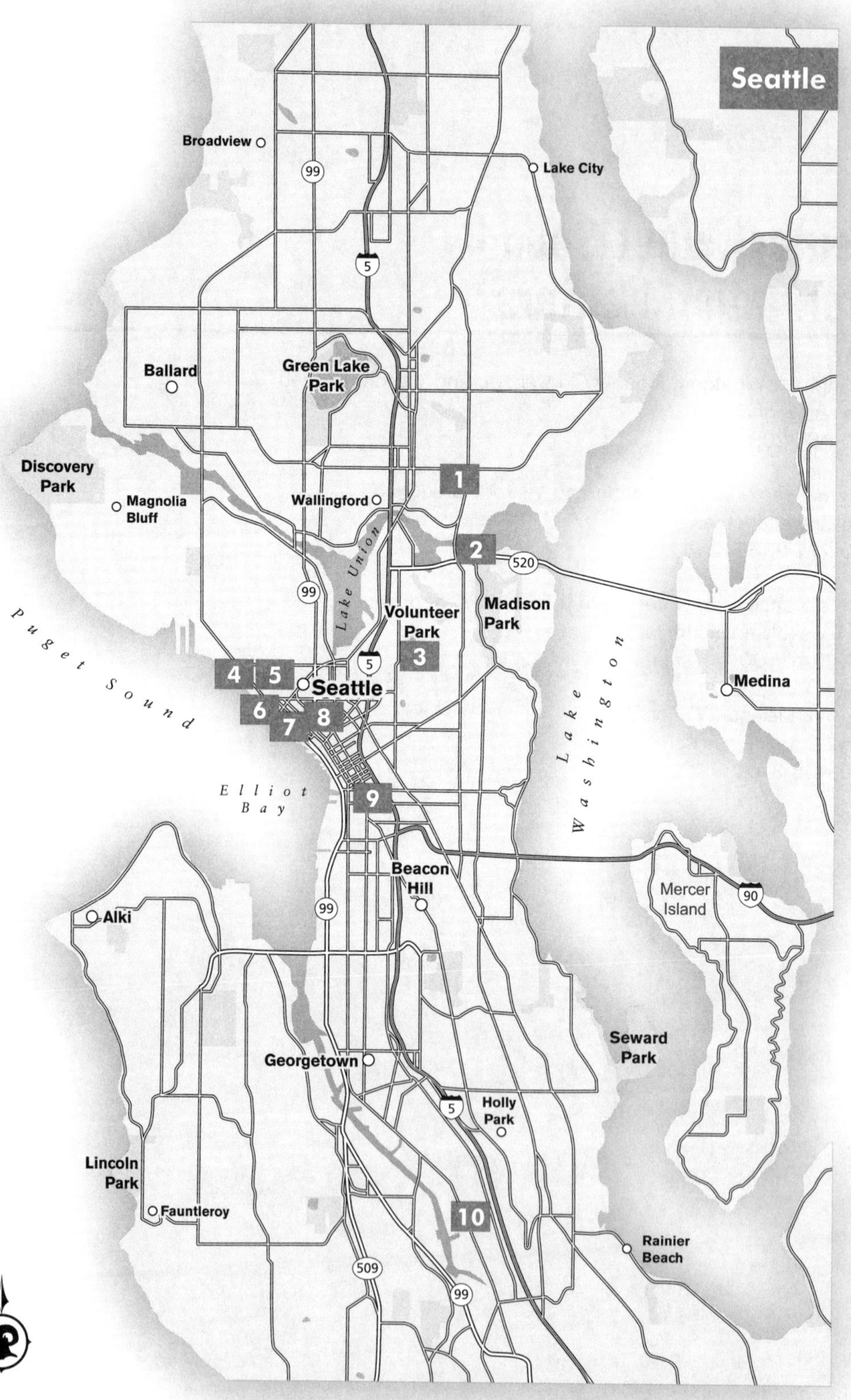
Seattle
Broadview
Lake City
99
5
Ballard
Green Lake Park
Discovery Park
Magnolia Bluff
Wallingford
1
2
520
99
Lake Union
Volunteer Park
Madison Park
Puget Sound
3
5
4
5
Seattle
Medina
6
7
8
Lake Washington
Elliot Bay
9
Beacon Hill
Mercer Island
90
99
Alki
Seward Park
Georgetown
5
Holly Park
Lincoln Park
Fauntleroy
10
Rainier Beach
509
99

Seattle

Seattle's best known iconic landmark may be the Space Needle, but it could just as easily be the Pike Place Market, the ferries that provide a major part of the area's transportation system, or the Experience Music Project. It's a bustling city full of life, hills, and, of course, rain!

Native Americans lived in this area for at least 4,000 years. The first Europeans to settle in the area were part of the Arthur Denny party, but that wasn't until 1851. Small settlements popped up—New York-Alki and Duwamps. Seattle gained its official name in 1853, when its citizens decided to "Americanize" and use a local Indian's name, Chief Sealth.

The Museum of Flight's main gallery

Seattle lays claim to Starbucks Coffee and Jimi Hendrix as natives, and it's home to dozens of great museums and fabulous historic homes. The waterfront offers good food, lots of gift and curiosity shops, and exceptional people, boat, and waterfront viewing opportunities. Walk up the hill a couple of blocks from the waterfront to Pike Place Market. Here, hundreds of vendors, thousands of colorful flowers, delicious foods, flying fish, and a handful of street musicians and entertainers provide plenty of happy diversions from the pressures of everyday life. So put on your walking shoes or jump in one of the famous amphibious ducks for a city tour. It's time to go exploring.

TRIVIA

1 Where can you see handmade water skis that were first used in 1928, thus introducing the sport to the Pacific Northwest?

2 Where can you witness Seattle's famous "flying" fish?

3 In which museum can you see Jimi Hendrix's first guitar?

4 Where can you see a Tlingit mortuary pole?

5 What museum features the Yick Fung Co. store as a key exhibit?

6 Where can you visit the 1916 biplane factory called the "Red Barn?"

7 What museum now shares a portion of the original Experience Music Project?

For trivia answers, see page 345.

1 Burke Museum of Natural History and Culture

WHAT'S HERE: **Exhibits ranging from North American dinosaurs and the Ring of Fire volcanoes to ancient cultures**

DON'T MISS THIS: **The American mastodon skeleton**

The museum is tucked into a corner of the University of Washington campus in Seattle. At the top of the steps leading to the front entrance, the imposing reproduction Tlingit mortuary pole is but a preview of what awaits inside. The original pole, which stood in a village near present-day Wrangell, Alaska, held the remains of a Tlingit Indian chief.

The museum has several million artifacts in its collection, but is able to exhibit only a small number at any one time. Since this a natural history and cultural museum, it includes numerous permanent exhibits on the life and times of Washington and the Pacific Northwest. Enter the first gallery and you've traveled back to a time before dinosaurs roamed North America. This is when simple animals like trilobites and corals were living under the ancient oceans. Walking farther into the gallery moves time ahead and suddenly there's the 140 million-year-old leg bone of a sauropod attached to a wall mural depicting the ancient animal. The exhibit cases hold many more fossils and bones, including those of a theropod from 140 million years ago and the partial head of a triceratops, which is only 65 million years old.

Exhibits reveal the Pacific Northwest's violent geologic past—and present. Throughout Washington, volcanoes dominate the landscape, two of the most prominent being Mt. St. Helens, which erupted violently in 1980, and Mt. Rainier, which has remained quiet long enough for glaciers to form on its sides. Exhibits explain how the earth's surface plates continue to move like giant puzzle pieces. Unfortunately, the relatively small San Juan Plate is moving toward the huge North American Plate, which isn't giving up any space. With no place else to go, the San Juan Plate is being forced to dive beneath its bigger cousin, resulting in lots of cracks in the earth's surface allowing for lava to move upward, creating volcanoes. With the huge Pacific tectonic plate also moving east, the result is the "Ring of Fire," a giant arc of volcanoes that starts in Asia and runs through Japan, Alaska, and down the Pacific Coast into California.

Entrance to the Burke Museum

A huge skeleton, looking very much like a modern elephant, appears on the tour. It's an American mastodon like those that lived here from about 3.5 million years ago to just 10,000 years ago, browsing on trees. Scientists think they disappeared because of a change in the climate—during the last ice age—or perhaps because these huge animals were easily found and thus overhunted by humans. It was those same ice age glaciers that gouged out the channels of the Strait of Juan de Fuca and Puget Sound through which so many ships travel today.

Head downstairs to the museum's lower level and the museum moves from natural history to cultural history. A dugout canoe is suspended over the staircase and a wall mural depicts a Native American village. Exhibits include numerous 11,000-year-old Clovis points (stone projectile points associated with the Clovis people) that range in size from three or four inches to about eight inches long. There are bamboo pipes, rattles, and numerous masks from cultures throughout the Pacific. Masks served ceremonial purposes, sometimes bringing ancestors back to life or enabling the wearer to become other beings, from birds to lions. Ceremonial mask dances sometimes were wild, accompanied by ringing bells and beating drums; others were quiet and serene. The museum's exhibit masks come from Queen Charlotte Island in British Columbia, Japan, and southwest Alaska. There are even carved Maori masks from New Zealand.

Exhibits include a look at different cultural foods such as rice, noodles, dried oysters, and chickens. Explained is the custom of leaving heads and feet attached to the butchered chickens in China—it represents rebirth.

Vehicle parking is available along adjacent off-campus streets. On-campus parking is available; although when classes are in session, finding parking can be difficult. Upon entering the campus, vehicles are charged a $12 parking fee on weekdays at the campus entry kiosks. If you leave in less than four hours, a prorated refund is given. The Saturday fee is $6 before 12 PM and free after 12 PM and on Sundays.

HOURS: Daily, 10 AM to 5 PM. Closed New Year's Day, Christmas, Fourth of July, and Thanksgiving.

COST: Adults, $8; ages 65-plus, $6.50; ages 5–18 and students, $5

LOCATION: Corner of the University of Washington campus at NE 45th Street and 17th Avenue, Seattle

PHONE: 206-543-5590

WEBSITE: www.burkemuseum.org

2 Museum of History and Industry

WHAT'S HERE: **A look at Seattle's colorful history**

DON'T MISS THIS: **The handmade water skis that introduced the sport to the Pacific Northwest in 1928**

Sitting near the shore of Washington Lake, the spacious museum is designed around several galleries, each featuring its own time line of Seattle's history. But even before entering the museum, pieces of Seattle's early history can be seen. Near the parking lot, the 5,000-pound bell displayed was purchased the year after Seattle's devastating 1889 fire. It represents the beginning of the city's efforts to professionalize and better equip its fire department. This warning bell sat atop the first fire station at Seventh Avenue and Columbia Street until its removal in 1919. Nearby is what looks like a giant doughnut, but instead is a stone once used to grind wood into pulp at Washinton's first paper mill (owned by Crown Zellerbach Corporation) located on the Columbia River.

Inside the museum, the time line of galleries begins with the early Native Americans and highlights Si'ahl's first encounter with Europeans when in 1792, George Vancouver's ship *Discovery* anchored off Bainbridge Island. Si'ahl, a young Indian boy, grew up to become leader of the Duwamish and Suquamish tribes and became better known as Chief Seattle. He remained friends with the settlers who came and ultimately helped convince his people to sign a treaty in 1855, giving 50,000 acres to the U.S. in exchange for continued hunting and fishing rights. Today, the city of Seattle and many of its surrounding towns sit on that land.

Exhibits highlight the battle between the U.S. and Great Britain over who was to control the Pacific Northwest. After the treaty that granted land south of the 49th parallel to the U.S., federal land policies were put into place that encouraged pioneer settlements. Encounters with the local Native Americans were not all peaceful during those early years. In 1855–56, a group of Indians who were not supportive of the treaties attacked the relatively new settlement of Seattle, which had only about 30 structures. The citizens retreated to the safety of an anchored warship. In subsequent years, Indian labor helped build Seattle, yet prejudices and discrimination remained.

The Boomtown gallery highlights Seattle's economic ups-and-downs from 1889 to 1940. In July 1897, the steamer *Portland* docked in Seattle and unloaded its 68 male passengers and $1 million in gold, kicking off the great Klondike gold rush. Before year's end 10,000 of Seattle's citizens had headed north to Alaska and Canada. Seattle continued to

Boeing B-1 Flying Boat

be the starting point for thousands of other gold seekers. Between 1898 and 1902, almost $200 million in gold passed through Seattle's assay office. Much of that wealth remained, fueling the city's tremendous growth—and vice. Twenty-four hours each day, the Red-Light District, with its dance halls, burlesque shows, brothels, opium parlors, and saloons, served miners and anyone else with a few dollars to spend. The exhibits include old poker chips, handcuffs, guns, and police nightsticks.

Transportation changed rapidly in the early 20th century. In 1906, the first automobile ads appeared in a Seattle newspaper. Eight years later, 20,000 of them were traveling Washington's primitive road system. Streetcar ridership declined and the ferries were redesigned to carry cars. In 1932, Highway 99 was completed, making a north-south automobile link between California and Washington.

Exhibits show the face of other social and economic changes around Seattle. Prohibition brought stills and illegal whiskey sales. Following the end of World War I, with government contracts suddenly cancelled, thousands of workers were being laid off. As a result, the country's first general strike took place in Seattle as 30,000 shipyard workers walked out in 1919. They were quickly joined by 35,000 union workers.

As the displays artfully show, World War II dramatically changed Seattle. Gone were the city's Hooverville shanties, the Great Depression–era city of unemployed and destitute. Prohibition was over, and with government contracts leading the way, the economy once again boomed. It wasn't a good time for the Japanese with President Franklin D. Roosevelt's order to move them to internment camps—photos illustrate families being moved and their homes lost. The Homefront gallery explores the war years, the Cold War, and the changes around Seattle as the suburbs first emerged.

The museum's vast artifact collection colorfully illustrates the many pieces of Seattle's varied history. There are photos of the 1962 World's Fair that saw the construction of the Space Needle; the changing timber industry that has supported untold thousands of Washington's families for more than a century; a look at Boeing and the aircraft industry; and the old trade in Native Alaskan baleen and ivory art pieces. There is the model of the *Kalakala*, the 1935 spaceship-like ferry that plied Puget Sound until 1967. And another Seattle icon is here—Lincoln Towing's "Pink Toe Truck." For many years, beginning in 1980, the bright pink tow truck, with its big set of pink toes protruding from the top of the cab, saw service and many parades around the city.

In one gallery, hanging from above is the first Boeing B-1 Flying Boat. In 1920, the small airplane began the first international airmail service flying between Seattle and Victoria, British Columbia. During the seven years it saw service, the two-person aircraft flew 350,000 miles, making 1,000 trips, and they never lost a single piece of mail. Aircraft continued to improve, especially during World War II. Following the war, the big Allison aircraft engine on display was taken from a surplus P-38 Lightning and placed in the *Slo-mo-shun IV*, one of the fastest hydroplanes of the time. Its radical three-point hull design influenced the design of every racing hydroplane that followed. After a severe wreck in 1956 that left the big wood-hull boat structurally unfit to race again, the boat was donated to the museum. A video shows the 1950s-era hydroplane in action.

Salmon fishing has been a Seattle economic mainstay. The salmon cannery gallery focuses on the history and the complexities of safely and efficiently processing and shipping fish to markets around the world. To illustrate the process, visitors are encouraged to race the Iron Chink, the mechanized fish cleaning and butchering machine. No, you don't use real fish, just a model salmon with "safe" knives. The old butchers couldn't win; can you?

HOURS: Daily, 10 AM to 5 PM; first Thursday of each month, 10 AM to 9 PM
COST: Ages 18–61, $8; ages 62-plus and students/military with ID, $7; ages 5–17, $6; first Thursday of each month, free
LOCATION: 2700 24th Avenue East, Seattle
PHONE: 206-324-1126
WEBSITE: www.seattlehistory.org

3 Seattle Asian Art Museum

WHAT'S HERE: **Vast collection of Asian art, from ancient to contemporary**
DON'T MISS THIS: **The outside view looking toward the Space Needle**

The museum building is impressive, though it lacks any overt Asian design themes. That has more to do with its original purpose, which was to house the entire Seattle Art Museum's collection. Following the construction of a new main Seattle Art Museum (SAM) downtown, this building, constructed in 1932 and organizationally still part of SAM, is dedicated to Asian art.

Each of the numerous galleries carries through with its own theme, such as Discovering Buddhist Art: Seeking the Sublime, which explores the imagery of Buddha. Six hundred years following Buddha's death, images of Buddha began appearing in parts of Afghanistan, Pakistan, and central India. His physical appearance was defined in 32 markings that extolled his greatness. He had blue eyes, webbed hands and feet, and a mole marking his forehead, often represented in statuary and paintings as a crystal or a jewel. Each of the hand positions relates directly to events from Buddha's life—birth, meditation, preaching, and the moment of death.

Seattle Asian Art Museum

Those physical images and the teachings of Buddha spread throughout Asia, and with that spread the expanded interpretations of his physical being as depicted by artists using different media (wood, stone, metal) began to change, while still maintaining the basic features of the original. The museum holds numerous art pieces that depict Buddha, his teachings, and the related rituals associated with Buddhism. Pieces from Japan include a standing bodhisattva from the 11th century made of wood, gesso, polychrome, and gold, and a seated Amitabha dating from the end of the 14th century, made of wood, lacquer, gold leaf, and a crystal inlay.

With more than 3,500 objects in its collection, the museum is one of the largest holders of Chinese art in the nation. A significant portion of the initial collection came in 1933 from the museum's founder Dr. Richard Fuller. Fuller focused his attentions on Chinese porcelain, jade, and snuff bottles. As a geologist, jade art intrigued him, so he collected pieces from the Neolithic period to the Qing dynasty (1644–1912). Several of his pieces are exhibited.

Also shown are examples of the paintings and calligraphy that are so closely associated with Chinese culture. The gallery presents three genres of Chinese painting: the naturalistic animal paintings from the 12th century; the abstract literati or ink-play; and paintings that seek refuge or solace in nature. An ink-on-paper piece—*Rock on Plants*—by Huang Fuzhou (1883–1971), reveals the artistry created by this well-known Chinese artist who painted with his tongue. His technique included taking a mouthful of ink and spraying it on paper or silk, then before it could dry, using his tongue to create the final artistic effect.

The museum's collections also include Chinese tiles. Tiles may have been used in China from as early as the Shang period (1600–1128 BC). The imagery found on many tiles was believed to bring good luck to a building's inhabitants. Other art pieces, such as those depicting horses, whose owners' real life relationships with the animals enhanced their projection of power and prestige, showed the animals in highly spirited positions wearing all of their elaborate regalia. The museum's third-century *Bear and Tiger Fighting* is a cast bronze piece that has been gilded in gold. It depicts a tiger aggressively attacking a bear, all wrapped in a circular ball design.

A 10th-century Chinese Yue jar (Zhejiang province) illustrates that trade was alive and well in early China. This yellow-green glazed "bamboo root" stoneware was used in Java funeral rituals. For those who love Ming period porcelain, where ornamental shapes beyond traditional pottery emerged, the museum has more than a few pieces in its collection. Examples include the early-17th-century piece with its molded and underglaze-blue decorations from Jiangxi province; its blue color possesses a purplish tone caused by the high-manganese cobalt mined in Yunnan province.

As practiced in most art museums with large collections, pieces are periodically rotated, partly because even a museum this large cannot exhibit all of its collection at one time. Special limited traveling exhibits also are an integral part of the Asian Art Museum's ongoing commitment to bringing the best of Asian art to Seattle.

Either before or following your visit, be sure to walk out to the end of the small plaza in front of the museum toward the reflection pond. The distant views of the Space Needle and downtown Seattle are well worth the short stroll.

HOURS: Wednesday through Sunday, 10 AM to 5 PM; Thursday, 10 AM to 9 PM
COST: Adults, $5; ages 13–17 and 62-plus, $3; first Thursday of each month, free
LOCATION: 1400 East Prospect Street, Seattle
PHONE: 206-654-3100
WEBSITE: www.seattleartmuseum.org/visit/visitSAAM.asp

4 Experience Music Project

WHAT'S HERE: **The history of rock and roll, with its roots in jazz, blues, and gospel**
DON'T MISS THIS: **Creating your own music with guitars, drums, computers, and more**

There are rock and roll museums and then there is Seattle's EMP, the Experience Music Project. Located only several dozen yards from Seattle's iconic Space Needle, EMP has become a Seattle icon of its own. When the museum opened in 2000, it created quite a stir—not only for what it housed, but for its appearance. Some folks didn't care for its soaring, swooping, gleaming metal walls.

The unique design came from Frank Gehry who purchased several electric guitars, cut them up into pieces, then arranged the pieces as inspiration for the museum's flowing lines. Some people insist that the museum's exterior looks a lot like one of Jimi Hendrix's smashed guitars. The mirrored walls' "Purple Haze" finish was created by dipping the steel shingles that cover the exterior walls into an acid bath. The 85-foot-tall building is cleaned once each year—a process that takes three months. Today, an entrance on the opposite side of the museum leads to the connected Science Fiction Museum.

Entrance to EMP store and restaurant

The interior is no less fascinating. Six hundred guitars, which play by themselves, swirl upward from the floor in a 35-foot-tall cyclone near the center of the museum. A large screen fills what is called the sky church and features pulsating visual and sound programs.

As with most museums that have collections numbering into the hundreds of thousands or even millions of artifacts, only a relatively small number can be exhibited at any one time. Rock and roll has always been in the business of entertainment. And part of that entertainment, sometimes overriding the musical artists, has been the art and promotion, from posters to costumes. EMP has collected more than 1,000 costumes and related memorabilia.

The museum does an excellent job of following the history of jazz, soul, gospel, country, and especially the blues, all of which have contributed to the foundation of modern rock and roll. But what would rock and roll be without the guitar? In the Guitar Gallery, more than 50 very rare guitars, both acoustic and electric, fill glass cases, the oldest an Italian gem from 1770. Signature guitars from the innovative minds of Orville Gibson, Leo Fender, and Les Paul are included in the exhibit that follows the evolution of guitars from their quiet origins to their screaming, rock concert sounds of today.

One of the museum's favorite rock and roll "sons" grew up in the Seattle area. Jimi Hendrix (1942–70) is a permanent fixture here, so you may even see his very first guitar, a Silvertone by Sears that still has fingering numbers on first three frets. But there are so many other great artists represented here through their records, costumes, and instruments, from B.B. King to Janis Joplin, from Bob Dylan to Heart, the Beach Boys, and many, many more.

A large part of EMP is most assuredly a hands-on museum. While you won't get to play any of those valuable, historic guitars, the third-floor Sound Lab has soundproof booths filled with guitars, amps, keyboards, and drum kits that you can play. There are recorded instructions on how to play instruments and how to record your songs. In one, a recorded voice guides you through a hands-on process where you can record a song that you mix from prerecorded music tracks. You decide how to balance each of the tracks with a set of faders and turn them into a finished product. Fortunately, the lines of people waiting for the labs are usually short and move reasonably fast as each lab session is timed. You have to leave when your 10 minutes or so runs out.

For music history fans, Sound and Vision: Artists Tell Their Stories offers hours worth of oral histories—stories told by the artists about themselves and their music. The collection includes hundreds of oral renditions from the likes of Pearl Jam guitarist Mike McCready, R & B legend Ruth Brown, record mogul Clive Davis, and country musician Marty Stuart. Visitors to the museum are encouraged to record their own stories about music and pop culture.

HOURS: Memorial Day weekend through Labor Day: daily, 10 AM to 7 PM; remainder of the year: daily, 10 AM to 5 PM. Hours can change for special events. Closed Thanksgiving and Christmas.

COST: Ages 18–64, $15; ages 65-plus, active military, and ages 5–17, $12

LOCATION: 325 5th Avenue North, Seattle

PHONE: 206-770-2700

WEBSITE: www.empsfm.org

5 Science Fiction Museum and Hall of Fame

WHAT'S HERE: **Science fiction at its best, from books and radio to television and film**

DON'T MISS THIS: **The Death Star model used in the *Star Wars* movies**

In 2004, the Science Fiction Museum and Hall of Fame opened in the same iconic Seattle building as EMP—Experience Music Project—both founded by Paul Allen, one of the cofounders of Microsoft. Sharing the same Frank Gehry–designed building is completely appropriate for a science fiction museum because the structure could easily be dropped into the movie set of some futuristic space world. Inside is not a huge gallery, but a series of smaller rooms connected by a twisting maze of short corridors and small hallways on two different levels, all with their own themes.

For those who grew up with James T. Kirk and the USS *Enterprise* (NCC-1701), one of the first exhibits is of the good captain's command chair. Many other *Star Trek* items, from weapons to uniforms, are here as well. Exhibits continue exploring the history of science fiction, from some of the simplest questions about "What if?" that started the science fiction craze, to the science fiction community's fan clubs and organizations that have celebrated and promoted this popular genre since its inception. There's even a 1939, hand-stapled copy of *The Who's Who in Fandom* and a copy of *Le Zombie*, a science fiction fan magazine from 1944.

Relatively new for the museum is the Science Fiction Hall of Fame that honors those who have brought science fiction to life. Four new members are added yearly, and they join some very amazing creators of science fiction, including Isaac Asimov, Ray Bradbury, Edgar Rice Burroughs, George Lucas, Mary W. Shelley, Rod Serling, and Steven Spielberg, among many others.

For the equipment techies, the museum's armory includes examples of the space hardware that is part of every movie and book, from scanners and communicators to tricorders and phasers. Most space suits were not designed to win beauty contests, and the collection of movie-designed outfits keeps that tradition alive.

A sampling of the space cities built by creative minds for movies can be seen, including computer-generated worlds of *The Matrix*, *Blade Runner*, and of course, *The Jetsons*. And one of the most feared artificial worlds, the model of the Death Star used in the *Star Wars* movies sits on its own pedestal. Temporary exhibits bring in other treasures. You might see

Science Fiction Museum

the B9 robot from *Lost in Space*, or perhaps the more ominous T800 Terminator, both of which have been here.

Throughout the museum, each of the themed galleries includes movie props, first edition books, costumes, posters, and more. There are almost always special exhibits that change every few months, each with a new look at a different aspect of science fiction.

HOURS: Memorial Day weekend through Labor Day: daily, 10 AM to 7 PM; remainder of the year: daily, 10 AM to 5 PM. Hours can change for special events. Closed Thanksgiving and Christmas.

COST: Ages 18–64, $15; ages 65-plus, active military, and ages 5–17, $12

LOCATION: 325 5th Avenue North, Seattle

PHONE: 206-770-2700

WEBSITE: www.empsfm.org

6 Pike Place Market

WHAT'S HERE: **Vendors selling everything from food to crafts**

DON'T MISS THIS: **The famous flying fish**

Pike Place Market is one of the oldest continually operating public markets in the country and one of Seattle's must-see tourist stops. The market opened in August 1907 as a place for farmers, fishermen, and other merchants to sell their products—and it's only grown larger over the years. Prior to the market's opening, most local farmers sold their produce through wholesalers who weren't always the most honest businesspeople. With support from a city council member, an ordinance was passed that created a public market. Even though the wholesalers attempted to sabotage the project, it turned into a roaring success as the locals flocked to the new market, buying everything the farmers had to offer. Politicians and business owners periodically have tried to change the market over the decades, at one point even wanting to tear it down to build a hotel and mall. Fortunately, the few successful changes that have been made appear to have been for the good.

If you enter the market from its main entrance where Pike Street turns right into Pike Place, you'll see two of the markets perennially famous icons—Rachel the Pig and the Pike Place Fish Market. Rachel is a 550-pound cast bronze piggy bank that has become kind of an unofficial market mascot. People, even big people, love climbing on the pig's back for photographs. Directly behind the pig is Pike Place Fish Market, an attraction that's made local, national, and international news shows over the years because of its flying fish—not real flying fish, but the kind thrown by the workers. Purchase a salmon or some other big fish lying on the ice counter, and the worker out front will shout a warning and fling the three-foot fish through the air to an employee behind the counter who prepares and wraps it. It happens quickly, so keep your camera ready.

The fish market may be the most well-known vendor at the Pike Place Market, but it's far from the only one. There are nine acres of market perched on one of Seattle's many steep hillsides. The main level includes dozens of food, produce, and flower vendors. Look for the elevator or take one of the stairways to the lower levels and there are a few hundred more shops selling everything from comic books to crafts. Several popular restaurants are also tucked into the different levels. Even if you don't want to buy, it's great fun just to wander through the market and maybe listen to musicians who post themselves in several places, accepting tips for their performances.

HOURS: Daily, some stalls open as early as 7 AM, especially the farmers; most other vendors open by 10 AM and close by 6 PM, Monday through Saturday; Sunday, 11 AM to 5 PM. Closed Thanksgiving, Christmas, and New Year's Day.

COST: Market is free

LOCATION: Several blocks around Pike Place and 1st Avenue, and Pike Street and Pike Place, Seattle. Parking garage is located at 1531 Western Avenue, although other parking is available.

PHONE: 206-682-7453

WEBSITE: www.pikeplacemarket.com

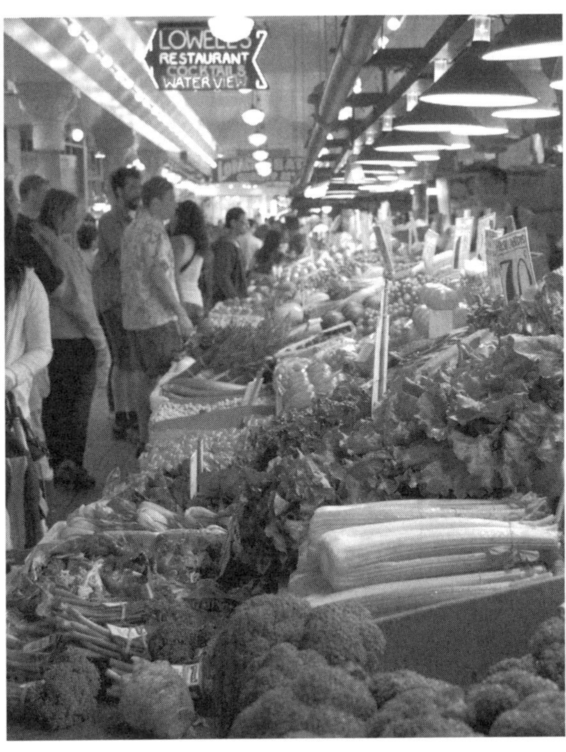

Pike Place farmers' market

7 Seattle Aquarium

WHAT'S HERE: Washington marine life, from fish to seals
DON'T MISS THIS: The underwater dome

From the outside, the Seattle Aquarium could be mistaken for one of the pier warehouses along the waterfront, in this case Pier 59. Once inside, though, it's obvious this is no warehouse. The museum completed an 18,000-square-foot expansion in 2007, so there's even more to see and do than before.

The first exhibit you pass upon entering the aquarium is Window on Washington Water. The 120,000 gallons of seawater contained inside 12.5-inch-thick glass hold salmon, rockfish, sea anemones, and other marine life that live among the rocks and kelp. Divers enter the tank three times each day and are able to answer visitor questions.

For those not too squeamish, here is an opportunity to touch live marine creatures. Life on the Edge is the aquarium's version of a tide pool, those shoreline pockets of water that are battered by crashing waves and often baked by warm sunshine, yet produce and support prolific numbers of marine species. Two large pools, with naturalists nearby to help youngsters and answer questions, are filled with such creatures as anemones and sea stars.

The ocean is alive with drifters, those sea creatures that lack the fins and tails that allow for easy movement when hunting for food. Instead, drifters relay primarily on ocean currents and the action of waves and wind to move them from feeding place to feeding place. So what are drifters? The best known are jellyfish, which come in many sizes and colors. The aquarium's "Ring of Life" is a glass doughnut filled with moon jellies. Special lights combine with the jellyfish's luminosity to create quite the spectacle. The jellyfish usually range in size from 10 to 16 inches in diameter and simply drift with the currents. As the jelly passes near anything that serves as a food source, it can sting its next meal with its tentacles before bringing it into its body to be digested. Another drifter? Octupi or octopus, if you prefer. The aquarium's giant Pacific octopus can be seen up close in another of the special tanks.

Birds and mammals are almost always around on Washington's hundreds of miles of shoreline. A large portion of the aquarium is dedicated to these creatures. Shorebirds have adapted quite well to living along the water's edge. Some are diving birds, capable of capturing food such as swimming fish. Others have long, stout bills that allow them to penetrate the sandy seashore and find food. Other shoreline creatures also found in the aquarium include harbor seals, fur seals, and sea

Seattle Aquarium

otters. If you've never seen these creatures swim, here is an opportunity to see them from both above and below at the underwater viewing area.

There is much more to see, from some of the strangest ocean creatures such as cowfish and potbelly seahorses, to the crashing coastline surf. One of the newest and most popular exhibits is the underwater dome. Head downstairs and you can stand beneath and be surrounded by a 400,000-gallon tank filled with hundreds of fish. The dome allows for 360-degree views. There is also a new cafe and gift shop.

HOURS: Daily, 9:30 AM to 5 PM, exhibits close at 6 PM. Open on Thanksgiving, Christmas, and New Year's Day, but with shorter hours.

COST: Ages 13-plus, $16; ages 4–12, $10.50

LOCATION: 1483 Alaskan Way (along the waterfront), Seattle

PHONE: 206-386-4300

WEBSITE: www.seattleaquarium.org

SEATTLE

8 Seattle Art Museum

WHAT'S HERE: **Extensive collection of art from around the world**

DON'T MISS THIS: ***Hammering Man***

Just a short walk from Seattle's historic Pike Place Market, the Seattle Art Museum dominates much of an entire city block. A fun way to see the museum is to take one of the self-guided theme tours that are offered. Check the lobby brochure rack when you enter for a series of suggested highlight tours or take a copy of the general guide map and spend several hours wandering through the museum's four levels and 35 galleries. The permanent collection numbers 23,000 objects, with about 2,600 exhibited at any one time.

As art pieces are rotated from storage to public galleries for viewing throughout the year, you might see such diverse pieces as a New Guinea wooden Asmat warrior's shield with its decorating art shapes representing a deadly female praying mantis or American artist Frederic Edwin Church's *A Country Home* (1854). You may see the Gela Mask made of wood, raffia, cloth, teeth, and other animal pieces. It helped dancers deal with problems affecting villagers. One of the galleries may hold *Claude Monet*, an 1890 charcoal-on-paper that was drawn by Theodore Robinson who befriended Monet in Giverny, France, or perhaps the candid portrait of Dr. Silvester Gardiner (1708–86) painted by American John Singleton Copley.

Chinese and Asian art pieces include a three-foot-tall Indian Buddha (possibly from the second century) made from schist. The collection includes numerous pieces of porcelain, which is a mixture of clay with other minerals, that when fired at a very high heat, fuses into the more durable product. The gallery is filled with examples of fine porcelain, some grouped by color, others by themes that include bugs, birds, and bees. Trade played an integral part in the spreading of porcelain throughout the world; one of the museum's examples is a gin bottle that was made in Japan, shipped to Holland where it was painted in the Japanese style, and finally sold on the Dutch market.

The fourth-floor galleries feature European art, a prominent aspect of the Seattle Art Museum's overall art collection. An example is *The Judgment of Paris* (circa 1516–18) painted by German Lucas Cranach the Elder. The piece represents a beauty contest that includes Mercury attempting to awaken Paris in the near darkness, both seemingly unaware of the nearby three almost identical nude goddesses—who generally draw most viewers' attention. Another piece that you might see and enjoy is Jacques-Andre-Joseph Aved's *Madame Brion, Seated, Taking Tea* (1750). The woman stares back at the viewer, somewhat smugly as she stirs her tea.

Contemporary art also has a place here. A self-portrait by Jacob Lawrence shows him in his attic studio where he and his wife lived in Seattle. He was a master of combining flat colors, strong shapes, and diagonal lines to create visual impact. There are many more pieces to enjoy as you wander the different floors and galleries, including numerous examples from Japan and Korea, Africa, and Mesoamerica. Native American, ancient Mediterranean, and Islamic art are also well represented. The pieces utilize many different mediums, including textiles, stone, metal, decorative arts, and fabric.

The first piece of art that you will see when you visit is actually outside the museum at the corner of 1st Avenue and Union Street. It's *Hammering Man*, a 48-foot-tall sculpture of steel with a mechanized aluminum arm that raises and lowers its hammer. There are *Hammering Man* sculptures in New York, Los Angeles, Germany, and Japan. Seattle's 26,000-pound version was placed here in 1992 and has been hammering away ever since.

Seattle Art Museum

HOURS: Tuesday through Sunday; 10 AM to 5 PM; Thursday and Friday, 10 AM to 9 PM. Closed Mondays, except major holidays. Closed Thanksgiving, Christmas, and New Year's Day.
COST: Adults, $15; ages 62 and over, $12; ages 13–17, $9
LOCATION: 1300 1st Avenue, Seattle
PHONE: 206-654-3100
WEBSITE: www.seattleartmuseum.org

9 The Wing Luke Asian Museum

WHAT'S HERE: **Creative joining of history, contemporary Chinese society, and guided tours of Seattle's Chinatown**
DON'T MISS THIS: **The recreated Yick Fung Co. store, originally opened in 1910**

Recently moved to a new and significantly larger location, this museum is continuing to expand both its collections and the permanent exhibit space. It is named in honor of Wing Chong Luke, (1925–65), Washington state's first Asian American to hold elected office. Luke was born in China, but by the time he was six, his parents had emigrated to the U.S. and settled in Seattle where they owned a small laundry and a grocery store. As the one of several Chinese harassed by school bullies, Luke soon won over the harassing students, in part by standing up to them and also through his drawings of cartoon panels that made them laugh. Luke excelled in school, becoming student president of Roosevelt High School.

Having just started college in 1944, he was drafted into the U.S. Army and served in Guam, Korea, New Guinea, and the Philippines, earning a Bronze Star. When the war ended, Luke returned to college earning a B.A. in political science and a law degree. He became Washington State's Assistant Attorney General from 1957 to 1962, serving in the Civil Rights Division. He was elected to the Seattle City Council in 1962, running on the slogan, "You are not electing a platform, but a Councilman." Always fighting discrimination in all of its forms, Wing Luke was a key figure in

The museum's Yick Fung Co. store

the passage of Seattle's Open Housing Ordinance in 1963 that provided punitive actions to fight racial discrimination in selling and renting real estate. Unfortunately, when he was returning from a fishing vacation in Okanogan County in 1965, his light plane crashed in the mountains, killing all aboard. The wreckage wasn't found for three years. Friends and supporters donated money to pay for the search, and the leftover funds were used to start the original Wing Luke Asian Museum.

With homelands ranging from Afghanistan, Nepal, Pakistan, Bangladesh, China, Japan, India, and other countries, the museum holds the potential for representing many different Asian cultures. The keystone exhibit is entitled Honoring Our Journey and documents the Asian-American experience with five themes: home, getting here, making a living, social justice, and community. Many Asians immigrated to the U.S. for the same reasons that Europeans and others had: escape from home country religious and political persecution, wars, and often the simple opportunities to make a better life. In the 19th century the California Gold Rush brought many Chinese to this country, and later, enticements by the railroads needing laborers attracted thousands more. In the 1890s, farming opportunities attracted Japanese frustrated with Hawaiian plantation work. Many of those who immigrated to the Pacific Northwest became part of the fishing industry in Washington, Oregon, and Alaska, the mining industry in Idaho, and more recently the health sciences and computer industry in the Puget Sound and Portland areas.

Even the museum building is part of Asian history in Seattle. It was built in 1910 and was named the East Kong Yick Building. It was paid for by 170 Chinese immigrants who wished to create a place where new immigrants could find a room, a meal, and comfort among those who spoke the same language. There were 50 rooms on the building's upper two floors that hosted not only Chinese, but workers from Japan and the Philippines. On guided "immersion" tours you can visit a one-room apartment, the hotel manager's office, the communal kitchen, and more.

One of the stops on the guided tours is a walk through the recreated Yick Fung Co. store. Much of the real Yick Fung Co. had operated only a half block away since 1910. The store was moved into the new museum as an exhibit, including the products that were on its shelves. The store's primary customers were Chinese restaurants—and not just local restaurants. Their imported soy sauce, chopsticks, spices, and other Chinese staples were shipped as far away as Idaho and Montana.

One of the more intriguing exhibits—and there are many—is the historic scrim, a theater curtain that was thought to have been lost since it was removed from the Kan Theater in 1915. The 15-foot-by-30-foot curtain, which served as a fire safety curtain, was painted with numerous, large advertising messages from local Japanese businesses. One of those early advertised businesses, the Maneki Japanese restaurant, survives today. The scrim now hangs in the museum's theater.

The museum staff offers tours of not only what they call the "immersion rooms," the restored historic boarding rooms on the top floor, but also tours of Seattle's Chinatown International District's shops and markets.

HOURS: Tuesday through Sunday; 10 AM to 5 PM; first Thursday and third Saturday of each month, 10 AM to 8 PM
COST: Adults, $8; ages 62 and over and grades 6 and above, $6; grades K–5, $5
LOCATION: 719 South King Street, Seattle
PHONE: 206-623-5124
WEBSITE: www.wingluke.org/home.htm

10 The Museum of Flight

WHAT'S HERE: **Aircraft, from some of the earliest to the Concorde**
DON'T MISS THIS: **The reconstructed original 1916 biplane factory in the Red Barn**

Being located in an industrial district near the Seattle waterfront makes complete sense for The Museum of Flight. As the world's largest private nonprofit air and space museum housing the largest aircraft collection in the western U.S., it tells the story of flight from the early days of the Wright brothers through today's space flights. The early history of aviation exhibits is housed in the original Red Barn where William E. Boeing began his airplane manufacturing business in 1916. The Red Barn exhibits include an aircraft factory workshop where Boeing's early 19th-century airplanes were built by hand from wood and canvas. Included are partially constructed aircraft illustrating the process.

It's impossible to know where best to start your tour. You can join a docent for a more informed tour, or simply go on your own as most visitors do. The six-story Great Gallery is the premier exhibit area where examples of aircraft from every era are exhibited. A storied DC-3, one of World War II's most venerable airplanes, sporting the Alaska Airlines name, hangs from the ceiling alongside many other equally famous aircraft. Nearby, with a wingspan nearly the same as the DC-3 but thousands of pounds lighter, is the MacCready Gossamer Albatross II, the first human-powered aircraft that was successfully flown (using bicycle pedal power) 22 miles across the English Channel.

DC-3 at The Museum of Flight

On the floor of the Great Gallery there are nearly two dozen more aircraft ranging from a reconstructed Wright 1903 Flyer to Vietnam-era aircraft such as the F-4 Phantom. Appropriately, next to the Phantom is the smaller Russian

SEATTLE

Mikoyan-Gurevich MiG-21, and another few feet away is the earlier MiG-15. Easily the largest aircraft in the main gallery is the Lockheed M-21, predecessor of the famed SR-71 Blackbird, the high-flying bullet of a spy plane. Sitting atop the M-21 is the only remaining Lockheed D-21B Drone, a mach-3-plus photo surveillance rocket that never quite worked the way envisioned. If you've ever wondered what it would be like to fly a mission aboard an SR-71, you have the opportunity to tuck yourself into the big SR-71's tiny cockpit, play with some of the controls, and imagine sitting there for many long hours. You can do the same in an F/A Hornet attack jet cockpit.

The Kid's Flight Zone is located off the main gallery. The zone includes flight simulators for kids (and adventurous parents), including one that allows you to sit in the seat of a hang glider, grab the overhead control bar and attempt to steer yourself off the top of a computer-generated image of a mountain and land in a bull's-eye target far below. Crashing into the trees or the adjacent hillside is common. Upstairs is a control tower that overlooks a very active airstrip. It includes exhibits and the same equipment that air traffic controllers use, including live radio traffic from the nearby real tower controlling the airstrip's numerous incoming and outgoing aircraft.

On the opposite side of the museum, past the Red Barn, is the realm of World War I and II aircraft, including the Italian-built Caproni Ca 20, considered the world's very first fighter aircraft. It was the only Ca 20 constructed because the government needed heavy bombers. The Caproni family stored the plane for more than 85 years before giving it to the museum. Touring the World War I gallery, you have an opportunity to try your hand at flight simulators, walk through a reconstructed bunker complex, and watch war-era history films in the French Farmhouse Theater.

Downstairs, World War II aircraft take over, with a Lockheed P-38L Lightning suspended from the ceiling. Scattered among the other exhibits are American, Japanese, German, and English fighter aircraft, with names like Spitfire, Messerschmitt, Corsair, Wildcat, and Mustang. In the Quonset Hut Theater, films of World War II aircraft battles are continuously screened.

When you think you've seen it all, take a walk across the pedestrian bridge to the museum's Airpark. Parked outside, several additional aircraft, including the retired supersonic Concorde, a Boeing 747, and a Boeing VC-137B, await your visit. The last was designated "Air Force One" anytime it was flying with Presidents Eisenhower, Kennedy, and Johnson. President Johnson even had a "doggie door" added for his pet beagles.

HOURS: Main Museum: Daily, 10 AM to 5 PM; open until 9 PM the first Thursday each month. Closed Thanksgiving and Christmas Day.
Airpark: Open generally May 1 through Labor Day, Thursday through Tuesday, 11 AM to 4:30 PM; remainder of the year, 11 AM to 3:30 PM. Airpark is also closed during inclement weather.

COST: Ages 18–64, $14; ages 65-plus, $13; ages 5–17, $7.50

LOCATION: 9404 East Marginal Way South, Seattle

PHONE: 206-764-5720

WEBSITE: www.museumofflight.org

Seattle Tours

T

Family/Kids' Adventure Tour

ESTIMATED DAYS: 1
ESTIMATED DRIVING MILES: 0

A few cities offer duck tours, and Seattle is one of them with its **Ride the Ducks of Seattle** (www.rideth educksofseattle.com). This is great fun for the entire family touring the best parts of Seattle in World War II amphibious vehicles. And partway through the tour of places like Pioneer Square, Pike Place Market, and the waterfront, to prove that the vehicles are indeed amphibious, you will be treated to a cruise on Seattle's Lake Union. The tours begin across the street from the **Space Needle** (www.spaceneedle.com), another fun ride. Take the elevator up to the restaurant that rotates slowly at the top of the 605-foot-tall structure built for the 1962 World's Fair. It offers a 360-degree panoramic view of Seattle and the waterfront. Tickets to the top range in price from $9 for kids to $16 for adults, but if you eat in the restaurant, the ride up is free.

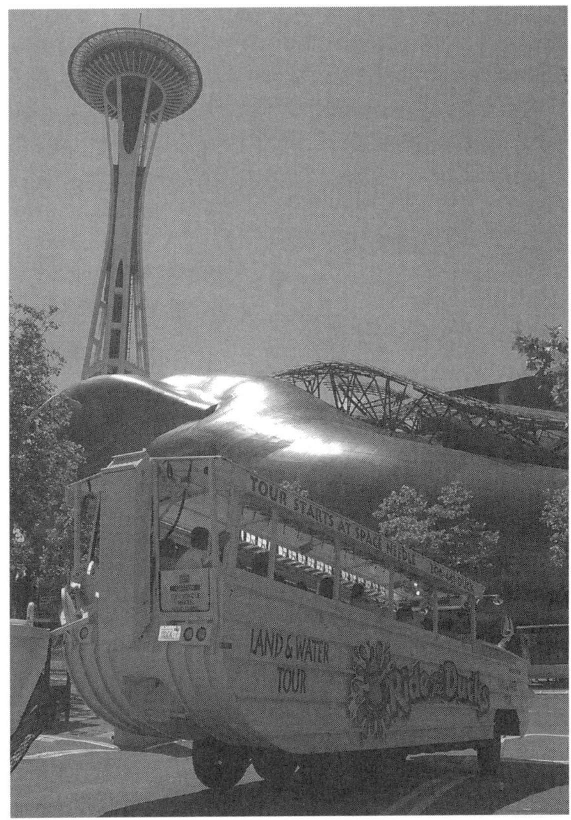

An amphibious duck on tour

Back down on earth, it's on to the **Science Fiction Museum and Hall of Fame** (page 255) where some of the world's best-known science fiction characters and their weapons and more await. In the same futuristic building, the **Experience Music Project** (page 253) resides. While older kids who are into

SEATTLE

rock and roll will enjoy the exhibits, everyone interested in music will love the hands-on areas where anyone, even those without musical instrument playing skills can make their own music. All of these sites are within a five-minute walk of Seattle's landmark Space Needle.

Seattle Waterfront Tour

ESTIMATED DAYS: 2–3
ESTIMATED DRIVING MILES: 1

Seattle's waterfront is a fun, vibrant place to spend an entire day. The perfect place to begin is at the historic **Pike Place Market** (page 256) where you can enjoy great food, lots of shopping, and even purchase fresh flowers for that special someone. Within easy walking distance from the front of the market, the **Seattle Art Museum** (page 259) awaits with its thousands of treasures and its iconic 48-foot-tall *Hammering Man* moving sculpture out front.

Walk down the hill on any of the adjacent streets to get the few blocks to the waterfront and the **Seattle Aquarium** (page 258) where examples of some of what lurks beneath Puget Sound and the Pacific Ocean can be seen. The waterfront features more restaurants and gift shops, including **Ye Olde Curiosity Shop** (www.yeoldecuriosityshop.com), a fixture since 1899. It's filled with novelty souvenirs, but also one of the oddest collections of historic artifacts and mummified bodies, two-headed calves, and a really ugly sea-creature of unknown lineage. Parking is at a premium around this part of Seattle, so when you find a space, it's best to park and walk.

Main entrance to Pike Place Market

Seattle Information Centers

Seattle Convention and Visitors Bureau
www.visitseattle.org
206-461-5800

Greater Seattle Chamber of Commerce
www.seattlechamber.com
206-389-7200

Washington's Cascade Range

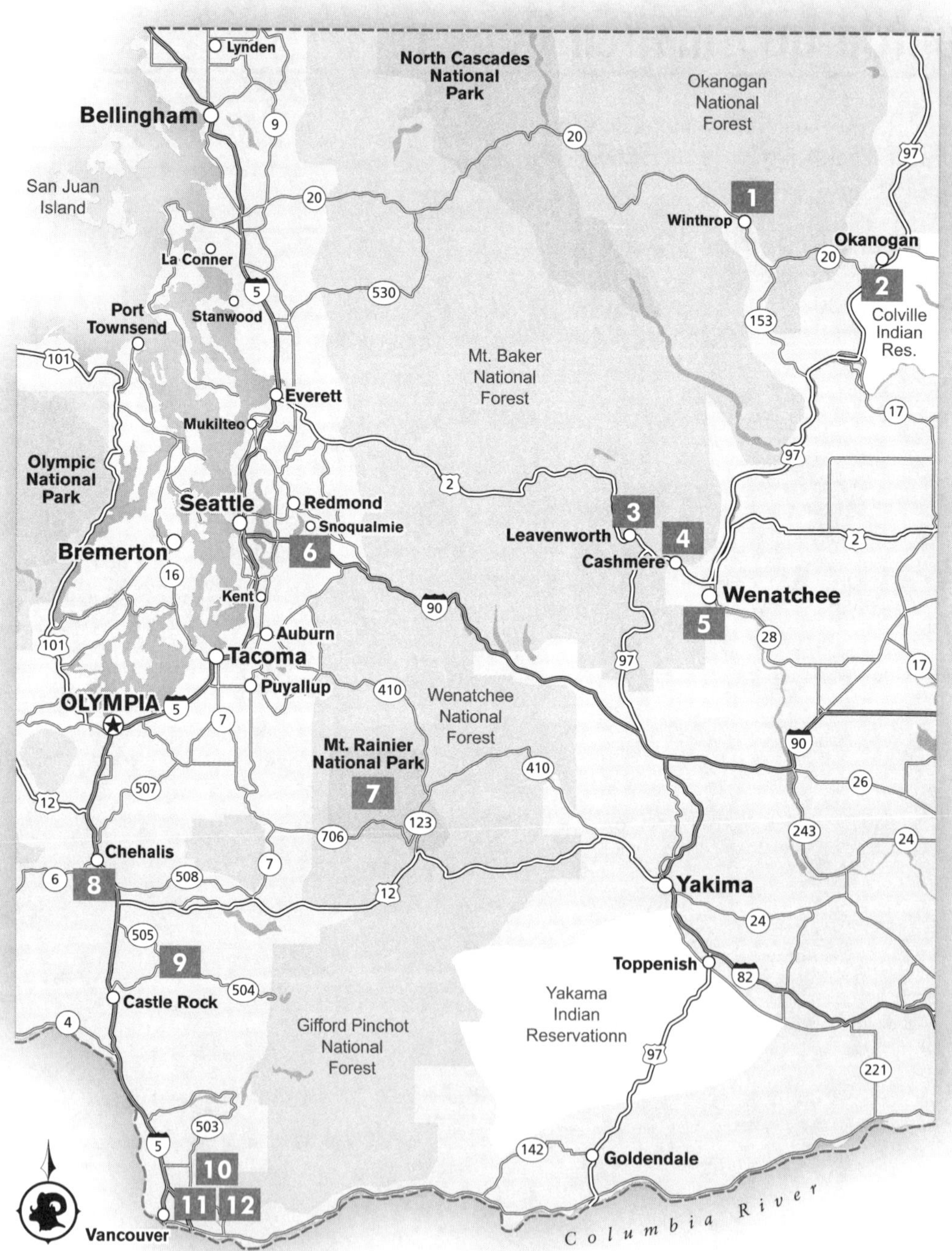
Lynden
North Cascades National Park
Okanogan National Forest
Bellingham
San Juan Island
Winthrop
Okanogan
La Conner
Colville Indian Res.
Port Townsend
Stanwood
Mt. Baker National Forest
Everett
Mukilteo
Olympic National Park
Seattle
Redmond
Snoqualmie
Leavenworth
Bremerton
Cashmere
Wenatchee
Kent
Auburn
Tacoma
Puyallup
OLYMPIA
Wenatchee National Forest
Mt. Rainier National Park
Chehalis
Yakima
Toppenish
Castle Rock
Yakama Indian Reservationn
Gifford Pinchot National Forest
Goldendale
Vancouver
Columbia River

Washington's Cascade Range

The Cascade Range passes through central Washington and is marked by tall peaks, including Mount Adams in the south and Mount Baker to the north. All are dominated by 14,000-foot, glacier-capped Mount Rainier and well-known Mount St. Helens, which still remains active following its catastrophic 1980 eruption.

Much of this great mountainous expanse is very lightly populated, with the exception of a few small towns along the southern Interstate 5 corridor, which we include in this section of the book. State and national parks and forests cover most of the Cascade Range,

Northwest Railway Museum

with tiny towns tucked into mostly isolated valleys where early pioneers were able to make their livings as farmers or later in the logging industry. Many of the people living here are descendants of those early pioneers, while others have come to exchange city life for the quiet solitude of nature.

Whether you travel here during summer, winter, spring, or fall, the views are spectacular and rivers seem to be everywhere, inviting you to cast a fishing line. Remember, during winter many of the highways through the Cascades are closed because of snow, especially the less-traveled secondary roads. Some remain closed all winter, while others are closed only until a snowplow can get through. Be sure to check road conditions if you are visiting during winter.

TRIVIA

1. In what national park will you find a mountain with 26 glaciers?
2. Where can you see a rare Rickenbacker Motor Company car built by a famous World War I German air ace?
3. Where can you see the world's largest collection of nutcrackers?
4. Where can you learn more about an apple-slapping machine?
5. Where can you see a volcano that erupted in 1980, sending superheated water and molten rock speeding through the surrounding valleys?
6. Where was the British Hudson's Bay Company headquarters located during the early 19th century?
7. Where can you learn the story about Russian aviators who landed unannounced in Vancouver after the first nonstop flight over the North Pole?

For trivia answers, see page 346.

1 Shafer Museum

WHAT'S HERE: A replica of a fictional Methow Valley pioneer settlement
DON'T MISS THIS: The log "Castle"

While most people would not think to refer to a simple log cabin as "The Castle," Harvard graduate Guy Waring thought differently. Near the end of the 19th century, Waring, having failed in his business pursuits in Washington's Methow Valley, returned to Winthrop, this time with a wife. He had convinced her to accompany him by promising to build her a fine home. Even the locals referred to his log home as "The Castle." Within a few years, Waring had become a successful businessman and owned every building in town except town hall. But his fortunes again changed, and in 1916 he claimed bankruptcy. He left his castle to his stepson Harry Greene and headed east.

In later years, Waring's castle became the town's Episcopal church. Finally, in 1943 local merchant Simon Shafer purchased the log castle and turned it into a museum. The Okanogan County Historical Society has since taken over the home and turned the entire homesite into a miniature historic town and museum.

Shafer Museum bell tower

Don't expect to see a large museum building when you get to the Shafer Museum—there isn't one. The museum complex looks like a small town that you enter by walking beneath the legs supporting a wooden bell tower. Inside the compound, gravel walkways lead from one building to the next, so wear appropriate shoes. Ask for one of the museum's brochures, especially if you have kids along. The brochure includes a quiz with several questions that most people—including kids—likely won't know the answers to, but that can be easily discovered while touring the museum's many exhibits.

One of the first things you may see is a Babcock press. It was not an apple press, but was a printing press that belonged to Claud Watkins who used it to print the *Methow Valley News* until 1976. Along with the printing press is a Linotype machine that made the hot lead type used to print newspapers. Nearby there are lots of pieces of farm equipment from past eras. An early part of the area's history is the homesteader cabin that Isaac Nickell built in the 1880s on his property near the mouth of Liar Creek. Trying to save his family's home from a wildfire, Nickell was severely burned, injuries that he eventually died from in October 1889. His cabin was moved to the museum site in 1951, where its dirt floor adds an additional touch of realism to the rustic nature of life here in the late 19th century.

The old stagecoach was one of the early museum artifacts that Shafer added to his collection. In the 1970s, a Japanese film company rented the coach to make a film about photographer Frank Matsura (see Okanogan County Historical Museum, facing page) who lived in Okanogan from 1903 to 1913. Slightly newer transportation can be seen in the 1914 Model T Ford touring car that is in beautiful condition. There is also a rare Rickenbacker Motor Company car built by World War I flying ace Captain Eddie Rickenbacker, a lover of fast planes who decided to build a fast car. His six-cylinder, partly aluminum car reached an astounding 95 miles per hour during a cross-country race.

In another log cabin structure, a kitchen has been set up that includes the blue-and-white kettle its owner used for 58 years. It was a bonus gift she received upon purchasing her Home Comfort Kitchen Range in 1894. There is also a waffle iron dating from the 1870s and a full-length, horsehide coat worn by a local stagecoach driver in the very early 1900s.

And the famous "Castle?" It's here. The hand-hewn log cabin that Guy Waring built in 1897 was constructed under his wife's careful supervision. Reportedly, she insisted that each log be within a half inch of level to guarantee tightly fitted walls that would keep out the weather. It worked.

Continue along the path to a structure originally built about 1900 as the town's post office. The owner moved the structure to Goat Creek were it became an assay office. Inside are numerous pieces of assay and mining equipment from gold pans to the assayer's furnace. Close to many miners' hearts was probably the painting of a young saloon girl wearing her revealing red dress—and the handmade signs advertising local drink: Squirrel Whiskey, $1 per gallon; Laughing Dew, $0.75 per gallon; and Crying Solace, $0.50 per gallon.

At the far end of the grounds is a collection point for many dozens of pieces of old mining equipment from Pelton wheels and trucks to stamp mills and matte shell molds (used for molten matte or impure metals). Inside some of the other nearby buildings are many more artifacts, including old clothing irons, guns, and cooking items.

HOURS: Memorial Day weekend through September: Thursday through Monday, 10 AM to 6 PM. Closed in winter.

COST: Donation

LOCATION: 285 Castle Avenue, Winthrop

PHONE: 509-996-2712

WEBSITE: www.shafermuseum.com

2 Okanogan County Historical Museum

WHAT'S HERE: Exhibits covering all aspects of the county's history
DON'T MISS THIS: The Fire Hall Museum next door

The museum's main gallery is filled with exhibits about the overall history of Okanogan County. They begin with the geology of the far distant past and end with what's here today. The display cases hold samples of the various rocks found in the area such as gneiss, a common rock formed from existing rocks that are placed under tremendous pressure and heat as deep as 10 miles below the earth's surface. Formed much differently is the sandstone sample that is made from soil deposits that build up in bodies of water such as ancient seas or lakes.

There is a quick look at American Indian life in the area, including the coming of fur traders, their impact, and the changes that soon followed. One of those changes was the construction of Fort Okanogan, built to support the Hudson's Bay Company. Trappers from miles around brought their beaver pelts here. In 1846, a treaty between the U.S. and Great Britain moved the U.S.-Canadian border north to the 49th parallel. By this time, the fur trade was nearly dead, with the last trading party coming to the fort in 1848. The fort fell into disrepair, and its remnants and surrounding 30 acres were sold to the U.S. in 1869.

The cattle industry was another of the area's economic strengths. Barbed wire, branding irons, and lariats can be found in the museum with maps and information about early day cattle drives. Next came gold! There was a short-lived gold rush in 1860 on the Similkameen River. It may have been spurred by the British surveyors helping to establish the U.S.-Canadian border the year before. It got another kick in 1886, when miners were allowed onto the Columbia Reservation. The rush was termed "The Comstock of Washington," although more people went broke than became rich. From 1886 to the market bottom in 1893, only about $6 million worth of gold and silver was recovered, as most of the ore was too low grade to be mined economically at the time. The mining exhibit includes some of the tools used by these hardrock miners. There are several mini-galleries that include local wildlife, at least the taxidermied versions of deer, Canada geese, salmon, and even a bighorn sheep.

The Fire Hall Museum next door

Head outside to the mini-Main Street with its numerous shops. You can wander through everything from a milliner shop, the Okanogan County Mercantile, and the Big Dan Saloon, the first to be granted an operating license by the Okanogan City Council in 1907. One interesting item is the round safe used at the Omak State Bank from 1907 until 1927. From there it did time in the county treasurer's office until it was moved—all 4,160 pounds of it—to the museum in 1994.

Frank Matsura's photography shop is of special interest. Matsura immigrated to the U.S. from Japan in 1901, taking a job as a hotel dishwasher. In his free time he took photographs of the community. In 1906 Matsura moved to Okanogan and set up a photography business. He continued taking photographs of the changes occurring in the county, documenting changes that new settlers and the resulting development brought—railroad construction, parades, new bridges, children, and the local Native Americans. He died suddenly in 1913, and a local judge saved Matsura's glass plates and nitrate films. In 1954, the judge gave them to the University of Washington. More of the collection went to the Okanogan County Historical Society when the judge died. The studio here was constructed to look as similar as possible to Matsura's photo shop as it appeared before his death, based on his own photos.

A little farther down this makeshift town's Main Street is a collection of horse-drawn equipment. The collection includes typical buggies of the time and various pieces of farm equipment such as the two-wheeled Fresno grader that was used to make road cuts and fills. It doesn't look much different from those used today, other than being smaller and not having an engine or operator cabin—and it was pulled by a team of horses. The apple shed with its sorting equipment was another big part of the agricultural scene here.

On the opposite side of the museum grounds is the Firehall Museum. It contains fire equipment from several eras of firefighting, including Omak's first motorized fire engine—a 1918 G.M.C. four-cylinder, three-speed truck. It had no siren, depending instead on the screams of the driver and passengers at "onlookers, dogs, and cats to get out of the way." That apparently was enough warning. Firefighting equipment improved dramatically by the time the city purchased its second-ever fire truck, another G.M.C., but one much larger with a six-cylinder Buick engine. It managed to continue fighting fires until the 1950s when it threw a rod while returning from a call. Both trucks are included in the museum's collection, along with numerous other historic firefighting-related tools.

HOURS: Daily, 10 AM to 4 PM
COST: Ages 12 and over, $2
LOCATION: 1410 2nd Avenue, Okanogan
PHONE: 509-422-4272
WEBSITE: www.okanoganhistory.org

3 Leavenworth Nutcracker Museum

WHAT'S HERE: **Largest collection of nutcrackers in the U.S.**

DON'T MISS THIS: **The six-foot-tall German-made nutcracker**

Most of us probably visualize an oversized and toothy toy soldier when thinking about nutcrackers, and this private collection has plenty of those from all parts of the world and in every imaginable kind of finery. Nutcrackers, those carved and brightly-painted wooden soldiers and kings, have been around since the 15th century. The original soldier nutcrackers really did crack nuts. The carved figures had oversized mouths that were opened by lifting a lever in the doll's back, a nut was inserted inside the mouth, and then when someone pressed down on the lever, the nut was successfully cracked open. Few modern soldier nutcrackers serve such a utilitarian function; instead, they festively decorate holiday scenes.

Nutcrackers have been used for thousands of years. The first were nothing more than stones used to pound open hard-shelled nuts. The oldest metal nutcracker known dates back to the third or fourth century BC and resides in an Italian museum. The museum has its own 2,000-year-old Roman nutcracker. Brass nutcrackers—the earliest were hand-wrought—existed during the 14th and 15th centuries. Later, especially in England, nutcrackers were made from molten metal poured into molds.

Arlene Wagner is the energy behind one of the world's foremost nutcracker museums. She is an accomplished dancer and ballet teacher who, coincidently, produced the Nutcracker Ballet for many years during the 1960s. Arlene fell in love with the holiday icon, just as the famed ballet's main character, Clara, did. With the help of her husband George, she started collecting nutcrackers from all over the world, and in 1995, they opened the Leavenworth Nutcracker Museum. To date, the collection is one of the world's largest with more than 5,000 pieces spread throughout a 3,000-square-foot, Bavarian-style building, located in downtown Leavenworth. Her favorite piece in the museum is a six-foot-tall soldier nutcracker made especially for her and her husband by Karl Roppl (since deceased) of Oberammergau, Germany. The nutcracker, with the exception of the handle, was carved from a single piece of Linden wood.

Leavenworth Nutcracker Museum

The museum is located upstairs and its large size is surprising. There are long rows of glass cases filled with nutcrackers. Most are the various carved and beautifully painted soldier nutcrackers, but there are hundreds of the more useable handheld nutcrackers. All are old, some are cute, others are intricately designed, and more than a few are modeled to look like people, with the nut-cracking portion of the device placed between their legs or in other body areas—a possible cause for a few visitors to blush. One of the collection's earliest pieces—a bronze Roman nutcracker—dates to between 200 BC and 200 AD. It was found in 1960 after being buried for more than 1,800 years and is one of only three known to still be in existence. It doesn't look much like a nutcracker, but that's what archaeologists have deemed it to be.

The museum has possibly the earliest multitool recorded, a 17th-century handheld device that was not only a nutcracker, but a pick, corkscrew, pipe tamper, cleaver, and screwdriver, with the nutcracker character's face etched on both sides of the device. There are exquisite silver-plated nutcrackers, including one from South Africa that is decorated with colorful beadwork, and screw-type porcelain nutcrackers from Germany. The betel cutters are a local refinement on nutcrackers. They came from India and Thailand and are used to cut areca nuts (mild narcotics), which are then mixed with lime and various spices. The concoction is wrapped in a betel leaf creating a "quid," which is placed in the jaw, similar to chewing tobacco. Unfortunately for the user, the betel nut eventually permanently stains the user's teeth and gums black.

An interesting display for anyone who collects nutcrackers (the soldier type) is the Buyers Beware exhibit. It shows original and valuable German-made Erzgebirge and Steinbach nutcrackers. Christian Steinbach is often called the "King of the Nutcrackers," and he has traveled to the Nutcracker Museum here in Leavenworth on numerous occasions to sign his pieces for collectors. The valuable authentic nutcrackers are shown next to their Chinese copies, which are often purchased by unsuspecting buyers traveling in Germany.

Wagner loves nutcrackers so much that she even authored a beautiful coffee-table book of her collection—*The Art and Character of Nutcrackers*, published by Collector's Press. Wagner will lovingly sign this perfect holiday gift for that nutcracker lover on your list from the "Nutcracker Lady." Visit the museum's website for more information.

This is a fun museum located in a fun town. In the 1960s the local business owners, hoping to lure tourists to the area in the face of the lumber industry's demise, decided to turn their town into a Bavarian-style village. With nature's alpine backdrop already in place, the transformation worked. Today the town is a bustling tourist attraction, with nearly everything from the buildings to the festivals, designed around their Bavarian theme.

HOURS: May through October, daily, 2 PM to 5 PM; November through April, Saturday and Sunday, 2 PM to 5 PM; or by appointment

COST: Adults, $2.50; students, $1

LOCATION: 735 Front Street, Leavenworth

PHONE: 509-548-4573

WEBSITE: www.nutcrackermuseum.com

4 Cashmere Museum and Pioneer Village

WHAT'S HERE: A museum and a pioneer town with relocated historic buildings

DON'T MISS THIS: The Mesoamerican pottery collection

This is really two museums in one and both are well worth the visit. The artifacts that have been recovered from the Columbia River area and held here is quite impressive. Several large glass-enclosed exhibits showcase everything from fishing spearheads, deer horn tools, and mauls to bone tube beads, turquoise pendants, and ceremonial knives and pipes. Unusual for most county and regional museums that focus on local history and artifacts, the exhibits also include a collection of Mesoamerican pottery and related items from the states of Colima and Michoacan in Mexico. Many of the pieces range in age from 1,200 to 1,400 years old.

Closer to home, the nearby Native American exhibits include examples of wild plant foods that the local Indians harvested. The small samplings include the common and Latin names, plus the Indian name: Bitterroot is *spa'tlem* to the Indians; huckleberry is *sisa'pt;* wild carrot is *so-wicht;* and Oregon grape is *Sqo'eyu.* Another plant exhibit extols the medicinal benefits of some of those plants: Wild ginger, bitterroot, and young larch tips were all used to cure stomach ailments, while yarrow and horsetail were used to aid arthritis relief. There are beautiful examples of Indian clothing from the Columbia Plateau, from finely beaded moccasins to feathered headwear.

As in many areas of Oregon and Washington, the Hudson's Bay Company played a role in the history here. One of the company's bright red-and-white flags that once flew over one of the trading posts is positioned near a large collection of artifacts from that era. Beaver traps were a common trade item as were rifles, bullets, and powder. Finding new uses for old things, especially trade items, the Indians transformed sewing thimbles into a series of bells.

Head downstairs to the mineral collection—it is quite impressive and not all is from the Pacific Northwest. There is epidote from Austria, azurite from Mexico, and sphalerite from Oklahoma. There are also examples of petrified wood. The museum's lower level also is home to its large natural history collection. Dozens of birds, including a bald eagle and a prairie falcon, and mammals fill the exhibits. Birds' nests with their eggs, all identified by species, provide a look at how different birds have very different needs for nests. Beyond the animals is the pioneer history wing with its many exhibits of local history, including a log cabin, women's clothing, a look at the history of the Boy Scouts, and a working scale model of a J.I. Case steam engine.

The museum's outdoor pioneer town

Head through the back door to the pioneer town outside. Twenty different historic buildings have been saved and moved to the museum site—and all have been furnished, most in appropriate period furnishings and supplies. Information about the owners and history of most of the buildings is posted on them. This is a fun place for kids to wander around the enclosed village compound. The 1880s Brender Canyon one-room schoolhouse is next to the barbershop, which is next to the 1896 general store. The store was originally built as a home, but needs changed. The transformation to general store brought a coffee mill, cracker barrel, and pot-bellied stove that likely warmed the bodies of many community members on cold winter days. The log cabin post office was originally built in 1872 in Wenatchee and operated as a trading post before becoming a post office. Gold played an important role in the settlement of the region. The assay office was built in 1879 by the Blewett Mines. More than $39 million in gold passed through this wooden building—back when gold sold for only $8 per ounce.

A caboose and the Railway Express office is part of the Great Northern Railway exhibit. When the railroad came, so too did many more travelers who needed hotel rooms such as those found at the museum's Mission Hotel, which was first used as a cabin in 1898.

HOURS: March 1 to October 31, 9:30 AM until 4:30 PM; November 1 to December 21, Friday through Sunday, 10:30 AM to 3:30 PM. Closed Easter.

COST: Adults, $4.50; seniors and students, $3.50; ages 5–12, $2.50

LOCATION: 600 Cotlets Way, Cashmere

PHONE: 509-782-3230

WEBSITE: www.cashmeremuseum.org

5 Wenatchee Valley Museum and Cultural Center

WHAT'S HERE: **History of Wenatchee, from the ice age to contemporary art**

DON'T MISS THIS: **The 1920s apple catapulting, wiping, sorting, and sizing machine**

The Wenatchee Valley Museum and Cultural Center is a large and imposing building. Walk through the large lobby and gift store area to the exhibits, and you will be propelled back through time, initially as far back as 140 million years ago.

The museum's main floor offers some real treats, including the restored Wurlitzer Theatre Pipe Organ. It first made music in the city's Liberty Theatre in 1919 providing the sound effects and music for silent films. The old organ can reproduce the sounds of a full orchestra, including clarinet, bass drums, xylophone, and even the clacking of a horse's hooves. Main Street exhibits lie past the Wurlitzer. There is a 1907 International

Auto Buggy, originally purchased in Spokane in 1909 reportedly for $1,000. In 1946, Henry Boersma purchased a load of scrap metal and buried in the heap was the Auto Buggy. He and a friend got the car running again and drove it in numerous parades over the years before it was donated to the museum.

On the main floor, a bank teller's window and a general store have been recreated from local historical buildings and artifacts. A printing shop, a Victorian-era living room, and a kitchen are included in the gallery exhibits, along with a farm shop and all of its tools.

The museum's second floor explores the Native American culture that thrived here before the pioneers began arriving in great numbers during the mid-19th century. For example, the early introduction of the horse from the Southwest in the 1730s changed Native American cultures dramatically. Suddenly, tribes could expand their hunting and gathering territories, sometimes clashing with other tribes. With the introduction of guns in the early 19th century by fur traders, life became both better and more dangerous for the Indians. Hunting, especially large mammals, became much easier, but horses and guns together allowed raiding parties to roam large expanses of the Great Plains and Great Basin, attacking peaceful villages. Horses and guns became barometers of wealth and power for Indians. Exhibits include a look at their changing lifestyles, but also include the more traditional aspects of Native American culture, from basket making to preparing hides for use as clothing.

In 1987, workers in an East Wenatchee apple orchard uncovered several large stone tools. They turned out to be part of a large cache of 13,000-year-old Clovis (stone weapon) points. Significant by themselves, these points were larger than any previously found, most ranging from eight to nine inches long. Subsequent digs uncovered hundreds of objects from tools to bone fragments. The site was later closed to future excavations. Several of those Clovis points are in the Ice Age Mystery exhibit on the second floor.

The Great Northern Railway, the development of which changed the way people lived and farmed throughout much of Washington, has its own exhibit. Here you will find a model railroad diorama that includes the line's bridges and tunnels. It was the Great Northern Railway that began to change the way the local apple growers plied their trade. With the development of insulated refrigerator cars, replenished with ice at each major depot stop, thousands of pounds of apples could be transported fresh to Midwest and East Coast markets.

Wenatchee's close connection with apple growing is evident with the museum's collection of apple crate art. A large gallery is dedicated to apples—planting, pruning, growing, and harvesting the fruit. Modern grocery store shoppers would not likely be so enticed to purchase the dull-skinned apples that came straight from the trees and were sold everywhere until the mid-1920s. It was

Wenatchee Valley Museum

then that farmers began washing their apples, adding the shine that we see on apples sold today, but not because they wanted to. They had been spraying fruit with arsenic of lead, and the FDA began forcing them to remove it prior to marketing. Numerous "rag-slapping" machines were invented that could wipe away the poisonous film, eliminating the need to wipe each apple by hand.

In the early 1920s, a machine became available that, not only would wipe off the apples, but then catapult them into waiting cloth baskets, with the lighter, smaller apples flying into the farthest sorting baskets, the heavier apples in the nearest baskets. The machine was not a commercial success, but the museum has a working model of the device. Hope that it's operating the day you visit—it's both noisy and fascinating to watch.

HOURS: Tuesday through Saturday, 10 AM to 4 PM. Closed Sunday, Monday, and major holidays.
COST: Adults, $5; ages 60-plus, $4; ages 6–12, $2
LOCATION: 127 South Mission Street, Wenatchee
PHONE: 509-888-6256
WEBSITE: www.wenatcheewa.gov/Index.aspx?page=32

6 Northwest Railway Museum

WHAT'S HERE: **Oldest continually used train depot in the Pacific Northwest**
DON'T MISS THIS: **A walk in the yard among the locomotives and cars**

The historic depot has been in constant use since its construction in 1890, although today only weekend fun train rides depart from and arrive at the historic building. When completed, the Seattle, Lake Shore & Eastern Railway (SLS&E) connected the farm- and timberlands around Snoqualmie with the markets in Seattle. Farmers and ranchers could now reach large markets with their products and get them there inexpensively while they were still fresh.

But the community changed in ways that benefited more than just farmers—the train offered city folks an opportunity to easily visit what quickly became one of the area's most popular attractions. The trip from Seattle now took only a couple of hours, not days. Snoqualmie Falls, the same waterfall that appeared on television's popular *Twin Peaks*, is not far away on the Snoqualmie River. As people discovered how easy it was to take day or overnight excursions here to visit the Snoqualmie Hop Ranch and the falls, business-minded individuals began catering to their needs. Restaurants and hotels were built, including the Snoqualmie Falls Hotel in 1919, and the nearby Snoqualmie Falls Lodge, today's Salish Lodge & Spa.

During its heyday, the Snoqualmie Depot's freight room included about half of the building, as everything from kegs of nails and produce to trunks and suitcases was stacked waiting for trains to arrive. And when the train did arrive, it often unloaded as much as it picked up, with horse-drawn wagons, and in later years trucks, backed up to load and unload freight. When the freight trains weren't busy with their freight business, passenger trains were busy with people coming to relax or perhaps to call the beautiful Snoqualmie Valley their new home. Passenger trains also carried the U.S. mail.

Some of those who came here to pursue a chosen business often found that there were other more lucrative business opportunities. The Reinig family arrived in 1890, intending to farm hops, but in 1902 they opened a grocery store. The Kinsey family was one of the first to purchase real estate after the town was surveyed and its lots created. They started several businesses, including a hotel and the post office.

Walking around the depot today is a trip back in time. Since much of the rolling stock—and there are a lot of locomotives and cars—is subject to being moved around by the volunteers here for various special events and programs, there's no telling what you might find where. For instance, there is the Polson Logging Company's 1915 wood-side dump car. It was used to help build new track into ever-expanding cutting areas at a time when big dump trucks didn't exist. The Kennecot Copper Company Alco RSD-4 #201 is the museum's workhorse. The big diesel locomotive is sometimes used to pull the Snoqualmie Valley's Railroad excursion trains. Like most diesel locomotives, the diesel engine powers a generator that creates the electrical power to turn the electric motors that move the locomotive. The 12-cylinder, 1,600 horsepower locomotive can reach 60 miles per hour.

This is snow country and even trains had to contend with the white stuff. The museum's Northern Pacific steam rotary snowplow was built in 1907; its job was to keep the tracks clear of snow over nearby Stampede Pass. The snowplow's boiler provided power to two steam engines that, through a series of gears, spun the nearly 10-foot-diameter cutting blade at 60 miles per hour, allowing it to cut through some of the deepest drifts covering the tracks. It took one or more locomotives to push the snowplow through the snow so it could do its job. Railroads continue to use similar plows today, although they are diesel or electric powered rather than steam powered.

Fruit Growers Express provided wooden refrigerator cars that were cooled by ice during summer long hauls to keep their produce fresh. The museum's car was built in the 1920s. For passengers—and usually the last car on today's depot excursion trains—the Oregon-Washington Railroad and Navigation Company Observation Car No. 1590 is a fine example of the famous Pullman cars. This car was built in 1913, and originally contained a buffet, parlor area, smoking room, shower, and barbershop. Its elegance was obvious with its African hardwood paneling and the inlaid hardwood patterns.

Northwest Railway Museum

Many railroad pieces from the collection, from locomotives to a caboose, can always be found on the tracks around the depot. More of the collection can be seen about two blocks away. The museum has recently added a new facility where restoration and preservation work is performed on historic cars and locomotives. A train shed is being planned that can protect additional pieces of the museum's large collection of rolling stock from the weather.

The depot has been restored to its late 19th-century appearance, although a few interior changes were made. What was originally the men's waiting room (separate from the women and children's waiting room) is now the gift shop and bookstore. From the exterior, the Victorian-style depot's bay window that allowed the stationmaster to see approaching trains remains in place. The old ticket window remains—that's where you purchase tickets for the train excursion rides.

HOURS: Depot open daily, 10 AM to 5 PM. Closed Thanksgiving, Christmas, and New Year's Day. Train rides are offered from early April through October, generally on weekends. Special holiday train rides are also offered.

COST: Depot admission is free; there are various fees for the weekend and special holiday train rides.

LOCATION: 38625 SE King Street, Snoqualmie

PHONE: 425-888-3030

WEBSITE: www.trainmuseum.org

7 Mount Rainier National Park

WHAT'S HERE: **Glaciers, fabulous vistas, wildflowers, and historic buildings**

DON'T MISS THIS: **The Longmire Museum and historic district**

Mount Rainier National Park is well known for the 26 glaciers that slowly press downward along its sides. Less known is the human history that is here, from the local Native Americans and the first American explorers to the early uses by pioneers who created a small resort complex at what is now the Longmire National Historic District.

While Native Americans may have respected or even feared the great snow-covered mountain, they regularly hunted on its slopes and in the valleys and meadows of the surrounding lands. As white settlers began learning about this volcanic mountain, they, too, began to come here. James Longmire and his family built and promoted the Longmire Medical Springs in 1888–89. Slowly, the mountain gained local and national fame. Mount Rainier climbers formed the Washington Alpine Club in 1891. Seattle and Tacoma businesses vied for tourists and new businesses by attaching their respective cities to promotions of the mountain. Tacoma unsuccessfully attempted to get the name of the mountain changed from Mount Rainier to Mount Tacoma.

Mount Rainier became the country's fifth national park in 1899, but that didn't end its troubles as far as the protection of its resources went. Local Yakama Indians who had hunted these lands for untold generations continued to hunt within the boundaries of the new park. Hunting did come to a halt, but not before numerous communications—as well as a few arrests—occurred between local park managers and the bosses in Washington, D.C., regarding treaty rights.

The small rustic building that is today's Longmire Museum has gone through many changes. It served as the first park headquarters from 1916 to 1928, having been constructed mostly of donated and salvaged materials at the total cost of $747.04. When it was abandoned and scheduled for demolition, a park naturalist successfully pleaded for it to be saved and used as a public contact station. Not much has changed inside the museum during the past 80 years or so. Original glass display cases hold original exhibits, and the old stuffed cougar looks at least that old. You can also find a few books, postcards, and other gift items inside for sale.

Outside is a slice of a giant Douglas fir that began life in the year 1293. In 1963, the Saint Regis Paper Company cut down this Douglas fir in the nearby Gifford Pinchot National Forest. Several of its annual growth rings have been marked with historical events that occurred as it grew over the centuries. For example, in 1315, a "little" ice age began causing Mount Rainier's glaciers to advance. The year 1480 brought a major eruption of Mount St. Helens about the same time that the world's population reached 500 million people. In 1786, Mount Shasta in Northern California erupted, and in 1800 Mount St. Helens did the same again. Between 1820 and 1854, Mount Rainier experienced minor eruptions and Nisqually Glacier had advanced to its lowest elevation, 900 feet below the current road bridge. In 1870, Hazard Stevens and P. B. Van Trump made the first documented ascent of Mount Rainier with guides James Longmire and Yakama Chief Sluiskin.

Not far away, the National Park Inn was constructed in 1917 in what became known as the "Rustic Style." But it is not the original National Park Inn. In those early days, railroads and various other concessionaires competed with each other, trying to attract the growing legions of tourists. Three inns once occupied this area. The first was built in 1906 and was dubbed the National Park Inn. In 1919, a new owner named the newer 1917 building the National Park Inn Annex. It was originally located across the road but was moved to its current location in 1920. After fire destroyed the original National Park Inn in 1926, the "annex" name was removed from the newer National Park Inn. It has been enlarged and refurbished over the years but retains that old "Rustic

Administration building in Longmire

Style" look and feel. The front porch faces the top of Mount Rainier, allowing guests to sit and enjoy a cup of coffee or cocoa and a spectacular view.

Also within the park's Longmire Historic District is the service station that was built in 1929 to provide gasoline and repair services for the increasing numbers of auto-driving tourists. Whole logs and large beams frame the porch that stretches its roof over the two red gas pumps that are mounted on glacial boulders and concrete. It no longer serves as a gas station, but is a small interpretive center filled with historic photos of the park.

The road from Longmire to Paradise is well worth the drive. The area received its name when John Longmire's daughter-in-law saw the subalpine meadow and exclaimed, "This must be what Paradise is like." When you see its summer wildflower displays and mountain views, you'll likely agree. There is a new Paradise visitor center filled with exhibits on the park. The old round, spaceship-looking Henry M. Jackson Memorial Visitor Center that sat here for years is gone. The new visitor center, unlike the old, has great views of the mountain. Maps, wilderness permits, and general park information is available at any of the visitor centers. Weather permitting during winter, the road from the Nisqually entrance that passes through Longmire is open to Paradise.

HOURS: The park is open year-round, although during winter, only minimal services are available at Longmire and Paradise. Summer hours vary at the different visitor centers and museums, but they are generally open from 10 AM until 5 PM; call for specific times or check website.

COST: $15 for a private vehicle, good for seven days

LOCATION: Mount Rainier National Park, Ashford

PHONE: Park information: 360-569-2211; Accommodations: 360-569-2275

WEBSITE: www.nps.gov/mora

8 Veterans Memorial Museum

WHAT'S HERE: **Extensive collection of mostly personal military-related items from uniforms to small arms**

DON'T MISS THIS: **The large flag from the USS *Abraham Lincoln***

Situated within view of the Interstate 5 freeway in Chehalis, the Veterans Memorial Museum's exterior provides few clues to its extensive collection of military-related items inside. The collection is organized into dozens of glass-enclosed cases lined up military-style along long rows and filled with surprises for military buffs.

While there are a few Civil War and pre-Civil War items, including an 1821 Harpers Ferry musket, most of the collection focuses on the U.S. military from World War II on. The collection includes an impressive assortment of rifles and handguns from numerous countries' militaries, including the U.S. Unlike most other firearm exhibits, this one displays the round that each weapon fires. There are even several light and heavy machine guns. One exhibit case is dedicated to various larger caliber ammunition that is used in the bigger guns, from 37mm to one 20mm round that came with a warning that it was not to be used with "forward-firing aircraft." That same case includes the brass casing from a round that the USS *Wyoming* fired at the celebration of the launching of the USS *Nebraska* on October 7, 1904.

For war movie buffs, some of the authentic World War II Air Corps items, used in the 1960s television series *12 O'Clock High* are here. The items, including the captain's leather Type A-2 Flight Jacket, were donated by Charles Foster, the copilot in all of the series' flight scenes. In a collection of World War II German military items, there is a rabbit-fur coat liner that was issued to a paratrooper. It was acquired during the Battle of the Bulge by the person who donated it to the museum.

The Japanese are not left out. There are numerous personal items, including wallets with Japanese money, personal family photos, and a "belt of 1,000 knots" made for a Japanese soldier in hope of bringing him good luck. The exhibit also includes a copy of the instrument of surrender signed by the Japanese and U.S. military officials.

The museum reveals a curious bit of World War I historical trivia, although certainly not thought trivial by the soldiers involved at the time. One method of communication used during the war was carrier pigeons, which carried messages when radios weren't yet available or weren't capable of handling military communications. In early October 1918, 550 men from the 77th Division were cut off and "lost," surrounded by the German army in the Argonne Forest. A human runner and six carrier pigeons had failed to get a message through from the lost battalion. Their last carrier pigeon—and their last hope—was Cher Ami, which means "dear friend." Cher Ami was released and the Americans watched as German gunners quickly shot it down. Soon though, the bird was flying again, and 30 minutes later and 25 miles away, it landed at division headquarters with the important message. One of the bird's legs was shattered, although with its critical message still attached, and its breastbone was broken and one wing badly hurt. The soldiers were successfully

…scued. Cher Ami won a special medal for gallantry and was returned to the U.S. for medical care.

Anyone who has been in the military will likely be attracted to the colorful back wall that is covered with hundreds of unit patches. There's a catalog to help museum visitors find specific unit patches. Some, like the 101st Airborne's screaming eagle, are relatively well known; others such as the Army Security Agency (ASA) patch, are much more obscure. But as you wander through the museum, you will see a display case that reveals some of the top secret work done by the ASA during its time in Vietnam. A member of ASA, Specialist E-4 James Davis was one of the first U.S. military personnel killed in Vietnam when his radio intercept and direction-finding team was ambushed by Viet Cong in 1961. For Vietnam-era veterans there is plenty here, from M-16s and AK-47s to claymore mines, uniforms, and all of the day-to-day equipment carried in rucksacks by soldiers in the jungles.

In May 2003, President George W. Bush landed on the USS *Abraham Lincoln* and made his "Mission Accomplished" speech. The huge U.S. flag that was flown in the ship's mess hall that day now covers one very large wall in the museum.

HOURS: June through September: Tuesday through Saturday, 10 AM to 5 PM, Sunday 1 PM to 5 PM; October through May: Tuesday through Saturday, 10 AM to 5 PM

COST: Adults, $5; students, $3

LOCATION: 100 SW Veterans Way, Chehalis

PHONE: 360-740-8875

WEBSITE: www.veteransmuseum.org

9 Mount St. Helens National Volcanic Monument

WHAT'S HERE: Three visitor centers on the highway to still-active Mount St. Helens

DON'T MISS THIS: Johnson Observatory film documenting the violent 1980 eruption

On Friday, May 16, 1980, crews of Weyerhaeuser loggers were cutting timber on the sides of rumbling Mount St. Helens. Two days later the volcano erupted, killing 57 people when an earthquake shook the mountain, causing the largest landslide ever recorded. The mountain's bulging north side broke free, releasing superheated groundwater and molten rock that exploded outward at 670 miles per hour. The superheated gasses incinerated everything in their path, from huge trees to wildlife. The mountain's snow and glacier melted immediately creating massive mudflows that rushed down the Toutle River canyon, destroying everything in their paths. Within seconds, Spirit Lake and its surrounding community were buried beneath 200 feet of volcanic mud, as a new Spirit Lake soon formed above.

Today, the forest is slowly reestablishing itself and much of the wildlife has returned, even as smoke and magma periodically escapes from the restless mountain. To witness the changes, there are several access points to the mountain, but the most popular—and the one with several visitor centers along the way—is via Highway 506 at Castle Rock (exit 49) and Interstate 5. The first place to stop is at the Mount St. Helens Visitor Center, only five miles from I-5. This is a good place to learn about the volcano, especially if you don't have another three hours or more to drive to the end of the Spirit Lake Highway and back in order to visit the Johnson Ridge Observatory.

Located at Seaquest State Park, the Mount St. Helens Visitor Center is a fun place for kids to explore the world of a volcano. The highlight for most kids is the walk-through volcano inside the center. Surrounding the mini-volcano are numerous exhibits and interpretive panels telling the story of the area and of the volcano's explosive 1980 eruption. Outside, a short trail winds through the adjacent wetlands, which is also great fun for kids. And on those clear days when its self-created clouds don't obscure the 8,364-foot summit, snowcapped Mount St. Helens looms 30 miles in the distance.

Your next stop along the Spirit Lake Memorial Highway should be at the Forest Learning Center (milepost 33). Operated in part by Weyerhaeuser, the lumber company that once logged most of the lands destroyed by the volcano, the center offers a different perspective on the eruption. Inside, the original forest has been recreated with trees, birds, raccoons, and a stuffed elk. Next to the forest is the "eruption chamber," a small theater that shows a short program about the blast and its aftermath. The exhibits that follow illustrate how loggers salvaged thousands of the fallen and incinerated trees and how foresters replanted the devastated lands. This is a learning center for kids with displays explaining forest regrowth and the ultimate regeneration of a completely devastated ecosystem. There is a real observation helicopter that kids can climb into and see the "tree farm" below.

alk outside to the observation areas overlooking the Toutle River canyon below. From here you can watch elk roam near the river as they did before the devastating blast. Binoculars help, but there are a couple of small viewing scopes along the ridge for visitors to use. If you want to get closer—but not too close—there is a trail that descends the 250 feet to the canyon below. It's a one-mile round-trip walk and much too steep in places to accommodate wheelchairs.

Back on the road, the last visitor center—and closest to the volcano's open mouth—is the Johnson Ridge Observatory. It's another half-hour drive, and if it's early summer count on passing patches of snow along the road as you climb higher. There are several viewpoints along the way—and plenty of wildflowers during summer. This is the largest and most popular of the three visitor centers (a fourth visitor center has been closed). As you proceed up the walkway from the parking lot, it looks like you are walking into the mouth of the volcano—well, not quite, but the view into the heart of the volcano's caldera is very impressive.

Inside the visitor center more exhibits help convey the power of the volcano's 1980 eruption. A large diorama-topographical recreation of the volcano and the surrounding mountains provides a very different perspective about the impact the eruption had on the surrounding lands and rivers. The best thing here, besides the view, is the movie, which is a must-see. The huge screen provides an amazing look at the eruption and the devastation it caused. And when the movie is over, the screen opens to an equally spectacular view of the volcano.

Outside the observatory, a short paved trail heads up along the adjacent ridge, providing more views of the surrounding mountains. Signs along the way interpret the damage inflicted by the heat and wind and explain how quickly plants and animals have returned to the totally devastated landscape.

Keep in mind that the visitor centers at the higher elevations can be windy and cold, even during summer. Be sure to dress appropriately in layers, especially if you plan to hike any of the trails.

Johnson Ridge Observatory

HOURS: **Mount St. Helens Visitor Center:** May through September, daily, 9 AM to 6 PM; off-season, daily, 9 AM to 4 PM
Forest Learning Center: Mid-May through mid-October, 10 AM to 5 PM. Closed in winter.
Johnson Ridge Observatory: Mid-May through mid-October, daily, 10 AM to 6 PM. Closed in winter.

COST: **Mount St. Helens Visitor Center:** Adults, $3; ages 7–17, $1
Forest Learning Center: Free
Johnson Ridge Observatory: ages 16 and older, $8. A U.S. Forest Service monument pass is required to hike on any of the trails at Coldwater Lake Recreation Area.

LOCATION: Spirit Lake Memorial Highway, from Interstate 5, exit 49 at Castle Rock, Washington

PHONE: **Mount St. Helens Visitor Center:** 360-274-0962
Forest Learning Center: 360-414-3439
Johnson Ridge Observatory: 360-274-2140

WEBSITE: **Mt. St. Helens Visitor Center:** www.parks.wa.gov/mountsthelens.asp
Forest Learning Center: www.weyerhaeuser.com/Sustainability/MountStHelens
U.S. Forest Service, Johnson Ridge Observatory: www.fs.fed.us/gpnf/mshnvm

10 Vancouver National Historic Reserve Visitor Center

WHAT'S HERE: **Information and exhibits about the history of the Hudson's Bay Company's trappers, early settlers, and the military**

DON'T MISS THIS: **The goods traded by the Hudson's Bay Company**

This expansive national historic reserve features several sites, including the reconstructed British Fort Vancouver (page 291), Officers' Row with officer residences in Vancouver Barracks that date from the mid-1800s, and Pearson Air Museum (page 293) at historic Pearson Field, which predates World War I. The area is a large park, with historic areas separated by large expanses of tree-covered lawns that are great for long walks or naps. A good starting point is the National Park Service Visitor Center near the East Entrance. The roads inside the reserve are well marked, so finding your way to the visitor center is easy.

The visitor center offers maps and park brochures, and inside there is an extensive interpretive gallery illustrating the area's long and complex history. Exhibits help tell the story about trappers and how they caught and processed thousands of beaver pelts each year. There is a look at the tools and practices of carpenters, coopers, and blacksmiths, as well as the trade goods, ranging from glass beads and guns to famous Hudson's Bay blankets and food supplies, that were the lifeblood of a thriving trade among Native Americans, U.S. citizens, British, and a few others.

…t across quiet, tree-lined Evergreen Boulevard from the visitor center is the old U.S. military's Officers' Row. The U.S. Army arrived here in 1849 as a result of the treaty with Great Britain that ceded what would become Washington State to the U.S. They were here to help keep the peace between the remaining British, the Indians, and the growing numbers of settlers. The soldiers began building troop barracks and residences for the officers. The oldest is the Ulysses S. Grant house, dating from 1849. Grant never occupied the house built of hand-hewn logs and later covered with siding, but he did serve at Vancouver Barracks. The Grant house features a fine-dining restaurant (call 360-906-1101 for information). Several of the historic homes have been restored with some now used as offices and gift shops.

HOURS: The historic homes' hours for public use vary. Visitor Center hours: fall-winter: daily, 9 AM to 4 PM; summer-spring: daily, 9 AM to 5 PM. The seasonal times change when Daylight Savings Time begins and ends. Closed Thanksgiving and December 24, 25, and 31.

COST: The visitor center is free; Fort Vancouver, $3 per person or $5 per family

LOCATION: 612 East Reserve Street, Vancouver

PHONE: 360-816-6230

WEBSITE: www.nps.gov/fova

Visitor center tool exhibit

11 Fort Vancouver National Historic Site

WHAT'S HERE: **Reconstructed fort that served as headquarters for the British Hudson's Bay Company**

DON'T MISS THIS: **The fort's kitchen and the cooking demonstrations**

Set amidst the forests of southern Washington and near the Columbia River, this reconstruction of Fort Vancouver is part of Vancouver National Historic Reserve. The original Fort Vancouver served as the headquarters for Great Britain's Hudson's Bay Company during the early 19th century. It was 1818, a time when the U.S. and Britain competed for control of what was then called Oregon Country. Britain thought it was gaining a competitive edge when in 1825 it moved the Hudson's Bay Company headquarters from near the mouth of the Columbia River upstream about 100 miles and built Fort Vancouver. It was a bold and beneficial move for the British. The new trading fort proved popular and successful with the beaver trappers and the newly arriving settlers.

Fort Vancouver's success lasted for 20 years, mostly under the direction of Dr. John McLoughlin, an organizational master who may have seen the proverbial writing on the wall. As head of the Hudson's Bay Columbia Department (Oregon Country), he was supposed to increase the taking of beaver—primarily for the hatmakers of the era—while doing what he could to keep the growing numbers of American settlers from taking over the lands that Great Britain was attempting to control. McLoughlin took advantage of the Americans, at least from a business standpoint, trading freely with them and even extending credit when needed. It was a practice that didn't make him popular with his boss Sir George Simpson, the head of Hudson's Bay Company's North American operations. Finally, in 1846, when the U.S. and Great Britain settled their land dispute by dividing the former American Indian lands along the 49th parallel, Britain discovered that their Fort Vancouver was now on U.S. soil. McLoughlin soon retired from his British post and moved to Oregon City, Oregon, and became a U.S. citizen. Unfortunately, over the next 20 years the fort was abandoned and finally destroyed by fire and decay.

In 1947, archaeologists began excavating the old fort grounds, ultimately recovering nearly 2 million artifacts. Using those artifacts and other documentation, reconstruction work was begun. Today, the fort's reconstruction includes a large vegetable garden just outside the main gate.

The fort is a great place for families to visit. There are plenty of opportunities for kids to explore the grounds and buildings, and there are usually docents around, especially on summer weekends, doing the things that the early trappers and settlers would have been doing here nearly 200 years ago. A favorite place for kids is the bastion at the far corner of the fort. Climbing the wooden ladder to the top of the bastion, with its views of the surrounding fort and grounds, is great fun.

Although the heyday of this wilderness fort was in the early 19th century, it was not without its comforts. Walk into the Chief Factor's residence—he was the boss of the trading post—and you'd think you were in a late 1800s city residence. The fine furniture, and other furnishings were of the finest available at the time, a testament to the ...al success hosted by Fort Vancouver. Behind the Chief Factor's house is the kitchen where meals were prepared for the gentlemen of the fort and for their guests.

Forts such as this were actually small cities within wooden walls. That is obvious here as you wander among the many reconstructed buildings. The two-story bake house contained two brick ovens where sea biscuits were baked for the fort's 200 to 300 employees; the blacksmith shop created the many metal tools and other objects needed; the Indian Trade Shop and Dispensary was where the doctor managed not only the hospital but an Indian trading operation; the Counting House served as the administrative center that tracked all of the incoming and outgoing goods and supplies; and the carpenter shop was where workers built wagons, windows, doors, and furniture for the houses they also constructed. There is a fur warehouse where the pelts were kept and a jail for those who were not willing to abide by the rules of the Hudson's Bay Company.

HOURS: Fall-winter: daily, 9 AM to 4 PM; summer-spring: daily, 9 AM to 5 PM. The seasonal times change when Daylight Savings Time begins and ends. Closed Thanksgiving and December 24, 25, and 31.

COST: Fort Vancouver, $3 per person or $5 per family

LOCATION: 612 East Reserve Street, Vancouver

PHONE: 360-816-6230

WEBSITE: www.nps.gov/fova

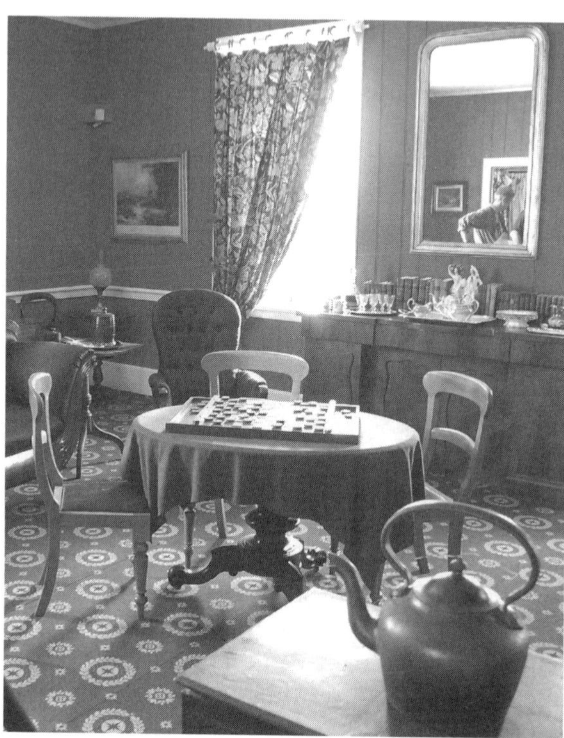

Comfort was not absent in the fort.

12 Pearson Air Museum

WHAT'S HERE: Large collection of historic aircraft at one of the country's oldest operating airfields

DON'T MISS THIS: The world's first bomber

There is plenty of history here, even before you enter the museum doors. The wooden hangar that houses much of the collection was built in 1918, making it the second oldest airplane hangar in the country. The military post was originally named Vancouver Barracks, and it conveniently had an adjacent field that suited early aircraft operations. But a few years later, the post was to see a name change because of a young flier, Lieutenant Alexander Pearson Jr. He had trained as a pilot in 1918, but World War I ended before he went overseas. He became a trainer for new pilots in Florida until 1919 when he was assigned to fly lead over a military convoy being sent across the U.S. The mission was a test to see how difficult it might be to move large numbers of military forces long distances across the country. One of the participants was Dwight D. Eisenhower, the future leader of the U.S. military in World War II and future president of the U.S. This was the trip that convinced Eisenhower when he became president to create the Interstate Highway System. Pearson's future proved to be far less successful. He died in 1924 when the wings of his Navy Curtiss R-8 collapsed while in a dive at an air race. The following year Secretary of War John W. Weeks ordered that the Vancouver Barracks airfield be renamed Pearson Field in honor of the fallen flyer.

The airfield has seen its share of history over the years. It was visited by a number of aviators who gained fame for one reason or another. The very first flight of an airplane here occurred in 1911 when Charles "Fred" Walsh flew in his Curtiss pusher-type aircraft. In following years, more flights were made at what become known as the Aviation Camp. In 1912, pilot Walter Edwards made the first airmail flight in the Pacific Northwest and the first interstate airmail run in the U.S. when he flew mail from the Waverly Golf Links in Oregon to his home field at Vancouver Barracks. In 1927, following his famous New York to Paris flight, Charles Lindbergh flew over the future Pearson Field, and in later years he landed here when visiting his brother-in-law who lived nearby.

Ten years after Lindbergh first flew here, a Russian Ant-25 unexpectedly landed at Pearson Field. The crew had just completed the first-ever nonstop flight over the North Pole and landed unannounced. The newly promoted commander of Vancouver Barracks, General George C. Marshall, greeted the fliers

World War II T-6 military trainer

ght them to his own home for baths and a meal. Apparently, while the Russian ked in tubs and enjoyed cognac with their bacon and eggs, a wind blew through their open bedroom windows scattering the $100 bills they had brought with them. The fate of the money is unknown.

The museum's collection of early 20th-century aircraft is a treat for flying buffs. It includes the world's first bomber, a 1913 Voisin III, one of only three remaining in the world; a 1941 Dehavilland Tiger Moth; and a 1941 Boeing Stearman. There are many more, including a 1953 Cessna 170 that flew around the world in 1956–57. In addition to the aircraft collection, the museum's exhibits tell many stories about early aviation history here, including the U.S. Army Signal Corps Balloon Service in World War I and the stripping of Sitka spruce from the surrounding forests for use in building World War I fighter planes, which were all wood framed.

The museum also explores the World War II aircraft "nose art," often scantily-clad "calendar girls" or cartoon character types of paintings affixed to the front of military aircraft. They were usually accompanied by names such as "Sleeping Dynamite," "Down de Hatch," and "Bottle Baby." The nose of a World War II-era military trainer has a sample.

If you'd like to experience being a pilot without leaving the ground, you can visit the museum's flight simulator room. The computer flight will show you that becoming a real pilot does indeed require practice. The museum also offers several aviation educational programs designed for kids ages 12 to 17 and special events for adults.

HOURS: Wednesday through Saturday, 10 AM to 5 PM. Closed Sunday through Tuesday.
COST: Adults, $8; seniors and active military with ID, $5; ages 6–12, $3
LOCATION: 1115 E. 5th Street, Vancouver
PHONE: 360-694-7026
WEBSITE: www.fortvan.org/pages/pearson-air-museum

Washington's Cascade Range Tours

Volcano Tour

ESTIMATED DAYS: 2–3
ESTIMATED DRIVING MILES: 140

Mount St. Helens (page 287) is the most famous of Washington's numerous volcanoes. The drive from the Interstate 5 turnoff at Castle Rock to the volcano's Johnson Ridge Visitor Center is about 45 miles. The visitor center sits on a ridge just 5 miles outside the main crater and the view into the crater is awe-inspiring, especially as you look around at the devastation and death caused by its 1980 eruption. The visitor center is closed due to snow during winter, and there will likely still be snow around the area in June and even July. There are two additional visitor centers along Spirit Lake Highway (State Highway 504) that focus on Mount St. Helens, including one in Castle Rock.

Almost directly north of Mount St. Helens is **Mount Rainier National Park** (page 282), home of another volcano. Mount Rainier last erupted about 150 years ago. Today, the 14,410-foot mountain is home to 26 glaciers. Several visitor centers and a small museum will introduce you to the wonders of this 235,000-acre national park, but time on some of the trails will be well spent. Many of the trails are short, but if you're craving a little more adventure, the 93-mile Wonderland Trail circles the volcano, offering commanding views of the mountain, its glaciers, and meadows filled with summer wildflowers.

Mount St. Helens Visitor Center

y History Tour

ESTIMATED DAYS: 1–2
ESTIMATED DRIVING MILES: 78

The earliest days of military history in the Pacific Northwest can be seen at **Fort Vancouver** (page 291). The reconstructed fort from the days of the Hudson's Bay Company control of the surrounding land is very impressive, especially if you arrive during one of the living history demonstrations. Inside the Vancouver National Historic Reserve, where the fort lies near the Columbia River, is another aspect of military history. The **Pearson Air Museum** (page 293) is the oldest facility of its kind in the Pacific Northwest, having been constructed in 1918. It is the site of many "firsts" in aviation history, including the landing site of the first nonstop flight over the North Pole. Unfortunately, it was Russian flyers who made the crossing and landed here unannounced.

A look at the more modern military history of the region is afforded at the **Veterans Memorial Museum** (page 285) located in Chehalis. The museum includes in its exhibits the personal items of many Pacific Northwest members of the military, ranging from weapons and equipment to hundreds of unit patches. The collection includes rifles and more from the Civil War, World Wars I and II, the Korean War, Vietnam, and the Middle East.

Pearson Air Museum

Washington's Cascade Range Information Centers

Leavenworth Convention and Visitors Bureau
www.leavenworth.org
509-548-5807

Southwest Washington Convention and Visitors Bureau
www.southwestwashington.com
877-600-0800

Lewis County Tourism
www.tourlewiscounty.com
800-525-3323

Eastern Washington

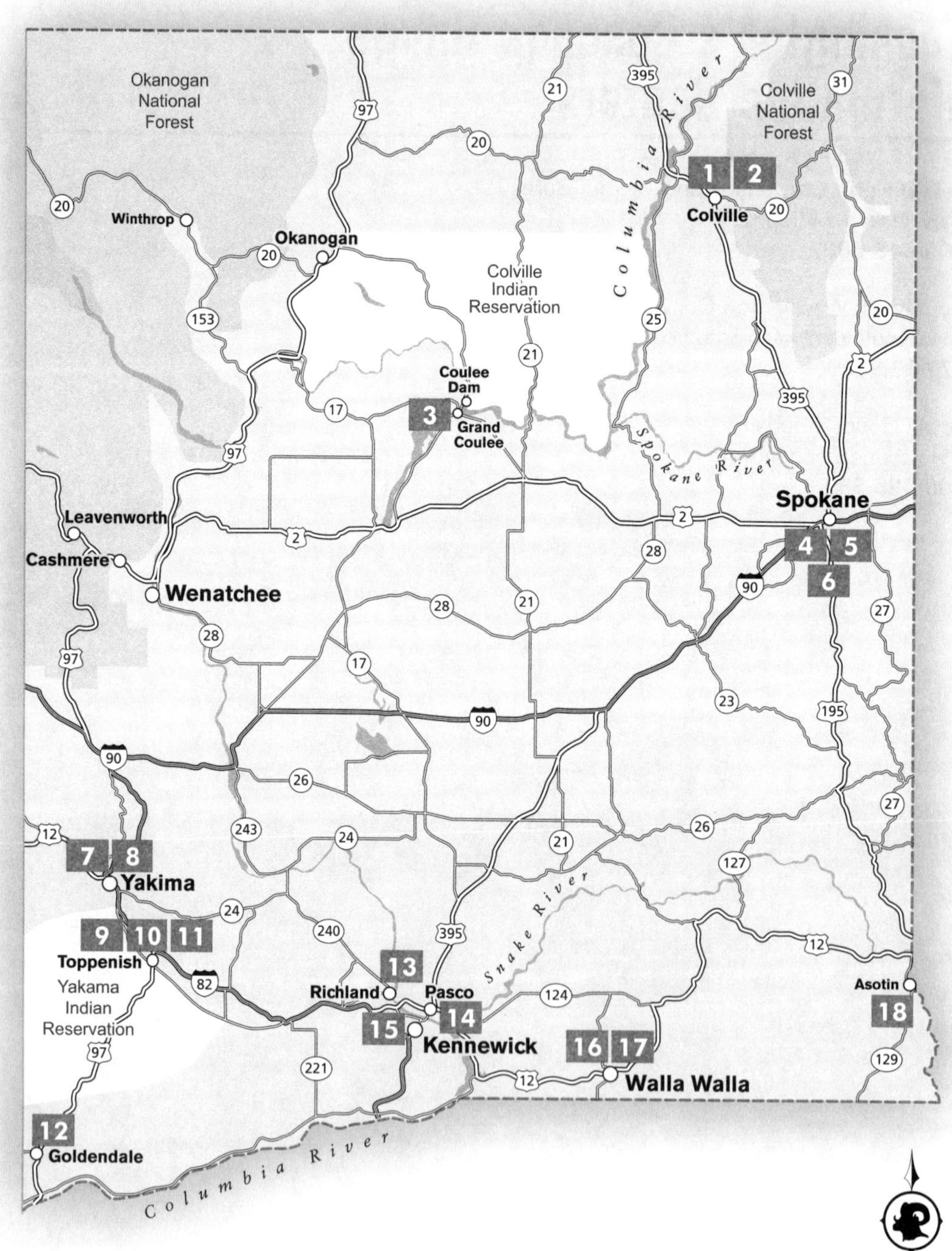

Okanogan National Forest
Colville National Forest
Winthrop
Okanogan
Colville
Colville Indian Reservation
Columbia River
Coulee Dam
Grand Coulee
Spokane River
Spokane
Leavenworth
Cashmere
Wenatchee
Yakima
Toppenish
Yakama Indian Reservation
Snake River
Richland
Pasco
Kennewick
Walla Walla
Asotin
Goldendale
Columbia River
1
2
3
4
5
6
7
8
9
10
11
12
13
14
15
16
17
18

Eastern Washington

Drive over the Cascade Range and drop into eastern Washington, and you will witness a significant change in the landscape. Gone are the lush green forests washed by rain and winter snow; you have entered a desert where precipitation has gone from 150 inches annually in the high mountains to only 9 inches on the eastern foothills.

As dry as Eastern Washington is, looking at a map shows that hundreds of streams and rivers crisscross the southwestern quarter of the state. Even the great Columbia River, with its beginnings in Canada, meanders southwest through Washington's dry southeast until it reaches the Oregon border and heads west on its journey to the Pacific Ocean. It was in this mostly isolated and uninhabited land that the U.S. military in World War II decided to build a city and conduct its top secret research into building the first atomic bomb. Numerous dams have been built, such as Grand Coulee Dam on the Columbia River, and smaller dams on other rivers in order to hold back water for irrigation and electrical power generation.

Asotin County Historical Society Museum grounds

Drive across these wide-open spaces and you will find hundreds of farms growing thousands of acres of wheat, with most of it dry farming, depending on the light seasonal rainfall for sustenance. Other places like Yakima, Kennewick, and Spokane depend, at least in part, on irrigation to grow crops ranging from apples to hops to grapes.

TRIVIA

1 Which structure took 12 million cubic feet of concrete to build?

2 What electric railroad has operated every year since its inaugural run in 1907?

3 What museum features a popular ingredient used in making beer?

4 Where can you see a collection of more than 100 different coffee grinders?

5 Where can you learn about World War II's Manhattan Project, a secret construction project to produce the world's first nuclear bomb?

6 Where can you learn about apples, apples, and more apples?

7 What park is named after a Agaiduka Shoshone woman who accompanied Meriwether Lewis and William Clark on their famous journey?

For trivia answers, see page 346.

1 Stevens County Museum

WHAT'S HERE: A museum that tells the story of this northeastern Washington county

DON'T MISS THIS: The exhibits down the hill in the small park

The museum complex is spread over several acres, from the hilltop Stevens County Museum and historic Keller House (page 303) to the historic structures on the flat below—a farmstead cabin, Colville's first schoolhouse, a trapper's cabin, blacksmith shop, the pioneer machinery museum, and more. The main museum holds a large and varied collection of local historical artifacts.

The first exhibits you'll see are the Native American cases. The collection of buckskin dresses is impressive, especially the bead work that is featured on some of the dresses, moccasins, and satchels. A couple of the exhibit cases take the beadwork a little further, illustrating the history of beads and bead trade and the use of "seed" beads. Small beads used to decorate cloth or skin garments that were first used in the 17th century, seed beads had very tiny holes, making them difficult to string. The Indians used sinew as a needle to pick up the beads and a fine awl to punch holes in the skins they decorated. The large assortment of beads illustrates the creativeness of these bead makers.

The museum has a dugout canoe that was hand hewn by a member of the Kettle River Indian tribe prior to 1910. It was used, instead of gold or currency, to make a $5 payment to the bank in Orient, Washington. It's an example of the canoes that provided transportation for trappers carrying pelts to be traded to the Hudson's Bay Company during the 19th century. And they didn't carry just beaver pelts. Nearly any animal that had a fur coat was fair game for the trappers. During 1830, members from the local tribes trapped and traded in part: 621 large beaver, 241 small beaver, 59 black bears, 58 brown bears, 19 grizzly bears, 103 fishers, 125 martens, 2,904 muskrats, 121 minks, and 3 wolves. The Hudson's Bay Company's nearby Fort Colville served as a British trading post for 45 years, finally closing in 1871. It was the longest-surviving British trading post in the Pacific Northwest.

The museum has dozens of exhibits that tell the stories of Colville's early pioneers. From clothes, religious items, and numerous historic photos, drawings, and lithographs to furniture, toys, office equipment, musical instruments, and tools, the museum's artifact collection ranges in age from the 1800s to more contemporary times.

Stevens County Museum

Down the hill below the museum is a park that holds many more exhibits, including several historic buildings that have been moved here. Colville's first schoolhouse originally occupied a site on

South Main Street. It was constructed for the education of John Hofstetter's children but was opened to other families as needed. The cabin was more intricately constructed than most log cabins; its logs were squared rather than left round, and they were connected with interlocking dovetail joints. Though the need for schools was increasing as more people settled the area, in 1891 fewer than one-third of the school-age children attended class. Often what education they received, they received at home with the Bible and a Sears Roebuck catalog serving as reading primers for many farm families.

The sawmill exhibit includes items from various mills, long since closed. For the early pioneers, trees were nothing more than a nuisance that needed to be cleared for homes and from potential farmland. That changed when timber became a valuable commodity. Between 1898 and 1910, the number of sawmills in Stevens County increased from 62 to 100.

A trapper's cabin, likely neater and less odoriferous than the original owner kept it, is also on the park grounds. A typical trapper might run a 12-mile trapline for martens or bears, and he would have to check it daily. The bear traps he carried each weighed 17 pounds, and he had to carry another 20 pounds of bait. Any animals he found in his traps had to be skinned on the spot and packed back to the cabin. Packs of heavy skins could weigh 100 pounds.

The blacksmith shop exhibit features tools and the bellows needed to fire coal hot enough to allow working iron to be forged into tools and hardware. There are also various pieces of pioneer machinery, including a large horse-drawn hay baler.

HOURS: May: daily, 1 PM to 4 PM; June through August: Monday through Thursday, 10 AM to 4 PM; Friday through Sunday, 1 PM to 4 PM; September: daily, 1 PM to 4 PM. Tours also available by appointment year-round.

COST: Admission good for museum and adjacent Keller House: Adults, $5; seniors, $3; grades K–12, $2; Family (same household), $10

LOCATION: 700 N. Wynne Street, Colville

PHONE: 509-684-5968

WEBSITE: www.stevenscountyhistoricalsociety.org

2 Keller House

WHAT'S HERE: Historic home built in 1910
DON'T MISS THIS: The original Gustav-Stickley furniture

Louis Young made a small fortune with his banking and real estate businesses. He also controlled a stage line that further added to his wealth. In 1910 when Young decided that he and his wife Anna needed a new house, they chose to build it on a hillside overlooking portions of Colville. Within the first year of its construction, fire severely damaged their new home. Louis and Anna decided to repair their home rather than demolish what the fire left undamaged and start over. They salvaged as much of the original materials as they could, but they also made many improvements. The interior woodwork was changed to quarter-sawn red birch, and they added beams to the first-floor music room, dining room, and vestibule. The first floor's oak flooring was cleaned, refinished, and moved upstairs, and replaced with new walnut-trimmed oak. They saved the original chandeliers as well as the leaded glass windows and had them reinstalled. Since the reconstruction, the home has not been changed.

What did change, however, was the name of the estate. When Young first purchased the property, he named his estate Lockwood. But following his suicide in 1914, Anna remarried and moved her new husband, Louis G. Keller, into the house. The home took on his name, thus becoming the Keller house, the name it carries today.

Anna had no children with either husband. She continued living in the home until her own death in 1963. Her second husband died in 1966 and willed the home to the City of Colville. It sat empty for several years until the Stevens County Historical Society became involved. Fortunately, most of the home's furniture, including all of the original Gustav-Stickley Craftsman-style furniture, had been in storage and was returned to the home,.

Upon entering the home, the era's love affair with the new Craftsman-style architecture and furnishings is immediately evident. The windows on each side of the brick fireplace are of leaded glass. The relatively small living room is furnished with a Stickley settee and library table. The other furnishings are from Switzerland and Italy. In the adjacent music room, the square grand piano is over a century old, although it is not original to the home; however, the photograph hanging above the piano and the small silver dog sitting on the piano belonged to Anna.

The most prominent display of the home's beautiful Craftsman-style oak furniture is in the dining room. The dining room table can be extended to seat

Keller House living room

20 people. The matching chairs, buffet, and serving table are all original to the house. The Tiffany lamp was saved following the fire, and there are samples of the family's dishes, both from the Young era and from the more recent Keller era.

There is a butler's pantry filled with drawers and wall storage cabinets, although the Kellers didn't have a butler. The butler's storage area must have served Anna well, because there is not much room in the small kitchen. There are several kitchen items here, such as canning jars and a pressure cooker.

Wandering through the remainder of the house reveals a furnished master bedroom, tile bathrooms that many people would love to have today, and guest bedrooms. Also, in several of the rooms, notice the wallpaper—some is original to the home, some is similar but new. Although the wall covering in the dining room looks like gold burlap, it is paper covered with gold gilt paint on embossed paper that is stenciled in the Art Nouveau foliate design.

HOURS: May: daily, 1 PM to 4 PM; June through August: Monday through Thursday, 10 AM to 4 PM; Friday through Sunday, 1 PM to 4 PM; September: daily, 1 PM to 4 PM. Tours also available by appointment year-round.

COST: Admission good for the Keller House and for the adjacent museum: Adults, $5; seniors $3; grades K–12, $2; family (same household), $10

LOCATION: 700 N. Wynne Street, Colville

PHONE: 509-684-5968

WEBSITE: www.stevenscountyhistoricalsociety.org

3 Grand Coulee Dam and Visitor Center

WHAT'S HERE: **Visitor center with exhibits about its construction**

DON'T MISS THIS: **A tour of the inside of the dam and its power generators**

With 12 million cubic feet of concrete, you could build a highway from Seattle to Miami, or you could build a sidewalk four feet wide and four inches thick that would wrap around the equator twice (50,000 miles). Or you could do what the U.S. government did in 1933 and begin building Grand Coulee Dam. Construction work on the dam wasn't completed until 1941, and additional power plants have been added over the years. Today, it is the largest hydropower producer in the U.S., capable of generating 6,809 megawatts of electricity.

From the visitor center parking lot, which offers a front-row view of the face of the dam, it doesn't appear to be nearly a mile long and 550 feet high. But when you realize that those tiny holes in the dam's concrete faces are spillways, each big enough to drive a full-sized pick-up truck through, the enormity of one of the world's largest concrete structures begins to sink in. And it needs to be big—Grand Coulee Dam controls an enormous amount of Colorado River water, or what once was the Colorado River. Today this section of the great river has been transformed into the calm waters of Franklin D. Roosevelt Lake, the reservoir behind the dam that meanders upstream for 151 miles to the Canadian border.

The visitor center is the best place to begin your exploration of the dam and its history. Be aware that weapons, purses, bags, backpacks, fanny packs, camera bags, or packages of any kind are not allowed inside the visitor center—and it is enforced. You can bring cameras, just not cases.

The visitor center exhibits extol the virtues of the dam, the irrigation it provides, the power it supplies, and the flood control that has prevented millions of dollars in flood damage over the years. Shortly after World War II began, the nation's leaders realized the potential for creating a nuclear bomb, and it became a task that had to be successfully completed before Germany could build theirs. Grand Coulee Dam provided the huge amounts of electrical power that was required not only at the super-secret Hanford Project down river, but also to other cities in the Pacific Northwest that were producing other needed war materials such as the tons of aluminum required to build thousands of aircraft.

Building such a project required a massive planning effort to undertake building towns for thousands of workers, constructing a railroad to get all the supplies in, mixing and pouring the foundation, diverting the river, and finally building the dam with several million more cubic yards of concrete. The visitor center touches on all these undertakings and the men who made it happen, from power monkeys to jackhammer men. Even back then, politics played a part, as former Grand Coulee Dam project manager Steven Clark observed: "The most difficult thing about managing Grand Coulee Dam is operating a multipurpose project in a world of special interests."

The dam created as many environmental and economic nightmares as it resolved. Salmon could no longer get upriver to spawn, and Native Americans and other people who relied on fishing lost their traditional spots under the new lake. "The promises made by the government were written in sand and then covered with water, like everything else," said a Colville tribal member. The answer, certainly not perfect, was to build fish ladders and hatcheries along the river.

In 1951, a feeder canal was completed and in celebration the 48 states and the territories of Alaska and Hawaii (both became states in 1959) each sent a gallon jug of water that was emptied into the feeder canal representing the benefits it provided to the entire country. Those old gallon jugs are in one of the exhibits. There are also core samples of the

Grand Coulee Dam

bedrock and a core sample that was drilled out of the third power plant, the last to be completed.

It's that third power plant that is connected to the dam across the river from the visitor center where tours are offered. And it's a tour well worth taking the time to experience. It begins with a search—you have to pass through a magnetometer that will check you for metal, and remember to leave any kind of carrying case behind. You must take a glass-enclosed elevator ride down the face of the concrete power plant, which gives some of the best views of the main dam you can get. Once inside the power plant, your guide will lead you into the belly of the facility where massive generators are turning. An incredible amount of engineering know-how goes into keeping these things working, and it's explained very well. Several exhibits along the way further explain what you are seeing, such as the six largest electric generators, and the world's largest gantry crane that is required to lift and lower their 2,000-ton rotors for scheduled maintenance or repairs. The tour takes 30 minutes and requires a half mile of walking.

HOURS: Memorial Day weekend through July: daily, 8:30 AM to 11 PM; August: daily, 8:30 AM to 10:30 PM; September: 8:30 AM to 9:30 PM; remainder of the year: daily, 9 AM to 5 PM. Closed Thanksgiving, Christmas, and New Year's Day.

COST: Free

LOCATION: Near the base of the dam in the town of Grand Coulee

PHONE: 509-663-9265

WEBSITE: www.usbr.gov/pn/grandcoulee/

4 Northwest Museum of Arts and Culture

WHAT'S HERE: Changing exhibits on history and art in six different galleries

DON'T MISS THIS: The Campbell House next door

The museum houses more than 68,000 fine art objects and material culture artifacts from the Americas, Europe, and Asia. Since this is a progressive art museum, exhibits are periodically rotated, and there is a constant flow of traveling and temporary exhibits throughout the year.

Explored through photographs and signage is a short history of museum collections, especially as it relates to Native American artifacts. It starts by looking at the 19th century, especially the later Victorian era when it became popular to collect pieces of Native American culture. The wealthy traveled the world, bringing home many treasures and pieces of art. This spurred amateur and professional collectors, and more than a few grave-robber entrepreneurs, to gather, trade, exhibit, and sell objects they saw as part of a "Vanishing Race"—the American Indians. Many of those early exhibits of Indian artifacts were showcased as the third leg of a natural triad—wild plants, wild animals, and "wild" people.

For decades, reputable museums freely exhibited Native American human remains and burial artifacts and relics. Even after the Federal Antiquities Act in 1906 prohibited digging for cultural artifacts on public lands, collectors still disturbed grave sites on private lands—and museums still exhibited the found items. Other federal laws inadvertently prevented Native Americans from practicing some of their religious ceremonies because the possession of such sacred Indian items as eagle feathers and bones was illegal. That oversight was corrected in 1978, and in 1990, the Native American Graves Protection and Reparation Act was passed, allowing recognized tribes to request and receive control of such sacred burial items and human remains from museums. Today, many museums work closely with local Native American tribes on exhibits and collections to ensure proper attention to sensitive issues and artifacts. This museum was founded in 1916, and it has undergone numerous changes regarding its collection of Indian artifacts and their exhibition. In partnership with surrounding Indian tribes, the museum showcases a fine collection of Indian artifacts, from beaded and buckskin dresses and basketry to pieces such as a peyote box, prayer fan, and gourd rattles.

The majority of the museum's galleries are not dedicated to the Native American collection, but to a wide assortment of subjects, much of it related to the Spokane area. The exhibits in them change regularly. As an example, the Walther Gallery has featured a Spokane time line that explores the timber industry and its impact—both the good and bad aspects—on the Pacific Northwest. Another gallery is dedicated to bringing the works of contemporary Pacific Northwest artists with penchants for including in their works, what the museum describes in one changing exhibit as exploring "our evolving, complex, and increasingly freighted relationship to the natural world."

There is always plenty here to see and do. It's best to check the museum's website in order to see what the exhibits will feature during your visit—or just stop by and be pleasantly surprised. The one part of the museum that doesn't change much is the historic Campbell House (page 308), which is located next door and open for tours during museum hours.

Northwest Museum of Arts and Culture

HOURS: Tuesday through Sunday, 11 AM to 5 PM. Closed Monday and major holidays (except New Year's Day).

COST: Adults $7; ages 62-plus and students, $5. Admission cost is for both the Northwest Museum and for the historic Campbell House tour, which is next door.

LOCATION: 2316 West First Avenue, Spokane

PHONE: 509-456-3931 or 509-363-5315

WEBSITE: www.northwestmuseum.org

5 Campbell House

WHAT'S HERE: **Historic English Tudor Revival home built in 1898**

DON'T MISS THIS: **The gold-filled burlap wall coverings**

Amasa "Mace" B. Campbell and his partner, John Aylar Finch, with money from investors, moved west from Ohio in 1887, to the Coeur d'Alene Mining District (Idaho). They invested $25,000 in an operating silver mine, which soon was making themselves and their investors very rich. Campbell returned to Ohio and married 31-year-old Grace Fox. The couple settled in Wallace, Idaho, a rough and tumble mining town, and in 1892, they had a daughter, Helen. Unfortunately, labor trouble in the mining district—and a collapse of world silver prices—made their home a dangerous place to live. The family moved to Spokane, where they built a new home. The turmoil in the mining district continued for several years, climaxing with the 1905 assassination of Idaho's governor and the implementation of martial law over the mining district.

The Campbell's new English Tudor Revival–style home was completed in 1898 following eleven months of construction. Changes and finishing work continued well beyond that time. The architect was Kirtland Cutter, an interesting character who apparently learned much of his design skills not from universities, but from traveling. He also owned and wore hairpieces, of varying lengths, to cover his balding head. By changing hairpieces, he could appear over a week or two to be in ever more need of a haircut—a sure sign that he wasn't really bald. Hair wasn't Cutter's only issue. Although Cutter told the Campbells that he designed their house to be one-of-a-kind, he apparently sold the same plans to another client in Spokane.

The new home was wired for electricity, eliminating the need for interior gas lighting that was more typically found in homes during that time period in Spokane. Its 10 fireplaces, some exceptionally elegant with marble and gold leaf, provided only part of the heat; a steam heating system was incorporated into the house to provide the majority of warmth. Portions of the home's well-worn wall coverings have been replaced with copies of the originals. One area where the original wall coverings remain is in the entryway with its heavy Gothic door and hardware. The walls were covered with burlap that had gold leaf rubbed into it. Other walls, such as those in the gilded French reception room, are covered in rose moiré silk. The two-level first floor was quite a design innovation for the time. Look closely at some of the heavy wood beams. They aren't solid, but instead are boxed wood beams. Apparently, the faux finishing touches were meant to save money, even though Amasa Campbell could easily have afforded the real thing.

Amasa died in 1912, but his wife and daughter continued to live here. Following Grace Campbell's death in 1924, daughter Helen donated the home to the city for an art museum. Unfortunately, since it was to be a museum requiring open gallery space, she sold all of its furnishings at auction. Even though all of the original furniture is gone, the Campbells had kept records, fortunately, of everything purchased for the home, from wallpaper to couches. Those records, along with photographs taken at the time, are being used to refurnish the home. Many of the rooms already have been furnished, such as the master bedroom, providing more than a hint of the luxury to which the Campbells were accustomed. The Campbells never had fewer than five servants working for them. As might be expected, the third-floor servant quarters were some of the rooms in the house where photographs weren't taken. The third-floor female servants' rooms are simple, with floors made from inexpensive fir. Fire regulations prevent them from being open for tours.

HOURS: Tuesday through Sunday, 11 AM to 5 PM. Closed Mondays and major holidays (except New Year's Day).

COST: Adults, $7; seniors (age 62 and older) and students, $5. Admission cost is for both the historic Campbell House tour and for the Northwest Museum, which is next door (page 306).

LOCATION: 2316 West First Avenue, Spokane

PHONE: 509-456-3931 or 509-363-5315

WEBSITE: www.northwestmuseum.org

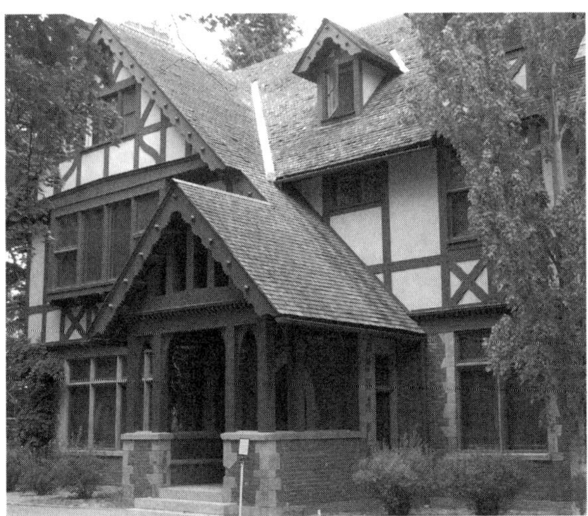

Campbell House

6 Mobius Kids Museum

WHAT'S HERE: A hands-on museum for younger children

DON'T MISS THIS: The daily art studio project

If you're traveling with younger children, from toddlers to kids younger than eight years old, then this is the place to visit. Many of the kids and their parents who come to Mobius Kids Museum are locals and visit regularly. But first-time kid-visitors will have a great time, while learning about art, other cultures, and science.

The museum takes its name from a mobius strip, a loop of material with a single twist that presents a continuous one-sided plane. For the museum, the mobius strip represents the endless possibilities, creativity, and sustainability that Mobius encourages.

For the youngest visitors, the Enchanted Forest is a place where toddlers and infants can crawl, climb, and explore. A tree slide and foam pond allow for extra challenges and fun. Parents can follow along and even create a woodland puppet show or read a book to their children. Bigger kids have fun playing in Geotopia, a miniature flowing river that teaches hands-on lessons about how water affects everything it touches. Kids can explore the effects of wind, water, and weather and how they all interact. There also are critters, live insects, and arachnids that include walking sticks (insects), Oswin the African millipede, and Leggy Peggy, the rosehair tarantula!

If bugs are too much, Cooper's Corner lets kids learn about traffic safety as they become crossing guards, learn how to properly fit a bicycle helmet, and deal with cars while riding bikes. A small "highway" allows some to ride mini-tricycles, while others can direct traffic.

Something for slightly older youngsters is *Bayanihan*, a Philippine word that refers to a community working together. Here kids can pass through a cultural portal to the village of Palo, located on a small island beyond the Philippines capital city of Manila. Kids learn to bargain for food at Jasmine's Sari-Sari Store, shop at a local fish market, and husk rice in the bahay kubo. They may "purchase" everything from imitation pineapples to fish.

The museum features numerous daily special programs for kids, as well as longer programs. The hand art studio is where creative young minds can get even more creative using paint, chalk, or whatever art medium is being used in the daily art project.

Interactive bike safety ride

HOURS: Monday through Saturday, 10 AM to 5 PM; Sunday, 11 AM to 5 PM. Closed Thanksgiving Day.

COST: General admission, $5.75; seniors (55-plus), $4.75; 12 months and younger, free

LOCATION: 808 West Main Avenue, Lower Level, Spokane

PHONE: 509-624-KIDS

WEBSITE: www.mobiusspokane.org

7 Yakima Electric Railway Museum

WHAT'S HERE: **Last original turn-of-the-century interurban railroad in the U.S.**

DON'T MISS THIS: **The historic 1910 car barn and substation**

The Yakima Electric Railway, originally constructed between 1907 and 1913, is located in downtown Yakima. The railway ultimately laid 44 miles of track, and it has operated every year since its inaugural run in 1907. Although today it operates on only five miles of its original track, the track and the overhead electrical power lines are original.

The Yakima Valley Transportation Company (YVT) was established at the last minute in July 1907, in an effort to assume a streetcar franchise that the city of Yakima had granted to a failing railroad company. The owners of YVT—company president Andrew Jackson Splawn and his six partners—had until the end of the year to get at least three miles of streetcar line into operation. It was an effort that few could match today. With borrowed and leased equipment, including two out-of-service streetcars from Tacoma, they began grading and laying track. By mid-December nearly 100 men were hard at work.

In early December, the two Tacoma streetcars arrived, carried on Northern Pacific Railway flatcars. They were in pretty sad shape, but they were made ready for operation. Splawn left Yakima for business in mid-December, instructing his chief engineer Edward Kenly to begin operations as soon as everything was ready. Kenly refused to initiate the company's first streetcar run until the inspirational leader had returned. Finally, on December 22, with Splawn back in town,

The railway's electric generators

everything was in place. Tacoma car #18 placed its pole against the new overhead electrical power lines—and it moved forward. A couple more runs followed, along with speeches about the bright future. The line opened to the public on Christmas Day 1907. More than 1,300 people paid their five cents to ride the new streetcar that first day.

The passenger operation continued for 40 years until buses and cars became more convenient. With passenger traffic dead by 1947, the YVT continued in business carrying freight using electric locomotives until 1985. In 1974, two trolleys from Oporto, Portugal, were purchased and brought to Yakima as a bicentennial project. Nearly identical to the original streetcars, they continue as the backbone of today's passenger-carrying trolley. But, unlike in 1907, today's operation is aimed at tourists, not commuters or freight. Two Brill Master Unit streetcars that were originally built for Yakima have been returned after a 42-year absence. One of the cars is operational and used for tourists and the second is being restored.

The car barn and powerhouse facilities that serve as a museum today look much as they did when constructed. The museum contains two of the original YVT electric locomotives, one from 1909 and the second built in 1922. Also on display is the belt-driven shop machinery needed to keep everything moving.

HOURS: The trolley usually operates from Memorial Day weekend through Labor Day; Saturday, Sunday, and holidays, 10 AM to 3 PM

COST: Adults, $4; ages 60-plus and ages 12 and under, $3; children on lap, free; family all-day pass, $15. All fares are good all day for as many rides as wanted. The museum is free.

LOCATION: Rides leave hourly from the car barn at 3rd Avenue and Pine Street, Yakima.

PHONE: 509-249-5962

WEBSITE: www.yakimavalleytrolleys.org

8 Yakima Valley Museum

WHAT'S HERE: **A detailed look at the history of Yakima**

DON'T MISS THIS: **The historic—and operating—soda fountain**

With Yakima Valley being one of the primary fruit-tree regions in the U.S., it makes sense that a large portion of the museum features a look at the history of this agricultural phenomenon in what is essentially a desert. In the 1880s, the Yakima Valley was an overgrazed wasteland. The short-lived grazing of cattle and sheep had destroyed the native bunchgrasses, and nothing grew on the rich volcanic soils except sagebrush. With only eight inches of rain each year, the region didn't appear to be suited to farming. But once irrigation was introduced, these desolate-appearing lands began producing some of the highest fruit yields ever.

During those early days, apple orchards were planted by hand, with the owners hoping the seeds would produce fruit on their 300 trees per acre within a decade. Today, nursery-produced dwarf trees are planted by machine and within three to four years, up to 3,000 trees per acre are producing mature fruit. Many other things have changed over the decades, and the museum's exhibits provide an excellent look back in time. The large display of colorful art that decorated the early wooden shipping crates is especially fun. In those early days of apple growing, there was an ongoing informal art contest as orchard owners tried to create the most attractive box labels—to get a little marketing edge over one's rivals. Exhibit labels even discuss the collecting and valuing of those old labels, since everything is now shipped in cardboard boxes and the art labels are history.

The apple exhibits include a look at everything from specialized equipment like the Lindeman-John Deere BO Crawler, a small bulldozer designed low to the ground so it can fit beneath the trees, to the special equipment used to make the original wooden fruit crates. You can learn about everything from pest management and how the trees are pruned and the fruit has been picked over the years to a look at the changing frost control measures that are taken on those overly cold spring mornings.

In another part of the museum, Supreme Court Justice William O. Douglas (whose term lasted from 1939 until 1975) is honored. His Washington, D.C., office furniture is the same as it appeared in 1980 following his death. Part of the exhibit is a replica, even though the museum owns the entire office contents. Included are his robe, various hats, chair, and numerous awards he received over the years. Take a close look at the robe—it

Yakima Valley Museum's soda fountain

is well worn and even has patches on the sleeves. The exhibit describes his career in law and his rise to the Supreme Court.

Throughout the remainder of the museum are collections representing all aspects of life in Yakima Valley. A 1902 Curved Dash Oldsmobile owned by a local insurance agent is here, as are old printing presses and even an early television studio. Many of the more common things that could be found around people's homes will likely be seen here—table settings from 1900 and from 1960, hundreds of "advertising" pencils, and bellows-type cameras. There are also horse-drawn wagons and clothes from past decades, including flour sack dresses made during the Great Depression by women with no money for store-bought clothes. In the center of one main gallery is a beautiful exhibit of brightly shining neon advertising lights, still selling their messages, from a cycling shop to a commercial office equipment company.

Outside the main museum is a completely functioning replica of a 1930s-era Art Deco soda fountain. You can go inside and enjoy lunch or an old-fashioned milkshake made from famous Tillamook ice cream.

HOURS: Tuesday through Saturday: 10 AM to 5 PM; Sunday, 11 AM to 5 PM. Closed Mondays and holidays except Martin Luther King Jr. Day, Presidents' Day, Labor Day, Columbus Day, and Veterans' Day.
Soda Fountain: Tuesday through Sunday, 11 AM to 5 PM (during school year); daily during summer, 11 AM to 9 PM

COST: Adults, $5; seniors, students, and children, $3; families, $12

LOCATION: 2105 Tieton Drive, Yakima

PHONE: 509-248-0747

WEBSITE: www.yakimavalleymuseum.org

9 Yakama Nation Museum and Cultural Heritage Center

WHAT'S HERE: **Cultural history museum of the Yakama tribe located on their ancestral lands**

DON'T MISS THIS: **The salmon harvesting diorama**

While the U.S. government tended to assign Native Americans to large tribes, especially when Indians were forced onto the reservation system, seldom were they cohesive nations. The Yakama (spelled differently than the modern Yakima geographic names) are a perfect example. Named to the Yakama Nation were the Palouse, Pisquouse, Yakama, Wenatchapam, Klinquit, Oche Chotes, and several others. A total of 14 tribes and bands became the Yakama Indian Nation under an 1855 treaty with the U.S. government, one of a number of agreements that forced the Indians to give up thousands of square miles, much of which has previously been designated reservations.

Owned by the Yakama Nation, the museum opened in 1980 and is one of the oldest Native American museums in the country. The symbolic longhouse designed into the museum's structure allows it to be recognized from quite a distance. The museum's many exhibits are a way for the Yakama people to tell their own story in their own way. For many visitors, walking through and viewing the full-sized dwellings and the hundreds of artifacts is quite rewarding. For those with an interest in the underlying spirituality of the Yakama people, there is even more here to learn. One of the first exhibits you'll encounter inside the museum is Spilyay, the legendary character often disguised as a coyote who taught humankind, through his daring and humor, how to survive and live harmoniously with all of nature. And there is sacred Patho, the first to greet the rising sun, the one who provides the source of life-giving water, serves as home to the salmon, and provides needed foods and medicines. You will encounter coyotes, as well as bears, beavers, and raccoons inside their dioramas. Each provided for the needs of the Yakama—the bear provided a warm coat for winter and fat for grease, while his claws and teeth were used as ceremonial decorations.

A traditional longhouse is part of the museum design.

One of the first full-sized homes is the Wulchi, an earth lodge dug partly into the ground. Although it was used seasonally by the roving Native Americans, the domelike structure was formed from bent tree limbs and covered with tules or other vegetation and finally mud to form a relatively permanent house. When its owners moved on to follow the changing food supplies, the house was closed, sometimes being used for storage, then reopened months later upon their return.

For all Indians who lived along the Colorado River, salmon served as the key to their survival. Before Captain Robert Gray sailed up the Columbia River in 1792 and renamed the river after his ship, the Indians here called it Nchiwana. It has been estimated that prior to 1800, between 10 million and 16 million salmon and steelhead migrated each year up the Columbia, the second largest river in North America. The museum's large diorama celebrating Celilo recognizes the important role the site served. Located near the present-day Dalles, Celilo Falls was the region's primary meeting and trading place for Native Americans. The exhibit includes wonderful photographs of fishing activities on the Columbia, the nets used for catching salmon, and the fish being split and dried over smoking fires for future consumption.

Nearby, the museum's tule winter lodge is of moderate size. These lodges were made large enough to house up to 15 families. As the extended family units that traveled together expanded, so too would the semipermanent winter lodges. Another structure that was required in a village was the sweat lodge. The Yakama sweat lodge or *pusha* (meaning "grandfather") was framed with willows and covered with animal skins. It was used daily for sacred songs and communication with the spiritual grandfather—and for mental and physical healing and cleansing.

There are many more exhibits in this expansive museum, including a close look at basket-making and the plants that provided the necessary materials for the myriad baskets. Another exhibit interprets the use of a time ball. For Native Americans here, time was not measured by days, weeks, and years. Instead, the time ball, with its knotted string that held pebbles, feathers, shells, and other objects as memory devices, measured time by day, night, seasons, and relationships between events. A new time ball was often begun at a marriage.

Another gallery interprets the changes that treaties with the U.S. brought to the Yakama culture. American Indians did not understand the concept of individual ownership of land, and often through misinterpretation, they agreed to treaty elements that were ultimately harmful for them. They were forced onto reservations where the Bureau of Indian Affairs attempted to "educate" their ancient and spiritual culture out of their children. The children were forced to wear uniforms and were required to speak only English, with severe punishments such as whipping and hunger if they failed to follow the rules.

One exhibit looks at the Yakama who have served honorably in the U.S. armed forces. The photos represent a sampling of those who have served through several wars in the different military branches. The case includes a few pieces of military equipment and medals, including a Purple Heart.

HOURS: Sunday through Friday, 8 AM to 5 PM; Saturday, 9 AM to 5 PM
COST: Adults, $5; ages 11–18 and 55 and over, $3; family, $12
LOCATION: 100 Spiel-yi Loop, Toppenish
PHONE: 509-865-2800
WEBSITE: www.yakamamuseum.com

10 American Hop Museum

WHAT'S HERE: **Everything related to the commercial growing and processing of hops**

DON'T MISS THIS: **The short video on growing and harvesting hops**

Beer is the world's longest produced and most widely consumed alcoholic beverage. It's been around for as long as 8,000 years, and it was certainly a part of life in ancient Egypt. Hops didn't become part of the brewing and flavoring process until much later, probably not more than 1,200 years ago. Some of America's early beer brewers included William Penn, George Washington, and Thomas Jefferson. Even the Pilgrims brewed their own beer.

If the ancient—and modern—process of brewing beer is a little fuzzy for you, then this is the place to learn more. While the focus of the museum is the local hops industry, there is an exhibit that illustrates all of the various changes that grains, water, and hops go through to create great-tasting beers. A short video program shows the hops growing and harvesting process—the focus of the museum's collections.

Farmers have been growing crops in this part of Washington for more than 150 years. Charles Carpenter was the first to grow hops on the eastern side of the Cascades, coming here in 1868 and planting rootstock taken from his father's hops fields in New York. The photos are of the original homestead cabin and the first hops kiln in Yakima Valley. Other photos show the Carpenter family at work over the generations.

If you've ever seen a hops yard with its high-climbing plants trailing their way up those long suspended strings, it's not likely you were aware that coconuts play such an important role in the continuing success of the industry. The hop plant's support "cord," those long lines that stretch to the ground from the tall support poles, is called "coir hop string." Much of the product comes from Sri Lanka and other countries where coconut trees grow in abundance. The tough fibers encasing the coconut shells are removed, dried, and twisted into the various thicknesses of coir required. It takes about 2,880 husks to produce enough string for one acre of hops, and there are 43,000 acres of hops grown annually in the U.S. Coir is renewable—and there are three crops of coconuts per year—and is a strong fiber with a rough texture that allows the growing hop vines to cling and climb; it stretches rather than breaks under the weight of the growing vines. Just as important, the string is cost effective, and it can be composted and returned to the soil after harvest. The

Early hop farming equipment

museum has lots of the string, much of it from Sri Lanka, exhibited in its various forms, from coir to bundles to bails.

As you'll learn at the museum, hops are an interesting plant. Through the centuries, they were believed to possess various magical attributes, including a natural sedative effect. Some people unable to sleep stuffed their pillows with the soft cones. Chemicals in the plant can produce those effects, although the potency can vary considerably, depending on the variety of hops and the age of their harvested flowers. Those same chemicals provide the bitterness and special flavors of beer.

Hops are one of the few plants that have both male and female plants, yet pollination isn't required to produce cones or for the plants to reproduce. Plant reproduction for agricultural purposes is done by separating new rhizomes (root structures) from the female plants, which can then be grown into new hops. The females produce the cones used in the beer-making process. The perennial plants can continue producing for as long as 30 years. The only things needed to keep them producing are added soil nutrients and new supportive coir hop string for each new crop.

For harvesting, the vines are cut from their support lines and poles, and the female cones are then separated from the plant. The seeds are removed, because they cause problems for some types of beers, then the remainder of the cones are dried and baled for shipment.

Throughout the museum there are pieces of equipment that have been used over the years for hop growing and harvesting. You can see everything from hand-planting tools and special harvesting baskets to the sewing machines that stitched together the burlap bags and a hop press and baling machine. There is a 19th-century "duster," a horse-drawn machine that sprayed the hops with various chemical concoctions designed to control hop aphids and spider mites. Tobacco juice, sulfur, soap, and whale oil were some of those early-day pest control agents. Throughout the exhibits you can see hops in all their many forms, from the small cones on an actual hop vine to processed hop pellets, hop extracts, and debittered hops.

HOURS: May 1 through September 30; Wednesday through Saturday 10 AM to 4 PM, Sunday 11 AM to 4 PM. Off-season tours may be arranged if volunteers are available.

COST: Adults, $3; students, $2, families, $7; under age 5, free

LOCATION: 22 South B Street, Toppenish

PHONE: 509-865-4677

WEBSITE: www.americanhopmuseum.org

11 Northern Pacific Railway Museum

WHAT'S HERE: **Restored train depot that includes locomotives and other rolling stock**

DON'T MISS THIS: **The outside yard where the rolling stock is exhibited**

As is often the case, it was a group of dedicated volunteers who brought the old Toppenish train depot back to life. Originally built by the Northern Pacific Railway in 1911, the depot was the area's transportation center for half a century. In 1961, the depot was closed for passenger service because competition from automobiles and airplanes had killed the demand for train travel. Twenty years later, the railway no longer had a need for the depot, even for freight, and it was completely closed. Local train and history enthusiasts leased the building, spent a few years restoring decades of deterioration, and finally opened the museum on July 4, 1992.

That's when the real work began. The Northern Pacific Railway Museum volunteers began searching for appropriate trains to begin their collection. The first piece acquired was the 1902 steam locomotive Northern Pacific Engine #1364. With that small beginning, many more pieces of equipment, including a rare Mann McCann Ballast Spreader, have followed. The steam-powered spreader was purchased by Northern Pacific in 1921 and used to pull ballast (the rock base) back onto the rail bed during summer, after it had slowly spread away from the tracks. During winter, the spreader's big front blade cleared snow from the tracks over Stampede Pass (until 1985). The museum has acquired an entire freight train, including its 1907 truss rod boxcar, 1931 ice refrigerator car, 1920s flat car, 1929 automobile car, 1932 wooden boxcar, 1923 Shell Oil tank car, and 1940 drop-bottom gondola. The 1908 wooden caboose brings up the rear of this historic freight train.

The restored train depot is as impressive as the growing collection of rolling stock. The brick building is partly a restored train depot and partly a museum focused on the history of the town of Toppenish. During the early days of train travel, there were separate waiting rooms where men could meet, conduct business, and smoke. The women and children had their own separate waiting room, which has been restored. What was originally the men's waiting room is now a large gift shop.

Locomotive 2152 in the museum's yard

The museum's exhibits include some of the fine china used on the Pacific Northern Railway's passenger cars. And there are menus featuring the fare for the day, as well as their low prices, at least by today's standards. A typical luncheon would include split pea soup with celery, chilled vegetable juice, panfried fillet of haddock with tartar sauce, braised rib ends of beef, creamed diced chicken with mushrooms (on toast), browned new potatoes, cauliflower, tossed green salad, Washington cherry pie, vanilla ice cream, coffee, tea, and milk—all for $1.90. Don't care for such a heavy meal? Try à la carte: A toasted sardine sandwich went for 40 cents or perhaps you would prefer the cold tongue sandwich for only 25 cents.

The museum features several exhibits related to the rather convoluted development of the town of Toppenish. The rich agricultural lands, coupled with adequate water availability through irrigation, made this part of the Yakima Valley very desirable to farmers. Land on which Native Americans originally lived was distributed in various ways by the U.S. government following 19th-century treaties and new laws. In 1887, Congress passed the General Allotment Act that allowed certain tribes to select large tracts of land (40–160 acres) for themselves and their children. While "white" landowners could sell their property, Indians had to wait 25 years after receiving their allotments before they had full title. So, until about 1905, since the site of Toppenish was part of the Yakama Nation Reservation, there were no fully owned Indian lands here that could be sold and built on. One of those claimants, Josephine Bowser Lillie Parker (1865–1932) was finally able in 1905 to subdivide some of her 80 acres and sell the new town's first city lots. At $25 to $140 each, they sold out quickly. The new town was named Toppenish, and Josephine is remembered as the Mother of Toppenish.

Other exhibit cases hold some of the early telegraph keys and related equipment, railroad signaling lanterns, a late 1800s Pullman berth, suitcases and mailbags ready for shipment, and an original Adams Motor Car used to do repairs on the tracks. It had a single-wheel motor and had to be pushed down the tracks to get started. The old stencil machines used to label shipping crates can be seen, as well as Railway Express Agency signs, paperwork forms, and packages, including movie films.

Be sure to take time to wander through the outside rail yard where the locomotives and cars are kept. There are informational signs attached to some of the pieces, identifying what the different parts are and what they do, such as the firebox, which is brick lined and burns coal at 2,000 degrees in order to create steam in the boiler.

The museum features special train ride events throughout the year, especially around Halloween, Thanksgiving, and Christmas.

HOURS: May through October: Tuesday through Saturday, 10 AM to 4 PM; Sunday, 12 PM to 4 PM
COST: Adults, $5; ages 12 and under, $3
LOCATION: 10 South Asotin Avenue, Toppenish
PHONE: 509-865-1911
WEBSITE: www.nprymuseum.org

12 Presby Mansion

WHAT'S HERE: 20-room Queen Anne Victorian mansion

DON'T MISS THIS: The large collection of antique coffee grinders

Less than a dozen miles north from the Oregon border and the Columbia River is Goldendale. Wheat and alfalfa brought affluence to the local farmers and, in turn, to the community. The day before 33-year-old town namesake John Golden left his home in Pennsylvania, he married 13-year-old (and nine months) Jane, and traveled with their parents—not exactly a honeymoon. Sometime after settling in Oregon, while John and Jane were traveling to Walla Walla in search of better grazing land for his cattle, young Jane became ill. While they stopped to let her rest, John spent time exploring the surrounding lands. He discovered that the bunchgrass in this area was plentiful, so this is where they settled. After saving enough money to purchase 200 acres, he had his new town surveyed, sold lots to folks who wanted to start new businesses, and gave several other parcels to the Methodist Church. Not only did his new town of Goldendale succeed, but Jane eventually gave birth to nine girls and two boys.

One of the beneficiaries of the area's trickle-down riches was attorney Winthrop B. Presby. Educated at Dartmouth College, he came west and worked for a while in his uncle's lumber mill, and later he became the local school principal (an elected position at the time). He decided to become a lawyer, which only required that an individual work under another lawyer or a judge for a while; that's what he did, passing the bar after two years of study. He also became mayor of Goldendale and later was elected to the state legislature.

In 1902, Presby built his Victorian home in its splendid Queen Anne style, adding imported tile from Europe. It only cost $8,000, even after the upgrades. Winthrop was married twice: His first wife was a pioneer girl who died of diphtheria not long after their marriage and birth of their child. Zoe, Presby's second wife, divorced him in 1913 after nineteen years of marriage, getting a $2,000 settlement and a $20 monthly stipend, which stopped a year later when Winthrop died in the house of "nerve exhaustion." A photo of Zoe hanging in the house shows a woman who knew what she wanted and probably got it. Following Presby's death, one of his creditors acquired ownership of the home, but he sold it for $12,500 in 1918 to Pearl Shepard, a local school teacher. Shepard lived in the home until 1959 when she sold it to the local

Presby Mansion

historical society for $2,500, donating the remainder of its value. The home now holds the history of Goldendale.

The house is filled with furnishings, most of it donated by local pioneer families. The hutch and sideboard did belong to the Presby family. They were sold at auction following Presby's death, and family descendants purchased them and gave them to the museum.

The kitchen floor is interesting—a gaudy pattern of different-sized red, black, and gray squares. Apparently when asked if it was original to the home, the last owner, quite elderly at the time, stated that her father put it in during the 1930s to replace the "really ugly" original floor.

As you wander through the home, some of the rooms are furnished as they might have been during the days when Presby owned the home, while others are filled with exhibits featuring everything from baskets made by the local Klickitat Indians to coffee grinders. In fact there is a collection of more than 100 coffee grinders of all sizes and shapes. One of the grinders is still attached to a small piece of wood that was part of the side of the covered wagon that brought it out west. There is even a furnished pioneer homestead cabin tucked into one of the rooms.

On the outside grounds are more exhibits, including a newspaper printing press, an old safe, and a reconstructed school room. In the carriage house are wagons, old tractors, a horse-drawn sleigh, and an old harvester.

HOURS: Change seasonally, call to verify: Monday through Thursday, 10 AM to 4 PM; Friday through Sunday, 10 AM to 4 PM

COST: Ages 13 and older, $4.50; ages 6–12, $1

LOCATION: 127 West Broadway, Goldendale

PHONE: 509-773-4303

WEBSITE: www.cityofgoldendale.com (no website dedicated to the museum)

13 Columbia River Exhibition of History, Science, and Technology

WHAT'S HERE: **Columbia Basin history focusing on the nearby top secret Hanford nuclear site**

DON'T MISS THIS: **A trailer from the largest trailer park in history**

Located near the banks of the Columbia River, the museum provides an overview of the Columbia Basin from the time of Native Americans through the coming of settlers looking for free farmland and new opportunities. The museum looks at the history of the Richland area: the Native Americans, the farmers, and finally the coming of the U.S. government and the military as part of the huge World War II Manhattan Project, destined to design, develop, and build the world's first nuclear bomb.

General Leslie R. Groves was placed in charge of the project. He ordered his staff to find a nuclear reactor site that had plenty of water for power generation at least 20 miles from the any town with a population of 1,000 or more. The nearest main highway or railroad had to be at least 10 miles away. The people living and farming the chosen area, some for generations, were ordered to leave within 30 days. They were paid for their land, but most felt the compensation was too little.

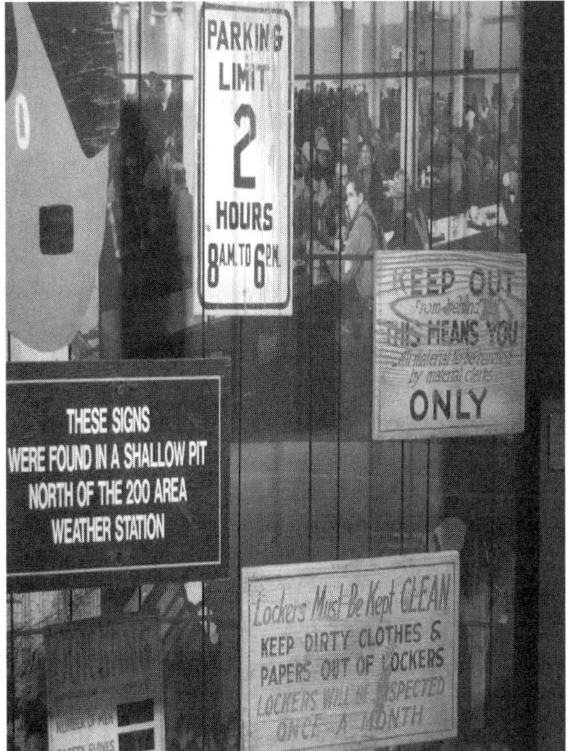

In April 1943, when ground was broken for the secret facility, there were only 6,700 people living along this 30-mile stretch of the Columbia River. One year later, 51,000 people were calling the temporary and secret construction city their home. New houses, dormitories, barracks, mess halls, and other facilities were built, with the better houses going to the top administrators, scientists, and physicians. The next best housing was filled with managers, engineers, and other professionals. For some of the blue-collar workers, small prefab houses were built, the one-bedroom, single-bath homes renting for $25 per month. For thousands of others, tiny 147-square-foot travel trailers were brought in and placed in the 3,600 spaces of what was to become the largest trailer park in history.

Signs at the secret city of Hanford

One of those original trailers, each of which housed an average of 3.7 people, is parked outside the museum.

Walk farther into the museum and you run into a guardhouse with signs warning about immediate dismissal if you aren't authorized to be here or if you are carrying cameras, binoculars, or any kind of signaling device—but it's just a replica of the 1944 facility. The recreated city includes numerous original signs such as street signs (North Street), building addresses (Bldg. 283), and notices to keep lockers clear of dirty clothes (monthly inspections). For today's students, there is a seemingly ancient mechanical device indispensable to architects and engineers of the time—a slide rule.

Much of the museum focuses on the engineering and special equipment required to handle both the initial and the ongoing development of radioactive nuclear materials such as plutonium. Following World War II, the facility became critical to the nation's Cold War security as the U.S. constantly developed improved nuclear weapons designed to counter the growth of the Soviet Union's growing nuclear arsenal.

Exhibits include a look at the million-gallon, double-sided containment tanks used to store radioactive waste—the early single-sided tanks leaked, allowing for about a million gallons of waste to escape into the ground. Manufacture of those old single-walled tanks was discontinued in 1964. Another exhibit that kids enjoy is the mechanical arms used to safely handle radioactive materials. The museum's exhibit works, so you can try your luck at moving those big robotlike arms. Fortunately, you will be moving around materials less dangerous than plutonium. Some of the professional operators are so skilled they can thread a needle with those robotic hands!

A fun and eye-opening exhibit allows you to use a Geiger counter to test for radioactivity. Some of the items you can test, with surprising results, include a Fiesta dinnerware coffee cup (you might want to use paper cups!), a common static eliminator available at photo supply stores, cloisonné jewelry, common salt, and even some real uranium. The Geiger counter does not lie.

Some exhibits are more technical, but ample explanations make them easily understood; the building of the Fast Flux Test Reactor used to test breeder reactor technology and make advances in important medical isotopes is just one example. There are plenty of very detailed reactor models to keep anyone interested in this technology busy for quite some time.

The museum includes a time line for each decade beginning in the 1940s that explains what was going on in the world and at the Hanford facility—from President Harry Truman deciding to drop the first atomic bomb on Japan to the ongoing cleanup efforts begun in the 1990s.

HOURS: Monday through Saturday, 10 AM to 5 PM; Sunday, 12 PM to 5 PM
COST: Adults, $4; ages 7–17 and seniors, $3
LOCATION: 95 Lee Boulevard, Richland
PHONE: 509-943-9000
WEBSITE: www.crehst.org

14 Sacajawea State Park and Interpretive Center

WHAT'S HERE: Interpretive center and museum dedicated to Sacajawea and the Lewis and Clark Expedition

DON'T MISS THIS: Views of the confluence of the Snake and Columbia rivers

Sacajawea State Park sits on a point of land in southeastern Washington, between the Columbia River and the place where the Snake River joins it. This site was the traditional Native American gathering place for fishing and trading. Salmon and other fish caught here were dried before the Indians departed to other areas throughout the year. That long tradition of this being an Indian-only trading place was interrupted on October 16, 1805, when the Lewis and Clark Expedition arrived and spent two nights camped here. Back then, there was only sagebrush, bunchgrasses, and prickly pear cacti, not the trees and large expanses of grass you see today. The American expedition joined in trading with the Indians before boarding their boats and continuing down the Columbia River to the Pacific Ocean, bringing to a close their epic journey of discovery.

The park and its interpretive center were named for the 17-year-old Agaiduka Shoshone woman who served as one of the expedition's interpreters and whom most people today know as Sacajawea. While camped here, she was able to converse with a captive Shoshone woman held by the local Walla Walla Indians, successfully interpreting for Lewis and Clark and the local tribes. One of the dozens of exhibits inside discusses successful communications during the expedition. Lewis spoke English to François Labiche, who spoke French to Toussaint Charbonneau, who spoke Hidatsa to his wife, Sacajawea, who spoke Shoshone to her brother, Cameahwait, the Shoshone chief. This process went on through the entirety of a very long speech that Lewis made. The chief's response went back through the same people to Lewis. A set of interpretive exhibit "wheels" with changeable statements from Lewis's speech and the English translations of the same Hidatsa, French, and Shoshone statements shows how difficult literal translations proved to be.

The park's visitor center, while relatively small, is filled with wonderful exhibits that follow the history and trail of Lewis and Clark. It begins with President Thomas Jefferson's desire to discover a Northwest Passage to the Pacific Ocean and the rich trading countries in the Far East. Of particular interest are the food rations and equipment that Lewis purchased for his journey. They included weapons, gifts for the Indians ($669.50 worth), navigational instruments, medicines, and clothing. They also carried portable writing desks on which they recorded more than

The Sacajawea Interpretive Center

1.2 million words describing their journey and their personal thoughts. Lewis also took a decanter and Clark his umbrella. Along with the food supplies, they carried 30 gallons of "strong Spt" (spirited) wine and more than 100 gallons of whiskey, the last of which they finished on July 4, 1805. The museum has replicas of the desks and casks of liquids the crew carried.

The exhibit includes numerous excerpts from the six journals that survived the expedition. Clark wrote about one curious spectacle—the sighting of a colony of prairie dogs, a species of animal that at the time was unknown to science: ". . . the Village of those animals Covs. about 4 acres of Ground on a Gradual decent of a hill and Contains great numbers of holes on the top of which those little animals Set erect make a Whistling noise and whin allarmed Slip into their hole." They tried unsuccessfully to catch one of the animals by digging up its hole; finally, by flooding a hole, they managed to capture one.

Exhibits recount the tearful reunion of Sacajawea with her brother when the expedition was attempting to trade for horses with the Shoshone before crossing the Rocky Mountains. During their successful trading the expedition encountered Spanish brands, bridle bits, and stirrups. By 1805, the extensive Native American trade networks had moved European goods to many areas of the continent. The expedition traded uniform coats (quite desired by the Indians), along with handkerchiefs, knives, and other small items. All appeared pleased with their trading successes.

As they entered the Bitterroot Mountains, Captain Clark recorded their misery: " . . . began to Snow about 3 hours before Day and Continued all day . . . I have been wet and as cold in every part as I ever was in my life . . . ." He didn't mention how 17-year-old Sacajawea was doing as she traveled with them, caring for her seven-month-old son.

The museum houses a large collection of artifacts, much of them Native American clothing and weapons, that would have been found here in the early 1800s. There is a quick look at the changes brought to the area as it was settled—the farming that began near here and the Northern Pacific Railway's construction site established in 1879 that soon grew into the town of Ainsworth. But when the construction site moved, the town of 1,500 people also vanished.

Today, the park offers shade trees, picnic tables, and a small dock on the river. The interpretive center is run primarily by a friendly group of volunteers, so calling in advance to check on hours of operation is advised.

HOURS: April through October; daily, 10 AM to 5 PM. The park is day-use only and is open daily 6:30 AM to dusk.

COST: Free

LOCATION: 2503 Sacajawea Park Road, Pasco

PHONE: 509-902-8844

WEBSITE: www.parks.wa.gov

15 East Benton County Historical Society Museum

WHAT'S HERE: Collection of local history from radios and televisions to quilts and Indian arrowheads

DON'T MISS THIS: Kennewick Man exhibit

The museum's collection begins even before you go inside. Scattered near the entrance are Native American petroglyphs found along the nearby Columbia River in 1939, pioneer farm equipment, and a section of the "Green Bridge," the first bridge built across the Columbia River between Kennewick and Pasco. It was a privately funded toll bridge that proved to be a financial success when constructed in 1922.

As you enter the museum, look down. The floor beneath your feet is made of petrified wood. The colorful and highly figured slices of ancient wood and minerals are arranged into 500 square feet of "tiles" and set in marble dust mortar. Gordon B. Maxey spent 16 years cutting and polishing the petrified wood that he had collected from California, Oregon, Washington, and Idaho. It once served as part of the floor of his own home, but following his death, the new owners of the home, Mr. and Mrs. D. L. McKeown donated the floor to the museum

The petrified wood that is perhaps millions of years old is joined by another very old artifact—Kennewick Man. In 1996, a skull was discovered along the shallow shore of the Columbia River, and additional searching turned up most of the skeleton of a man thought to be about 9,000 years old. Scientists estimated that he lived into his 50s, but led a tough life. Sometime in his life he was hit by a spear point that was stuck permanently in his hip bone, his chest had been crushed, and he probably had a crippled left arm, although he had all of his teeth and no cavities. An infection of some sort ultimately killed him. The museum has a casting of the original skull, which is now held by the Burke Museum of Natural History and Culture in Seattle (page 247). There is also a display of the bones, laid out so you can see what this ancient guy may have looked like, at least as a skeleton.

The museum's single-floor gallery holds a wide assortment of displays that represent the county's history. One of the exhibits encourages visitors to touch it; a telephone operators' switchboard that was taken out of service in 1968 has all its plugs and switches and a sign encourages you to pull the plugs and flip the switches. Nearby is a collection of 1920s-era Pathe records that were played on a windup gramophone. One of the donating family's members once played the records in his barn as he milked the cows.

A collection of early clothing irons

One exhibit illustrates that what was technologically changing in the world of television in the 1950s is similar to what is occurring today with the beginning of the era of digital television; the museum's ultrahigh frequency (UHF) converter created the same consternation 50-plus years ago. KPTV in Portland was the first television station in the U.S. to broadcast on one of the new UHF frequencies, Channels 14 through 83. Anyone wanting to receive the new channels was required to purchase a converter, at least until the new sets being sold began including the new channels.

The museum has a Wurlitzer jukebox with song titles typewritten on the song selection directory. The musicians provide a clue as to the age of the big machine—Mama Cass, Dean Martin, Mills Brothers, The Lettermen, Herb Alpert, and Lynn Anderson. And then there is the "Cyclops," television maker Philco's 17-inch Predicta television that sold for about $280 in 1959. Its space-age design was meant to attract buyers, but the brand was failing. Wandering through the rest of the museum reveals everything from a 1920s dental office with its ancient-appearing X-ray machine, to old cameras, quilts, and sewing machines. There is an AP teletype machine, a large collection of military uniforms, and a Saxony spinning wheel that was used in Tennessee in the 1870s before making its way to Washington. Another spinning wheel, originally used in Norway in 1850, was brought to Iowa in 1880, before finally coming by wagon to Kennewick, Washington, in 1904. Those who must iron their clothes will feel good that they don't have to use the old gas-heated and early electric irons. None appear user-friendly or particularly safe.

HOURS: Tuesday through Saturday, 12 PM to 4 PM
COST: Adults, $4; seniors, $2; ages 5–17, $1; active military, free
LOCATION: 205 Keewaydin Drive, Kennewick
PHONE: 509-582-7704
WEBSITE: www.owt.com/ebchs

16 Fort Walla Walla Museum

WHAT'S HERE: **Expansive fort grounds with extensive history museum and pioneer village**

DON'T MISS THIS: **Historic cemetery with graves of soldiers who died fighting local Indians**

The North West Company chose a site near the confluence of the Walla Walla and Columbia rivers to build a fort and trading post in Nez Perce Indian country. The company soon merged with the Hudson's Bay Company. That fort burned in the late 1820s and was rebuilt only to be destroyed by fire again a decade later. It burned once more during the Indian wars that occurred throughout the West during the 1850s. By this time, the fur trade era was over, along with the need for the fort.

But the area was not to be without a fort for long. A couple of temporary military Fort Walla Wallas were built in 1855 and 1856, east of the current city of Walla Walla. Finally, in 1858, the permanent new fort was completed. As you walk up the Penner Trail and onto the main grounds, you will pass what was once the corner of Rose Street and Myra Road, which was a corner of the old fort. Fort Walla Walla served as a cavalry outpost until 1910. After the closure, it reopened for a short time as a training post for the 146th Field Artillery. The only original buildings remaining from the 1858 fort became part of the Veteran's Administration Hospital when it took over the property in 1920.

Today Fort Walla Walla is made up of three separate areas: Pioneer Village, the exhibit halls in the fort's buildings, and the military cemetery in the park just outside of the fort's main entrance. The Pioneer Village looks just like what it is supposed to look like—a small pioneer village. The site's 17 original cabins (moved to the site), with the school, jail, and other buildings have been filled with artifacts that could have been found here back in the 19th and early 20th centuries. Some of the buildings include a doctor's office log cabin that was originally within

Gravesite memorial tombstone

the old fort (the fort encompassed one square mile, the equivalent of 640 acres). The desk was actually here at the fort and used by Dr. Dorsey S. Baker in the late 1800s. The railroad first reached here in about 1880, and the depot is filled with artifacts from several early railroads in the area. The barbershop contains one of the oldest barber's chairs (manufactured around 1870) in the Pacific Northwest. No early town was complete without a blacksmith's shop. Although the building is a replica, the equipment inside is mostly from the 1880s.

The Prescott Jail is always one of the more fascinating buildings for the kids. With no jail of their own, the town of Prescott finally authorized the construction of a jail in 1902, a place that could house drunk and rowdy cowboys arrested for fighting and similar offenses. It was built from 2-inch-by-6-inch timbers spiked together; the window was a small hole in the door. One night a group of drunken cowboys attacked the jail with their ropes and horses, attempting to tip the structure over. They failed. A fire in 1915 that destroyed most of Prescott's business district didn't reach the jail. It was saved and is now part of Fort Walla Walla's Pioneer Village.

Inside the main fort's outer row of buildings is where the majority of the museum's exhibits reside. The exhibit hall buildings, the first of which was built in 1969, are not historical. Exhibit Hall 1's exhibits periodically change, but generally include a collection of Native American woven bags, baskets, and beaded items and a diorama depicting Walla Walla headman Yellept's gift of "a very elegant white horse" to Meriwether Lewis and William Clark.

Exhibit Hall 2 includes a horse-powered stationary threshing machine—and its horses, although they aren't real—and a description of how wheat grain kernels were separated from the chaff and straw. Other harvesting equipment includes a water wagon and even a cookhouse that was pulled to the harvesting site. It contains a woodstove, icebox, tables, and for the men's comfort—fly traps.

Exhibit Hall 3 features the only exhibit in the U.S. of an entire 1919 Harris combine and Shandoney hitch. The combine "combines" the work of two earlier machines, by cutting and threshing the grain. By incorporating a locally developed self-leveling device, the local growers could use the big horse-drawn machine on their hilly lands without the danger of it rolling over—doubling the amount of land they could plant and harvest. The 33 life-sized fiberglass mules are attached via the Shandoney hitch to provide the pulling power. The hitch was also modified so that no single mule had to pull more than its share of weight.

The last two exhibit halls contain stagecoaches, wagons, fancy buggies, and even a branding iron collection. There is also firefighting equipment and even a recreated part of the Washington State Penitentiary here. The prison exhibit includes two steel "bucket cells" that were constructed by Prison Industries to match the original 1886 cells. The 6-by-7-foot cells are furnished just as the originals, including the bucket that served as each prisoner's toilet. It was emptied once each day by the inmate.

The old cemetery just outside the fort is the final resting place for numerous soldiers, many of whom died in battles with local Indians. One headstone (shown on page 329) reads: IN MEMORY OF ENLISTED MEN 1ST CAVY KILLED IN ACTION NEAR WHITE BIRD CANYON IDAHO JUNE 17, 1877. Others mark the gravesites of individual soldiers—officers and enlisted, alike.

HOURS: April through October, daily, 10 AM to 5 PM
COST: Adults, $7; ages 13–18, $6; ages 6–12, $3
LOCATION: 755 Myra Road, Walla Walla
PHONE: 509-525-7703
WEBSITE: www.fortwallawallamuseum.org

17 Kirkman House Museum

WHAT'S HERE: **1880s Italianate mansion**
DON'T MISS THIS: **The rare Weber piano that was shipped around Cape Horn as a birthday present**

This 1880s home has been through tough times, but has survived to become one of Walla Walla's best preserved (and restored) mansions open to the public on a regular basis. Touring the home won't provide any idea of how most of the people in Walla Walla lived during the late 19th century, because the Kirkmans lived in luxury. The home was built at a cost of about $7,000 by English-born William Kirkman who came here in 1872. It took six years to construct this brick home with its Corinthian columns and the Greek figurehead keystones.

William Kirkman had come to the U.S. at age 20, and initially planned to sell tapestries and fabrics, but ended up dabbling in gold mining. He had lost almost everything he ever made before entering the cattle business as a partner with John Dooley, known as the "King of Cattle." They ran cattle on their Figure 3 Ranch, with its lands stretching from Pasco to Spokane and Sprague to the Snake River. He was the first to reap the financial benefits of shipping cattle out of the Washington Territory via the railroad. Kirkman came to own more than 1,200 acres where he ran both cattle and sheep.

Kirkman House

On a trip with his wife and two oldest children to England in 1892–93, his first time back since leaving 40 years earlier, an illness he had been fighting returned. He stopped to meet his wife Isabella's family in Ireland before returning to the

U.S. Unfortunately, he died in Wisconsin as they were heading home to Washington on the train. Together, he and Isabella, whom he had met in San Francisco and married in 1867, had 10 children, but only four survived to see adulthood.

The Kirkman family lived here until 1919, when Isabella donated the home to Whitman College, which their four surviving children attended. The home became a boys' dormitory, and a physics student who lived here, Walter Brattain, later shared the 1956 Nobel Prize in physics for the invention of the transistor. In the 1920s, the house was sold and became an apartment for the next half century. The new use brought about many interior and exterior changes. By 1972, even though the house was on the National Register of Historic Places, it was empty and abandoned. Five years later the Historical Architecture Development Corporation purchased the home, and restoration was begun to turn it into a historic house museum.

This Italianate home was built of local brick, with sandstone used to accent the corner walls and portions above and around the windows. Remarkably, the original glass fanlight over the front door has survived more than a century of often hard use. Extensive work was completed inside to restore the home to its original elegance. Also original to the home is the oak parquet floor with its walnut inlays at the entryway. The upstairs hallway has the original faux finish walls—downstairs it has been recreated.

Several rooms, including Mrs. Kirkman's bedroom, the children's bedrooms, and the parlors, have been furnished with period pieces. Some Kirkman furnishings, including the Weber piano in the middle parlor, remain. It was ordered from New York, and then shipped around Cape Horn and up the Columbia River before being put on a wagon for Walla Walla. The box-style piano with its ivory keys, dubbed a "coffin on legs" by some detractors, was a birthday present for Fannie Ann, the Kirkman's eldest daughter. Its 85 strings (rather than 88) run from side to side allowing for its compact size. One of the common practices of Victorian times was the making of wreaths from the woven strands of human hair. Mrs. Kirkman's elaborate effort made from her family's hair is on view here.

HOURS: Wednesday through Saturday, 10 AM to 4 PM; Sunday, 1 PM to 4 PM. Closed Christmas Eve and Day and New Year's Eve and Day.

COST: Adults, $5; seniors and children, $3

LOCATION: 214 North Colville Street, Walla Walla

PHONE: 509-529-4373

WEBSITE: www.kirkmanhousemuseum.org

18 Asotin County Historical Society Museum

WHAT'S HERE: **Museum of local history with historic outbuildings**

DON'T MISS THIS: **The 1901 pole barn out back, with its 200 branding irons**

This simple block-constructed 1920s building was once used as a funeral parlor. Today, covering its two levels are hundreds of artifacts donated by locals. This is not a formal museum where everything is orderly and labeled, but a treasure chest of history waiting to be discovered. When you run across something you'd like more information about, simply ask one of the volunteers who can likely answer your questions.

Filling the first floor are numerous hutches and sideboards, most containing smaller finds, from clothing items to tools. There's an old ship's steering wheel from a river steamer and an office desk with several different typewriters, an adding machine, and one of those metal-bladed fans that might be seen in movies from the 1940s. You can find an 1890s music box, a 1920s-era telephone switchboard, and an organ from 1900. Around most of upper wall of the large main floor gallery are photographs of people who lived and likely died in and around Asotin. Poke around a bit more and you'll discover the glass case holding a 10,000-year-old mastodon tusk that was discovered in nearby Critchfield Canyon.

In the basement the main exhibits include women's clothing, wigs, and a few kitchen items. There is a veteran's display with uniforms, flags, and photographs. There is also a wonderful collection of original newspapers from around the area dating from December 7, 1941, when Japan bombed Pearl Harbor, and others from August 15, 1945, declaring the end of World War II.

Outside, behind the main museum there are several historic buildings that have been moved to the site. The largest is the pole barn that was originally built above Asotin Creek in 1901. It has the typical horse-drawn buggies, but something not seen too often is the horse-drawn ice cutter. Most fascinating perhaps are the 200-plus branding irons that line the walls. Each is labeled prominently with the name of the brand and the owner's name. In the machine shed is a 1949 Harris combine that was still operational when donated to the museum. The 1929 International Farmall tractor had a single owner before coming to the museum. When Dwight Halsey purchased it new for his ranch, it was the first tractor in the area that featured the new tricycle-design front wheel.

Near the pole barn is the Theon house that was moved here in 1986. It was built in a town that essentially died because of its poor water supply. Today it is furnished as a late 19th-century house. In 1927, the Ray's Ferry-Hackaberry School,

Asotin County Historical Society Museum

a one-room schoolhouse, was moved here and furnished from several other schools from the area. Kids like Forgey's log cabin, which was originally built in 1882 near Ayer's Gulch. It was used as a small grain bin before being moved to the museum grounds. There is even a sheepherder's cabin, fully furnished, including a whiskey bottle. Under a shelter is the slowly crumbling remains of a replica river barge once used on the Salmon River. A man by the name of Captain Guelke used a similar barge to haul supplies up the Salmon River to miners and homesteaders.

HOURS: Tuesday through Saturday; 1 PM to 5 PM. Non-summer hours can vary, so call to confirm; museum is also open by appointment.

COST: $2 donation requested

LOCATION: 215 Filmore Street, Asotin

PHONE: 509-243-4659

WEBSITE: www.asotincountymuseum.com

Eastern Washington Tours

Far Eastern Driving Tour

ESTIMATED DAYS: 2–3
ESTIMATED DRIVING MILES: 75

Eastern Washington is a big place with small communities scattered sporadically acreoss its wide open spaces. Tucked up near the far northeast corner of the state on U.S. Highway 395 is the tiny town of Colville. At a higher elevation, it, unlike much of the remainder of arid eastern Washington, is surrounded by forest. One of the town's early businesspeople was Louis Young. The home he built later became known as the **Keller House** (page 303), which is today a house museum. Fortunately, much of the original furnishings remain in the home, including the beautiful and numerous Stickley-made Craftsman-style pieces. Next door to the Keller House is the **Stevens County Museum** (page 301), well worth the time to wander through.

The largest city in the far eastern reaches of Washington is Spokane. Another of eastern Washington's successful businesspeople built an even more elaborate home for his family here. The **Campbell House** (page 308) was built as an English Tudor Revival home in 1898. Today, the furnished mansion is open for tours as part of the adjacent **Northwest Museum of Arts and Culture** (page 306). Spokane is also known for its beautiful Riverfront Park that fronts the Spokane River. This is a must-see destination, especially if you have kids. The park boasts an antique Looff Carousel and a gondola ride that goes out over Spokane Falls. Wine lovers should take the drive up to **Arbor Crest Winery** (www.arborcrest.com), if not for their fine wines, then certainly for the cliff-top view of Spokane and the Spokane River from its historic Cliff House.

Stevens County Museum

Highway 97 Agricultural and Rail Tour

ESTIMATED DAYS: 1–2
ESTIMATED DRIVING MILES: 22

Yakima is one of the best apple-producing regions in the world. It's also home to the last original turn-of-the century interurban railroad in the U.S. The **Yakima Electric Railway Museum** (page 311) was originally constructed in the early 1900s, but the overhead electrical lines that power the cars are original—and still work. Besides the original car barn, several of the restored cars still operate during the summer months, mostly for tourist passengers.

There is another railroad museum in nearby Toppenish. The **Northern Pacific Railway Museum** (page 319) features a restored train depot and numerous pieces of historic rolling stock, including steam locomotives and even a rare Mann McCann ballast spreader, circa 1921. As you drive around this quaint town, be sure to look for the wall murals that decorate many of the sides of downtown businesses. Actually, they are impossible to miss.

Part of what the railroad did for the community of Toppenish was to ship agricultural products, and one of the biggest of those products was, and remains, hops. Hops are vital to quality beer production and the importance of the hop industry to this part of Washington is highlighted inside the **American Hop Museum** (page 317). It's a fun museum, but don't expect beer samples. You may be able to get a few hop flowers if you ask nicely.

Northern Pacific Railway Museum

Family/Kids' Summer History Tour

ESTIMATED DAYS: 1–2
ESTIMATED DRIVING MILES: 92

Begin in Yakima with a fun ride on the **Yakima Electric Railway** (page 311) and then a visit to the railway's museum to see where all the electrical power comes from and how this railway has managed to remain operational since the early 1900s.

For a look at some more advanced technology, drive southeast on Interstate 82 toward the Tri-Cities area and stop at Richland. The **Columbia River Exhibition of History, Science, and Technology** (page 323) provides a fascinating look at the history of nuclear power in the Pacific Northwest. Any student looking for a science project can find a few ideas here. In addition to numerous exhibits on the area's history developing nuclear energy and nuclear bombs, there is also an opportunity for kids to manipulate "radioactive" objects with robotic arms and hands. There's even a critical nuclear engineer's "calculator," better known as a slide rule, from the 1940s that most of today's students have likely never seen. The museum is situated adjacent to a public park on the shores of the Columbia River.

Then it's time to follow the Columbia River along Interstate 82 once again to its confluence with the Snake River. Movies, cartoons, and books have told the story of Sacajawea, the young Indian woman who was the primary guide for the Lewis and Clark Expedition. She and the men of the expedition camped on the shore where the Snake and Columbia rivers join forces. This is now the site of **Sacajawea State Park and Interpretive Center** (page 325), which focuses much of its interpretive exhibits on the young Shoshone woman. There is a large park here with picnic tables and even a small pier for fishing if you want to spend the afternoon under the shade trees.

Hanford's 1940s temporary worker housing

Eastern Washington Information Centers

Greater Yakima Chamber of Commerce
www.yakima.org
509-248-2021

Spokane Regional Convention and Visitors Bureau
www.visitspokane.com
509-624-1341

Walla Walla Valley Chamber of Commerce
www.wwvchamber.com
509-525-0850

Tri-Cities Visitor and Convention Bureau
www.visittri-cities.com
800-254-5824

Trivia Answers

OREGON

Portland and the Columbia River Gorge

1 **Which Portland museum is designed for kids?**

Oregon Museum of Science and Industry

2 **Where can you learn about the first dam built across the Columbia River?**

Bonneville Dam and Lock Interpretive Center

3 **What mansion sits on a 1,000-foot-high bluff overlooking Portland?**

Pittock Mansion

4 **Where can you see exhibits about the history of windsurfing that include the very first board built in 1964 by inventor Newman Darby?**

Hood River Museum

5 **Where can you get a glimpse back 15,000 years when a glacier dam broke, releasing the water from a 3,000-square-mile lake down the Columbia Gorge?**

Columbia Gorge Discovery Center and the Wasco County Historical Museum

6 **What historic national landmark, built as a rest stop in 1918, offers a spectacular view of the Columbia River?**

Vista House at Crown Point

7 **Which museum has an underground tunnel connecting its two primary galleries?**

Portland Art Museum

Oregon Coast

1 **Where can you tour a historic lighthouse ship?**

Columbia River Maritime Museum

2 **Where can you see a metal bathtub with an accompanying view of Astoria and the Columbia River?**

Flavel House

3 **What state park was once the only place on the U.S. mainland that a Japanese ship successfully attacked during World War II?**

Fort Stevens State Park

4 **Where can you tour a hangar that once housed the largest aircraft in the world?**

Tillamook Air Museum

5 **What is the oldest and highest lighthouse in Oregon?**

Cape Blanco Lighthouse

6 **What state park is the site of lumberman Louis Simpson's two mansions?**

Shore Acres State Park

7 **Where can you see one of the largest Monterey cypress trees in existence?**

Chetco Valley Museum

Oregon's Interstate 5 Corridor

1 **Where can you visit a childhood home of President Herbert Hoover?**

Hoover-Minthorn House Museum

2 **Where can you learn about the history of the Oregon Trail and also view Willamette Falls?**

Museum of the Oregon Territory

3 **Where can you go on a tour and watch "America's Favorite Treats" being made?**

Harry & David

4 **What 19th-century Victorian Queen Anne Revival home did a 25-year-old architect design for a prominent physician?**

Shelton-McMurphey-Johnson House

5 **Where can you see 10,000-year-old sandals made from sage bark?**

University of Oregon Museum of Natural and Cultural History

6 **Where can you purchase flour ground on a 130-year-old mill's still-operating, water-powered grinding wheels?**

Butte Creek Mill

7 **Which museum was once an 1880s Italianate-style courthouse built using 150,000 bricks?**

Jacksonville Museum

Oregon's Cascade Range

1 **Where can you see a springtooth, a chisel plow, and a rodweeder?**

Sherman County Historical Museum

2 **Where can you learn what *yáamâ*, *i'ánk*, and *tuhudya* (from three Native American languages) mean in English?**

The Museum at Warm Springs

3 **What museum features a large volcanic rock with several initials and the year 1813 carved by members of the Pacific Fur Company?**

Des Chutes Historical Museum

4 **Where can you see forest animals, a historic homestead ranch and sawmill, and Native American and early settler artifacts?**

High Desert Museum

5 **Where can you see spindle bombs, "squeeze-up," and pumice?**

Newberry National Volcanic Monument Lava Lands Visitor Center

6 **Where can you find the deepest lake in the U.S.?**

Crater Lake National Park

7 **Where can you see a "balloon bomb" that was once launched in aerial attacks by the Japanese against the U.S. during World War II?**

Klamath County Museum

Eastern Oregon

1 **Where can you see "War Paint," a famous bucking bronc now "preserved" for visitors' viewing pleasure?**

Pendleton Round-Up and Happy Canyon Hall of Fame

2 **What museum used to be a firehouse?**

Eastern Oregon Fire Museum

3 **Where can you see some of the Oregon Trail's original wagon ruts, plus a life-sized diorama of a wagon train heading west?**

National Historic Oregon Trail Interpretive Center

4 **Where can you see two criminals' skulls from a county's first hanging?**

Grant County Historical Museum

5 **What historic Victorian home can you tour whose former owner left an endowment of $22 million to help pay the college expenses of the town's future high school graduates?**

Adler House

6 **What Chinese doctor's office and general store was locked up and forgotten about for 20 years before its treasures were rediscovered in the 1970s?**

Kam Wah Chung (State Heritage Site)

7 **Where can you see a quilt made in 1854 that future U.S. president Abraham Lincoln was said to have helped sew?**

Harney County Historical Museum

WASHINGTON

Olympic Mountains and the Pacific Coast

1 **What museum features a prominent exhibit of its town's historic red-light district?**

Jefferson County Historical Museum

2 **Where can you see a shot-line gun used to aid passengers in escaping a stranded or sinking ship?**

Fort Worden State Park

3 **In what national park can you visit the Hoh Rain Forest, which averages 14 feet of rain each year?**

Olympic National Park

4 **Where can you see an item that has been used as a weapon of war for hundreds of years, a form of transportation, and as a child's toy?**

World Kite Museum

5 **Legend has it that the steaming tears from two dragons unable to win in battle created what special place?**

Sol Duc Hot Springs

6 **Where can you see hundreds of objects discovered in an Indian village, which was buried by a landslide 500 years ago?**

Makah Cultural and Research Center

7 **Which fort protected the Washington side of the mouth of the Columbia River during World War II?**

Fort Columbia (State Park)

Greater Puget Sound

1 **Where can you learn more about a 1913, seven-horsepower Indian motorcycle that only cost $250 new?**

Lynden Pioneer Museum

2 **Where can you see RCA's first AC-powered radio, built in 1926?**

American Museum of Radio and Electricity

3 **What museum and accompanying tour takes visitors through the world's largest building?**

Future of Flight Aviation Center and Boeing Tour

4 **Where can you see an SRC, an ROV, and DSRV?**

Naval Undersea Museum

5 **What is the name of the destroyer that came under attack in the Gulf of Tonkin, marking the official U.S. entry in the war against North Vietnam?**

USS Turner Joy *(Naval Memorial Museum Ship)*

6 **Where can you see a giant puppy named Leroy?**

Tacoma Art Museum

7 **A large Tiffany chandelier is located inside the fourth-tallest masonry dome in the world, which is part of what historic building?**

Washington State Capitol

Seattle

1 **Where can you see handmade water skis that were first used in 1928, thus introducing the sport to the Pacific Northwest?**

Museum of History and Industry

2 **Where can you witness Seattle's famous "flying" fish?**

Pike Place Market

3 **In which museum can you see Jimi Hendrix's first guitar?**

Experience Music Project

4 **Where can you see a Tlingit mortuary pole?**

Burke Museum of Natural History and Culture

5 **What museum features the Yick Fung Co. store as a key exhibit?**

The Wing Luke Asian Museum

6 **Where can you visit the 1916 biplane factory called the "Red Barn?"**

The Museum of Flight

7 **What museum now shares a portion of the original Experience Music Project?**

Science Fiction Museum and Hall of Fame

Washington's Cascade Range

1 **In what national park will you find a mountain with 26 glaciers?**

Mount Rainier National Park

2 **Where can you see a rare Rickenbacker Motor Company car built by a famous World War I German air ace?**

Shafer Museum

3 **Where can you see the world's largest collection of nutcrackers?**

Leavenworth Nutcracker Museum

4 **Where can you learn more about an apple-slapping machine?**

Wenatchee Valley Museum

5 **Where can you see a volcano that erupted in 1980, sending superheated water and molten rock speeding through the surrounding valleys?**

Mount St. Helens National Volcanic Monument

6 **Where was the British Hudson's Bay Company headquarters located during the early 19th century?**

Fort Vancouver (National Historic Site)

7 **Where can you learn the story about Russian aviators who landed unannounced in Vancouver after the first nonstop flight over the North Pole?**

Pearson Air Museum

Eastern Washington

1 **Which structure took 12 million cubic feet of concrete to build?**

Grand Coulee Dam (and Visitor Center)

2 **What electric railroad has operated every year since its inaugural run in 1907?**

Yakima Electric Railway (Museum)

3 **What museum features a popular ingredient used in making beer?**

American Hop Museum

4 **Where can you see a collection of more than 100 different coffee grinders?**

Presby Mansion

5 **Where can you learn about World War II's Manhattan Project, a secret construction project to produce the world's first nuclear bomb?**

Columbia River Exhibition of History, Science, and Technology

6 **Where can you learn about apples, apples, and more apples?**

Yakima Valley Museum

7 **What park is named after a Agaiduka Shoshone woman who accompanied Meriwether Lewis and William Clark on their famous journey?**

Sacajawea State Park and Interpretive Center

Index

H

I

J

K

O

P

Q

R

S

T

U

About the Authors

Together, authors Ken and Dahlynn McKowen have 50-plus years of professional writing, editing, publication, marketing, and public relations experience. They have had more than 2,000 articles, stories, and photographs published, and are the authors or coauthors of *Chicken Soup for the Entrepreneur's Soul, Chicken Soup for the Soul in Menopause, Chicken Soup for the Fisherman's Soul, Chicken Soup for the Soul: Celebrating Brothers and Sisters,* and the *Highroad Guide to the California Coast.* For publisher Wilderness Press, their books include national award-winner *Best of California's Missions, Mansions, and Museums* and the *Wine-Oh! Guide to California's Sierra Foothills.*

The McKowens are the owners of Publishing Syndicate (www.PublishingSyndicate.com), which provides writing and editing services for publishers. They also release a free monthly writing and publication e-newsletter for new and established writers and offer for sale several e-books relating to the craft of writing and getting published.

The couple have two additional businesses under the umbrella of Publishing Syndicate: www.PlacesToDiscover.com, a site that showcases travel destinations for tourists and offers stock stories and photographs to the print media, and Ranger Ken: Discovering Nature school programs (www.RangerKen.com). A former California State Park ranger, Ken takes nature into elementary schools via campfire programs. Through the sale of *Ranger Ken* educational coloring and activity books that Ken pens and Dahlynn illustrates, they offer opportunities for parent-teacher associations to raise money for their schools.

When they're not traveling the world, the McKowens reside near Sacramento, California, where they spend their free time volunteering at their local elementary school.

A Few Organizations that Support Oregon and Washington's Mansions, Museums, and More:

The **Oregon Historical Society** was founded in 1898 to preserve and interpret Oregon's past in thoughtful, illuminating, and provocative ways. The *Oregon Historical Quarterly*, the organization's journal of record for Oregon history, has been published continuously since 1900. The society maintains extensive collections, including 25,000 maps, 30,000 books, photographs, and millions of feet of film, videotape, and microfilm. **www.ohs.org**

For more than 60 years the **Southern Oregon Historical Society** has been collecting artifacts and stories related to its history. The organization maintains several historic buildings, including the Jacksonville Museum, the 39-acre Hanley Farm, the Beekman House, and the U.S. Hotel. **www.sohs.org**

The **Oregon State Archives** is part of the Secretary of State's Office and is responsible for maintaining the state's oldest documents, including the Oregon Constitution, as well as earlier records from the state's provisional and territorial governments. **http://arcweb.sos.state.or.us**

Founded in 1978, the **Oregon Museums Association** provides resources and services to museum professionals and more than 200 museums and cultural institutions throughout Oregon. **www.oregonmuseums.org**

The **Washington Secretary of State's office** maintains an extensive and rare collection of publications and newspapers related to the state's history. Numerous other documents, including census and naturalization records, are available. Much of the collection is available online. **www.secstate.wa.gov/archives/**

Founded in 1891, the **Washington State Historical Society** is dedicated to collecting, preserving, and vividly representing Washington's rich history. The society maintains several facilities, including the Washington State History Museum, State Capitol Museum and Outreach Center, and the Research Center in Tacoma. **www.washingtonhistory.org/wshs/default.aspx**

The **Washington Museum Association** provides support services to museums, including acting as a clearinghouse and information network for museum-related information. **www.washingtonstatemuseums.org**